D0986969

When the computer age began about a quarter-century ago, its participants were active in such unknown territory that charting its limits was difficult, forecasting its future development all but impossible. But now that this revolutionary era is history, its veterans have the experience and confidence to look twenty years ahead—if tentatively, and with some internal dissension. This book presents the predictive insights of some of the most honored of these veterans of computer science and information processing. Four of the authors have received the Association for Computing Machinery's highest honor, the Turing Award; two have received the Nobel Prize in Economics; two are, or have been, chief executives of major corporations; and several others are academic and research leaders in their respective disciplines. All of the contributions were written expressly for the book, and have not been previously published. And all are written in a manner that the general reader will find fully accessible.

The first group takes up the impact of the computer on individuals. The computer in the home is discussed by Joel Moses (MIT); "the return of the Sunday painter" by Nicholas P. Negroponte (MIT); individualized automation by Michael L. Dertouzos (MIT); "convivial computing" by Terry Winograd (Stanford); computers and learning by Seymour A. Papert (MIT); and computers and government by J. C. R. Licklider (MIT).

The next two articles discuss trends in traditional computer use. Victor A. Vyssotsky (Bell Laboratories) writes on the use of computers for business functions, and Sidney Fernbach (Lawrence Livermore Laboratory) on their use in scientific work.

The book's third part explores socioeconomic effects and expectations. Daniel Bell (Harvard) has contributed "The Social Framework of the Information Society," and Herbert A. Simon (Carnegie-Mellon) discusses the consequences of computers for centralization and decentralization. The impact of computers on world affairs is taken up by Robert G. Gilpin

MIT Bicentennial Studies

The Computer Age: A Twenty-Year View

Edited by Michael L. Dertouzos and Joel Moses

(Princeton); regulation and computer services by Roger G. Noll (California Institute of Technology); modelling by Martin Shubik (Yale); and the economics of information by Kenneth J. Arrow (Harvard).

Trends in the underlying technology are traced in the next part. Hardware prospects and limitations are evaluated by Robert N. Noyce (Intel Corporation). This is followed by B. O. Evans (IBM) on communications; Marvin Denicoff (Office of Naval Research) on sophisticated software; Marvin L. Minsky (MIT) on the "representation of knowledge"; and Alan J. Perlis (Yale) on some current research frontiers.

The final part of the book includes an invited critique by Joseph Weizenbaum (MIT) and rejoinders by Daniel Bell and Michael Dertouzos. The comments of a second "house" critic, John McCarthy (Stanford), have been incorporated as they apply throughout the book.

Michael L. Dertouzos is Director of MIT's Laboratory for Computer Science (formerly Project MAC). Joel Moses is Associate Head for Computer Science and Engineering of MIT's Department of Electrical Engineering and Computer Science. Their volume is the sixth in the MIT Bicentennial Studies series.

ARY
OLLEGE
C. 28144

The MIT Press
Cambridge, Massachusetts,
and London, England

Second printing, December 1979
Copyright © 1979 by
The Massachusetts Institute of Technology

All rights reserved. No part of this book may be reproduced in any form or by any means, electronic or mechanical, including photocopying, recording, or by any information storage and retrieval system, without permission in writing from the publisher.

This book was set in VIP Helvetica by Grafacon, Inc.,
and printed and bound by Halliday Lithograph
in the United States of America

Library of Congress Cataloging in Publication Data

Main entry under title:

The Computer Age

  (MIT bicentennial studies)
  Includes index.
  1. Computers and civilization. I. Dertouzos,
Michael L. II. Moses, Joel.
QA76.9.C66F87   301.24'3   79-13070
ISBN 0-262-04055-7

Contents

301.243
D 438

110563

V
Critiques

Series Foreword

As part of its contribution to the celebration of the U.S. Bicentennial, MIT has carried out studies of several social and intellectual aspects of the world we inhabit at the beginning of our third century. Our objective has been to inquire how human beings might deal more intelligently and humanely with these factors, most of which are closely linked to developments in science and technology.

The papers prepared for these inquiries are being published in a Bicentennial Studies Series of which this volume is a part. Other studies in the series deal with linguistics and cognitive psychology, the economics of the new international economic order, administrative and economic factors in air pollution, the social impact of the telephone, and world change and world security.

It is our hope that these volumes will be of interest and value to those concerned now with these questions and, additionally, will provide useful historical perspective to those concerned with the same or similar questions on the occasion of the U.S. Tricentennial.

Jerome B. Wiesner

Preface

This book started as an idea in Stockholm during the 1974 International Federation of Information Processing Societies Conference. We had just been appointed to lead the MIT Laboratory for Computer Science and were naturally questioning the future of computer science research and the specific directions that our laboratory should take. Our discussions with colleagues and our own observations left us with conflicting impressions of the field. On the one hand it seemed to be growing steadily in terms of machines manufactured and new applications introduced. Many once esoteric and complex tasks, such as the development of systems for operating and managing computers, had become relatively commonplace. On the other hand, many of the computer's early promises, some dating as far back as twenty-five years ago, remained largely unfulfilled. Yet such promises were being put forward again, partly because of an improved understanding of the problems and partly because of expected major advances in the underlying hardware technologies. The question we had to confront—whether the field of computer science was relatively mature and evolving slowly or in its infancy, with a revolutionary impact yet to come—is apparently shared by the general public, which has to reconcile visionary predictions of intelligent servants, or an information revolution comparable in impact to the industrial revolution, with the mundane everyday tasks and simpleminded errors of computers in billing or airline reservations.

To help us answer this question, we thought of asking several noted people to contribute their points of view to a study of the future of computers and information processing. We did not feel that a broad, statistical canvassing technique was appropriate because we were concerned with the long-term future of a field that is traditionally difficult to predict. Instead, we focused on individual viewpoints and tried to attract authors with either a record of predictive/analytical ability or the power to initiate change by virtue of their positions. The selection of authors was carried out by a steering committee consisting of Daniel Bell (Harvard), John

McCarthy (Stanford), Victor Vyssotsky (Bell Labs), and the editors (MIT). The committee tried to focus on topics expected to be important in the next twenty years. For example, technological developments in the computer field might make possible automation of the dispensation of services and the production of goods, understanding of natural language, new ways for educating and entertaining mankind, new ways of communicating, conducting business, and governing, and in general, the assumption by the computer of progressively higher levels of what is now considered human skill, knowledge, and intelligence. Whether such feats are technologically practicable is the subject of considerable debate, along with the social effects of such technological progress, and it is also part of the purpose of this study to address these issues.

In addition to the essays themselves, the study also included critical evaluations by John McCarthy* of Stanford and Joseph Weizenbaum of MIT. Many of McCarthy's comments have been incorporated in editorial postscripts to the essays; Weizenbaum's critique appears as a separate essay at the end.

Several of the authors of this study presented their preliminary results at a Convocation of Communications sponsored by MIT and AT&T in celebration of the centennial of the telephone and held at MIT on March 9 and 10, 1976. Funds for the overall study were provided by AT&T, IBM, the Office of Naval Research, and the MIT Laboratory for Computer Science and are gratefully acknowledged here. Special thanks are due to Dorothea Scanlon, Herb Hughes, and Marsha Baker for helping with administration and manuscript preparation.

Michael L. Dertouzos
Joel Moses

* John McCarthy is professor of computer science and director of the Artificial Intelligence Laboratory at Stanford University. A recipient of the Turing award, he is widely known for his development of the LISP programming language and for his role as co-founder of the field of artificial intelligence.

Introduction

THE HARDWARE REVOLUTION AND THE SOFTWARE PUZZLE

The past twenty years have witnessed an incredible anti-inflationary trend in the computer field—the reduction of the cost of the underlying components (hardware) that make up computers at the rate of about 30 percent per year, amounting to an overall cost reduction of a factor of one thousand for the same level of performance. This trend has made possible the widespread use of computers in data processing applications like payrolls, insurance, credit cards, and accounting, as well as national defense and government. More recently it has made possible use of relatively cheap low-performance microcomputers in automobiles, calculators, cash registers, hobby computers, microwave ovens and other appliances. It has also made practicable very high performance, large-scale machines that have been programmed to help in medical diagnosis, to understand a limited repertoire of spoken English sentences, or to play a fairly good game of chess.

This cost reduction trend has apparently not yet reached its limit. Noyce, in his essay on hardware technology, sees no physical barriers to a further improvement in cost/performance of as much as one thousand in the next fifteen to twenty years. Assuming that there are no other barriers, such as lack of sufficient investment in research and development, this projection means that machines that are very sophisticated by today's standards should cost no more than a color television set in the last decade of this century.

Communications, another important technology for computers and information processing, is also undergoing revolutionary changes. Evans discusses the emergence of computer-to-computer communications via satellite as a major new technological force. The interconnection of geographically distributed computer systems into networks adds a further dimension to the potential for information processing. Thus it appears that not only will machines be significantly less expensive and more powerful but also capable of sharing, pooling, and coordinating information from many sources.

However, while this hardware revolution has made computers affordable and promises to make them even more so, perhaps until the turn of the century, it is not enough in itself to accomplish many of the visionary promises of an information revolution. The missing ingredient comes under the heading of software technology and includes the operating systems, languages, and applications programs that tell the hardware what to do. In retrospect, the rate of improvement in the cost/performance of software during the past twenty years has been much smaller than that of the hardware. As a result, the software cost now exceeds the cost of the hardware in many computer systems. The prospect for the next twenty years is murky, although research in this area is both vigorous and ambitious. For instance, Perlis's essay describes some of the work being done to systematize and standardize the art of programming, which is succeeding in reducing its cost and in producing more correct programs. This approach is a relatively conservative one, since it proceeds on the assumption that we must come to terms with the complexity of existing software systems before we can venture out to break new ground.

Partially offsetting the fear that the cost of conventional programming techniques will continue their historic trend is the promise of intelligent programs, that is, programs in which the computer exhibits some intelligence. These programs began to be developed in the late 1950s in the field of artificial intelligence. Winograd's essay discusses new developments in this field. In order to obtain a more natural communication between man and machine using English, the computer will need to become more knowledgeable about the real world, about human goals, and about commonsense reasoning. Minsky examines the basic issues involved in getting a computer to represent commonsense knowledge, while Moses weighs the potential impact on the home of programs that are knowledgeable in specialized areas.

Unlike the predictably favorable cost performance trends of the hardware, the software prospects present us with a puzzle, an important ingredient of which is the extent of intelligence that will be practically achievable by future programs. Unfortunately, premature and often very ambitious past claims about what intelligent computer programs will soon be able to do, along with the inherently controversial nature of machine intelligence, have resulted in a skeptical attitude by many people. Nevertheless, recent research results with programs that exhibit some "understanding" of English, of circuit design, or of mathematics are indeed promising and seem to justify an optimistic attitude.

IMPACT OF COMPUTERS ON INDIVIDUALS AND ORGANIZATIONS

The contrast between hardware and software forms a topic under which several of the essays may be classified. Another important topic involves the extent to which computers are expected to affect individuals and organizations, as well as the extent to which individual authors present an idealistic, often revolutionary view of the future or one that is relatively more realistic and evolutionary.

Until the last few years, computers were sufficiently expensive that only organizations, often only large organizations, could afford to own or use them. The remarkable decrease in the cost of computer systems makes it possible for individuals to own their own computer systems or for organizations to own so many powerful systems that individual members can act as if they owned one. At present, personal systems based on microcomputers have limited power, yet in the coming decade the power of personal computers will increase greatly. As a result, computers and, more generally, information processing will have a direct impact on many individuals. Since such direct involvement of computers with individuals has been minimal until recently, the next two decades are likely to bring revolutionary changes.

Several essays deal with the impact of computers on individuals. Moses's essay considers the variety of domestic services that might become available in the next decade or two. He believes that the introduction of computers into homes will powerfully affect interactions between family members and could increase the self-esteem of individual members of the family. Negroponte's essay deals with applications involving graphics and pictorial images. He sees a future in which individuals paint on a computer screen and create films using computer aids. Dertouzos's essay deals, in part, with the use of computers for individualizing services and products, such as computer-based systems that produce shoes tailor-made for each customer. Winograd hopes the interaction between individuals and computers will become considerably more "convivial" than it is today. Papert's essay deals with the potentially revolutionary impact of computer systems on the education of children, since computers will allow the child to explore aspects of the world on his own.

While the future impact of computers on individuals may be revolutionary, as the authors of some essays predict, their impact on large organizations is more likely to be an evolutionary one, mainly because large organizations have been the traditional users of computers. Being complex enterprises, they are also resistant to change. Three of the authors deal with traditional sectors of computer applications—in business data processing, in scientific computation, and in government. Vyssotsky sees an evolutionary development in which computer systems gradually automate more and more of the business functions currently performed by clerical personnel. Fernbach sees a future in which scientific computation in large laboratories will rely not simply on the very big computers, as in the past, but on a broad range of machines, including special purpose minicomputers. Licklider's essay on computers and government presents a scenario in which the government fosters the development of a national computer-based network called MULTINET, which affects not only the way the government does its work but also the way individuals at home communicate with each other and with the government as well. This essay thus combines the two aspects of the topic, the computer's impact on individuals and organizations.

SOCIOECONOMIC VIEWS OF THE COMPUTER

Whether they are concerned with hardware/software or individuals/organizations, most of the essays mentioned so far see the impact of computers and information processing from a primarily technological point of view. In contrast, the essays in part 3 concentrate on their sociological and economic effects. Many of these authors find the impact of computers and information processing to be largely an indirect one.

Simon's essay considers whether the use of computers tends to favor the centralization or decentralization of organizations. After pointing out the complexities of this issue, he concludes that computers do not force either centralization or decentralization and can be used to effect essentially any level of centralization that an organization may wish. Noll's essay weighs the advantages and disadvantages of regulation of computer services. Based on past performance of regulatory agencies, he recommends continued deregulation, although he sees various forces that may lead to some regulation in computer communication, for example. Gilpin's essay examines the impact of computers on world affairs. He points out that, contrary to Marxist principles, technology generally has only an indirect effect on society, although computers have, for example, aided the rise of the multinational corporation and strengthened both offensive and defensive weapons systems. Shubik's essay deals with computer modeling of social and economic systems and concludes that while improved computer systems and more extensive data bases would certainly be helpful, the critical need is for more people who can make reasonable models. Arrow's essay treats information as an economic signal in the marketplace. As such, information has some unique features, in that once obtained it need not be obtained again. Arrow analyzes the value of information primarily from an information theory point of view.

Bell's essay presents a sweeping view of the role of information processing in our society. As the coiner of the phrase, "the postindustrial society," he points out the increasing role informational activities play in our society, affecting almost every facet of human endeavor. While the social impact of technology may be only indirect, as Gilpin points out, the cumulative effect of computers and information processing may be very great.

Weizenbaum's critical essay is unique in that it focuses exclusively on negative social factors that may accompany or impede the information revolution. He is, for example, concerned about irreversible effects on human values, undue delegation of responsibility to computers, lack of accountability in the diffuse authorship of large programs, and the inability of the often-touted future uses of computers to meet pressing social needs. While Bell, in his reply to Weizenbaum, does not dismiss these fears out of hand, he claims that the strictures Weizenbaum draws in his own essay are based on a misreading and therefore lack validity.

THE EDITORS' VIEW OF THE FUTURE

The editors' future scenario for computers and information processing rests on four technoeconomic developments that go beyond the continuing hardware revolution. They are personal computers, more intelligent programs, hidden computers, and distributed systems.

To summarize current expectations regarding personal computers, relatively inexpensive machines are likely to find their way into a large number of households, where they will be used for recreation, education, control, and communication with other informational resources.

Intelligent programs represent recent trends and the hope that we can break away from the tedious, mechanistic nature of programs that "can only do what you programmed them to do." High-risk, high-payoff research in natural-language understanding by computers and the incorporation of higher levels of intelligence in programs that dispense legal, financial, and medical services are already in progress. The extent to which these developments will be successful cannot now be accurately gauged. However, a trend toward gradual improvement seems plausible.

Hidden computers are a parallel to hidden electric motors. When asked how many electric motors we have in our homes, we at first think of only three or four and are invariably surprised when the actual number turns out to be closer to twenty. Similarly, the inexpensive microcomputers of today, which are already finding their way into our automobiles and appliances will undoubtedly proliferate into a large number of computers hidden from immediate view, because our attention will be focused instead on the functions they perform.

Geographically distributed systems, consisting of intercommunicating computers, are needed because people and hence the collection and use of information are geographically distributed. Such an arrangement of computing resources is natural because it matches in the data domain the long-existing structure of traditional organizations and interorganizational communications. To that end, local computing resources are envisioned as being quite autonomous, remaining under the control of local groups. Data communication between such systems is viewed as an integral part of an overall distributed system and represents a common denominator for conducting informational transactions.

The principal use for such distributed systems is likely to be in the office automation area, which is broadly viewed as the automation of inter- and intraorganizational informational transactions. At the beginning, such transactions will probably entail the processing of electronic mail and messages and the automation of certain routine office procedures. Later, it is envisioned that the large number of organizations and individuals interconnected through such a distributed system will form an informational marketplace where information can be bought and sold in roughly the same way as today's goods and services. This information network, in combination with intercommunicating personal computers, could radically change our way of life by the turn of the century.

When it comes to the socioeconomic effects of the computer, we tend to be optimistic. While we agree with Weizenbaum that misunderstandings about the computer's "power" and a tendency to blame the machine will undoubtedly be present, we believe that, on balance, people will comprehend the proper level and function of these machines. Our optimism perhaps carries us a little too far in our belief that the dehumanizing influence of computers will be counterbalanced and exceeded by the societal benefits of individualized products and services, by the reduction and predigestion of the information avalanches that face us daily, and by improvements in the quality of our living and working environments.

I
Prospects for the
Individual

1
The Computer in the Home

Joel Moses

A visitor to an American home in the last decade of this century might note several scenes not present in today's homes. For example, while a six-year-old child might be seen playing with toys, these toys are different from those currently available because they are computer-controlled, and the child has programmed their actions. One toy is tracing a figure on a piece of paper spread on the floor. It is doing this without human intervention. The child is seen watching the pattern being drawn. If he decides that the figure is not to his liking, he walks over to a typewriter and keys his corrections to the program controlling the toy's movements.

In another part of the house two teenagers are seen playing Space-War, a game played on a TV-like screen, which may be thought of as an extension of Ping-Pong. In Space-War each side has a rocket with a number of missiles. The game is made more complex and interesting than Ping-Pong because the rockets move in curvilinear fashion owing to the presence of a gravitational field generated by a star depicted by a bright spot in the center of the screen.

Later one of the teenagers is seen reading a book. The pages of the book are displayed on the face of a hand-held screen, and are turned by pressing buttons on the console attached to the screen. On a nearby screen the other teenager is comparing his favorite baseball team's current batting statistics with statistics taken at a similar point in the schedule a year earlier. The father appears to be reading the newspaper on yet another screen. He uses the console to obtain more detailed information on a news item of particular interest to him. The mother is seen paying this month's telephone bill. No checks are visible. Rather, the bill is viewed on the

Joel Moses is professor of computer science and engineering at MIT and associate head of the Department of Electrical Engineering and Computer Science. For many years, he has led the project that developed the MACSYMA symbolic manipulation system, one of the largest systems for solving nonnumerical problems in engineering and science.

screen, and various keys are punched on the console informing the bank to pay the telephone company the full amount.

This scenario indicates some of the computer-based services that could appear in the home in the next two decades. The implications of the widespread introduction of these services into the home are already the subject of some debate, and I shall therefore consider a number of the technical, social, and economic issues that must be resolved if the home computer becomes a reality. I shall emphasize the computer-based recreational hobbies and educational services over others like menu planning, income-tax aids, and computer programming, because although they will not be easily achieved, I believe they will have a great impact on the individual and his relationship to others.

I am assuming that the components of the home computer system are cast along fairly traditional lines. These are a central computer; a main fast memory for the computer; a larger-capacity but slower backup memory (such as a cassette); portable TV-like consoles with typewriterlike keyboard attachments; and a connection to an outside communication network, such as the telephone network, which permits the home computer to connect to central computers and their information storage and also to computers located at other homes. I shall assume that the cost of the basic system will be comparable to that of a color television set, with the monthly cost for using the network and its services comparable to today's telephone service cost.

The market for home computer systems has grown phenomenally in the past few years. Such systems have been sold largely to people who have made a hobby out of their home computers. My discussion will concentrate more on computer systems for the general populace which will have greater power and offer far more capabilities than any that are likely to be available in the next few years. At the same time, I do not wish to underestimate the impact of systems with significantly less power which could become widely available in the next five years. Electronic games are already bringing computer-based recreation into many homes, often without computers. Word-processing services in the home, such as those for editing papers, do not appear very far away, nor does use of the telephone network for computer-mediated transmission of letters (electronic mail) or payment of bills.

COMPUTER-BASED RECREATION

Visitors to university computer centers are often regaled with a variety of computer games. Currently popular computer-based games are Jotto, a word game, chess, and Space-War. Many thousands of attachments to TV sets for playing Ping-Pong-like games are expected to be sold this year for under $100. It is reasonably safe to assume that with the expected cost reduction in computer hardware in the next two decades, a variety of computer-based games and related recreational services will be available in many homes.

There is a popular tendency to play down the importance to one's life of recreation that is not very demanding physically. Partly this is a carry-over of the Puritan ethic, a feeling that one must earn one's leisure time. Thus, while few deny the need for recreation, many act as if they feel that they should work hard at play as well as at work. In addition, one effect of television has been to degrade the creative aspects of recreation and overemphasize its purely entertaining aspects. One effect of computer-based recreation will likely be a deemphasis of the increasingly passive or exceedingly physical modes of leisure and the reintroduction of an older active and interactive mode.

The popular electronic Ping-Pong game is an example of a two-person game requiring some physical dexterity. Probably the most interesting such game is Space-War, invented in Cambridge, Massachusetts, around 1960. Space-War is a two-person game that utilizes a TV-like screen. Each player is given a spaceship which moves on the screen and which can be turned, sped up, or slowed down by moving knobs on a console. Each ship has a number of missiles which are used to shoot down the opponent's spaceship. The game is made more complex by introducing a star in the center of the screen which creates a gravitational pull, causing the ships to move in a curvilinear fashion. Ships that move off the top of the screen reappear at the bottom; those that leave from the right appear in the left part of the screen. The geometry of the space, which resembles that of a torus, also has its counterintuitive aspects. The game offers the players some unusual experiences, and they learn how to execute some of the same maneuvers required by spaceships.

Computer programs have played chess at a good amateur level since 1967. Though no current programs play at the level of a world champion, they can easily defeat over 90 percent of the amateurs in the country. Current programs possess two features that make them very useful in the home. For one, chess programs are forgiving. They let you take a bad move back without complaining. They do not gloat after they win or become very gloomy after a loss. For another, chess programs can be tuned so that they play just a little bit better or worse than their opponent, making it possible to let one's temperament dictate how often one loses to such a program. The author must admit to having lost several hundred matches to one of these programs over the last ten years.

There are certain drawbacks to current chess programs. They do not use well-defined plans for attack or defense. Rather, they tend to play a cautious game, waiting for the opponent to make a tactical mistake. They are also unable to describe the purpose of their moves or the strengths and weaknesses of the opponent's moves, as a human tutor might. Such weaknesses present a challenge for designers of chess programs in the next decade.

One of the strengths of computers in a recreational environment is the great variety of things that can be done with the same basic system. One would not expect the emergence of a computer in the home to create a sudden and long-lasting chess or Space-War mania in the country, but one would expect a "Game of the Month" club to appear, along with increased playing of the classical games.

COMPUTER-BASED HOBBIES

Games are not likely to be the only recreational uses of computers in the home. Computer systems could also aid in various traditional projects in the home that often have a recreational component. For example, a computer system could help to design new dress patterns. Patterns might be used to guide a computer-controlled saw to cut wood for a chair, in an extension of the way in which machine tools are now guided in industrial applications. Nicholas Negroponte's essay, "The Return of the Sunday Painter," discusses how computers could permit people to "paint" on the surface of the screen (see chapter 2).

An era in which computer-based applications in the home were widely prevalent might make it possible for an individual who so chose to become expert in a wide array of activities, since with the help of computer systems he could reach a reasonable level of proficiency relatively quickly. In addition, those who shared a common interest might use the computer-communication network (which I shall discuss later) to form an electronic version of a club. A club for those interested in, say, Chinese pottery of the Ming dynasty might meet on the air on Wednesdays at 7:30 P.M. in order to view and discuss a particular vase.

One effect of the mass media in the past century has been to homogenize experience by providing everyone with the same TV shows or newspaper columns. The mass media also tend to reduce most individuals to insignificance by building up a few personalities to superhuman proportions. Computer-based hobbies can work to reverse this trend by allowing different individuals to specialize in different areas and build up their self-esteem by virtue of their proficiency.

COMPUTER-BASED EDUCATION IN THE HOME

One of the early predictions made about television was that it would have a great impact on education. It is fair to say that whatever positive impact the medium has had has been late in coming and not as great as its adherents had hoped for. Although proponents of the home computer risk falling into a similar trap, I nevertheless believe that computers in the home will be of very great value in education.

One of the major differences between computers and television is that a computer and its associated hardware and software leads to an active rather than a passive involvement. It is argued by some, notably Professor Seymour Papert of MIT (see chapter 5), that the deepest educational experiences for a child occur as a result of working on projects of fairly long duration. In order to facilitate such projects and to channel them into educationally rewarding directions, Professor Papert's group has devised a number of "supertoys." One such toy, which looks like an inverted fruit bowl, is called a turtle and can be made to crawl on the floor under the control of the computer. It can be programmed by a seven-year-old child to draw various patterns, such as a circle or a human figure, on paper laid on the floor. If the figure being drawn is incorrect or not to the child's liking, he can modify the program and redraw the figure. Another turtle project is a simple program that causes the turtle to wind its way through a maze of boxes on the floor. Through such projects children can learn geometric skills and develop intuition and have a great deal of fun in the process. Another supertoy is a music box that can be programmed to repeat a set of notes with variations. Such a toy gives children who are not yet skilled in playing musical instruments an enjoyable way of making music on their own.

A more traditional form of computer-aided education is based on the concept of drill and practice. For example, a slide appears on the display screen saying that George Washington was the first president of the United States. A later slide asks who was the first president and gives five choices. If the child answers correctly, he advances to the next section; otherwise he repeats the section. Such programs are quite successful in certain situations, such as memorizing vocabulary.

The drill and practice form of computer-aided education has often been criticized. The kind of teaching program many of its critics would like to see is one that offers a conceptual understanding of the material being taught rather than one based on a script composed of multiple-choice questions. Unfortunately there are as yet few programs with this property. One example is the Sophie system, which teaches naval recruits how to repair electronic circuits. Remedying this lack of sophisticated software in the next two decades is a challenge for workers in the field of computer-aided education.

Computers are already in use in the nation's grade and high schools, most commonly in high schools, where they are used to teach ways of programming computers to solve mathematical problems. There are sizable efforts under way to introduce systems based on the drill and practice model, such as the PLATO system marketed by the Control Data Corporation. The penetration of computer-based education into the schools can be expected to increase in the next two decades. It is quite likely that the learning experience and the sheer enjoyment that children will derive from computer-based education in the home will speed up the introduction of such educational technology into the schools.

In addition to its value for children, computer-aided education in the home can be of value to adults as a means for obtaining continuing education, which is acquiring more and more importance in our society as the average age of the population rises. While many adults go to schools and colleges in the evenings and some take courses via television, there are many who are held back by the timing constraints imposed by these forms of education. The educational computer program in the home could presumably be run at any available time, and the computer system might even remind the student to continue a course if he had been avoiding it for a while.

AUTOMATIC CONTROL OF APPLIANCES IN THE HOME

Millions of families already have rudimentary forms of computers in their homes. Interestingly enough, most of the owners of these computers are unaware of their existence, because they are the forerunners of a generation of silent, invisible, and very cheap computers (microcomputers) which can be used to operate various appliances.

These rudimentary computers are the ones used to control electronic calculators. The function buttons of calculators provide such a simple language for getting a computer to solve a computational problem that the user is often not aware that he is programming a computer. It is the restricted nature of the service to be performed that makes the interaction with the computer so easy. Home appliances also perform well-defined services, and most of them can be expected to be controlled by computers in the next decade or two. At first the appliances will have independent microcomputers; later they may be linked to the central home computer. A computer-controlled range could regulate the heat in the oven quite carefully (say within $1°$ of the desired temperature). It could be made to turn on a back burner after the oven had been at $370°F$ for thirty minutes, for example. A washing machine might be able to accept a more complex description via push buttons of the range of fabrics in a particular load. It would then try to regulate the temperature and washing cycles so that all the clothes were properly washed.

Large buildings are already making use of small computers in order to optimize the consumption of energy. Such control of heating and cooling plants saves enough in energy costs to pay for the computer system after only a few months of use. Similar savings could be had in the home if temperature sensors throughout the house were connected to the home computer. Such a computer could also be informed when people leave the home and when they are expected back and could have good plans for regulating heat and air conditioning at night.

The impact of computer control would be more revolutionary and controversial in the case of appliances such as automatic vacuum cleaners, which would clean wall-to-wall carpets and sweep under the furniture by themselves. Such vacuum cleaners would presumably use tactile sensors to locate the furniture and to avoid close contact with pets or babies. Similar appliances can be imagined for cooking in the kitchen or cleaning in the yard. Again it is likely that the wide range of services provided by such devices will have the greatest impact. Safety and cost factors will, of course, play a paramount role in determining their eventual usefulness. Michael Dertouzos discusses how related computer-controlled devices, largely outside the home, could produce custom-made apparel, such as shoes (see chapter 3).

COMMUNICATION AND HOME COMPUTERS

So far I have largely stressed "stand-alone" applications of the home computer—that is, they do not depend on a communications network. I believe that such applications will be the first to become available, and the current computer hobbyist and video games markets tend to confirm this view.

Coupling a home computer with a communications network will permit many new services and raise many new issues such as privacy and potential impact on existing services (for example, the Postal Service), along with a number of issues related to communications, government regulation, technological alternatives, and potential requirements for capital investment.

There are various alternatives to existing communication services, depending on the characteristics of the technology in use. The telephone network can currently be used to transmit digital information at rates from 10 characters per second to 960 characters per second. At the latter rate, the usual TV screen can be filled in under two seconds. A modem, the device that permits the encoding and decoding of the signals over the telephone lines, presently costs under $10 per character in the transmission rate. These costs can be expected to be reduced markedly with new electronic technologies and larger markets. For services such as electronic mail, the telephone network's transmission rates, especially at the high end of the scale, will present no problems. The problems arise when one considers transmission of books and especially of pictures. The transmission of different pictures into each home will force the use of technologies with broader bandwidths than those currently available for the telephone network.

Electronic Mail, News, and Related Services

Many people have noted a trade-off between doing a computation locally, for example at home, or doing it remotely and communicating the results. When the information changes rapidly, as in the case of news, there is no way to avoid some form of communication. The trade-off in such cases is between physical transportation of the information and electronic communication. There are two major information services to the home that are currently delivered by carriers rather than entirely by phone or radio and television. These are the mail and the newspaper. My concern here is with how these services could be delivered via a communication network and the home computer.

Let us consider the various classifications of mail. First, we shall remove parcel post from further consideration. If you send your aunt a sweater, she had better get that sweater rather than an electronic image of it. First-class mail is another story. Much of first-class mail to the home is composed of bills, and much of the mail sent out by homes consists of payment of such bills. Electronic communication can make a significant contribution here. Second-class mail is largely comprised of magazines. Magazines are facing grave financial crises because the cost of mailing them has risen so high. Much of the rest of the mail is so-called junk mail, which is advertising in one form or another. Mass advertising is in large part a gamble—the advertiser is betting that a certain percentage of the recipients will actually buy the product or service. This situation could stand some improvement as far as both parties are concerned. There remain personal letters and Christmas cards. The latter category accounts for a significant fraction of the mail, but one wonders whether an electronic reproduction of a card will be satisfactory to the sender or the recipient.

One scenario that can be considered for the automation of the distribution of bills goes as follows: The electric company sends the information in its bill to your home computer. When you decide to check on your electronic mail that day you see the bill's contents on your screen with all the usual information such as kilowatt-hours used. If you are satisfied with the bill you can press some buttons on the console and cause a message to be sent to your bank requesting it to pay the bill from your account. This process thus avoids the mailing of the bill, the writing of a check, and the mailing of the payment. If you are not satisfied with the bill you can send a reply to the electric company via the network stating the reason for non-payment.

Let us consider the service in greater detail. Since the bill itself contains only a moderate amount of information, say a hundred words of text, the current telephone network is faster and probably no more expensive even today than the mails for this purpose. The idea of coupling the bank into the process of paying bills over the network is an example of what is called an electronic funds transfer (EFT) system. An EFT system similar to the one just described for the home is used in certain retail transactions as well. The information on a sale, along with the buyer's account number and password, is fed to the bank automatically, causing the buyer's account to be reduced accordingly, after which a message is transmitted to the seller's bank to increase his account by the amount of the sale. The combined use of such a system in the home and in stores would drastically cut down on the volume of checks in circulation. Some banks already offer the simple half of this transaction—that is, one can call the bank and request it to pay the required amount to the sender of one of the usual monthly bills, such as the electric bill.

An extension of the electronic bill-paying service would allow one to send a typewritten or even handwritten message to a relative or friend on the network. Message sending has, in fact, been one of the most common uses of a major existing computer network, the government's ARPA network. Computer programs can make the job of addressing such electronic letters very convenient. Once the computer knows your mother's network address, then you may just write a letter to "Mom," and the proper addressing is done automatically. The letter can be expected to be in her mail file either the same day or the next. This mode of communication has many of the advantages of a telegram over a telephone call. The message will arrive even if your mother is on the phone or not home at all when you send the message. The recipient has a chance to look this message over quite carefully. If the communication network had sufficient bandwidth one might even be able to attach a doodle or a recent photograph to the message.

A potentially important use of message transmission is for transmission of identical messages to a group. The computer could keep the addresses of all your bridge club members. Then you need only send a message to "Bridge Club Members." This form of communication could substantially increase the number of groups one would be able to join. A side effect would be that one's mail would tend to increase, but since messages over the network would contain the name of the sender (telephone calls do not), one could direct the computer to ignore mail from unwanted senders.

Let us now consider the possibility of transmitting news over the network. The morning news could be transmitted overnight and stored in the computer's memory, to be read from the console in the morning. Although the amount of information to be transmitted is quite large (especially if one includes digitized photographs and diagrams), we might be able to get away with the current telephone's capacity, though a technology with a bigger bandwidth (like cable TV) might very well turn out to be preferable. The reason is that a single paper is being transmitted to many transcribers, and the time available for transmission is hours rather than seconds.

One potential difference between electronic news and our current newspapers is the length and variety of the articles. The news stories need not be limited by current page size. Thus articles may be of greater length and contain more background information than at present. Furthermore it may be possible for subscribers to obtain news of particular interest to them by having the computer store stories containing certain key words in the title and ignore many others. The *Wall Street Journal* is already using a satellite to transmit news copy to various printing plants around the country. Many newspapers and magazines use computers to store copy, justify it, and prepare it for photocomposition. Thus electronic news in the home appears to be in line with the present evolution of this field. In fact, the BBC sends certain news information over the air which can be picked up by owners of television sets with special attachments.

Much of the income derived by newspapers comes from advertising. With the advent of a home computer network, advertisers may change their mode of operation, but the consequence of such a change for newspapers is entirely unclear. Advertisers currently use mass mailings and newspapers partly in the hope of getting a message to a customer at about the same time he or she wishes to buy a particular product or service. This aspect of advertising is a fairly inefficient process. Quite often the consumer does not receive the information he wants, and the advertiser reaches many people who are not interested in the message at that time. One possibility is to collect current advertising copy for a whole class of products, say groceries, in the memory of a central computer. Consumers would have access to this information in the home and might even be able to place an order at home in a manner similar to that of a Sears catalogue.

Magazines should be able to use the network in a manner quite similar to newspapers, with the possible difference that one might be able to pay for the right to read a single story or two rather than the whole magazine. The impact of a potential loss of advertising is likely to be consequential here also. Of course, there are now magazines such as *Consumer Reports* that are viable even though they do not accept any advertising at all.

Electronic mail will, of course, have a tremendous impact on the U.S. Postal Service. The Federal Communications Commission or Congress could forestall it by postponing the introduction of such a service until sufficiently many carriers and mail sorters have retired, but there may in fact be no need for such action since half the employees of the Postal Service are over fifty years of age.

THE ELECTRONIC LIBRARY IN THE HOME

The dream that one might be able to read any book in a large library such as the Library of Congress just by pressing the right keys on one's console and reading the pages from a display screen has been around for quite a while. Presumably the texts of the books would be stored in digital form on some medium that can be read by a computer. The contents of a single page could be displayed on the TV-like screen; by pressing a button one could effectively flip pages. Ideally the contents of a new page would appear on the screen very quickly, say in under a second.

What would be required in order to make this dream a practical reality? Assuming a page of text contains 300 words on the average, or about 2,000 letters, it has about 10,000 bits of digital information. At 300 pages per book, the Library of Congress, with 20 million volumes, will thus contain about 10^{14} bits of textual material. By contrast, a single photograph has something on the order of a million bits (10^6) of digital information. But since the number of photographs is smaller than the number of pages of pure text, we can still estimate the capacity of the library at about 10^{14} bits. This is approximately one thousand times the capacity of the largest computer memories now available, so in order to make a copy of its contents available for use with the home computer, one would need to employ a new technology or a highly modified existing technology, such as video tape. Current business and scientific users of computers have only recently awakened to the value of a storage medium with just the properties required by a copy of a library (i.e., very high capacity, relatively slow access, relatively slow read-in rates, and no writing capability beyond the first time). Nevertheless, we cannot be reasonably certain that such a technology will be widely available in homes by the last decade of this century.

On the other hand, if a computer-readable copy of the library were kept in a central computer, thus sharing the memory costs among thousands of subscribers, the contents of a book could be transmitted a page at a time on demand over a communications network, such as the telephone network. However, at current telephone rates for digital information (between 10 and 960 characters per second), it would take about several seconds for a new page to appear on the screen, which may not be an acceptable rate for most purposes. And even if the system were clever enough to keep ahead of the reader, it would get bogged down transmitting a digitized picture, which would require several minutes at current rates.

Another possibility is that one could improve the transmission capacity of the telephone networks by improving the switching elements underground or even changing all the cables to use fiber optics. This would involve a multibillion-dollar capital investment and would take a decade or two to carry out over the whole country. One hesitates to speculate about such a possibility, in part because of the feeling that digging up the streets of our cities is such a large undertaking that the results would have to satisfy our needs for many decades to come.

There exists yet another communications technology that could possibly handle all the requirements—cable TV. With cable TV one might be able to transmit different books to hundreds or thousands of simultaneous readers in a given locality. There are various arguments advanced as to why cable TV has not got off the ground, such as difficulties with local regulatory bodies and lack of sufficient service to the community; the home computer could very well lead to the widespread use of cable TV. Satellites could potentially offer another broad-band technology suited to applications in the home.

But even supposing we could resolve the storage and communication problems in the next two decades, we would still face another technology that has had five hundred years to develop—the technology of bookmaking. Consider some of the characteristics of books: they are fairly small, lightweight, and very portable (imagine taking a TV-like console to read in bed), easily marked up (for the purpose of recalling previously read material), and possess high communications bandwidth (for maps, reproductions of paintings, and so on). For the technology of display consoles to achieve these characteristics in the laboratory stage is likely to require well over a decade, and even then some compromises will probably be unavoidable.

Another issue that would have to be confronted in a world of electronic home libraries is that of copyright. How would the rights of authors be protected? One could charge the readers a fee for each book they read from a central memory, but the payment to be obtained by publishers and authors for a copy of a full library sold to the home appears a more complex matter. The advent of a computer communication network with its potential for rapid access to articles and books will surely have a major impact on the publishing field.

COMPUTERIZED FACT RETRIEVAL

A special part of a library in the home is composed of reference books, such as encyclopedias, record books, and dictionaries. A user of reference material is usually after only a tiny fragment of the information contained in such volumes. Thus the total amount of information to be stored and the amount needed to be transmitted at any given time is not nearly as great as in the case of a full electronic home library, making it possible to avoid many of the problems associated with the latter. In fact, in the case of reference material, computers can potentially offer better service than consulting reference works in the library.

As in the case of the electronic home library, one might be able to purchase a full copy of the reference books in the form of a cassette tape or obtain the desired information through the telephone network. One advantage that the network approach possesses over both the home copy and the present system is that the network could maintain up-to-date versions of the material. The centralized information could presumably be kept current with about the same manpower needed to keep reference books current, at the same time avoiding the delays entailed in publication and distribution of the volumes.

A more basic difficulty with reference works is that one cannot always determine how to find the information one seeks, no matter how well classified the volumes may be. A simple example of this type is that of finding the correct spelling of a word when an incorrect one is known (actually there now exists a book for just this purpose which contains many common misspellings). This is a situation in which computers could do very well, given an appropriate classification of the information and some capacity to conduct a dialogue in English within a narrow domain of interest. In particular, the misspelling situation could be handled by knowing the common misspellings, knowing heuristics for ways in which people tend to misspell, using some knowledge of phonetics, some trial and error, and so on. Furthermore, there would be no need to look up a word in a pocket-sized dictionary. The computer could store the information contained in the largest dictionaries, giving out as much detail as the user might request.

Another application of fact retrieval in which computers could perform better than standard reference volumes occurs in situations where one can store all occurrences of a particular class of events. Examples are stock sales and baseball games. Suppose you wanted to know how often your team won Sunday doubleheaders last season or the won-lost record of left-handers in Fenway Park. Such information could be compiled in a record book, but it is not likely to be if the question is of a nonstandard kind. A program could search the record of all games played by your team last year or all games ever played in Fenway Park and answer these questions with little difficulty. The problems of structuring information on financial transactions or baseball games is clearly within the state of the art, and an English-language question answering system, if sufficiently restricted in subject matter, should be within the state of the art in the next ten years. Such a natural-language program will, however, require a large memory for grammatical information, semantic word meanings, and the like. Terry Winograd discusses the general implications of such programs for the interactions between humans and computers (see chapter 4).

Fact retrieval services generalize into advice-giving services. One of the most often mentioned services for the home is a program that aids in the preparation of income taxes, such as helping the user to take as many legal deductions as are available to him. One advantage of such a service would be in unusual situations, where the program could point out existing tax rulings—something the local H. & R. Block representative is not likely to be able to do. The next two decades may also see homes containing programs that dispense legal or medical advice, such as antidotes to poisons found in household cleaning fluids, although most advice-giving programs will be slated for use by doctors and lawyers in their offices. There is much research at present on diagnostic and disease management tools for doctors. Examples are programs that recommend how much digitalis to give a patient or that determine which one of about a hundred different infections a patient seems to have.

OFFICES IN THE HOME

A relatively radical proposal for trading transportation for communication is the concept of the office in the home. Underlying this concept is the belief that many employees, especially those in white-collar jobs, could stay at home one or two days a week and still perform essentially the same duties that they now do via the network. An advantage claimed for this concept is that less travel to the office would mean a reduction in pollution and energy consumption. Such a system would demand an exceedingly close coupling of the office in the home with the regular office. Assuming that the person staying home is the proverbial paper shuffler, then the memos he or she would receive must be communicated to the home and back to the office at approximately the same rate as before. This places a strain on the network. If one were to allow interviews in the home office, then a picture-phone-like facility would be necessary as well. At this point it is difficult to imagine how such a concept would affect one's interactions with colleagues and other members of the family.

The office in the home would presumably use much of the same hardware, software, and communications technology that are likely to be used in the "automated office" in the coming decade. The automated office concept assumes a marked reduction of paper flow, since individuals will be able to read the required documents on the console. If a document needed to be printed, it would be done on copying machines directly attached to the network of consoles. Preparation of the documents themselves could be notably simplified by having powerful editing and text-justifying software in the console computer.

The office in the home concept can be of great importance to people who find it difficult to leave the home. Mothers with small children might be able to have part-time jobs at home by working at a computer console during their free minutes. People with certain emotional and physical problems which make it difficult for them to interact with other people outside the home may find that the computer network gives them an important outlet.

HARDWARE-SOFTWARE REQUIREMENTS

The basic hardware bottleneck in the introduction of sophisticated computer services in the home is likely to be the size of the main and backup memories. A computer with a main memory of about ten million bits will probably be satisfactory for most services. A reasonable guess for the sale price of the home computer is about $500, or the price of a color TV set. The current value of a medium-speed computer with the desired memory size is about $500,000, although cheaper and decidedly more expensive computer systems with such specifications are clearly available. Is there any reason to expect the cost of the system to be reduced by a factor of nearly one thousand in fixed dollars in the next two decades? The answer is yes if we extrapolate from the experience of the past two decades. It is an adage in the computer business that the cost of a given computation goes down by 30 percent every year. In fact, certain manufacturers appear to price their equipment accordingly. When extrapolated for twenty years, the 30 percent reduction rate yields a decrease of a factor of about a thousand. Noyce's essay on the physical limitations of large-scale integration (LSI) technology tends to support this expected reduction in the cost of hardware, but if it fails to materialize, one could always cut down on the services available in the home, or use lower performance systems, or use the network for various services that cannot be obtained at home.

The major reason for favoring a relatively powerful home computer is that a sizable software system will be needed for the support of natural-language interaction, for fact retrieval systems, and generally for the support of the wide variety of services I have described. Thus in addition to the hardware required and the communications requirements, one has to consider the cost and availability of software for performing the various services. Currently software costs are outstripping hardware costs in most computer installations. The computer in the home may provide a different experience. At present a particular piece of software may be used in anywhere from a single installation to approximately 50,000 installations, with a majority being used at fewer than a hundred installations. If we assume that software could be used in ten million homes, with the cost amortized over several years via a rental charge, then even a multibillion dollar software cost could be recouped.

One factor that will affect the cost of the home computer is whether the system is sold by a single company or several competing companies. If we assume that available services will continue to grow gradually, as they have already been doing in the recreation area, then the market will be competitive. This may require home owners to pay for a multiplicity of hardware systems, multiple versions of similar software, and so on. Competition, of course, will likely produce some very good products, along with many mediocre ones, and possibly some undesirable ones. A gradual entry into the home may provide sufficient lead time for the basic research that needs to be done on issues like natural-language query systems. The argument for a more monopolistic market is based on the need for a large capital investment in software, hardware, and communications equipment in order to deliver good service from the start. On the other hand, we do not yet know which services are likely to be most useful, and a competitive market will point these out.

SOCIAL IMPACT OF HOME COMPUTERS

Some people maintain that the introduction of computer-based services in the home will only further the process of making us incompetent in areas in which we were previously competent, as the introduction of hand calculators may have done in the area of arithmetic. There are others who believe that the range of services potentially available through the home computer is not sufficiently interesting and useful to families and that few of them would purchase a system even if it were to cost as little as a color television set. It is hard to argue against such claims at this time. Data regarding the acceptance of relatively rudimentary recreational and educational services in homes in the next five to eight years should give us some information on these points. Others do not deny the value of services like computer-based education but argue that our understanding of the software issues involved in producing viable services are woefully insufficient. Thus they recommend that we wait until the services become very much better than they are now before unleashing them on the market. I have much sympathy with such a position, yet I wonder whether the market forces in our economy can be controlled sufficiently to make such an approach effective. Moreover, there is good reason to suppose that a child presented with bad educational material in the home will ignore it, given the choice.

A distinction must be made between the social impact of a home computer system that is not connected to a communications network and one that is. Some services such as electronic mail cannot exist without such a link, but there are many that can, such as recreation, education, device control, and fact retrieval.

The issue of privacy, so often raised in discussion of the social impact of computers, takes on slightly different forms in the home. If your home computer is not connected to a communications network, then the private information that you have placed in the computer's memory is physically located in your home. Thus unless electronic snooping becomes much more refined than it is now, a thief who wants to steal such information will be forced to commit a burglary. The deterrent in such a situation is the same as in the usual case where someone breaks into your home and rifles your desk. Unfortunately our legal system has not yet determined a punishment that fits a crime like this. The punishment for breaking and entering may be insignificant when compared with the value to the individual of the information lost. Furthermore, the information you may have in your file at home may be truly private (such as love letters).

Most of the debate on privacy so far has dwelt on data bases that collect information like age and bank balance easily obtained from some other data base, such as a registry of births and deaths. Nevertheless, the potential for loss of information is considerably enhanced if the home computer is linked to a network. Even if we suppose that the links are such that the network cannot get information from the file at home that the user did not specifically transmit, we would still have the technical problem of enforcing such a restriction. If we wish to be able to keep private information in the memories of central computer networks, then the problems become much more acute. In spite of recent breakthroughs in the development of "unbreakable" encryption codes, in the long run we may want to have what John McCarthy has called a "Privacy Bill of Rights."

The government may play a major role in the operation of such a network of home computers. Licklider's essay, in fact, discusses a government-sponsored network, dubbed MULTINET, that would link home computers with various agencies of the government (chapter 6). Another way in which the government may be involved is in the area of regulation. Noll's essay on this subject (chapter 12) paints a bleak picture of past experience with regulated industries, yet he admits that it is unlikely that a national network of computers will escape regulation entirely. Several national policy commissions have already examined various issues such as privacy, electronic funds transfer, and copyrights. Though many laws and regulations have been proposed, the home computer field is still largely unregulated.

A large national network need not be established all at once. It could start in small communities and grow over time. This approach requires less capital in exchange for a reduced level of service. Some have proposed that the federal government sponsor a pilot experiment in which a community of, say, fifty thousand is linked via telephones to central computers. Some such experiment appears to be a good way of beginning the informal public policy debate over the home computer. An experiment with as few as 200 homes provided with a comprehensive home computer system and communications network could yield much insight into the technical and social problems that remain to be resolved, and especially which approaches and services should be avoided in the future.

The home computer will not arrive all at once. Various computer-based recreational, educational, and control services will appear in many homes in the next ten years. Current systems composed of a black-and-white television set, a keyboard, and a microprocessor-based computer are already available for under $500. The coming decade will, one hopes, give us sufficient time to prepare for the impact of what may well turn out to be the most powerful technology to be introduced in this century, one that could profoundly affect our lives both as individuals and as members of families.

EDITORS' POSTSCRIPT

Most idealistic projections of the impact of computers on individuals are vulnerable to the criticism that similar projections were made about the telephone, radio, and television in previous decades. Such projections have not been fully borne out, a point raised by Weizenbaum's essay. At the same time, the reader should note that Moses makes relatively long-range projections extending fifteen or twenty years into the future. Thus, as McCarthy has pointed out in his critique, he tends to deemphasize the fact that many services, such as electronic mail, might become available in the next five to ten years, services that could have a noticeable impact on the home relatively quickly.

2
The Return of the Sunday Painter

Nicholas P. Negroponte

Rarely have two disciplines joined forces seemingly to bring out the worst in each other as have computers and art. A mixture of mathematical exercises has predominated in the search for ways to use computers in general and computer graphics in particular for the purpose of achieving a new art form, or simply art, or both. The symmetry and periodicity of the Lissajous figures (easily generated curves on TV screens), transformations into and out of recognizable patterns, and the happenstance of stochastic* processing epitomize the current palette of gadgetry used by either the playful computer scientist or the inquiring artist in the name of art. While the intentions may be good, the results are predominantly bad art and petty programming. In almost all cases the signature of the machine is far more apparent than the artist's.

In computer science communities, computer art is for the most part a Calcomp contest.** We can imagine sprocket holes framing the top and bottom or sides of a line drawing, curiously signed with line work that is usually much richer. However, it is exactly in such banality that I find my theme. That is, the art form lies not in the product but in the process of creating and playing with it, an activity currently limited to a few but predicted to be available to all.

We can confidently postulate more tactile and graphic computers of exceptionally low cost. Similarly, we can picture users ranging from children to adults, from workmen to professionals, delighting in the mannerisms of something like an electronic finger painting. Along these lines we can imagine the performing and the visual arts drawing closer together, designs becoming more ephemeral, and every man an artist.

Nicholas P. Negroponte is associate professor of computer graphics at MIT. His interests are in the human-to-machine interface, particularly new modalities of interacting with machines at the sensory level as well as at the level of application.

* Use of randomness by programs, thereby generating different and unpredictable results.

** The Calcomp Corporation sponsors an annual contest of computer art.

Shudder! Does this mean that the fine arts might lose their purpose of creating and recreating metrics for beauty and meaning, along with their position as historical landmarks of cultural complexity and contradiction? Not at all. What will happen twenty years hence is that the impact of computers on the visual arts will be enormous in our everyday lives but comparatively small in terms of the breadth of an artist's activities. We can expect computer graphics to invade our homes and our work life, but we should not expect all canvases to be cathode-ray tubes. Nor should we expect a computer aesthetic to pervade every aspect of creativity, any more than we see the heroes of Dostoevski in the laws of relativity.

This hypothesis is derived from evidence provided by the visual arts themselves, as their products, processes, and participants move further and further away from what we now know as art. Computers will characteristically be able to break down barriers between the arts, between work and play, between the haves and have-nots.

All following arguments anticipate achievements in artificial intelligence and personal computers and a richness of media for man-computer interaction analogous to a private world's fair. We can imagine computer-driven celebrations that would make today's most psychedelic environments look like funerals. Furthermore, current trends in video approaches to computer graphics, three-dimensional displays, flat displays, color displays, and developments in input techniques are fashioned more after the paintbrush than the T square. But these are not the crucial issues.

PRODUCTS

A Metaphor Cannot Be Hung Upside Down

Recall a romantic and personal event. Perhaps it takes place in a far-off land, on a beach, under a full moon, and you are wildly in love. You put a pebble in your pocket. Then, for a week or a year or half a century, this pebble sits on the mantel. To you, it sits more nobly and beautifully than a Brancusi because of all the meanings you ascribe to it and the memories it evokes. It has value to you as a metaphor, and as such it is personal art.

An artist, in the most general sense, is a maker of metaphors. We can conclude that an acclaimed artist of some accomplishment has successfully made metaphors to which a broad cross section of a culture can ascribe meaning. This is what distinguishes you from Picasso and the pebble from a Picasso sculpture.

Within the realm of "products" this distinction is important, first because I will shortly argue that the major impact of computers will be in the personal art forms and second because shared metaphors of Art with a capital *A* are partially shaped by professional critics. With regard to a more

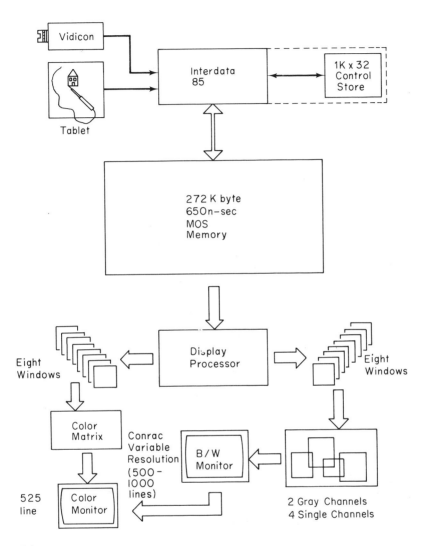

2.1
PAINT Experiment Display Configuration

2.2 (See next page)
Transformations by Vera Molnar, The Concourse Gallery, 35 Marylebone Road, London NW1, June 10 to July 2, 1978. Her catalogue opens with a quote from J. J. Winckelmann: *Kleine Schriften und Briefe,* 1755: "Der Pinsel, den der Künstler führt, soll im Verstand getunkt sein" (The paintbrush that the artist handles should be dipped into knowledge.)

traditional kind of art object, I divide the importance of computers into two functions: contributing to the common metaphors and acting as a new medium.

Automata found their way into the metaphors for art in the seventeenth and early eighteenth centuries, modeled after the mechanisms of clockwork. A great mathematician like Leibniz would even have argued that celestial intervention was not necessary to maintain them. In the late eighteenth century and through the nineteenth, we find metaphors derived from the steam engine; the optics of a steam-filled railway station helped lead us into impressionism. In the case of both clocks and engines, the art was intended for the amusement of a mercantile aristocracy. In some instances, there was no metaphor; the automaton itself was the product, and the artist reacted with concern. For example, Eugene Delacroix wrote in his journal on August 3, 1885, "I went to the Exposition; I noticed the fountain which spouts giant artificial flowers. The sight of all those machines makes me feel badly. I don't like that stuff which, all alone and left to itself, seems to be producing things worthy of admiration."

Explorations of contemporary metaphors for art, reflecting an electronic age, were the subject of three consecutive art exhibitions: *Cybernetic Serendipity* at the Institute of Contemporary Arts in London (August 1968), *Information* at the Museum of Modern Art in New York (June 1970), and *Software* at the Jewish Museum, also in New York (September 1970). Of the three, *Software* offered the most sophisticated imagery and the most complex machines, but each provided a rich repertoire of new metaphors upon which to build and with which to compose. None offered art per se.

MIT contributed a "piece" to *Software* called SEEK, purposely named with a verb. It deserves mention inasmuch as it was a product of processes orchestrated to interact with an animate world. While it was an inspired assemblage of hardware and software, it rightfully could be called a "hack" in some dialect of computerese.

SEEK consisted of a simple block-piling mechanism with five hundred two-inch cubes it could pile on a grid within a large glass box. Prior to opening night it did just that, using a simple space-allocation program to assure many nooks and crannies and remembering the position of each block. On opening night a small colony of gerbils was introduced into the system. Scurrying about within this parsimonious architecture, they knocked over blocks and set many askew, causing a dreadful mismatch between the real world and the computer's model of it. SEEK's task was precisely to manage this mismatch, which it did in two ways. In the case of slightly displaced cubes, the machine fastidiously realigned and restored the neighborhood. In the event of major dislocations, the program interpreted the movement as purposeful (i.e., the gerbils wanted it that way) and put the blocks in their new places. For the observer this meant a new

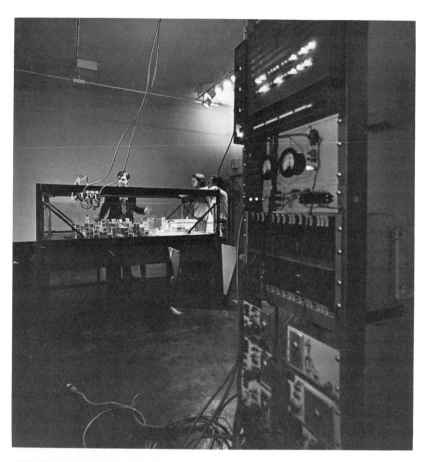

2.3
SEEK

architecture, which changed from day to day according to how the little animals inhabited it. The purpose was neither to find the essence of gerbilness nor to liken people to gerbils or the blocks to foreign policy (as was suggested). The intent was simply to show an interactive system observably dealing with unpredictable events, from an unsettled heap of blocks to its own malfunctions.

Reviews of the show failed to keep SEEK intact, to see its animate and inanimate aspects as equally purposeful. *The New York Times* (September 18, 1970) reported that ". . . a mechanical grappler rearranges them [the blocks] to wall the furry creatures in"; *Art News* (December 1970, in a snide editorial entitled "Gerbil ex Machina") wrote, "The gerbils could use their blocks to achieve positive, socially meaningful ends, but not just mess around with them"; and the *Wall Street Journal* simply found it and computer art in general ideologically "kinky."

Copyrights Instead of Signatures and the Xerox Original

We can observe the medium much more easily than the metaphor, at times too easily. A generalized criticism of computer graphics in art is that it is a caricature of McLuhan's cliché, the medium is the message. One of A. Michael Noll's earliest works, *Gaussian Quadratic* (1963), sets the stage for

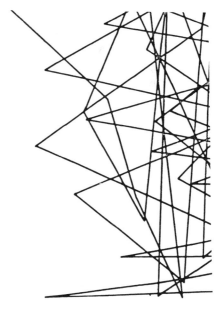

© AMN 1965

2.4
A. Michael Noll's *Gaussian Quadratic* (1965), its lower-left-hand corner

line makers and stochastic processing, in this case of ninety-nine zigzags. What is most revealing is the work's copyright, dated two years later. Noll was one of the first to realize and hint at the proprietary problem, one that has come to plague the entire computer industry, one for which the art world had previously accepted a signature as a patent. We would be hard put to define the notion of forgery in most products of computer art.

In 1963 the magazine *Computers and Automation* instituted an annual art contest, the winner of which was usually on the cover of their August issue. To date we find as winners of the contest the results of transformations that, like good stunts, capture our attention by their cleverness and unrealizability without computer aid. This is true in both static and dynamic graphics.

In 1967 six Japanese formed the Computer Technique Group (CTG) to produce static graphics with an IBM 7090 and a Calcomp 563 plotter. Their work is still a landmark, though the group has been disbanded. Their material epitomizes the kaleidoscopic adventures of computer graphics in art, in some sense saturating the transformational grammar of interpolation. The illustrations, ten years old, are classics in their own right.

The art form of dynamic graphics is epitomized in the work of John Whitney (for example, *Permutations*) and Peter Foldes (for example, *Hunger*). They are chosen as examples not only because of their acknowledged contribution to computer animation but also because both animator-artists embarked on the use of computer aids following extensive careers in which they worked without them. While Foldes is assisted by his humor and Whitney by his sound, both suffer from the short-lived but overwhelming signature of the machine. Ultimately the metamorphoses and periodicities have none of the richness of *Bambi*.

All of these examples are taken from the basic line-making paradigm of early computer graphics, involving both plotter and cathode-ray tubes. More recently we find computer graphics moving toward raster scan technologies, most noticeably television, but also toward large flat displays of light-emitting diodes, plasma, or thin film transistors.* These techniques are beginning to merge the complexities of video, to offer on-line color, and to mark computer graphics with a shape-oriented bias, not yet saturated by a CTG. The work at the New York Institute of Technology is notable, and similar work is being conducted at MIT. Hard copy is attained through a Xerox color copier on-line to the display.

PAINT—AN EXPERIMENT

Some of the accompanying color illustrations are taken from an experi-

---

* Alternative techniques to television-technology displays.

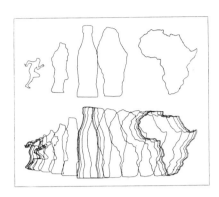

2.5
Two works from the CTG Group, circa 1968

2.6
Two frames from Peter Foldes' *Hunger*

ment funded by the National Science Foundation. Accomplished artists and young children were invited to use a color raster scan display system. The purpose was to observe the period of training required for skilled artists to overcome the propensities of a machine.

In the May–June 1972 issue of *Art in America,* Robert Mueller postulated a system with which "a person could draw by hand directly into video, in full color, using regular brushes or pens (but without pigments of any sort). This provides an extremely delicate control, right down to a single hairline of video input at any given point. And since this input is immediately converted into electronic signals, it can release a repertoire of arbitrary shapes. . . . Shapes can be 'played' . . . bands of color . . . brush to the surface. . . ."

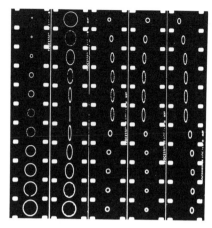

2.7
A sequence from John Whitney's film *Permutations*

In the September–October issue that followed, Professor Harold Cohen responded with a letter stating, "At the present time, video—regarded as a black box—presents the user with far more complex picture processing abilities than does the computer: but even here the range of abilities has turned out to be disappointingly limited. Thus Mr. Mueller's image of the artist of the future painting with a paintless brush on a television tube with one hand—because it is after all the artist's touch that counts—while twiddling knobs with the other: dressed, presumably, in smock and beret, and cracking walnuts with his left foot: this image is as silly as misguided."

Ironically, the display configuration used for the PAINT experiment matches almost exactly Mr. Mueller's fantasy (and some participants may wear berets). Computer enthusiasts should note that it consists of 272K bytes of MOS memory shared by a minicomputer (with control store) and an elaborate display processor. The user has a multiplicity of tablet and touch-sensitive inputs, through which he can deploy brush strokes, patterns, textures, line work, picture, and text. The products combine a world of picture processing with a world of graphics—hitherto well-separated disciplines.

PROCESSES

Shaking Hands with the Viewer

Georg Ness of Erlangen, Germany, has the distinction of having held the first one-man (!) computer art show in early 1965. His has been followed by

many other exhibits, frequently adjuncts of comic relief to some ponderous computer conference. In almost all cases, with the exception of
emerging video artists, the art is that of mathematical lines.

In contrast, the beginnings of a more exciting computer art can be found
in notions of interaction between viewer and art. Such processes have
their origins in kinetic works as far back as the Bauhaus. The works of
Moholy-Nagy (*Light-Space Modulator*) and Calder (*A Universe*) were
dynamic, though closed, systems. Intricate movements were well-planned
paths through space and had well-planned causes and effects and well-
planned timing.

Seemingly less well-planned kinetic art is found in a cybernetic approach where stimuli are taken from an unpredictable environment. The
response of the art form is derived from a model of appropriate behavior
rather than a regulatory process. While examples of interactive art have so
far used only meager computing elements and almost no memory, we can
see the beginning of a process of viewer participation where the waving
hand becomes the baton and voices become the stimuli of kinetic
sculpture. In its extreme form, this kind of visual art becomes a performance, conceivably a silly-looking dance by a passing observer stepping
on the toes of more self-conscious and sedate spectators.

One example of an interactive art form is Wen Ying Tsai's *Cybernetic
Sculpture No. 15* (1968). It used sound sensors to solicit data which in turn
controlled and modulated strobing lights flashing on an array of gently
swaying stainless steel rods. The clap of a hand caused a frequency
change and hence different patterns of movement, as if the viewer were
the choreographer of dancing wheat fields. In another example, Lillian
Schwartz's *The Proxima Centuri,* an illuminated globe in a box withdraws
into the box upon sensing a human presence. Otherwise, assured of
human indifference, the plastic ball reflects complex images.

Imagine more moody pieces. Simple extrapolations of interactive art can
embellish the behavioral model to include inputs from the weather, time of
day, Dow-Jones Average, and the results of sports events, elections, or film
ratings. In some sense, this could be the art form of off-track betting. Or,
with more fantasy, we can imagine a future of the visual arts populated
with patronizing pieces of sculpture and caustic canvases that recognize
the viewer to be male or female, rich or poor, bewildered or blasé, you or
me. In this fiction, the artist runs a kennel for cuddly art forms that get to
know their future owners, who in turn get to know and love them.

Computers Working with the Artist

A yet more complex form of interaction can be found in the processes of
interaction that constitute a partnership of computer and artist, bent upon

making art jointly. The computer medium illustrates a cooperation similar to Vassarely's factory of people filling in the proper colors, doing the tedious graphics, following the direction of the master. In contrast, here I am considering the joint authorship of ideas as well as graphics. Think of it as computer aids to conceptual art.

This process can be likened to the more practiced work in computer-aided design in mechanical engineering, electrical engineering, architecture, and the like. The future importance of computer partnership in these areas will lie in their subtle mixture and augmentation of talent and competence. To date, however, these partnerships, between architect and computer, for example, are achieved through well-defined divisions of labor. While the machine is admittedly doing more than the graphics, it is given a readily computable task, usually considered dull by humans, in order to liberate the designer as well as to aid in calculations. The assumption is that humans will be more creative and do better work by virtue of a tranquility and concentration previously unattainable in the tedium of daily practice. In fact, it has never worked this way. This is partly because computer-aided design still involves the implementation of well-formed, thoroughly debugged ideas, which are in effect designed completely off the computer on the backs of envelopes.

Some research into computer aids is focused on bringing design aids into areas of greater ambiguity and inconsistency, acknowledging that these vagaries are indigenous to the design process, not mere noise. For example, work in sketch recognition is geared to inferring the graphic intentions of the user, sometimes carrying several candidate interpretations to avoid the nagging and distracting "Do you mean . . .?" In the case of sketches we postulate that the scribbly nature of line work is an effective representation of thought; one neither doodles with a T square nor prepares legal documents with a crayon. Nevertheless, regardless of intentions, we still lack the precedent of a designer using a computer in what he would consider creative endeavors.

Computers in the arts, as aids to instead of media for the artist, can be viewed as a worst case for computer-aided design. The task is not well-specified, functions are intertwined with meanings, and the user is characteristically temperamental, inarticulate, and unpredictable. And in the operations research sense, the product has no utility function.

One can imagine a working relationship similar to that of an author and a good librarian. The computer participates as an aid to browsing through material, widening the scope of the artist's metaphorical magic. Otherwise, we are stymied by a lack of examples that can be extended to human partnerships. Gilbert and Sullivan or Rodgers and Hammerstein epitomize partnerships in music, but one did the lyrics and the other the melody,

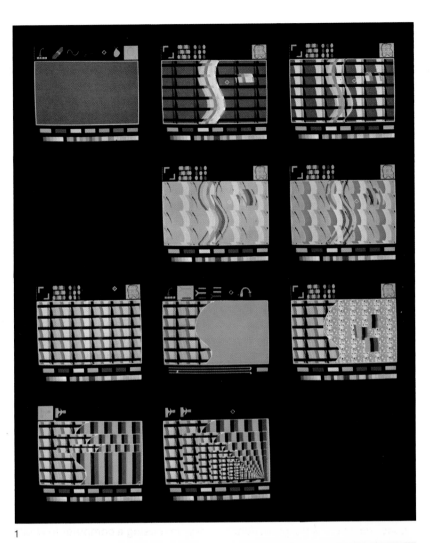

1

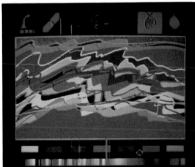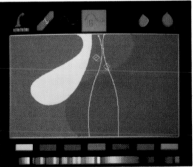

2

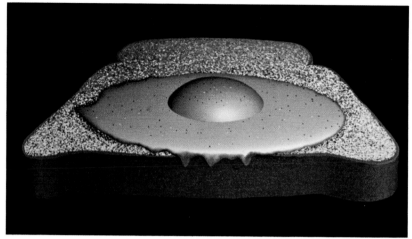

3

4

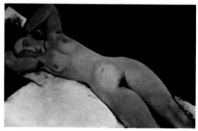

5

1
A sequence of fourteen steps through the composition of an illustration with a computer program affectionately called PAINT. The patterns and colors are flooded onto a display screen in images explored by American artist Ralph Coburn and the author. These panels were used as the October/November cover of the *Technology Review*, designed by Nancy Pokross. This particular computer program uses pictograms at the top of the screen to describe graphical functions within any graphical mode selectable from a menu of ten. At the bottom of the screen is a palette of primary and secondary colors.

2
The two illustrations were done by British painter Edgar Millington-Drake, Spring 1976, using the same computer program PAINT. One purpose of this page of "paintings" is to illustrate different styles manageable by the same computer program.

3
Egg Toast by Alvy Ray Smith, New York Institute of Technology, 1977. In contrast to the other color images, this illustration enjoys a very high spatial resolution, considerably greater than television as we know it today. The image was created in sections or "windows," on-line and subsequently photographed off-line.

4
This six-foot-high display is currently achieved through rear projection television technology. However, large and flat displays exist in laboratory environments and will be available in the near future. Their importance will be in the concatenation of the performing and visual arts, especially when touch-sensitive.

5
A Modigliani displayed with only 1000 colors selected from two different sets. The significance of the display is twofold: only 10 bits of data at each picture element are necessary to achieve such "full color," and the indirection of color assignment allows for yet further transformations.

working in distinctly different media. In literature it is equally difficult to find examples, except in technical writing! And when we do find them, we have enough evidence to presume that each party did a well-defined chunk and that they did not, for example, exchange roles between sentences or trains of thought.

In the visual arts, there are (only) two famous partnerships: Charles and Ray Eames and Jean and Sophie Taeuber Arp. The first two may be a questionable example for the fine arts, though they are certainly important figures in the development of the theory and practice of the graphic arts. The Arps apparently collaborated on collages made during the period 1910 to 1925. These two examples offer an interesting clue to the nature of these partnerships. Both pairs are husband and wife, from which we can infer that they knew each other well, shared common experiences, and evolved a personal language of communication and interaction.

Idiosyncratic Systems

"Okay, what is the meaning of this?"
"Meaning of what?"
"You know."
"What do you think?"
"Oh, that's it, is it?"
"Yes."

This is a commonplace and archetypical exchange familiar to spouses, lovers, and good friends. It caricatures a conversation driven by inference making and interpersonal hypotheses. The point is that both parties know each other well and use that knowledge for both data compression and descriptions that might otherwise be almost unexplainable. The latter is important to the case for computers aiding artists, as it is through shared experiences that people gain ease in talking to people. You can, for example, use the term John-like, derived from the salient features of your dear friend or worst enemy John, to describe somebody or something that otherwise might require the subtleties of great writing to portray.

The computer and the artist can be likened to director and actor, knowing each other on many levels. On the simplest level, the machine has a model of the artist that acts as a predictive mechanism for gauging responses. On a more complex level, the computer has a model of the artist's model of it, which provides evidence for what can and cannot be left to inference. And finally, following the formula of R. D. Laing and his colleagues, we have the computer's model of the artist's model of its model of him. This tongue-twisting logic leads to a working definition of acquaintanceship, where the first and third converge, taking into account oscillations caused by mood, climate, physical states, and the like and jeopardized only by absentmindedness, crises, drugs, and drink.[1]

The purpose of such a joint venture is to achieve the fullest and deepest intracommunication. I have likened computer-aided design to talking about Cézanne with a Martian via telegram. Most efforts in the field have concentrated on the telegram aspect of the comparison; here we are dwelling on the Martian. The kind of machine intelligence that would be needed to make personalized as opposed to simply personal computers would additionally offer a working relationship marked by constructive antagonisms, compliments, criticisms, and an atmosphere hostile to complacency.

The proof must be more general than the fact of artists playing with computers. People should enjoy the amenities of idiosyncratic systems in their everyday lives. The artist is offered, in some sense, as the extreme case.

PARTICIPANTS

The Vulgarity of the Many

A standard and even twentieth-century attitude toward visual eroticism is exemplified in the acceptance of a book on a sexual theme if it is sold in a limited edition and at a high price. If it is relatively cheap and has wide distribution, it is called pornographic or, more recently, therapeutic. Similarly, art forms maintain their value by avoiding the vulgarity of mass production. We are most aware of this in the United States, where we have a high density of bad graphic and industrial design, from the printed page to the television set to the table setting. Other countries, most western European ones, enjoy good design in subways, household goods, and even food packages. This in itself blurs the division between art and reproduction.

The major impact of computers in the visual arts will be on our daily lives, not necessarily on high and fine art. The observers will be participants. Processes will be products.

The computer will contribute to the dissemination of the visual arts by virtue of its media, particularly through television. Already we unwittingly observe computer-generated logos undergoing complex analog and digital transformations during station breaks. At network costs between $2000 and $4000 a minute, we are beginning to see dynamic and color computer graphics in the household. At the same time, in bars, airports, and some homes, we find television games and hobbyist computers that evidence the modest beginnings of interactiveness. The extrapolation and proliferation of the combination of these is analogous to having a real bear versus a stuffed one.

While these may appear to be vulgarized art to the art historian, they really represent a simple proposition, not threatening to the profession. Consider the meaning we ascribe to children's drawings when they are the work of our own children. A piece depicts stages of learning and an outpouring of (usually) simple emotions. Frequently, with the blatant exception of finger painting, a child's art portrays a collection of characters, which often have names and always have meaning. The point is that we hang the piece, maybe frame it, surely enjoy it for a great many reasons, none of which has to do with matters of formal composition, color theory, or aesthetics. Such is the paradigm that might be applied to computers in the visual arts of the many.

The Burden of Leisure

Currently in the United States, a small fraction of the population works to feed the rest. And since 1957, for the first time in history, white-collar workers outnumber blue-collar workers. We all know about the 35-hour week, that decreases to 25 hours and then to 0; this is an acknowledged probability, concern, and nightmare.

A Club Méditerranée attitude toward the growth of leisure is to expand the opportunity for playful, bucolic living, away from the mechanics and vicissitudes of daily urban life. The model is one of leisure amplification, getting the most out of your two weeks, a model derived from the aristocratic man of leisure who belongs to a privileged class. In his inaugural address at Imperial College in 1958, Dennis Gabor pointed out that the analogy was faulty inasmuch as the leisured classes in older societies could command the services of other people and, more importantly, believed themselves to be elites. And for the average member of the privileged classes, life was often made bearable only by hard drinking.

A different, more appropriate, and less pessimistic model is offered by the arts. For example, in school, "arts and crafts" is a subject commanding a peculiar position between Latin pedagogy and soccer practice. Arts and crafts combines work and play, whence comes our model. Many scientists enjoy an adult life of arts and crafts in that the line between their work and play is indeed thin. The researcher learns to play with ideas abstractly. The computer programmer plays with concepts more tangibly. These are some of the greatest luxuries of our time.

The visual arts are one example of promulgating a work-play redundancy. A great deal is done for its own sake. Winning or losing is usually less important than playing a good game. And frequently pleasures are shareable only with a cross section of intimate friends.

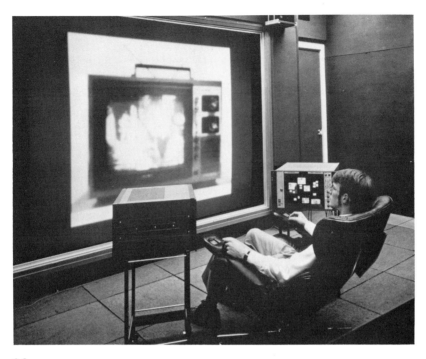

2.8
Media Room. Homes of the future will have rooms akin to this illustration into which
a user can immerse all sensory apparatuses. This particular application is a "Spatial
Data Management System," with a fictitious country called Dataland displayed
to the user's right. In front appears an item in one particular neighborhood of
Dataland. In this example this item is a "virtual" television for which the user
can make animation, with which the user can look at old movies, or through
which the user accesses the networks. The user's controls are touch- and pressure-
sensitive instrumentation in the arms of an Eames chair.

The sets for science fiction films usually include wall-size televisions,
automated kitchens, and some kind of household robot. However, we
rarely see people interacting with this gadgetry except as a means to some
end. Nevertheless, think of our Sunday painter reincarnated with an easel
of electronics and a palette of computer graphics. His work is as invigorat-
ing as a game of tennis, his challenge is that of chess, his product is as
ephemeral as a child's drawing. In this fantasy lies the potential for the
major impact of computers on the visual arts of the future.

NOTE

1
See, for example, Laing's *Interpersonal Perception* (New York: Springer, 1966).

3
Individualized Automation

Michael L. Dertouzos

Automation is not new. It has been with us for several generations as a consequence of the industrial revolution, which managed to reduce human and animal muscle power from a once-dominant to a now-obsolete productive resource. The future of automation has been the subject of considerable speculation. Science-fiction writers, cartoonists, philosophers, and technological forecasters have alerted us to the dangers of a course that seems inevitably to lead to an impersonal and heartless society driven by the goals of productivity, efficiency, and uniformity.

What *is* new today is the onset of the information revolution with its progressively less expensive computers and more knowledgeable programs. Given its technical and economic advantages, the impact of the information revolution on automation promises to be substantial. It is my contention that it will in addition profoundly affect the quality of our lives and will in fact reverse some of the impersonal and dehumanizing consequences of the industrial revolution.

Broadly speaking, automation is the process of replacing human tasks by machine functions in the production of goods and the dispensation of services. By this definition it encompasses almost all of our productive efforts. My discussion will be restricted to the automation of the production process, often called factory automation, and the use of computers in instrumentation and control, that is, for monitoring and adjusting ongoing processes such as the automatic piloting of aircraft. Even with this restriction, however, the productive activities covered by the topic represent about a third of the world's gross national product, which indicates the immense potential significance of automation. I will start with a hypothetical example of a process that appears to be technologically feasible and might well become part of everyday life in the future.

Michael L. Dertouzos is professor of computer science and electrical engineering at MIT and director of MIT's Laboratory for Computer Science. His research interests are in the use of computers to control physical processes.

A SHOEMAKING SCENARIO

Your need for a new pair of shoes takes you to the nearest regional manufacturing and distribution center, better known as "Auto Shoe." Since this is your first visit you are directed to a foot-measuring station (fig. 3.1). After removing your shoes, you place your feet in two strange-looking shoelike contraptions and attach the dozen or so straps that according to the instructions will measure your crucial contour lines. Still somewhat nervous, you turn the tension-adjusting knobs and feel the straps tightening around your feet. The instructions say that you should adjust the knobs until the pressure on each foot feels right—just like a well-fitting pair of shoes. Adjustments done, you press the "go" button and receive a small card containing your name and the coded measurements of both feet. The instructions conclude with the suggestion that if you like the fit of your new shoes you should file the card in your home computer for use at a later time in this or other Auto Shoe centers.

You then proceed to the shoe-design station, where a few representative samples of the latest shoe styles can be seen and handled. The ever-present instructions explain that since the number of possible shoe designs is too large to be represented by individual samples, you must consult the computer-driven color display screen of styles if you wish to see additional variations. Since you are after a conservative brown leather shoe you have little trouble making the basic choice, but you appreciate the opportunity to add a personal touch in the form of brass grommets for the laces.

Confident of your choice, you forgo the opportunity to see an image of yourself wearing your chosen shoes on the large vertical display screen. Instead, you place your money card in the appropriate slot and press the order button. The green light notifies you that fifteen dollars have been transferred from your bank account to Auto Shoe and manufacture has begun.

Curious about the process, you elect to spend your waiting time on the observation platform instead of in the computer-game room. The guiding display screen explains that material selection is in progress. A special mechanical arm collects the parts that will go into your shoes from what looks like a vertically stacked stockroom. Large sheets of leather, obviously intended for soles and uppers, are placed and registered on a cutting table. There, an automated stylus cuts the necessary patterns, directed by a sizing program that converts the coded measurements of your feet into two-dimensional forms. You are impressed by the fact that the machine seems either to see or remember where it has cut before, since it is cutting the new patterns with a minimum of waste.

While the sheets are returned to the stockroom by the arm, the precut

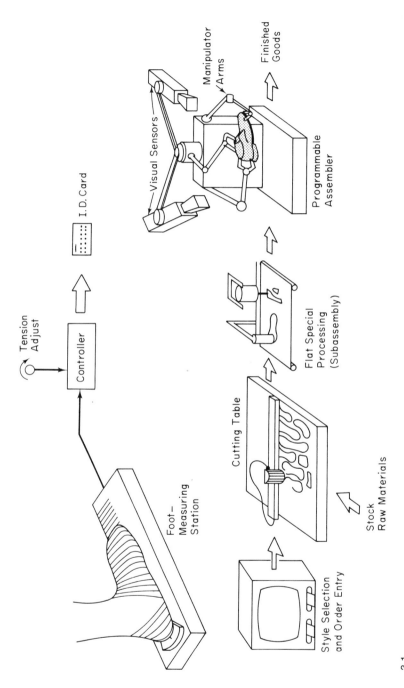

3.1
Automated Shoemaking

pieces are further processed by special-purpose machines—holes are punched, grommets inserted, and some gluing and sewing seems to take place while the pieces are still lying flat. The processed parts are then passed to what looks like an automated assembler, equipped with three multiple-joint arms and two television-camera inspection units. Two of the arms hold the shoe components in place, conveniently presenting them to the third arm which is busy stitching, gluing, and pressing. The inspection units appear to monitor the position of the parts and the progress of the work, directing the arms in the assembly process.

Eleven minutes have passed since the order button was pressed; your shoes pop out through the delivery chute. They fit rather well, explaining why Auto Shoe is doing such a booming business. Nearby, a customer presents himself to the complaint department, disappointed with the results of Auto Shoe's experimental program for ordering shoes through home computers. However, he is appeased with the gift of his ill-fitting shoes and winks at you knowingly. As you leave, you can't resist asking the factory manager about the implications of this automated activity on the more conventional shoe industry. His well-rehearsed answer informs you of the decaying nature of the shoe business in the United States; of the huge governmental subsidies that are needed to keep factories open; of the miserable working conditions, low wages, ancient capital equipment, and balance-of-payments deficits attributed to the low cost of foreign labor. He concludes with the observation that besides reviving this dying industry, the new process leads to a better product, tailored to the individual consumer, at a lower cost, thereby improving our way of life.

With a few exceptions and qualifications, the technology needed to support this hypothetical automated shoe factory is either here or almost here. Selection of parts in an automated stockroom has been demonstrated and implemented. Computer-driven sizing and cutting is already being done in certain sections of the garment industry. The conversion of foot measurements into two-dimensional patterns is straightforward in principle, as is the development of an electromechanical device for obtaining these measurements. Display screens have already been used to combine computed or stored pictures with images obtained by television cameras. Integration of various information-oriented functions, such as production orders with accounting data and funds transfer, have already been partially implemented and present no technical obstacles.

Perhaps the least practicable of our hypothetical factory's components is the automated robot that assembles a shoe from its major subassemblies. Laboratory-type machines that are similar in principle, combining a television camera and one or more manipulators, have been built at Caltech, the Draper Laboratory, MIT, and Stanford and have been used to perform simple, well-defined tasks, such as selection of building blocks from a random pile and assembly of a precision shaft with its bearing. Some of the potential capabilities and present difficulties of these machines are discussed in the following section, since they will undoubtedly affect the future course of automation.

PROGRAMMABLE ROBOTS AND VISION

Industrial robots are available today. They consist of electromechanical or hydraulic manipulators that can grip objects, rotate them, lift them, and in general move them in a prearranged manner dictated by a sequence of stored commands. These commands are often written ahead of time by programmers. More advanced machines can be walked through their intended assembly operations by a human operator for the purpose of learning a desired motion. Later, the machines mimic the acquired motions, typically at a higher speed, in order to perform their assembling functions. Some of these machines also have a modest sensory capacity, in order, for example, to control the pressure of a grip or the torque applied to a bolt. Their main function, however, is to repeat a preset, predetermined motion, in the same sense that a tape recorder repeats prerecorded sounds.

While these industrial robots are useful in their present form—automobile manufacturers use them to weld vehicle frames—they are severely limited in comparison to human assemblers in at least two ways: they lack appropriate sensory information, and they lack knowledge specific to the task they must perform.

The sensory task of these machines is almost as difficult as that of a blindfolded man who without using his sense of touch is supposed to reach out with a wrench and tighten a few nuts as the work goes by on the assembly line. I say "almost" because the machine can position its arm more accurately than a blindfolded man, placing it, for example, within fifty-thousandths of an inch of the desired position. However, the work is not always precisely where it should be. The resulting combined errors in work and manipulator position prohibit the use of these machines for finer operations or where the parts have not already been accurately positioned. By contrast, human assemblers in the electronic microcircuit industry can bond wires under a microscope with positional accuracies of one-thousandth of an inch or better.

Human assemblers generally acquire, organize, and use a great deal of information specific to their tasks. This knowledge, along with the more general knowledge and common sense that they possess, enables workers to understand what they see, follow alternative strategies, formulate new approaches, and set different goals in response to changes in their work

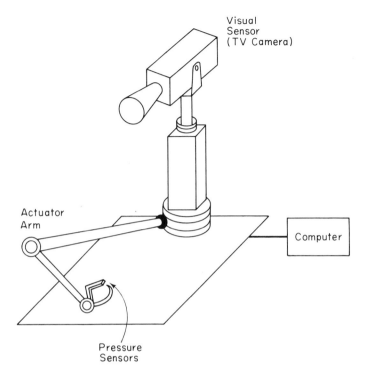

Visual
Sensor
(TV Camera)

Actuator
Arm

Computer

Pressure
Sensors

3.2
General-Purpose Programmable Robot

environment. Since the ability of human assemblers to deal with variability is largely what distinguishes their performance from the repetitive and mechanistic behavior of today's industrial robots, it is not surprising that some researchers in this area are currently trying to develop a general-purpose programmable robot (fig. 3.2) equipped with sophisticated sensors, notably vision, and a computer large enough to process and understand the sensory data. The term *general-purpose* means that the machine, like a general-purpose computer, can be programmed to do different tasks, such as assemble motors under one program and inspect parts under another.

The principal technical difficulties associated with such a machine lie in the software, that is, in the way information is processed, rather than in the equipment that is used. In fact, the biggest difficulty lies in making the computer understand what is seen by the machine's visual sensor. The sensor, similar to a television camera, measures light-intensity levels at a large number of image points, roughly corresponding to the large number of dots that make up a newspaper photograph. The results can be thought of as a list of perhaps a million numbers, representing the light intensity at each one of a million picture points. With current technology, there is no difficulty in obtaining such a list and storing it in the computer's memory, typically in a few thousandths of a second. The difficulty lies in deducing from this list that the image represents, for example, a motor with its cover partially assembled and a bolt missing at the upper right corner—the kind of information needed to direct the manipulator to insert the missing bolt in the proper hole. The computer's problem in interpreting what it sees is not hard to understand if we imagine ourselves trying to achieve the same objective not by looking at the object itself but instead at the printed list of a million light-intensity numbers. Indeed, our own ability to understand and analyze a visual image, while not yet fully understood, seems to rest on two fundamental notions: the identification of elemental visual features such as lines, edges, and basic shapes, most probably by the eye-brain neural network attached to the retina; and the identification of higher-level objects, such as bolts and motors, which are represented in terms of elemental and intermediate-level objects, probably accomplished deeper within the cortex. In the latter task, it appears that our own history of acquiring, structuring, and using knowledge is significant. How can a primitive tribesman, for example, analyze the scene as we do, if he has seen neither a motor nor a bolt and if the notions of engaging and rotating a bolt are totally unknown to him?

The future prospects for a vision-dependent general-purpose programmable robot are governed by research results in these two areas, namely the recognition of elemental visual objects and the processing of information by knowledge-based programs. I believe that progress in the first area will depend on the development of special-purpose multiple-processor retina machines containing hundreds if not thousands of processors dedicated to the identification of basic visual objects. The recent development of inexpensive microprocessors similar to the ones found in pocket calculators is a crucial step toward making such systems economical.

Research in the second area—the development of knowledge-based programs—is still in its infancy. While programs have been written that demonstrate the use of specific knowledge in specific contexts, we do not yet have a theory or a transportable model that can acquire, structure, and use knowledge in a systematic way. Nevertheless, the effects achieved to date are rather impressive. In a recent experiment at MIT, programs using an English vocabulary as a knowledge base have been able to detect English Morse code messages through high noise levels, roughly in the same way that by concentrating we can detect an interesting conversation through an otherwise noisy cocktail party. Winograd's natural-language programs also exhibit this power (see chapter 4). While it is still too early to know what factors might limit the computer's ability to store and use knowledge, indications are good for achieving progress in this area. In fact, we can be cautiously optimistic about a good retina machine as well, so that the development of an adequate vision-dependent programmable robot sometime in the next twenty years seems a reasonable prospect.

Progress in programmable general-purpose robots, however, need not depend on vision research, since it is possible to achieve considerable results with senses simpler than vision, as the successful employment of visually handicapped people shows. The tactile sense is particularly useful in this context, and "seeing by feeling" may in fact be the practical short-term solution to the difficulties of automated vision.

Examples of tactile sensing abound in our automated environment, especially in control systems. Limit switches, pressure sensors, position detectors, angular position encoders (detectors), and similar devices are used in a variety of applications, from home appliances and burglar alarm devices to sophisticated guidance and navigation systems that keep airplanes and ships on course. Automatic control systems such as these have been with us for a very long time, using gravity, waterfalls, and later steam and electricity as their energy source. The difference between a control system and a programmable robot is more one of complexity than of substance, and the control systems of the future will probably evolve in the direction of what we now call programmable robots.

FUTURE PROSPECTS OF AUTOMATIC CONTROL SYSTEMS

A control system is characterized by an objective, such as keeping the temperature of a liquid constant or maintaining the course of an airplane. Such a system can be disturbed by deliberate changes in the objective, such as raising the desired temperature of the liquid or changing the desired course of the airplane; and by unexpected changes in the physical environment which throw the system off balance, such as changes in the air temperature surrounding the liquid or pressure and flow disturbances in the atmosphere in the case of the airplane. The control system has the single mission of maintaining the desired objective even if we change that objective, and despite the presence of unwanted disturbances.

Control is usually accomplished by using appropriate sensors to measure the error between the desired objective and the actual status of the controlled object, and then by using actuators to apply corrective energy so as to reduce this error to zero. The sensors measure a physical quantity, such as temperature or speed, and translate it into an electrical quantity, such as voltage, which can be handled by electronic equipment; the actuators do the converse, delivering mechanical, thermal, or other forms of energy as instructed by electronic commands. The control system, or servomechanism, continuously and automatically performs the tasks of measuring the error, calculating a corrective action, and applying that action so as to keep the error at a minimum. Typically, the corrective action is simply proportional to the error or to the rate of change of the error or to the sum of these and like quantities. As a result, the overall system obeys and can be analyzed in terms of linear differential equations —a mathematical topic that is well understood. A large number of today's control systems are built with electronic components such as transistors, resistors, and capacitors, which evolved primarily as part of the post–World War II electronic technology that is responsible for most contemporary advances in control automation.

It should be apparent that control systems and programmable robots have many similar features. Both have sensors and actuators, both have objectives, and both calculate how to actuate these objectives on the basis of what they sense. The difference between them is that control systems as we know them today are at a lower level of complexity. It is, for example, much easier to measure automatically the temperature of a liquid, or even the pressure, flow, and temperature parameters of a process control factory, than it is to analyze and understand a simple visual image made up of a few white blocks against a black background. It is also easier to calculate corrective actions in the case of a control system, even if it means solving fifty equations, whereas it is considerably more difficult to decide what compound motions are needed to assemble a motor when the parts are not always in their original position. Thus the control systems of today may be thought of as primitive versions of the programmable robots of the future. In retrospect, it is not surprising that the imagination of a great mathematician, Norbert Wiener, expanded the notion of control to cybernetics, thereby attempting to explain certain animal and human activities in terms of control and communication models.

What makes the programmable robots and the control systems of the future potentially so much more powerful than the electronic control systems of the present is, of course, the use of computers. Besides the inexpensive hardware offered by solid-state technology, the crucial element contributed by the computer is its ability to understand and execute sophisticated tasks expressed in terms of programs (procedures or algorithms). The descriptive power of procedures is indeed very powerful, enabling us to instruct the system to adopt different alternatives when different situations are encountered, even to devise new strategies when old ones fail and to learn from its mistakes. To many advocates of this view of the computer, procedures are the ultimate model, through which almost everything, anthropomorphic behavior included, can be expressed. This, of course, remains to be seen. We have always been anxious to explain the puzzling phenomena around us or within us in the language of the latest discovery—early models of the brain were mechanical, full of gears and levers; they were replaced with hydraulic models, then electronic cybernetic models; now the model is procedures.

In any case, regardless of the ultimate epistemological and philosophical consequences of this argument, procedures are sure to replace the electronic control systems of today. Figure 3.3 shows a computerized control system of the kind that we are already beginning to encounter in automobiles. It consists of one or more microcomputers, a memory, and several sensors and actuators. Also shown is a large computer that helps program the smaller machine. Suppose that such a control system were destined for your automobile. Its designers would type the strategy to be carried out by the system in a convenient (to engineers) language, using the large computer. The large computer would translate the strategy from the designers' language into the much more detailed language of the microprocessors in the small machine. The translated program would fill up the memory of the small machine, which would then be disconnected from its parent and placed in an experimental car. There it would carry out its instructions, perhaps adjusting the fuel-air mixture for maximum economy and routinely monitoring oil pressure, speed, generator current, and similar quantities, alerting the driver only when necessary or, if requested, through a single display screen. The designers, having observed the control system at work, would make any necessary changes, reprogramming the little machine until it was made to operate satisfactorily. The microprocessor control system could then be manufactured en masse and installed in every automobile. In fact, engineers in Detroit have been working on similar although simpler on-board computer systems for at least five years, and computerized cars are now beginning to appear in the marketplace.

Such programmable control systems have many new applications besides automobile monitoring, such as controlling home appliances, medical instrumentation, agriculture, and so on. Programmable computerized controllers such as these will eventually replace almost all of today's electronic control systems because they are more flexible and more powerful in carrying out strategies; they cost the same as electronic controllers; and they can send and receive information to and from other computer systems, making it possible to set up networks of controllers and integrate management and accounting data with operational information.

NETWORKS AND INTEGRATED AUTOMATION SYSTEMS

The general-purpose programmable robot and the microcomputer-based controller are two components essential to the future development of automation. A third is the distributed system, or network, which is made up

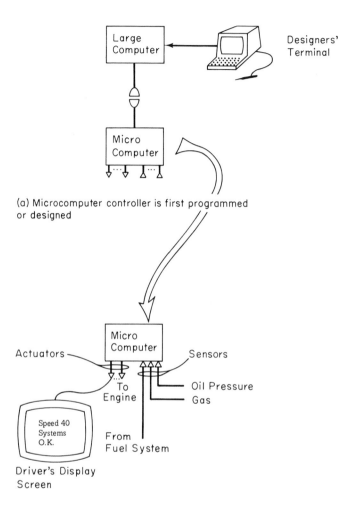

(a) Microcomputer controller is first programmed or designed

(b) Once satisfactory, it is manufactured and installed in every car

3.3
Programmable Controller

of a number of interconnected robots, programmable controllers, and computer systems. Such a supersystem extends beyond the domains of automated assembly and control into some clerical and possibly managerial functions.

Imagine an automated traffic control system made up of computer-based controllers, one for each major intersection of a large city (fig. 3.4). Each controller activates the traffic lights and senses the traffic load of its own intersection. In addition, each controller communicates with its (four) neighboring intersection controllers, so that the network of wires linking the controllers follows the network of city arteries. The purpose of this distributed control system is to improve traffic flow within the city. We could begin to understand and program such a system if we imagined that instead of computer-based controllers there was a policeman at each intersection who could communicate via telephone with police at neighboring intersections. Such a network could improve traffic flow in a number of ways, for example by relieving the local load of each intersection; by alerting neighboring intersection controllers of shifting traffic loads, since messages follow the same routes as cars but travel much faster; by clearing desired routes for emergency vehicle use; by diverting traffic away from congested areas; by recognizing that a controller is disabled and routing messages around it; and by easily admitting new controllers into the system as the city grows and new lights are added.

Much remains to be learned about what would make a good programming strategy for such a distributed system or, for that matter, for similar computer-based networks of controllers. What is significant, however, is that such a system would function at a higher level of complexity than a single controller. Knowledge about traffic control would be localized to an intersection if applicable only to that intersection but would be communicated if applicable to other intersections. This separation of knowledge into local and distributed forms seems important in roughly the same sense that aggregates of human beings can, through communication and cooperation, achieve things that a group of isolated specialists would find it difficult or impossible to achieve.

If we now change the setting from traffic control to a small factory (fig. 3.5), the distributed system becomes a network of controllers and general-purpose robots involved in assembly and inspection. Additional machines that handle only information can now be connected to this network for the purpose of order handling, inventory control, accounting, production planning and control, plant maintenance, forecasting, and management reporting. It is not difficult to visualize how such a fully automated factory might work—not unlike a well-run factory of today, with procedures appropriate for dealing with many contingencies, but surpassing it in efficiency.

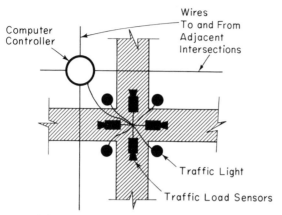

(a) Each controller handles its own intersection

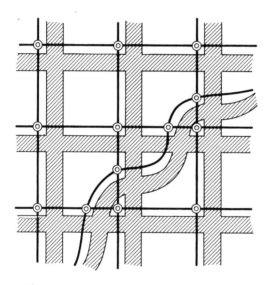

(b) Adjacent controllers communicate with
wires that follow traffic routes

3.4
Traffic Control with Distributed Controllers

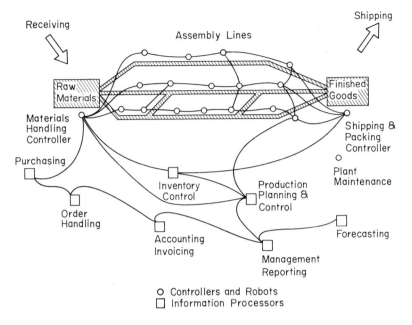

Receiving

Assembly Lines

Shipping

Raw Materials

Finished Goods

Materials Handling Controller

Purchasing

Order Handling

Inventory Control

Production Planning & Control

Accounting Invoicing

Management Reporting

Shipping & Packing Controller

Plant Maintenance

Forecasting

○ Controllers and Robots
☐ Information Processors

3.5
An Automated Factory Organization

Further examples of automated networks might involve the more sophisticated control of complex vehicles like ships and airplanes and secondarily automobiles, as well as transportation systems, where a great deal of sensed data must be monitored, processed, integrated, and converted to specific actions. Such networks can be "democratic," as in the case of the traffic control system based on distributed rather than centralized authority, or "regimented" networks with a clearly defined chain of authority, consisting for example of a machine with several subordinate machines that in turn command other subordinate machines, and so on. As the interconnection of machines into networks becomes a reality, we will probably discover that there are various ways of organizing these machines, as indeed there are various ways of structuring conventional organizations.

SOME SOCIOECONOMIC OBSERVATIONS

The direct cost of using automated robots and controllers will undoubtedly be a major economic factor in the future course of automation. If we assume that the capital cost of a programmable robot is recovered in three years, and if we make some additional assumptions about the running costs of such a machine, we see that it would have to cost less than

CARNEGIE LIBRARY
LIVINGSTONE COLLEGE
SALISBURY, N. C. 28144

$50,000 and equal or exceed the productivity of an unskilled worker before it could compete with the latter. Inasmuch as the technology of sensors and actuators is not expected to undergo drastic changes, it appears that three-quarters of this cost should be allocated to sensors and the manipulator arms, leaving some $15,000 for information processing. At the current rate of cost reduction of processors and memories (about 30 to 40 percent per year; see Noyce's calculations in chapter 15), which is expected to last well into the 1980s, such a sum could well support a storage capacity of four million bytes and a processing power of one MIPS.* On the basis of what we know today, this amount of computing power would be more than adequate without vision and perhaps barely adequate with some elementary vision. These estimates are necessarily uncertain, yet it appears that the cost-performance capabilities of programmable robots could become competitive with unskilled workers by the turn of the century. The programmable controllers, on the other hand, need not reach such a threshold of competitive ability before they can be used. As the cost-performance ratio of programmable controllers improves, they will gradually replace today's electronic controllers in almost all applications of automated control.

Direct costs, however, are only one of the factors affecting the future course of automation. Other costs and other criteria will contribute, perhaps more critically, to the expansion of its role in our economy. The use of automation to revive a decaying industry, as in the shoemaking scenario, would offer an alternative to the progressive erosion of the human labor segment and the eventual elimination of that industry from our GNP. Another situation in which computerized automation would be invaluable is in environments hazardous to humans. Whether in mining and excavation, in the toxic atmosphere of a painting room, or in the high-temperature environment of furnaces and casting processes, an automated working unit could protect the health, indeed the life, of human workers by replacing all or part of their activities. Then there is the execution of repetitive and mindless tasks where human knowledge and problem-solving capabilities are not only unused but probably abused for lack of stimulus, like turning the same six bolts on the same wheel of the same car on the same assembly line eight hours a day, five days a week.

To my mind, however, the biggest benefit of computerized automation lies in the tailoring of products and services to the most variable of demand centers—ourselves. Before the industrial revolution, craftsmanship and attention to the individual gave rise to products and services that,

---

* A byte is a unit of information equivalent to a letter or symbol; a MIPS is a processing rate of one million instructions per second. The combined capacity is available today in machines costing approximately $500,000.

though not many in number, were adapted to their recipient. The low cost of mass-produced goods was achieved at the expense of this individualization, through the efficient generation of homogeneous and impersonal products and services. The process has been gradual, and the cost benefits have blunted our senses to the point where we hardly question the current state of affairs. Our dwellings have become prefabricated and uniform cubicles; our furniture, clothing, and footwear are either constant in size or force us into preordained proportions. We must go through hundreds of newspaper pages to read the fraction that interests us, while we are bombarded by an ever-increasing amount of junk mail. Our transactions with large service industries—insurance companies, credit agencies, utilities, banks, the government—continuously remind us that we are no more than a string of numbers that must follow preset patterns and procedures. Even art, vacations, and religion have become part of the homogeneous mass dispensation.

Computer-based automation can help reverse this dehumanizing trend without decreasing the cost benefits of mass production because the computer is capital- rather than labor-intensive and can be programmed to meet the needs of consumers. With today's construction technology, houses could be designed by computer to suit the individual; to speculate a bit further, they might even be built out of raw materials through a network of programmable robots. The result would be housing that was both less expensive and more varied. Other examples suggest similar approaches. Knowledge-based programs installed in our home computers could act as information fillers, listening to the wire services and other incoming messages and printing only what interests us. Junk mail too could be reduced with advertising in reverse, where the consumer broadcasts a need and the manufacturers reply by offering products and services that fulfill the stated need.

Increased automation could also lead to problems. In the same sense that today's machines and vehicles have weakened our muscles, we can expect that tomorrow's automated robots might weaken the basic skills that they replace. An early form of arithmetical atrophy is already evident with the mass proliferation of inexpensive pocket calculators. This atrophy could spread, and we might come to rely too heavily on our automated assistants. Another problem might arise from the mismatch of automated capability and demand. In our eagerness to modernize we might overburden the machines by asking them to perform tasks for which they are only superficially or marginally suited, thereby producing shoddy results. Finally, we might experience psychological adverse effects if some of our capabilities were shown to be replaceable by machine functions.

The displacement of humans by machines is certain to be the most fearful and far-reaching consequence of automation. Earlier, I spoke of machines replacing humans in decaying industries, hazardous environments, and in the performance of mindless tasks—presumably areas where such a change would be tolerable, indeed desirable. Of course, lacking an alternative, people would rather do mindless tasks or even expose themselves to danger than be out of work, and a more automated world might raise the specter of conflict over this issue between different segments of our population. For example, the occupants of automated housing would enjoy the benefits of reduced costs as well as a more suitable living environment, since labor is almost half of total construction costs, but the construction labor force would be up in arms over the loss of work.

While the prospect of such a polarization can help to identify potential problems, it is nevertheless not realistic. What seems more realistic is that the rate of progress in automation will be necessarily slow for both technological and social reasons. There are still many uncertainties about the future evolution of programmable robots. Progress in automated controllers, although easier to foresee, is not likely to be much faster than the current rate of growth of automation. After all, numerically controlled machine tools were first developed in the 1950s; now, almost thirty years later, even though they are commercially available, they represent only 1 to 2 percent of all machine tools. Similarly, even with successful programmable robots, whether of the "feeling" or "seeing" kind, progress in using them is likely to be slow. At first they will function as assistants to human assemblers, since they will undoubtedly need constant supervision. Computers continue to be complex systems that undergo frequent failures even in simple contexts, let alone in the sophisticated situations that I have described. The costs and efforts needed to program such machines and to maintain their programs in the presence of changing factory situations is not going to be a trivial task. In fact, it may require personnel considerably more skilled and initially equal in number to the personnel that is supposedly being displaced.

In spite of the promise that computers offer, the leap in imagination, as has been the case in the past, will probably continue to be bigger than the leap in practice. We should not forget that nearly three decades after the development of modern computers, and in spite of intervening promises and successful demonstrations in other domains, we are still using these machines primarily to add and subtract and to store and retrieve information. And even if all of our technological problems were solved, it does not seem likely that workers and employers alike would accept rapid changes that result in massive unemployment.

Another factor that tends to retard rapid development and may even hide some unexpected surprises is the presence of layers of technological complexity. Looking at the past development of computers, we see that any given technological advance, whether in equipment or in programming, was capable of reaching only a limited level of additional complexity. A new development, such as a larger memory or a new language, had to come along to raise the limit of complexity to a higher level and lead to new results. At the same time, the past offers us no assurance that we will continue to reach new layers of complexity in our pursuit of advanced automation.

These negative factors, however, should not be viewed as ironclad obstacles to the future progress of automation. I mention them here primarily to put the much-discussed issue of human replacement by machines into a more balanced perspective. The industrial revolution did not eliminate labor; it merely shifted the muscle-intensive segment of labor to higher levels of skill and professionalism over a span of several generations. The information revolution is likely to have a comparable effect, converting labor segments characterized by low levels of skill and intelligence toward higher professional levels or toward new occupations. Such a shift could be a beneficial one, in that it would raise our intellectual baseline. Even more exciting is the associated prospect of exploring the potential benefits of informational resources, which unlike material and energy resources are not known to rely on finite and exhaustible reserves. By introducing flexibility, economy, and individualization of goods and services into our way of life, computer-based automation could provide the driving force that ensures long-term progress. To deny that we shall strike out in such new directions is to deny the fundamental versatility and adaptability of human beings and our inherent desire to possess more than we own and achieve more than we have already accomplished. That the future of automation will take this direction, with its attendant humanizing consequences, is more probable on technical, economic, and social grounds than the more spectacular and much-touted dehumanizing alternative.

EDITORS' POSTSCRIPT

Although the relatively optimistic forecasts made by Dertouzos are based on technological and sociological assumptions that may not prove justified, many of them are offered as plausible extensions of present technology. To the extent that we may be at least one scientific revolution away from the technological level required to reach the stated objectives, as McCarthy has suggested in his critique, the future may turn out to be even more surprising than this essay suggests.

4
Toward Convivial   Terry Winograd
Computing

Dialog 1:
Bank clerk: Thank you for waiting, Mr. Bell. I'm sorry to have to tell you that your credit application was not approved.
Customer: Why not? My credit should be perfectly good.
Clerk: Because the computer said so. We put in all the information you gave us, and the computer set the credit limit at zero.
Customer: But why? Was it my salary, my other debts, my medical history, or what?
Clerk: The computer decided on the basis of the facts you gave us.
Customer: But what things does it think about in deciding?
Clerk: I'm telling you, the computer just takes all of the information and decides. I don't know just how it goes about it—I'm a banker, not a computer expert. But this computer handles all of our banking information reliably, and I'm sure there were good reasons.
Customer: Well, ask it whether it had anything to do with my job problems. I think it is easy to misinterpret what has happened over the last few years if you don't take my illness into account.
Clerk: What do you mean, "ask it"?
Customer: Just type in something so it will tell you whether that was the problem.
Clerk: You don't understand. This is a computer, not a person. You give it the information, and it decides the credit limit. You can't ask it questions.
Customer: Well, then tell it about this letter from the doctor, saying that since the operation my back troubles are completely cleared up, and I won't be having all those sick leaves anymore.
Clerk: You sure don't know much about computers. You can't just tell it stray things. You can only put in the information it asks for. You do what it says, you don't make up new things for it to do. Now please, we're very busy. If you're not satisfied, you can fill out one of these complaint cards. Print your last name in columns 1 through 20. . . .

Dialog 2:[1]
Excerpts from a dialog between a person and a simulated robot operating on a set of toy blocks like those shown in figure 4.1.

Terry Winograd is assistant professor of computer science at Stanford University. He is well known for his contributions to natural-language computer programs, and through his 1972 doctoral thesis became one of the first researchers to demonstrate the feasibility of programs that understand English.

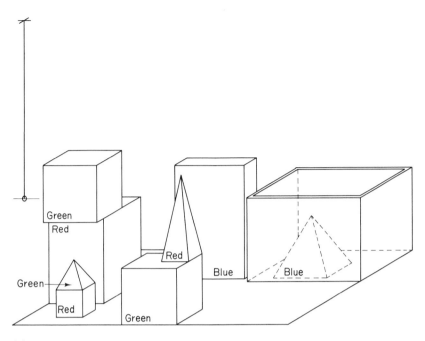

4.1
"Pick up a Big Red Block"

Person: How many blocks are not in the box?
Computer: Four of them.
Person: Is at least one of them narrower than the one which I told you to pick up?
Computer: Yes, the red cube.
Person: Can the table pick up blocks?
Computer: No.
Person: Can a pyramid be supported by a pyramid?
Computer: I don't know.

Person: Will you please stack up both of the red blocks and either a green cube or a pyramid?
Computer: OK *(carries out the action on the display screen).*
Person: Had you touched any pyramid before you put the green one on the little cube?
Computer: Yes, the green one.
Person: When did you pick it?
Computer: While I was stacking up the red cube, a large red block and a large green cube.
Person: Why?
Computer: To get rid of it.
Person: Why did you do that?
Computer: To clean off the red cube.

Person: A "steeple" is a stack which contains two green cubes and a pyramid.
Computer: I understand.
Person: Are there any steeples now?
Computer: No.
Person: Build one.
Computer: OK *(builds a stack made up of two green cubes and a pyramid).*

Dialog 3:[2]
These are excerpts from the middle of a dialog in which a doctor is using a computer program to help choose the best antimicrobial therapy for a patient.
Computer: In light of the site from which the culture was obtained, and the method of collection, do you feel that a significant number of ORGANISM-1 were obtained?
Doctor: WHY?
Computer: [1.0] It is important to find out whether there is therapeutically significant disease associated with this occurrence of ORGANISM-1. It has already been established that:
[1.1] the site of the culture is not one of those which are normally sterile, and
[1.2] the method of collection is sterile.
Therefore, if:
[1.3] the organism has been observed in significant numbers
Then: there is strongly suggestive evidence (.9) that there is therapeutically significant disease associated with this occurrence of the organism
[Also: there is strongly suggestive evidence (.8) that the organism is not a contaminant.]
Doctor: HOW DO YOU DECIDE THAT AN ORGANISM IS PSEUDOMONAS AERUGINOSA?
Computer: Rules which conclude that the identity of the organism is pseudomonas-aeruginosa generally use one or more of the following pieces of information:
the site of the culture
the gram stain of the organism
the morphology of the organism.
Furthermore, the following relationships hold:
The gram stain of the organism and the morphology of the organism tend to appear together in these rules.
RULE 184, RULE 116, RULE 047, RULE 85, and RULE 40 conclude that the identity of the organism is pseudomonas-aeruginosa. Which of these do you wish to see?
Doctor: HOW DID YOU DECIDE THAT ORGANISM-1 MIGHT BE A PSEUDOMONAS?
Computer: I used RULE 85 to conclude that the identity of ORGANISM-1 is pseudomonas. This gave a cumulative certainty factor of .24.

One can pick up any popular magazine today and find articles singing the praises of computers and the benefits they will bring to all of us side by side with articles lamenting the increasing "computerization" of our society. The exchange in dialog 1 is becoming all too familiar as the rapidly decreasing costs of computers make them more and more a part of our everyday lives, affecting everything from office work to the games we play. It is practically certain that computers will have far-reaching effects on the structure of our social institutions, many of them beyond our ability to predict or even envision.

But using computers and "being computerized" are very different things. The problem is not in the nature of computers but in the ways we choose to use them. Our fictional bank clerk is wrong about what computers can do. They are not incapable of responding to the customer's naive requests for an explanation, and the flexibility to accept unexpected information should in fact be part of any computer system that makes decisions affecting people's lives. Dialogs 2 and 3 are taken from actual sessions with computer programs designed to interact with people within specialized domains such as medicine and the simplified world of a block-manipulating robot. My concern will be with such "noncomputerized" interactions with computers, along with other research being done in programming computers to be more "convivial" tools. I will describe ways in which programs are being designed to work with the natural modes of human thought and communication, rather than demanding a "computerized attitude" on the part of those who interact with them. We are just beginning to have examples of such programs, and we can expect them to become much more widespread in the future.

THREE DIFFERENT WAYS OF LOOKING AT COMPUTERS

The dialogs I have presented are surprising to many people. They violate the stereotypes of computers expressed in clichés like "Computers are just superfast giant adding machines," and "Computers only can do what they have been programmed to do." Strangely enough, this includes many of the people who work with computers and those in positions to decide how they will be used in business, education, and the other institutions of our daily lives. Paradoxically, it is often the "experts" who perpetuate the mistaken impressions attributed to the bank clerk in the first dialog. To understand this paradox, we need to look first at the history of computers together with the attitudes people have adopted toward them.

The evolution of computers is often described in terms of "generations," each representing a major new advance in the components from which computers are made. First-generation systems were built of vacuum tubes; the second generation replaced these with smaller, more reliable transistors. The third generation is based on integrated circuit chips, which combine hundreds or even thousands of components in a single tiny device. Noyce describes current research on fourth-generation systems in which entire computers are built on a single silicon chip (see chapter 15). In a parallel way, we can speak of three generations of metaphors which have been used to explain what computers do during the thirty years since they first reached the public consciousness.

The Computer as a Number Processor

The earliest computers were designed to carry out large mathematical calculations needed for tasks such as designing weapons and analyzing the results of complex processes in physics, a function captured in the popular characterization of computers as giant adding machines. The nature of the calculations was well understood; similar calculations had been carried out by hand or on mechanical calculating machines for years. All the computer did was add a new degree of speed and accuracy, making it possible to carry out calculations far too large for people working with traditional methods. From this standpoint the computer did not represent a qualitatively new kind of device and therefore could lead to no major changes in the society that used it. Much of the popular view of computers still runs along these lines, and the extensive use of computers in this role in highly publicized ventures such as moon landings tends to reinforce it.

The Computer as a Data Processor

Although the high cost of early electronic computers meant that they were used primarily for scientific and military applications, the ideas behind data processing are much older than the ability to construct electronic computers. As far back as the end of the last century, Herman Hollerith was able to mechanize work in the Census Bureau using punch cards almost identical to today's IBM cards. A computer can process vast numbers of individual data items, storing them away in a data bank and then searching this data bank for information. In this way it carries out work that would otherwise require an army of clerks, filing and retrieving information and filling out forms, bills, and addresses.

The majority of computers in use today are operated in this data processing fashion. The computations they carry out are not complex or based on higher mathematics but are highly repetitive jobs like adding up invoices, processing checks, and recording airline reservations. Many of the objectionable aspects of "computerization" have their source in the efficiency-oriented mentality that goes along with this kind of computing. An obvious example is the design of systems that convey the attitude that a person is "just a number" by insisting on identifying individuals by numbers instead of by name, as we are accustomed to do in the rest of our interactions.

In fact, programs are perfectly capable of dealing with names, including all of the complexities created by people with the same name, the use of nicknames, name changes, and so on. But in order to do this, they must be built in a different style—one that embodies some of the knowledge a person would use in doing the same task.

The Computer as a Knowledge Processor

The metaphor that has most fascinated people over the years is that of computers as giant brains. Ever since the first mechanical calculating devices were invented centuries ago, people have spun fantasies about mechanical minds—robots designed to serve humanity but with the potential to compete for dominance as intelligent masters of the world. Within the past twenty years, we have begun to build computer systems that have some claim to a kind of intelligent behavior and are referred to as knowledge-based systems or intelligent programs. Much of the most exciting research in computer science lies in this area, known as "artificial intelligence." The motivation for this research comes both from the desire to build useful machines and the desire to expand our understanding of how our own minds work through building and studying devices that mimic intelligent behavior.

The goals of artificial intelligence encompass a broad range of different behaviors that we think of as intelligent. There has been much work in "robotics," the attempt to build computer-controlled devices that see, touch, and move around (see chapter 3). There are programs that play games like chess and checkers, programs that aid in medical diagnosis and treatment, programs that prove mathematical theorems, and programs that do complex analyses of scientific data. Building programs within each of these domains has required an understanding of the reasoning processes that go on in people solving the problems; equally important has been the construction of a "knowledge base" containing the specialized knowledge needed for the task.

The view of computers as knowledge processors is a third-generation attitude which has only recently begun to have practical implications in the design and use of computers. There is a major shift in emphasis between programming a data processor to maintain and use a "data base" and constructing a program that makes use of a "knowledge base." In a data base, the conceptual organization is simple, and the problems are simply those of scale and efficiency. In organizing a knowledge base, on the other hand, there is no simple definition for what should be included or when it can be used. We need to capture the commonsense knowledge that every person can draw upon in carrying out a task. This knowledge structure is many times more complex than most of the data bases now being processed on computers and must be built on many different levels.

The major thrust of research in artificial intelligence is in defining what we mean by a "knowledge representation" and trying to describe those areas of human knowledge that are useful as part of computer systems.

I have already mentioned the paradox of computer experts having out-of-date views of what computers can do. The problem is that the people who work with computers today have differing sets of priorities. The pragmatists see computers primarily as data processors and are concerned with the ways they can be used to increase the power and efficiency of our social and economic system. The romantics see computers as a way of expanding human potential, as tools that enable us better to understand and work with our environment. They emphasize that in working with computers we do not have to become mechanized ourselves. Papert, whose essay on computers in education is an example of the romantic approach, believes along with many others that computers should be the servants of the children who program them rather than masters of efficient drill (see chapter 5). Minsky emphasizes another facet of the romantic approach in his description of work in artificial intelligence aimed at providing theoretical tools for cognitive psychology, in which computers are used not to process data but as models for understanding the human mind (see chapter 18). Much of the research I am concerned with here leads in this direction. Programs that use natural language and deal with natural forms of explanation are built on current theories of psychology. Through experimenting with them, we gain new insights into human language and its underlying thought processes.

Weizenbaum's critical essay points out some of the dangers of taking the computer as a metaphor for the human mind (see chapter 20). In developing and explaining our theories, we scientists who work within artificial intelligence have a responsibility to keep them in mind. This does not negate the value of the computational metaphor as one of the most interesting of the many different views of humankind now being explored.

CURRENT RESEARCH IN BETTER COMMUNICATION WITH COMPUTERS

Most of the communication with computer systems today is in one of two specialized forms. People in positions like the bank clerk in the first dialog are able only to provide data or ask for information in a limited, fixed format. Other people, who program these computers, use a specialized programming language. Most of the available languages have been designed with numerical calculation and data processing in mind and are not well suited to more natural forms of representing knowledge. The usefulness of computers would undergo a qualitative change if this distinction between "programming" and "using programs" were broken down and it became possible to communicate with computer systems in a more natural way. Three areas of current research are aimed at this goal: natural communication, spoken communication, and explanation systems.

Natural Language and Communication

One step toward making computers more convivial is the development of systems that interact in a natural language such as English or Chinese. We would like computer systems in general to have the ability to answer a range of questions like those we might ask at an information desk or to carry out commands like those we would give to an apprentice. Dialog 2 is an example of one such program, built at MIT several years ago. The program simulates on a TV screen a simple robot system, consisting of a single mechanical arm which manipulates toy objects on a tabletop. A person types commands, questions, and new information to the program in English, and the program responds with answers and by moving objects around on its TV screen simulation. The program contains a good deal of knowledge about the world of blocks, which it uses in planning how to carry out complex operations and in answering questions like "Can the table pick up blocks?" In addition, it keeps a memory record of everything that has gone on so far in the dialog, so that it can understand references to past events and answer questions about what has happened and what reasoning it used in deciding on its actions.

Most of the effort in building this program went into analyzing the ways in which different words and phrases are used to communicate meanings. It contains a grammar that enables it to analyze the structure of English sentences, along with subroutines for interpreting the meaning of individual words in context, and a number of special programs for dealing with a wide range of language phenomena. For example, the program has to be able to find things referred to by pronouns ("it," "that," etc.), understand the use of the definite article to refer to recently mentioned objects (as in "the block"), recognize the use of questions (such as Will you . . .?) as implicit commands, and figure out what is desired in a shortened question such as Why? In addition to following commands and answering questions, the system allows the user to define new terms and state new facts to be used in further reasoning.

Within its limited vocabulary (about 200 words) and set of concepts, the program I have described is reasonably good at understanding complicated sentences. It is able to seem natural largely because it converses about a limited world of toy blocks and carries on a dialog in which each of its actions is a response to a specific question or command. If we tried to apply it to a less rigid situation, for example getting it to serve as an apprentice builder, we would soon find it frustratingly incompetent at recognizing what our commands and questions meant. This is because it doesn't apply other aspects of knowledge to the task of understanding language.

When you first think about the problem of getting a computer to use English, it seems that the hardest part is the rules of the language—grammar, spelling, and the meanings of words. In fact, although these details are indeed difficult to master, they cover over a much thornier problem, which has to do with the basic nature of human communication. When you talk to another person, you know that you share a large body of commonsense knowledge about physical objects, events, thoughts, motivations, and all the other aspects of the human world. In asking a question, stating a wish, or giving information, you put in just enough detail so the other person can figure out what you intend. You can leave a tremendous amount unsaid because you know the other person will be able to fill it in from basic knowledge and experience. In order to achieve this same kind of "natural communication" with a computer, we need a way to build in the same sort of reasoning people use to understand one another.

Dialog 4:[3]
From a dialog in which the computer is helping a person schedule an airline flight.
Computer: What time do you want to leave?
Traveller: I must be in San Diego before 10 AM.

Dialog 5:
From an experimental dialog carried out by people over a teletype link.
Clerk: Do you want the flight arriving at 8:00 PM?
Traveller: When does it leave?
Clerk: 6:30 P.M.
Traveller: How much?
Clerk: $25.50 round trip.

Dialog 4 shows some conversation fragments of a system called GUS which communicates with a person in English to help make travel arrangements. Dialog 5 was gathered in an experiment in which a person played the role of travel agent, using a teletype so that the user interacted in the same style as he would with a computer system.

In Dialog 4 the computer must make use of knowledge at several different levels. Superficially, the answer has nothing to do with the question. The computer asked when the customer wanted to leave, and in response the customer said something about when he needed to be somewhere. A human listener immediately realizes that—

a. the response is relevant to the question.

Whenever we use language, we make a number of assumptions about the nature of conversation and the goodwill of the people we converse with. If the response had been, "Isn't it a nice day out today?" a human listener would be confused and would make an effort to understand how the current weather could affect the departure time for the planned trip.

b. being somewhere is a consequence of going there.

This is an example of the kind of painfully obvious fact that we aren't even aware of knowing when we understand language but that must be made explicit if the program is to understand what is going on. The system was discussing a flight to San Diego, not an event in San Diego, and the program's knowledge base must provide for the reasoning needed to draw the connection.

c. the time of leaving determines in a systematic way the time of arrival, which in turn determines the time you will be at the destination.

As with (b), this seems trivially obvious. In fact, it takes an elaborate program with a good deal of knowledge to handle the kinds of simple time relationships that every child masters in his or her first few years.

Dialog 5 is even more difficult. The question "How much?" has to be interpreted in light of what a traveler would reasonably want to know. Simple rules for handling sentence fragments might lead to the mistaken interpretation, "How much of the flight leaves . . .?" and the corresponding nonsensical answer, "The whole thing." The system needs to have knowledge not only about the information a travel agent has but also about airplanes and the typical needs and interests of the people who use them.

In addition to work on dialogs, there is a great deal of current work on understanding sequences of sentences that tell some kind of story. The emphasis in these programs is on joining the new information with a preexisting body of knowledge. Dialog 6 is an interaction with SAM, a program that uses simple stories as inputs, on the basis of which it makes inferences and answers questions. SAM has a knowledge base consisting of a set of scripts that represent the normal course of events for a few simple situations like going to a restaurant or taking a bus trip. This program is still very primitive, handling only a few stock situations and drawing a few basic inferences it is preprogrammed to look for (such as surmising that the reason for leaving a large tip was because of quick service). But it points the way toward programs that can make extensive use of stored knowledge of "the way things are" to help fill in unstated facts in stories.

Dialog 6:[4]
Input: John went to a restaurant. The hostess seated John. The hostess gave John a menu. John ordered a lobster. He was served quickly. He left a large tip. He left the restaurant.
Paraphrase (produced by SAM): John decided he was going to go to a restaurant. He went to one. He asked the hostess for a table. She told him

he could go to it. He went to it. She went to it. He sat down in a chair. He got a menu from her. He read it. A waiter saw John was at the table. The waiter went to it. John ordered a lobster. A chef cooked it. The waiter got it from the chef. The waiter served it to John quickly. He ate it. He asked the waiter for a check. John got it from the waiter. John remembered the waiter had served the lobster to him quickly. John left the waiter a large tip. John paid the check. He left the restaurant.
Person: Why did John go to a restaurant?
SAM: So John could eat a meal.
Person: Did the waiter give John a menu?
SAM: John got a menu from the hostess.
Output of a simple story comprehension program.

Interactive Systems and Spoken Communication

One of the greatest limitations on interacting with computers is the fact that all input and output must be in writing. There is a tremendous difference between speaking with a person and communicating by writing. Those people with whom we only correspond can be close and useful friends, but there are many things they simply can't do for us because they demand a more interactive conversation. The systems described earlier are relatively interactive in that a response to a typed question comes back after only a few seconds. In many systems, the computer is operated in "batch mode," in which an entire set of commands must be gathered up and entered all at once, usually in the form of a deck of punched cards, and the response comes after a delay of minutes or hours in a single batch of printout.

Interactive systems are one of the major topics of current computer research, along with personal computers that can bring all their resources to bear on interacting with a single user, providing instant reaction and performing complex processing to interpret the input and produce a response. As computing power becomes cheaper, it will become feasible to provide systems that can do the difficult job of analyzing spoken inputs as well. Our ability to program computers to use speech is still very limited. In both understanding what is said and generating responses, we are able to handle isolated words with some success; connected conversation is possible only on a primitive level. But over the next ten years, we can expect to see a number of applications in which the techniques are sufficiently developed to be practical.

It is impossible to predict how the way we use computers will change when they are able to accept spoken inputs and produce a wide range of spoken outputs. Certainly it will become more convenient and natural, for both current users of computers and those for whom the more mechanical forms of interaction have been barriers make computing seem an alien process. Many of the uses of the computer projected for the future—whether in the home, the office, in industry, or in education—will really come into their own only when a person can give a command to a computer merely by speaking.

Inventions like the telephone and automobile caused major shifts in the structure of the institutions that made use of them. Their existence had an impact for which more primitive but analogous devices like telegraphy and trains offered no precedent. In the same way, speech-using computers will become common (and seem indispensable) in situations where we cannot now even imagine that a computer could be useful.

Speech generation: Anyone who goes to movies or watches television has heard fanciful examples of computer speech. The robot who monotonically intones "DOES NOT COM-PUTE" is a stock character of science fiction. There has been a long history of research into speech generation, much of it done at Bell Telephone Laboratories, and many different techniques have been developed, with different degrees of quality and flexibility. Programs for computer-aided instruction have made use of a variety of techniques for producing spoken answers and messages. Other systems provide data, such as the telephone company system that intercepts incomplete calls and reads out the exact number dialed. The greatest problem is in producing sentences that are not simply prestored patterns, with appropriate rhythm and intonation (the rises and falls of pitch that accompany every utterance). Current systems produce utterances that are understandable but whose intonation patterns are nonexistent or highly unnatural.

Just as the question-answering systems described earlier demonstrated the vital importance of a large knowledge base in understanding language, the experience with building speech-generation systems has offered new insights into the major role played by intonation patterns in communicating meaning. It has become clear that intonation cannot be thought of simply as a matter of conveying additional emphasis or emotion but is essential to the structuring of basic meaning in messages. It is hoped that within the next few years these studies will provide a theoretical base for tying together a reasoning system and a speech generator to achieve a high degree of naturalness.

Speech understanding: Speech understanding has proved to be an extremely difficult problem. There now exist systems that can be trained to recognize individually spoken words from a vocabulary of several hundred choices. These are of use in interactions where the user selects from a small set of options what the computer is to do. A number of recent projects have aimed at developing systems capable of recognizing normal, continuously spoken language, and they have provided a good deal of new insight into the problems of organizing systems with multiple knowledge sources.[5] Reasonable success has been achieved with systems that work within extremely limited domains, where the user has only a few options for what to say. Other systems try to combine the analysis of spoken forms with the kinds of language understanding I discussed earlier, but it will be a number of years before these become good enough for practical use.

Explanation Systems

In talking about natural language and speech, we have been dealing with the form of communication. If computers are to be convivial tools, it is even more important to deal with its content. A system that is interactive and uses spoken English can still be intransigent and uncooperative. When computers are used for tasks that go beyond the simple kinds of calculation and data processing we see today, they will move into domains where it is not sufficient just to provide "the answer." As an example, a program to aid in medical diagnosis cannot be written in a way that is guaranteed to provide the right answer in every case. Even if our theories of programming made it possible to provide such guarantees (which they currently do not), medical diagnosis itself involves many facts whose meaning is uncertain, tentative, and probabilistic. If a program is to be useful, it must operate in a mode much more like a human consultant, in which it can offer interpretations, explain the reasoning behind them, and modify them on the basis of new information.

Users of complex systems cannot assume, as our bank clerk did, that the knowledge at their disposal is accurate or even suited to their purposes. The quality of the results depends on the quality of the information they are based on, and methods are needed of checking and modifying the information a computer uses at all levels. Today only a few programs on the frontiers of computer science research have the ability to explain their actions. Dialog 2 includes an exchange in which the program explains the planning involved in choosing a particular sequence of actions done to carry out a command. Dialog 3 is a segment of a conversation between a doctor and a system that helps select antibiotic therapy for infections. This program will soon reach the level of expertise and conviviality where it may be useful in real medical settings. A major part of its future develop-ment lies in expanding its ability to explain the reasoning involved in each of its decisions.

The eventual importance of explanation systems is not limited to life-and-death matters like medicine. Like natural-language and spoken com-munication, this style of cooperative interaction will have an impact on every use to which computers will be put. There are good reasons for building self-explanation facilities into every complex computer system, whether it is computing accounts and sending bills, controlling the flow of traffic in a city, or keeping track of airline reservations. If the bank in our opening story had installed a system with an explanation facility, the clerk would not have had to stop with the answer, "Because the computer said so," but could have found out just why and immediately taken action if the decision was based on wrong information. As computers are used in more and more of the processes that affect our lives, it will become critical to insist on this sort of responsiveness.

The most obvious and direct reason for adding explanation systems to complex programs is that it extends the number of people who can make use of the system and makes interaction easier. An airline reservation system that could deal directly with customers would have broader usefulness than one demanding specially trained personnel. In order to do so, it would have to be able to explain what it was doing and what information it needed, and to answer questions, as illustrated in Dialog 4.

WHERE ARE THINGS HEADED?

Earlier I classified attitudes toward computing in terms of generations and as romantic or pragmatic. My discussion of convivial computing has clearly been from a third-generation romantic perspective. In looking further into the future, I will try to look at the problems from a more pragmatic viewpoint. Stated simply, the question that needs to be answered is, If all of these things are so great, why aren't they happening now, and when will they, if ever?

The first and most obvious response is that our ability to program convivial systems is still in an early stage. The examples I have given are all from research programs that are much smaller and more specialized than the systems' real applications would require. Several years of further research will be needed before the body of techniques for designing convivial systems is well enough worked out to be generally used. This is purely a technical problem, though, and one whose future seems clear.

However, the question, Where are things headed? can never be answered solely on technological grounds. It is all too easy for scientists and engineers to assume that providing devices that could conceivably be used as tools in solving problems is equivalent to providing solutions. In practice the realities of economics and social power will do more to determine the future uses of computers than resolution of the technical and scientific problems.

For most tasks now widely handled by computers, the least costly alternative is to continue with rigid "computerized" systems. Most of the institutions controlling the development and use of large computers place the highest priority on efficiency and cost reduction. In the long run, consumer preferences may have an effect on the nature of services provided, but in the short run, decisions are made on narrower economic grounds, with an overriding emphasis on the quantity rather than the quality of the goods provided. People have been persuaded to accept a view of computers that leads them to tolerate the kinds of impersonal interaction that is cheapest to provide.

In addition to institutions that are not disposed to provide convivial computing because of the expense, there are others with a vested interest in the "mystification" produced by the impersonality and inaccessibility of their computer systems. The bank that attributes its credit decisions to an inscrutably wise computer program is not as easily held up to public scrutiny and accountability as one that explains its decisions on an individual basis. The recent use of computer printouts by the U.S. military to deceive the press about our bombing policies (see chapter 20) is an extreme but not isolated example of mystification.

Even within the computer profession, one often encounters an attitude that things should not be made "too easy" for computer users who aren't computer specialists. This is not based on an attempt to deceive or avoid accountability but is a product of the self-esteem that comes from being able to master difficult and abstruse systems. It has the same effect, though, of reinforcing the image of the computer as impersonal and inscrutable rather than accessible and convivial. Such an attitude can prevent people who have the knowledge to make decisions about systems from doing so, like the clerk in the dialog who claimed ignorance about the criteria for making credit decisions—"I'm not a computer expert." A major goal in designing new computer systems is to make it possible for the relevant experts to have direct access to what is in the programs, whether they be bankers, doctors, or just people who want to build their own personal systems.

In the next ten to fifteen years, we can expect the following things to happen:

1. The techniques for convivial computing will be developed to a point where it is possible to make major changes in the way people interact with computers. This will include advanced explanation systems, strong natural-language capabilities, highly satisfactory speech generation, and a moderate degree of speech understanding.
2. The costs of computing will drop to a point where it is economically feasible to apply these techniques, and this will be done in those places where there is a demand for less "computerized" computers.

We need to be concerned about the possible side effects of these developments. It is impossible to predict all of the new computer uses or their consequences. However, there are some obvious opportunities for misuse, which must be checked. As an example, Weizenbaum points out

The Computer Age:
A Twenty-Year View

edited by
Michael L. Dertouzos
and
Joel Moses

that speech understanding systems could greatly extend the potential for surveillance of ordinary citizens.[6] Computer monitoring of telephone conversations would make use of the same technical tools that are being developed to increase the average person's capabilities for natural interaction with computer systems. There is no way to manipulate the technology to prevent such misuses. The issues are social and political, and the public must be given the necessary technical knowledge to understand the problems and influence what is done.

Finally, some things we can hope for and work toward:

1. There will be more computer systems designed to explain what they are doing, and less mystification about what computers are and what they can do.

2. The increased accessibility and conviviality of computing will make computers and programming the province of anyone who wants to learn about them, rather than the private domain of a highly educated few.

These things will not happen just because the technology exists but will require efforts in public education and a broader concern among those who work with computers about the effects they will have on our lives.

EDITORS' POSTSCRIPT

The number of people who can interact with computers today is perhaps no more than several hundred thousand, because of the difficulty of learning complex languages, systems, and procedures. If the natural-language gate to computers opens up, then these machines will become accessible to many millions of people, as is the case for the telephone— which will profoundly affect our way of life, probably beyond what this essay predicts. However, the technological problems that must be solved before this can happen are indeed formidable. As McCarthy points out, a dialog program that accepts "I must be in San Diego before 10 AM" almost certainly does not understand "must" well enough to know when to ask whether chartering a plane is warranted. Such issues, which involve making the commonsense world comprehensible, will undoubtedly critically affect natural-language computer program research and may delay or impede progress in this very exciting and promising area.

NOTES

1
Terry Winograd, *Understanding Natural Language* (New York: Academic Press, 1972).

2
Edward H. Shortliffe, *Computer-Based Medical Consultation: MYCIN* (New York: American Elsevier, 1976). See also Randall Davis and Douglas Lenat, *Automated*

Acquisition of Expertise (New York: McGraw-Hill, forthcoming).

3
Daniel G. Bobrow, Ronald M. Kaplan, Martin Kay, Donald A. Norman, Henry Thompson, and Terry Winograd, "GUS, A Frame-Driven Dialog System," *Artificial Intelligence* 8, no. 2 (April 1977): 155–173.

4
Roger C. Schank and Robert P. Abelson, *Scripts, Plans, Goals, and Understanding* (New York: Halsted Press, 1977).

5
See Allen Newell *et al.*, *Speech Understanding Systems* (Amsterdam: North-Holland Publishers, 1973), and D. Raj Ready, *Speech Recognition* (New York: Academic Press, 1975).

6
Joseph Weizenbaum, *Computer Power and Human Reason* (San Francisco: W. H. Freeman, 1976).

5
Computers
and Learning

Seymour A. Papert

The kinds of questions usually raised in discussions of the potential impact of computers on education are far too narrow in their vision. In fact, they constrain us in our ability to consider, or even to see, the more fundamental set of issues raised by a theoretical consideration of education, computational models, and the human psyche. I am convinced that these issues in a very concrete sense will confront us in their most urgent and acute forms within the next five or ten years. What we refuse to face now will, like the return of the repressed, come back to haunt us.

Faced with a computer technology that opens the possibility of radically changing social life, our society has responded by consistently casting computers in a framework that favors the maintenance of the status quo. For example, we typically think of computers making credit decisions in an otherwise unchanged banking system, or helping to teach children to read in an otherwise unchanged school system. We think of computers as helping schools in their task of teaching an existing curriculum in classrooms instead of confronting the fact that the computer puts the very idea of school into question. The invasion of computer technology into education is inevitable. By operating with a limited and deformed vision we are increasing the ultimate social cost of correcting the mistakes we are now making, mistakes that grow out of our collective resistance to coming to terms with what the computer is going to mean in our lives. I will begin by addressing the social implications of some models of how the computer is being used in education, after which I will present some of the powerful technical possibilities, many of which are now operant, that dramatize the absurdity of continuing to think about computers, or about education itself, in traditional ways.

Seymour A. Papert is professor of mathematics and Cecil and Ida Green Professor of Education at MIT. For many years he was codirector of the Artificial Intelligence Laboratory at MIT and head of its LOGO project, which deals with the use of computers in the education of children.

CRITICAL STRATEGIES

One can classify the uses of computers in education in many ways. For example, one can distinguish between drill and practice (computer as automated teacher), simulations* (computer as automated world), and learning simple programming languages (computer as toy computer). Traditionally, these uses have been perceived as different, and I myself have treated them as different in order to contrast situations where the computer programs the child and where the child programs the computer. However, here I want to take a different tack and stress the underlying sameness of these forms of computer use. What they have in common is that they share a model of education which leads them to reinforce traditional educational structures and thus play a reactionary role, opposing the emergence of radically new forms of education.

How then do drill and practice, simulation, and simple programming languages articulate the dominant structures of the traditional model for education and the dominant forms of educational practice? I will begin with drill and practice, a model that sees the computer as an automated teacher, doing essentially the same job as a "real" one in an automated but otherwise unchanged school environment. In this model the computer is used to put the students through their paces in a series of repetitive exercises, such as $17 + 13 = ?$. The manipulative nature of this model is often curiously reinforced by the use of precious pseudopersonalizations in the computer's interaction with the child. For example, if Johnny happened to answer 31 in the above case, the computer might reply, "No, Johnny, wouldn't you like to try again?" The designers of this software would not insist on the centrality of these personalizations to their enterprise, but I would like to suggest that they are symptomatic of particular attitudes toward knowing that are embedded in such computer-aided instruction. Impersonating the teacher is not such a long step away from automating the teacher, or at least automating the most superficial aspects of teaching.

Drill and practice programs in common use, for example those of Patrick Suppes,[1] undoubtedly succeed in their immediate goal of improving the performance scores of "lagging" children. Studies typically show that a child who has been advancing only half a standardized year per academic year in elementary school arithmetic can frequently begin to advance two years per year with computer drill and practice. Thus he will be "caught up" in no time at all. I have no doubt that more sophisticated programs could achieve even more impressive results, but in my view, the point is not to congratulate ourselves or our computers about having

---

* Such as planetary motion on a screen.

"caught him up" but rather to ask a series of hard questions about why he had to get caught up and what it is that he is catching up to.

Using an analogy; suppose for some reason that a hypothetical teacher, X, wanted to make me recite some Sanskrit poetry. Undoubtedly drill and practice of meaningless Sanskrit monosyllables would get me reciting the set piece. I have no doubt that a well-programmed computer could get me there faster than could Teacher X acting alone. This would be particularly true if X had me in a classroom with thirty other Sanskrit learners. Underlying this process of rote learning would be a dissociation of my spontaneous thought processes from my verbal product.

Some people have observed that the process of elementary education consists of such a dissociation, of "bringing a child to give the right answer" independently of what he is thinking. Elementary-school-age children themselves reflect on this experience of dissociation. In a survey of third graders who asked, What do you do to learn?, nearly half of the children questioned referred to a process they called "making your mind a blank and saying it over and over again." But there is another way of learning to recite Sanskrit poetry—learn some Sanskrit. I can learn many hundreds of lines of English poetry in the time it would take me to memorize one meaningless line of Sanskrit syllables. The children for whom mathematics comes easily learn their multiplication tables many hundreds of times faster than the ones whose catching up I have discussed. "Gifted" children seem to know mathematics in the same sense that I know English. The children who have been caught up have been caught up to something very different, what I refer to as a denatured mathematics because it is mechanical and has a rote structure that has nothing to do with mathematics as a form of knowledge. This mathematics is not only denatured but is also alienating, distancing the child from his own thought processes as well as from the true nature of mathematics.

Of course I do not mean to confine my criticism to the results of learning "mathematics" by rote through computerized drill and practice. Old-fashioned methods of rote learning of tables and working endless problems on squared paper are possibly even worse. So it might seem unfair to criticize the computer, which at least is effective. But I want to point out how paradoxical it is to use the computer to drill denatured mathematical facts into the child when it could be used in a fashion analogous to teaching Sanskrit in my analogy. The computer is the one tool through which we know how to heighten the child's experience of mathematics in its intimate relationship with how he situates himself dynamically in space and time, a relationship that is closely tied to the development of the deepest symbolic structures. Thus there is an important sense in which a rote use of the computer involves a double contradiction. We are using the computer as a sophisticated way of doing a kind of mathematics we wouldn't be doing at all except for the limitations of an earlier technology—pencil and paper. We are using the one technology that offers the promise of getting us out of this box, but we are using its power to squeeze ourselves ever more tightly into it. Why are we doing this?

The answer to this question has a social as well as a technical dimension. First, a theory of knowledge underlies this use of the computer. We are socialized into thinking of mathematics as a collection of number facts. This atomistic theory of knowledge leads naturally into a model of teaching as the achievement of a set of discrete behavioral objectives and of learning as the repetitive performance of prescribed exercises. The teacher plays the role of an authority figure who prescribes the exercises and judges their performance, while the child learning mathematics is also learning how to accept authority in a way prescribed by school and society. Replacing a human teacher by a machine changes nothing, except perhaps that it makes the process more effective by giving it a mechanical image that is in fact more resonant with what is really going on.

Drill and practice also reinforce one more feature of current education, the concept of a curriculum, which appears to most educators as inseparable from effective communication of knowledge. The drill and practice model raises to a higher power the idea that education without curriculum equals chaos.

While the drill and practice model may seem an easy target, other models of current computer use are more sophisticated. Consider for example, a vision of the computer as a laboratory through which simulation experiments can be performed. Simulating a universe model has some interesting features, particularly in contrast to drill and practice. The student is engaged in a more active process. For example, one of the most widely used set of programs of this type allows a high school student to carry out simulated experiments in demography. By entering parameters such as the statistics of birth and death, the student can see played out into the future the consequences of conjectures about the conditions under which one might get zero population growth. Compared with most social studies programs, this approach engages students with concepts that can make the subject come alive. But here again, we must ask what it is that comes alive. I spoke of a denatured and alienating mathematics; now we confront a denatured and alienating sociology, an overly mechanistic view of what society is like. We see the same processes in the uses of computer simulations in the teaching of physics. In a typical example, students are asked to perform experiments to discover or confirm various laws of physics through simulation. As with drill and practice, using the computer as a social-physical science laboratory implies an epistemology. One might argue that the epistemology under attack is the epistemology of the school science lab rather than the epistemology of simulations as such, and I do not mean at all to imply that simulation as such is an educationally conservative practice. But I do say that simulation as practiced within the traditional educational structure is quickly absorbed, despite the often radical intentions of its creators, to become a reinforcing agent of the traditional rather than a vehicle of the new.

The epistemology implicit in simulation of traditional experimental situations is conservative in several respects. First, although there is much talk of a "logic of discovery," this is based on a fiction. What the student is free to discover is nothing but what the situation has been set up to make him discover. Second, although there is much talk of the student as active and engaged, he is still operating passively. In an important sense he is still being programmed by the computer rather than programming the computer himself, a distinction that leads me to a consideration of a third common use of computers in education, where, indeed, the student is actually given the chance to program.

The way in which programming has been introduced is a revealing example of how the best intentions can become self-defeating. Clearly the first step seemed to be to find an extremely simple language that high school students could easily use. BASIC appeared to be such a simple language. What could be simpler? The language uses no sophisticated ideas; it has only a handful of primitive concepts, and everything the student needs to know can be spelled out on a page. But to see the logical trap, consider a scenario that opens the question of other ways of defining what is simple and what is complex. Suppose that a master linguist presented us with the idea of simplifying the acquisition of language by children by offering them a language with only a hundred words. These hundred words would of course be carefully chosen so that every possible thought could be expressed in them. We might jump at the chance; we might perceive this language as simpler to learn. But what do we mean by "simpler" and what do we mean by "learn the language"? Indeed, the children would learn its vocabulary very quickly, but they would spend the rest of their time struggling with its constraints. They would have to search for devious ways to encode even mildly complex ideas into this small vocabulary. Thus it is with the well-known programming language BASIC. Its vocabulary is quickly learned, but its programs quickly become labyrinths. Some students take to it very easily, just as some students take to mathematics very easily no matter how badly it is taught. They become captured by the power of the computer and find in it an enriching medium of expression. But their numbers are few. For the vast majority of students who learn to program in BASIC, learning to program means learning a few set pieces of programming from a textbook and devoting the rest of their time at the terminal to playing computer games. Attempts to "simplify" programming have backfired and have created a kind of pathology. This pathology has its own symptoms: instead of writing programs, thousands of high school students with the privilege of access to computers are sitting at their terminals playing simple computer games like ticktacktoe.

This pathology is not unique to the computer world. Once again it is in harmony with a prevailing assumption in education, the idea that the more knowledge is cut up the more easily it can be fed out one crumb at a time. However, this idea leads to a vicious circle, since the individual crumbs, though small, have no meaning in themselves, so that the task of fitting them into larger structures is beyond the capacities of the learner because he is left with no independent resources. The teacher is thus left with the task of programming the instructions, the "curriculum" of exercises each of which can be digested but not metabolized.

Why then is BASIC so widely used? Two reasons come to mind. The first relates to the epistemological prejudice that favors BASIC because it is "simple," despite the accumulation of evidence that its simplicity does not translate into learnability. The second reason is more fundamental. The typical teacher of BASIC is content to have very limited successes.* This is all that he, like any teacher, is accustomed to expect. Moreover, of those who have glimpsed the possibility that all students might become creative programmers, many recoil at the prospect of facing thirty students, each of whom understands what he is doing better than the teacher does. Thus, for the traditional educational system the limitations of BASIC are its advantages.

The third reason for BASIC's popularity is technological. It provides a rationalization, a kind of "cover story" in which various elements of the computer world (computer manufacturers, teachers, publishers) find themselves in a kind of complicity. Together they are protecting the primitive use of the computer in "easy" ways which do not seriously challenge the status quo and do not require deep thinking, imaginative planning, or taking risks. The rationalization for the continued use of BASIC creates a mythology of what is technically possible. If you ask someone in the computer world, he will typically say that one of the reasons we use BASIC is because it is economical. Historically, this was true, since BASIC could be run on small machines, the kind of machines that were first available to high schools. This situation has radically changed in a period where the cost of the more powerful computers is not significantly higher than the smallest ones. Indeed, the major cost in a school installation is now the terminal, irrespective of what computer it is connected to and what lan-

---

* Although some of the most exciting and excited teachers I have known are trying desperately to achieve an educational utopia through the inadequate instrument of a too-limited computer system.

guages it is going to be talking. If you ask a teacher, Why BASIC?, you will hear as an answer the same story and the fact that many textbooks are available; if you ask a publisher he will tell you that the teachers want BASIC. When I asked an influential member of a federal agency with power to influence policymaking in this area, he said that the cost of reprogramming the computers now used in high schools would be monumental. It took me many hours to convince him that the cost of reprogramming the teachers after their numbers have multiplied in the next five years would be hundreds of times greater.*

This reprogramming (both of the machines and the teachers) will be inevitable because the technological trends that already make it possible to go far beyond BASIC will eventually bring the presently utopian vision of computers within the reach of everybody. The emergence of the personal computer has launched a social process (one out of many convergent ones) capable of realizing this vision.

The technological imperative to stick with BASIC echoes very general processes typical of the social appropriation of a new technology which I will show with an example drawn from outside the area of computers and education. The example is based on a story illustrating what I shall call the QWERTY phenomenon. QWERTY is a sequence of letters on the typewriter keyboard and was commonly used to name the present disposition of keys until the defeat of all rival arrangements made a specific name unnecessary. It is interesting to ask people why the keys are so disposed. Most imagine vaguely that the arrangement optimizes some aspect of typing; the fingers move less, it represents the diagram distribution of English, and so on. But the truth is very different. The history of QWERTY is a mixture of ingenuity in dealing with the very marginal technology of the earliest commercial typewriters and inept bungling. The goal of the designers of QWERTY was to minimize the frequency of immediate succession of strokes which would cause a barely workable mechanism to jam as a result of the slow return cycle (a bug that some of us still remember in the typewriters of our youth). Thus, if the intention of the QWERTY designers had been achieved, the arrangement would be almost exactly the opposite of what is needed to optimize typing. Fortunately they bungled, so that the actual arrangement is almost random.

How did QWERTY become established? The explanation is obvious: once enough people had learned touch typing the social cost of change became too great to be overcome by demonstration that other arrangements facilitated learning, or reduced fatigue, or whatever. QWERTY had

---

* The hours of work were wasted, since the person I had "reeducated" left the agency soon after. The hard lesson is that the real source of the problem is not what isolated individuals think or know.

dug itself in for several generations and will stay for a few more years until the computerized typing machine allows a sufficiently graceful transition to something else.

When we look at the pattern of computer development, the possibility of QWERTY-like phenomena is very apparent. For example, many features of the BASIC story are analogous to the QWERTY story: they are perfectly rational when seen historically as adaptations to early and very marginal computer technology, and they survive by a process of social fixation into a period when they no longer have any rational technological reason for existence. The only reason for the continued existence of BASIC is its social implantation.

If it seemed to be the case that computers will affect education only in a marginal way, comparable, say, to that of the typewriter in schools or even to that of the typewriter in business, the story of how society learns to use it would be certainly interesting but hardly fundamental; its little deviations from an ideal would be no more significant than the QWERTY episode. But I believe that the computer's impact will be more comparable with that of fuel-burning technologies in modern transportation or of chemistry in medicine or of electronics in telecommunications. The manner in which society learns to use it is a much more serious affair, and the social costs of doing it badly will be higher than those incurred through first developing the automobile and then worrying about its side effects in the form of pollution of the atmosphere, deformation of the cities, death on the roads, and so on.

SYNTHETIC STRATEGIES

Present strategies of computer learning have very direct social implications, and this will be no less true in the future. In 1973 Christopher Jencks[2] published a book in which he argued on the basis of empirical data that schools do little to redress the inequality of life chances. Certainly he could find no evidence that the introduction of TV, movies, language labs, and other educational hardware made a significant difference. Nor did the innovative curricula of the 1960s. My argument is that powerful computers could have done so.*

This is because the computer can enter the educational process in a profoundly different way than has so far been the case. Since the late 1960s I have been involved in a project that captures many of the features of what I see as a positive direction for the future of computers in educa-

---

* There were perhaps a few computers in the high schools in Jencks's sample, but their numbers were too small to have any impact on the study. In any case, they would have been used in one or another of the conservative modes I have discussed and would not have made a difference.

tion. This project involves a computer language, LOGO, and a computer-based learning environment, the MIT Children's Learning Lab. A visitor to the lab is likely to encounter a scene in which children interact with computer-controlled devices. One such device, the one we find most evocative for young children, is the turtle (see fig. 5.1). In the turtle we see very dramatically many of the ways in which this environment differs not just from traditional forms of computer use but from the models that govern education in noncomputerized schools as well. It is relational before being abstract, the child himself is in control, and the results of the child's programming are limited only by his imagination. In no sense are we talking here about set exercises or prefabricated simulations.

The turtle is a cybernetic animal. It moves under the control of the computer, which is programmed by the child. The child writes an instruction, PEN DOWN, FORWARD 100, and the turtle drops its magic marker and moves forward 100 units, tracing a line as it goes. If the child then says RIGHT 90, FORWARD 100, RIGHT 90, FORWARD 100, RIGHT 90, FORWARD 100, the turtle has traced a square. To SQUARE can then be encoded in the computer's memory, so that the child does not have to repeat this long set of instructions but can simply use the command to SQUARE. For young children, the operation is conceptualized as teaching the computer a new word, and how to teach becomes not only a metaphor for how to program but a theme of the child's activities in the learning lab.* Suppose the child wants to program the turtle to trace out a circle and he asks us what to do. Instead of telling him what instructions to write, we say, "Stand up, walk in a circle," and perhaps after a few false starts the child proposes to the teacher that what he is doing is "turning a tiny tiny bit and moving forward a tiny tiny bit." The child then tries that with the turtle. We have told him how to express the instruction to keep repeating any sequence. And so the child writes RIGHT 1, FORWARD 1, with instructions to repeat, and to his delight, the turtle traces out a circle. This is the way the child will develop many programs of his own invention. The teacher does not have to suggest that the child stand up and play turtle at each point. The idea of drawing upon his own body geometry becomes part of the culture into which he has been socialized.

What have we seen in this simple example, and how is it different from the images I have sketched of children doing drills, of children simulating population growth, and of children programming a computer to write in BASIC to solve simultaneous equations? First of all, the child is learning

---

* An example of a conceptually meaningless limitation of BASIC is that it does not allow new commands to be introduced in this sense. At best it allows new "mathematical functions" to be introduced and given names such as FN3. The possibility of an exchange based on natural language and natural thought structures is lost. There can be no excuse for this limitation of BASIC. It is pure QWERTY.

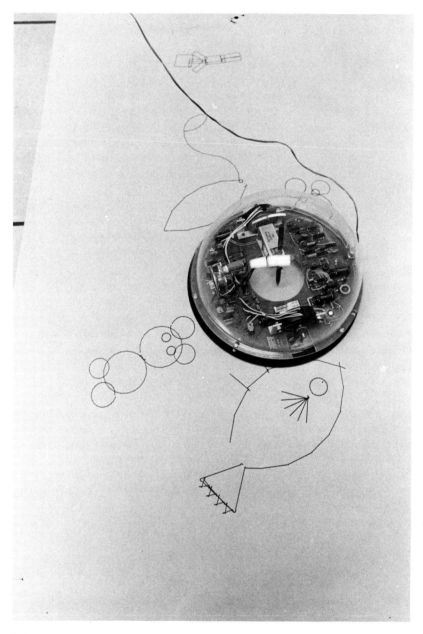

5.1
A Mechanical Turtle Scribbling

by being brought into a relationship with his own intuitive knowledge structures, in this case of his own body. He is learning to see formal mathematics as a symbolic language, a different style of articulating and elaborating what he already knows. Mathematics, instead of being alienating, is profoundly egosyntonic. I do not mean this in any metaphorical sense. The youngest children relate to the turtle by limiting its movements with their own bodies and having turtles imitate their movements. As they gain more mastery of the programming language, these primitive imitations become more expressive.

The suggestion that deep psychological structures are being touched on is confirmed by a few case studies of work with LOGO turtles and autistic children. These children used the turtle as a first object to communicate with; ultimately they communicated through the turtle with their human teacher.[3] Work with the turtle not only changes the child's relation to himself, it changes his relation to the teacher. The authoritarian model is broken. The teacher becomes a partner with the child in a joint enterprise of understanding something that is truly unknown because the situations created by each child are totally new. Children who have been socialized into traditional schools and into schools where the usual kind of so-called "discovery" strategies predominate find this hard to believe. Let us not delude ourselves that we fool children into thinking they are "discovering" things that are already well known to the teacher. One of my favorite anecdotes from the LOGO experience is about a child who jumped up in the middle of a debugging session and said in a tone full of astonishment, almost disbelief, to his teacher, "You mean you *really* didn't know how to do it?"

Just as marked as the change in the child's relation to himself and to the teacher is the change in his relation to knowledge. Knowledge is now a source of power to do what he could not do before. One sees this most dramatically when a child moves from simple programs designed for a mechanical turtle that traces patterns on the floor to programs for a "light turtle" that operates on a TV-like display screen. Compared with what was possible with paper and pen, the new possibilities offered by the complexity, precision, and animation of computer-generated graphics seize the imagination with their power (see fig. 5.2). Children are fascinated by doing things with lines, light, color, and animation that they have never done before, but beyond the novelty of the experience is the awareness that they themselves are able to do something such as animation that they previously associated with television, something they watch as passive observers. An epistemology of true and false is shattered or rather recast as part of a broader epistemology with the pragmatic dimension of knowing how to make things work. The question is now no longer right or wrong, gold star or not, for the steps in a little exercise but a goal that

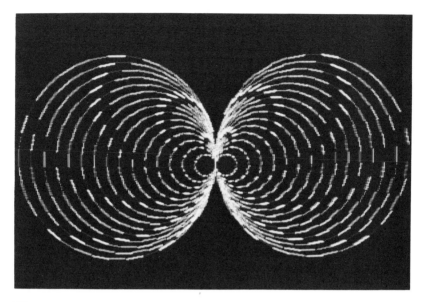

5.2
An Elaboration on the Turtle Circle Drawn by a TV Turtle

might be reached only after several weeks' time. The question posed when something doesn't work at an intermediate stage is how to fix it. I think it is a significant fact of what I shall call the computer culture that it has a name, "debugging," for this important intellectual operation which is significantly unnamed in both the popular and the standard educational culture.

The traditional teacher can scarcely avoid being ambivalent about such a changed relation to the child. Much as he might envy the situation in which the child does not need to be "motivated," he can scarcely face with equanimity the possibility of the child's really taking off on his own. What is more, in most learning environments the child in the anecdote who was incredulous at discovering that he and his teacher were sharing a mutual ignorance would be quite threatening for the unprepared teacher. Quite obviously, if part of what is supposed to happen in a classroom is getting children used to accepting authority, they have to believe that the teachers "know." This points to the way in which the project goes beyond suggesting how computers can be integrated into schools and becomes one of rethinking what our society expects schools to do.

Where does the notion of curriculum fit in? I see learning in this kind of environment as more than anything else like the child's acquisition of language, which is certainly not guided in any sense by curriculum but is a process of acculturation. Such processes work through the personal appropriation of knowledge from the surrounding culture. I see the computer as an agent for exposing the child to a set of possibilities for acculturation, whether in mathematics, in science, or in language itself.

This image of learning suggests a critique of what a school is all about and even raises the question if such demarcated institutions as schools make any sense. I sympathize with Ivan Illich's vision of a deschooled and decentralized society[4] but think that his proposals are totally utopian without a look at education through the prism of the computer culture. The presence of the computer is what will make a deschooled society possible and even necessary, because if my vision of the way computers will be used is realized, it will come into conflict with the rational structure of schools on every level, from the epistemological to the social.

My attitude toward Illich extends also to many other educational visionaries. Dewey, Montessori, Neill, all propose to educate children in a spirit that I see as fundamentally correct but that fails in practice for lack of a technological basis. The computer now provides it; it is time to reassess the practical possibilities for instituting what previous generations have dismissed as romantic. I have said enough at least to raise serious doubt about whether Jencks's gloomy conclusions would extend to a reform of education based on a widespread computer presence with LOGO as a model. These doubts should become even stronger when we look at the probable impact of something that we know is happening even now—the proliferation of the personal computer. Already the advent of the microprocessor, the "computer on a chip," has made possible the presence of at least 15,000 computers in the living rooms of American families.

The next few years will see an explosion in the numbers of privately owned computers. Much more significantly, they are about to cross a power threshold that will support the LOGO-like use of them. When this happens, there will be for the first time a viable alternative to schools and the possibility that education will once more become a private act. What I envisage is private in many more senses than a return to an eighteenth-century tutor and pupil model. The tutor served an aristocracy, and the knowledge he transmitted fostered socialization into an elite as much as and together with the "content" of the lessons. The computer has the potential of serving everybody—it will soon be as inexpensive as a television set.

Although the sinister possibility exists that only an elite will appropriate the new computers, this need not happen; I hope it will not. But it is a plausible, even very likely scenario that over the coming decade a significant number of families will come to see the private computer as a viable alternative to public school, less expensive and more effective than private school. Under these circumstances a movement to withdraw from the schools could quickly become a class issue. For example, rising demand for more educational materials for the personal computers would make them yet more valuable and so lead into a self-reinforcing cycle. Such a movement could create a situation in which a future Jencks might find that educational technology had indeed affected inequality—not by reducing it but by amplifying it. If, as the LOGO experience suggests, interaction with the computer can put the learner into contact with his most private self, it can also nurture in him an image of himself as an independent intellectual agent.

EDITORS' POSTSCRIPT

The reader of this essay should keep in mind that prior technologies such as television were also expected to transform education, an expectation that has largely not been borne out. Weizenbaum's essay claims that the movements led by Dewey and Montessori were hindered not by a lack of a technology but by the institutional nature of the schools. He argues that schools have become prisons of sorts for children and that this issue must be addressed first.

NOTES

1
Patrick Suppes and Mona Morningstar, "Computer-Assisted Instruction," *Science,* October 17, 1969, pp. 343–350.

2
Christopher Jencks *et al., Inequality: A Reassessment of the Effect of Family and Schooling in America* (New York: Harper & Row, 1973).

3
The best-documented individual case study is in Sylvia Weir and Ricky Imanuel, *Using LOGO to Catalyse Communication in an Autistic Child,* Edinburgh University Department of Artificial Intelligence Research Report no. 15 (Edinburgh, 1976). See also Paul Goldenberg, "Special Technology for Special Children: Computers as Prostheses to Serve Communication and Autonomy in the Education of Handicapped Children" (Ph.D. diss., Harvard University, 1977).

4
Ivan Illich, *De-Schooling Society* (New York: Harper & Row, 1972).

6
Computers and Government   *J. C. R. Licklider*

Most individuals and organizations can plan only a few years ahead. By and large—although few governments accept it as a main domain of responsibility—the part of the future that is ten to twenty-five years away is left by default to government. One of the aspects of the future that government influences significantly is the development and use of computer technology. It has been observed that people tend to overestimate what can be accomplished in a year and underestimate what can be accomplished in a decade. It will be important to keep in mind, therefore, that the end of this century is almost as far forward in time as it is backward in time to the mid 1950s; the "giant brains" of the 1950s will fit on a single chip today. The interaction of government with computers that I shall examine will involve a technology in the course of advancing as far beyond today's technology as today's technology has beyond SEAC, SWAC, and EDVAC—some of the earliest computers.

Although, for brevity, I shall often use the term *computer* alone, I shall usually intend to associate communication and information with it. Thus *computer technology* may be read, whenever appropriate, as *computer and computer communications technology* or *computer-based information technology*.

THE FUNCTIONS OF GOVERNMENT

For purposes of discussion, I have divided the specific functions of government into seven categories. The first three, which include the protective and regulatory functions, should be self-explanatory. The government carries out fostering functions, which make up the fourth category, when it fosters the health, education, and welfare of individuals and organizations.

J. C. R. Licklider is professor of computer science and engineering at MIT. In the early 1960s, as director of the Information Processing Techniques Office in the Advanced Research Projects Agency of the Department of Defense, he was instrumental in envisioning and funding the development of time-shared computers and advanced research in artificial intelligence and computer science. His involvement with the Department of Defense (he was director of the same office in the early 1970s) and his direction of the MIT Laboratory for Computer Science in the late 1960s have equipped him uniquely to write on the topic of this essay.

The fifth category, the service functions, include the mail, the telephone system, transportation, and public utilities. Collecting revenue, conducting elections, instilling patriotism, disseminating propaganda, and the maintenance of government operations come under a sixth category, what I call the self-sustaining functions of government. Finally, there are the metafunctions of government, which include the collection and assessment of performance statistics, the planning and promulgation of activities to be engaged in by the government and the governed, and more fundamental acts of self-definition, such as declaring independence.

It should be noted that when I speak about an activity of government, I refer almost exclusively to the executive branch of the federal government, although this includes not only full-time workers on the government payroll but also the many contractors who are likely to perform the actual work when a government "does" something.

Basic Assumptions

The nature of the advances in computer technology that will be realized during the remainder of this century will depend upon many factors, of course, but it may be taken for granted that the number of computers extant will continue to increase, along with the computing power of a typical machine. Computers will come more and more to pervade the socioeconomic system.

The progressive incorporation of computers into the organizations and processes that constitute the socioeconomic system will be essentially a matter of programming. I shall therefore often use the term *programmation* instead of computerization, which seems to place too much emphasis on hardware, and instead of automation, which seems not to leave enough room for people, through programming and through interaction with programs, to influence what is going on.

It seems clear that programmation will have short-range economic or military advantages even if it is not wisely planned and well executed—but that if it is not, it will be disastrous in the long run. The implication that programmation will proceed, one way or another, even if government does not do much about it raises the issue of government responsibility for and involvement in planning for the future.

It is one of my basic assumptions that the technologically developed countries are in fact only a short way down the road of technological development, having passed through the early material-energetic stage but having only recently entered the informational stage of the industrial revolution—that the remainder of the century will be a period in which information will be in the ascendant. At the same time, computers and programs will be the subject of contention.

For example, the field of artificial intelligence—in particular, the part of it concerned with knowledge-based systems and natural language—is inherently amenable to fairly rapid development but at the same time especially susceptible to misgivings and misjudgments on the part of the natural intelligences with which it might eventually compete.

TWO SCENARIOS

Since we need a context to discuss the issues raised by the interaction of computers and government, I will sketch two scenarios for the development of computer technology in the United States between now and the year 2000. The first scenario is pessimistic: computer technology and government's use of it continue to advance, but no dramatic changes occur, and the year 2000 is new sheet metal on a souped-up 1970s chassis. In the second scenario, the development of computer technology is if not revolutionary at least planned, and specific advances are deliberately fostered and given sustained support. In particular, recognizing the potential significance of computer communication, the government organizes all the resources of society to develop and exploit networking in socially as well as economically productive ways.

Scenario 1

The United States government continues to be a major user of computers but does not push computer development as it once did. Large-scale integration of semiconductor devices levels off after 1985, but electron-beam technology yields 10^{15}-bit stores with 0.1-second access to any bit. Such stores cost about one cent per megabit. In the year 2000, the cost-effectiveness of other computer subsystems is about one hundred times what it is now.

IBM explores many new concepts and technologies but preserves functional compatibility with its established systems. It develops satellite communication systems to interconnect its computers and markets integrated information networks (incorporating its satellite communication technology) suitable for geographically distributed corporations, but it stays out of the computer communication service field because it fears that initiatives there might attract governmental regulation to other parts of its business.

With facilities that are still in the process of conversion from "analog voice" to "digital data," the Bell System offers point-to-point and dialed digital transmission services but not packet-switched* services, which it seems to consider more a threat than an opportunity, as do the European

* Another method of communicating digital data.

national telecommunication authorities. Only in Japan's sphere of influence are computers and communications tightly integrated: the Japanese government has fostered a sustained and coordinated national project involving the computer industry, the communications industry, and the universities.

Because their networks are diverse and uncoordinated, recalling the track-gauge situation in the early days of railroading, the independent "value-added carrier" companies capture only the fringes of the computer communication market, the bulk of it being divided between IBM (integrated computer communication systems based on satellites) and the telecommunication companies (transmission services but no integrated computer communication services, no remote computing services).

Controlled sharing of information in computer systems and networks has been neglected because the military, diplomatic, and intelligence people (who control most of the government's computer development funds) want to maintain their exclusive secrecy. Instead of trying to bring all pertinent information and expertise to bear upon the solution of a problem, they keep their many computers and data bases in guarded vaults, out of the reach of unauthorized persons and insulated from one another. As a result of intensive development, personal identification techniques are almost perfectly reliable.

In the research community, software art has become more and more sophisticated, but with only minor effects outside the laboratory. In the "real world" of government computing, the overriding software problem is the chaos that has resulted from the proliferation of programs and programming languages and from starting de novo on new projects instead of building on existing software. The prevailing response has been to standardize languages at the level of FORTRAN, COBOL, and DOD-I (the all-purpose programming languages prescribed by the Department of Defense) and to simplify and systematize everything possible.

Governments use computers more than ever before, but the pattern of use has not changed markedly over the years. The protective functions of government still account for most of it, primarily in code breaking, with intelligence analysis second, logistics third, and command and control fourth. But almost all military equipment is computerized in one way or another, so total computer use for all weapon systems far exceeds their use in code breaking. In the regulatory, fostering, service, and self-sustaining functions of government, the main role of computers is data processing. Social Security, Internal Revenue, law enforcement, and the census are the major nondefense users of computers. They share the cost of maintaining the National Roster, the ultimate personnel data base with a file for every person, natural or corporate.

Electronic funds transfer has not replaced money, as it turns out, because there were too many uncoordinated bank networks and too many unauthorized and inexplicable transfers of funds. Electronic message systems have not replaced mail, either, because there were too many uncoordinated governmental and commercial networks, with no network at all reaching people's homes, and messages suffered too many failures-of-transfer.

Data bases are often extremely large, dealing with entire populations and nationwide inventories. Highly efficient batch processing defines the environment within which data are managed. Interactive data management has proved to be too inefficient with very large data bases, even with the 0.1-second random-access storage hardware. Digital image processing is highly developed in respect to encoding, compression, and enhancement, but not interpretation, which requires human expertise. Though officially secret, it is widely known that of all federal employees, surveillance photointerpreters are the most numerous. Natural-language understanding and speech-understanding computer systems have never been developed to a point of practicality because they require too much processing; feasibility demonstration systems back in the early 1970s were not cost-effective. There is some use of knowledge-based computer systems in space, subterranean, and other "hostile environment" applications, but by and large the main uses of computers, the ones essential to the operation of the socioeconomic system in the year 2000, involve no more than fairly routine data processing—just very, very much of it.

Scenario 2

On the whole, computer technology continues to advance along the curve it has followed in its three decades of history since World War II. The amount of information that can be stored for a given period or processed in a given way at unit cost doubles every two years. (The twenty-one years from 1979 to 2000 yield ten doublings, for a factor of about 1,000.) Waveguides, optical fibers, rooftop satellite antennae, and coaxial cables provide abundant bandwidth and inexpensive digital transmission both locally and over long distances. Computer consoles with good graphic display and speech input and output have become almost as common as television sets. Some pocket computers are fully programmable, as powerful as IBM 360/40s used to be, and are equipped with both metallic and radio connectors to computer communication networks.

An international network of digital computer communication networks serves as the main and essential medium of informational interaction for governments, institutions, corporations, and individuals. The Multinet, as it is called, is hierarchical—some of the component networks are themselves networks of networks—and many of the top-level networks are national networks. The many subnetworks that comprise this network of networks are electronically compatible and physically interconnected. Most of them handle real-time speech as well as computer messages, and some handle video.

The Multinet has supplanted the postal system for letters, the dial telephone system for conversations and teleconferences, stand-alone batch-processing and time-sharing systems for computation, and most filing cabinets, microfilm repositories, document rooms, and libraries for information storage and retrieval. Many people work at home, interacting with coworkers and clients through the Multinet, and many business offices (and some classrooms) are little more than organized interconnections of such home workers and their computers. People shop through the Multinet, using its cable television and electronic funds transfer functions, and a few receive delivery of small items through adjunct pneumatic tube networks. Routine shopping and appointment scheduling are generally handled by private-secretary-like programs called OLIVERs which know their masters' needs. Indeed, the Multinet handles scheduling of almost everything schedulable. For example, it eliminates waiting to be seated at restaurants and if you place your order through it can eliminate waiting to be served.

Governments do their "paperwork" in subnetworks of the Multinet. In the process, they generate huge data bases, but the fact that they are computer-processable keeps their sheer volume from limiting their usefulness. Task-control programs know, for example, who has to sign off on, coordinate on, or simply read each item, and by what date. They regulate the flow of information through the offices and agencies, preventing the accumulation of backlogs and keeping track of productivity. They also enforce rules of access and dissemination that have been painfully worked out over the years, ensuring executive privilege to working papers and at the same time making available to Congress, for example, data that the rules say Congress ought to have.

The security features of the Multinet make it possible to control access selectively at any level, from the basic item of information to the highest-level subnetwork. Some of the functions of the defense and law enforcement sectors of government are carried out in subnetworks to which other, ordinary subnetworks have no access at all. Other sensitive functions, such as proprietary commercial functions and funds transfers, are protected at lower levels so that the government can monitor them selectively. The security rules and procedures have been developed with such exquisite care and so fully tested, proven, demonstrated, and explained that almost everyone accepts their validity and effectiveness. They are regarded as essential parts of the networks; indeed, they have been more difficult to realize than the hardware and transmission-level software.

Once in a while there is a flurry of rumors about international espionage within the Multinet, but widespread belief in them is precluded by the fact that entrances to and exits from national networks are under national control, access control is so highly developed, and complete audit trails are recorded. More frequently, a national government is accused of monitoring more assiduously than the law allows, but in the United States, at least, no one has yet come up with audit trails to prove it.

Networking has greatly increased the effectiveness as well as the efficiency of many of the functions of defense. Command and control is now based upon on-line, interactive data management, modeling, problem solving, and communication. The command and control function is very closely coupled to intelligence analysis and dissemination (which embraces the same kinds of activity) and even to some components of intelligence acquisition. That is, many intelligence functions can be carried out within the span of a single command decision process. State, Defense, the CIA, and other departments and agencies are interconnected so effectively that organization charts do not seriously interfere with teamwork. Indeed, the network protocol graph has largely displaced the organization chart. The FBI and state and local law enforcement agencies are internetted* in protocol-controlled patterns, of course, with one another and with offices in the defense complex.

The government uses the Multinet to monitor and regulate the day-to-day operations of business and industry. Stock markets, for example, operate within the Multinet, as do stockbrokers and buyers and sellers and the financial departments of corporations, and the government monitors and records every transaction. Government access—indeed, all access—to the data pertinent to regulation is controlled by the already mentioned security rules and procedures. Many government services are executed in or delivered through the Multinet. Weather forecasting, market reporting, the census, and the modernized post, telephone, and telegraph services are obvious examples, but there are many others, such as mediation, licensing, insurance, statistics and indicators, and library services. Much of the function of revenue collection is part and parcel of computerized commerce and electronic funds transfer, which are of course carried on within the Multinet. Advisory polls and formal elections have been carried out through the Multinet since 1990, when the universal ID system, based on computer recording and identification of fingerprints, was set up on a nationwide basis.

* Connected via computer communications networks.

ISSUES AND PROBLEMS

Whether the future moves toward Scenario 1 or Scenario 2—or toward some other pattern of events that I do not have the imagination to envision—will depend to a large degree, I think, on the resolution of many already discernible issues and problems related to specific functions of government.

Computers and Defense

The protective functions of government are more or less clearly separated into two sets, the external protective functions (such as defense) and the internal protective functions (such as enforcement of criminal law). Both are usually given high priority by society and the government, external ordinarily even higher than internal. Moreover, there appears to be a strong natural affinity between computers and defense.

The altered context in the defense sector The defense sector has been the main governmental developer and user of computers and is the main focus of the government's expertise in computer science and technology. In the 1950s and 1960s, the defense community of the United States saw itself as having a broad and long-term responsibility for the technological foundation of national power. Future-oriented study groups—scientists, engineers, and military people working closely together—explored the gamut of possibilities in such areas as nuclear-powered aircraft, overseas transport, air defense, battlefield surveillance, ballistic missiles, limited warfare, space warfare, and cold warfare. If the defense community concluded that the country needed a new industry (such as titanium or solid rocket propellants), a new industry was created. If the defense community thought it would be good to have larger, faster computers, it ordered some—and a computer firm figured out how to build them, at government expense. When Congress complained about the cost of such initiatives, defense spokesmen replied that they were essential for national security and, moreover, generated new businesses, new industries, and new economic strength. Defense got increasing appropriations, year after year, and forced massive developments in high technology for two decades.

As early as 1962, Secretary of Defense McNamara was telling the services that they could no longer develop every system they could think of, that plans had to compete with one another, and that only a limited number of projects promising high payoffs could be pursued. McNamara's edicts had an effect on expenditures: they sounded so good to Congress that he got even more money than before, and the services spent it. But the Vietnam War achieved what McNamara had intended, and more. Then came Watergate, with its involvement of the FBI and the CIA, and the investigations into the CIA's ultraintelligence operations.

As far as long-term planning and support of technological development are concerned, the situation in Washington today is quite different from what it was in the 1960s. Although the Mansfield amendment, which in effect limited weapons research and development to situations with clear-cut defense payoffs, is no longer in force, congressional staff members and defense officials insist that defense budgets be justified on the basis of what they will do for defense alone, and it is harmful to his cause if the justifier says, "Incidentally, this development will also have important educational and medical applications." It is very good to economize in executing an established function; it is not very good to achieve a new defense capability if it increases costs. There is not much long-term investment capital in the defense budget;* every project must "pay off" in three to five years; the stress is on application rather than discovery and invention; and the successful research proposal identifies in its first paragraph the weapon system development project that is its technology-transfer target.

Despite the changes, defense is still the sector of government that supports computer technology most vigorously and imaginatively, and it is the mainstay of research and development in areas like interactive computing, networking, data management, graphics, image processing, natural-language understanding, and speech understanding. It is therefore a very serious matter that local and short-term optimization has become so dominant. For the sake of future national security, it is essential to remove the inhibition about long-term thinking in the defense community. For the sake of the nation's future strength in the computer field, it is essential either to redeclare the legitimacy of defense's husbandry of advanced computer technology or to incorporate the responsibility (and authority and funds) for it into some other agency's charter. Both alternatives raise further issues, of course. The latter runs into the problem of finding another agency with as natural an involvement and as much in-house expertise in information technology. The former runs into the problem of the estrangement caused by the Vietnam War, which is now part of the larger problem of distrust of Washington.

Special computers and ad hoc software   The computers that are incorporated into weapon systems are diverse, and most of them are special. Some military computers are general-purpose as far as computation is concerned but built to withstand hostile environmental conditions. Others are special-purpose because they have to interact with equipment that ordinary general-purpose computers cannot deal with. Still others are very special because they are built as integral parts of larger systems, de-

---

* Editors' note: Written before the 1979 budget, with its increased research and development component, was made public.

signed, developed, programmed, and procured as components of weapon systems rather than as computer systems.

The diversity and specialness of weapon-system computers have created a situation in which software is the villain. Often there is not time or money to create the automatic translator that would permit programming in a high-level language, so the computer (assembly) language tends to be as special as the computer itself. Software preparation starts from scratch for each new system, and the software has to be changed to compensate for almost every improvement introduced into the weapon system after its preliminary design. The resulting "slippages" and "overruns" are regarded as intolerable by everyone concerned, and the software people get the blame—much of it, but by no means all of it, deserved.

An important factor in this unhappy situation is short-term and local optimization: as long as development and procurement are organized in terms of individual weapon systems, it is difficult to fund at a high enough level and continue for a long enough time programs such as the All Application Digital Computer, which was an attempt to develop a machine suitable for a wide range of military applications. Another factor is the lack of exchange between the weapon system software community and the software research community—between the people who have the problem and the people who are set up to find solutions. A third factor is the advance of microprocessors. Microprocessors make it almost irresistible to design the computing part of a system in terms of its function in the system, to optimize for speed and compactness and local efficiency.

The problems of diverse and special computers are important to the future of computers and government because they account for a major part of the frustration and aggression with which much of the defense community now reacts to computers and software. The following seem like reasonable steps toward solving them:

1. Matrix organization of weapon system development, with rows for weapon systems and columns for subsystems such as computers, communications, and propulsion
2. Injection of engineering discipline into software development
3. The multiapplication philosophy of the All Application Digital Computer
4. Programming language and automatic programming research to overcome the obstacles that stand in the way of using high-level languages and advanced software development methods in weapon system applications
5. Reinvolvement of major parts of the computer research community in military computer projects

Weapons system evaluation   Because they go on continuously, the battles of the marketplace provide early and abundant feedback about the value of commercial products. Military battles, on the other hand, are separated by intervals during which there are no clearly valid indications of relative effectiveness—and when an actual trial by fire does come along, it returns a conglomeration of distorted observations from which you may possibly deduce who won but not how or why. There is thus a shortage of "truth points"—points of confrontation that would permit the true evaluation of performance needed to guide the development of military technology. The shortage of truth points presents both a problem and an opportunity for computers. The problem is simply that it makes the military environment less propitious than it would otherwise be for the evolution of computer technology. The opportunity is that computer technology, suitably developed and exploited, might increase the number of truth points dramatically.

If all the interfaces among weapon subsystems were digital and all the components were controlled by or through computers, it would be possible to simulate military engagements with a high degree of realism and validity by operating actual components, subsystems, or even systems in simulated environments. Computer-based simulation would make it possible to exercise, test, experiment with, and evaluate weapon systems every day instead of every war. The defense community seems to be slow in recognizing the potential of programmation to revolutionize military preparedness, but the progressive infiltration of computers into weapon systems will eventually create the conditions for what W. R. Sutherland has called "exercising the fleet while it is in the harbor."

There is another sense in which the military environment provides too few truth points for efficient development of computer technology. Only a few people are actually involved in a typical million-dollar budget decision: an administrator or two, two or three technical people, and a couple of congressional staff members. The first and last may not understand the technical issues involved in the decision nearly as well as the political and the fiscal issues, and they may have only a few minutes to devote to the matter. This is a rather frightening exposure to the vagaries of small sample statistics, but one can say in favor of the process that it is at least largely free of the indecisiveness that characterizes large committees.

Oversophisticated and undersophisticated systems   The defense community has a long history of undertaking very ambitious system development projects involving computers. Some of them, such as the SAGE air defense system, proved to be marvelously stimulating to the development of technology but so sophisticated as to be almost unworkable and unmaintainable in the real world of military operations. Repeated experience with such frontier accomplishments has led to the cautious philosophy reflected in maxims like, "If it won't work under ten coats of gray paint, it has no place on a ship." The trouble is that there is no way—for example, in radar, sonar, and electronic warfare—that simple, unsophisticated systems can do many of the things that military systems have to do. Sophistication is required—yet sophistication has so often made systems inoperable and unmaintainable. The dilemma is whether to retrench or push forward in the hope of breaking through to a level of sophistication capable of solving the problems sophistication causes. Most computer scientists seem to take the second horn of the dilemma quite seriously, whereas most members of the defense community are skeptical.

Standardizing programming languages and methods   The diversity of the programming languages used is the source of much of the trouble that besets defense software. Should the diversity be eliminated through standardization by edict? (The Department of Defense made COBOL standard over a decade ago to clean up a Tower of Babel situation in data-processing software development.) At present, there is a move to require that all weapon system programming be done in a single DOD-wide programming language. An essential part of the move is to define the language.

In the more inclusive field of programming methodology, the trend is toward integrated software development systems in which such functions as specification, costing, programming, debugging, documenting, and updating are coordinated and systematized, usually within the philosophy of structured programming and often within the context of on-line interaction. Many software firms are involved in defense software development, and it seems likely that before long each one will have its own integrated "software factory," highly efficient in and of itself but different from all the others—and putting out software incompatible with the software put out by the others. Should the Department of Defense make a single software development system the standard before too many different systems have become established, or should it defer standardization until the choice is clear?

In both programming languages and programming methodology, it seems desirable to limit diversity in software development* but to encourage creativity and wide-ranging experimentation in software research. But software art is advancing so fast that a few more years of research will make the most advanced languages and systems obsolete. Even worse, these advanced languages and systems have not been set up and organized for widespread use and are not familiar to most weapon system programmers. Any programming language or system that could be put into widespread use within a year would be obsolete at the start, and any really effective one would require a five-year start-up period.

---

* Production in the software field is of course just a matter of copying digital records. Development is the main activity.

The only solution is to find a way of eating one's cake and having it too, because in such a rapidly advancing field there will never be a right time to stop improving and standardize what we have. The most promising approach, I think, is that of the Advanced Research Projects Agency's network-based National Software Works (NSW), which will link geographically distributed software development resources and provide protocols for their use. The NSW may be able to create order out of the diversity of software development methods and systems without hampering research. Indeed, it provides an excellent framework for software research as well as software development, since it offers an ideal path for technology transfer from one to the other. But there is a difficulty even here: The manager of a weapon system development project is not likely to be willing to interrupt the course of the project to change his approach to software, yet that is the only point when there is enough money to pay for the change.

Other issues and problems   The following are a few of the many other issues and problems that are shaping the future of computer development and application in the defense sector:

1. The critical importance of controlled information sharing and the relative neglect of research and development in computer system and network security;* the near impossibility of making the most widely used operating systems secure, and the huge expense of replacing them with new ones with designed-in security features

2. The attainability (and cost-effectiveness) of automation in critical military and intelligence functions such as target recognition (built into missiles) and interpretation of surveillance photographs

3. The attainability (and cost-effectiveness) of speech understanding by computer, essential if computers are to be used routinely by almost all military personnel, and the conflicting approaches required by (a) speech input to computers in semantically and syntactically constrained task environments and (b) monitoring semantically and syntactically unconstrained messages to detect items of special interest

4. The attainability (but undisputed cost-effectiveness if attainable) of intelligent computer programs that provide consultation on the maintenance of complex devices and systems

5. The substitution of simulation and modeling for actual experimental testing in, for example, the evaluation of the aerodynamic designs and configurations of nuclear explosives; the extension of simulation and modeling into areas not governed by well-established differential equations

* There are excellent research and development projects in this area, but the total funding falls far short of what is needed to meet the requirements of widespread networking.

6. The use of a computer network to provide a rapid, efficient, unifying communication system for NATO

7. The conflict between (a) the desire of a commander to have full and rapid access to all the data at his level and below and (b) the insistence of the commander that he and his staff filter and interpret data going up the chain of command in order to protect his superiors from drawing incorrect conclusions; the implications of that conflict for information system design and data management

8. The protection of military computer communications—especially packet-switched communications—against countermeasures such as jamming, spoofing, and disruption of traffic flow

Computers and Internal Protection

The internal protective functions of government include the functions of criminal law enforcement by police and courts, some of the functions of the national guard, and some aspects of protection against espionage, sabotage, and terrorism within the country. The involvement of computers in this sector is sensitive because there is no clear line between protection against antisocial behavior and repression.

Law enforcement networks and data bases   To obtain a perspective on the interaction of computers and government in internal protection, we must project a future in which there are not only police and FBI networks and data bases but also networks and data bases for computerized commerce, electronic funds transfer, customized news, general reservations, computerized communications, and so on. In such a context, a major part of criminal law enforcement will be concerned with violations of law that occur literally within a network. (How else could one rob a bank or hold up a liquor store?) And the main source of information about the whereabouts of suspects—and probably also the best kind of alibi—would be audit trails within computers.

In theory if not in practice, most of the issues raised by criminal violations of this kind can be decided preclusively. The obvious way to prevent misuse of audit trails, for example, is not to have audit trails; the obvious way to prevent theft from a computer is not to have a computer or if you have one not to put anything of value into it. But there is no chance of maximizing the value of computers to the society through blanket preclusion. It is essential to develop a system—part technological, part legal, part administrative—that will make it easy to obey the law, that will facilitate effective enforcement of the law, that will be prohibitively difficult to subvert, and that will keep such good records that subversion will be detected when it does occur, even if a law enforcement agency is the subverter. It is not obvious, of course, that such a system can be developed, but it is very obvious that the situation will become intolerable if computerization and programmation proceed without it.

Computer system and network security   Ever since World War II, computers have been used to process classified information, and for more than a decade computer security has been a serious focus of research and development. However, the main approach to computer security has been to put the computer in a vault, to control human access to the vault and the information flowing from it, and assuming job A has a higher security classification than job B or must for some other reason be isolated from it, to try to erase all trace of A from the computer before using it to process B. That approach addresses neither the problem of multilevel security (storing or processing mixed security classes of information at the same time) nor the problem of computer communication security (maintaining security in a computerized communication system or in a distributed multicomputer network).

Computer system and network security should be viewed as the other side of the coin of information sharing. What is needed is a systematic technical solution to the problem of sure and convenient access by individuals and groups to the resources they have selectively been authorized to use, at the same time denying access to individuals and groups not so authorized. The solution must include audit trails, authorization channels, and facilities for continuous testing and evaluation. The problem of determining who should be authorized to use what and how is, of course, a separate matter, since it depends on the context.

Two approaches are being taken to the solution of the technical problem as it relates to computer-operating systems. Both involve selecting out all the components that are fundamental to security and organizing them into a single subsystem (a "security kernel"), which is subjected to a thorough engineering analysis. In the first approach, the security kernel must be simple enough for human minds to be able to determine whether it is or is not secure. It seems plausible to at least some experts that an effective security kernel can meet this demand. In the second approach, the design and implementation of the security kernel would be analyzed and verified not by people but by programs, programs similar to those used in proving theorems. That approach strikes many as fanciful, but I find it more plausible than the first. A workable security subsystem will be hierarchical in structure, with perhaps a few dozen components at the top level and a fan-out factor of ten or so from one level to the next over three or four levels. It will not be long before program-verification programs can handle systems of that complexity—although I would not trust many human minds to think them through flawlessly.

The overall problem is larger, however, than the problem of security in isolated operating systems. It includes the problem of security in networks involving several or many computers and several or many data bases with controlled sharing down to the level of individual items. In this larger context, the issue is essentially whether to continue along the present course, which will yield a mix of easily penetrated networks and impregnable computers in vaults—neither of which will adequately protect the rights of individuals—or to mount a security research and development effort large enough and long enough (perhaps ten or fifteen years) to yield, if one is possible, a truly durable solution. This is an expensive issue as well as an important one, because effective security cannot be achieved within the context of existing computer operating systems.

Computer system and network facilities for ombudsmen   Even if a good technical basis for securely controlled sharing of information is developed, the administrative rules governing sharing will have to be defined and understood, and computer networks and data bases will have to be trusted by potential users and (in democracies, at least) by potential referents, that is, by the public. The obstacles to meeting these requirements may be even harder to overcome, since even with increased education about computers, the technology involved will necessarily remain obscure to many of those who will need to understand and be convinced. Such a situation calls for ombudsmen, but the ombudsman's role can be played effectively only if special facilities to support it have been designed into computer systems and networks.

Let us assume—although the assumptions are far from trivial—that informational ombudsmen, having been especially selected for trustworthiness, are in fact trusted by the operators, users, and referents of networks and data bases. There must then be legal protocols to define the responsibility, authority, and access privileges of ombudsmen and computer and communication facilities to support them in their work. The question is Who should define the protocols and design the facilities? These tasks are not in the direct line of any organization's chartered or assigned responsibility, but they are basic and essential.

The idea of designing facilities for ombudsmen once more raises the problem of providing a technical basis for system and network security. Some person, suspicious that some secret data bank contains misleading information about him, will surely suspect that the system is more complex than even the highest ombudsman realizes—and that an all-powerful manipulator (a would-be dictator? a system programmer?) is busy altering files and covering up audit trails. What is needed is a design and a way of implementing it that do not in fact have such a superior level and can be proved to everyone's satisfaction not to have one.

"Tailing" technology   It is a responsibility of government to protect law-abiding citizens from criminals, rioters, and terrorists, and in order to discharge that responsibility the government may monitor the movements of actual or suspected criminals, rioters, and terrorists. A repressive government may, in addition, keep track of citizens it suspects of dissidence. Alarms have been raised about the possibility that electronic funds transfer records, for example, could be used for this purpose or even that the activities of ordinary citizens suspected of nothing could be routinely monitored on security grounds.

Computer-based voiceprint and fingerprint identification have been investigated, and while voiceprints may not be useful in applications involving large populations, fingerprints of course are. No doubt a fingerprint identification system using sensors inside glass doorknobs could, at great cost, be made to identify all ye who enter here without gloves. I recall a half-serious proposal made around 1960 (a few years before it became feasible) that a miniature transmitter be built into every automobile license plate and that it repeatedly transmit the license number at a low power level, to be picked up by receivers in the streets and relayed to a central computer. The same idea could be applied to individuals instead of automobiles; a repressive government could insist that everyone stick his or her ID card into a slot at every intersection. If people complained about the inconvenience, implanted code transmitters signaling to street-corner receivers or chemical labels checked by street-corner analyzers could be used instead of ID cards and slots. The sensing scheme is not the critical thing—the critical thing is that well before the end of the century there could easily be enough computer power and communication bandwidth to make such schemes feasible. And it would be hard to beat the system. For example, if someone avoided the sensors he would create a suspiciously null record, and if he exchanged ID cards with someone else, supplementary photographic or fingerprint systems would catch both "criminals."

Other issues and problems   Among the many other prospects offered by the role of computers in internal protection, two stand out in my view:

1. The use of computer-based education, made available through networks to prisoners in their cells, to rehabilitate convicts; the use of the same networks to motivate the prisoners with work that is readily measured and scored as well as productive—and to get something useful out of them instead of just time

2. The implications—which include the near elimination of the false alarms that make so many present-day systems impractical—of microcomputers and networks for multisensor home and plant security systems

Computers and the Regulatory Functions

In a computer-based socioeconomic system, many more aspects of behavior could be monitored than is now the case, and control based on monitored data could be much finer and tighter. It is widely believed, and probably true, that such control is necessary (though not sufficient) for stability in systems as complex as economies and societies. But what should the control be designed to optimize? How tight should it be? Which of the monitoring and control functions, if any, should be handled by the government? These are some of the questions that must be answered.

Programmation of monitoring and regulation The regulatory functions of government are of two kinds: functions that have already been programmed for routine execution by people or computers and functions that still require the inclusion of human judgment on a case-by-case basis. As the process of programmation proceeds and as advances in artificial intelligence give computers some judgmental capability, some of the functions now requiring human judgment will be shifted into the first category. Other functions will retain human judgment, but it will take place within a computer context through on-line interaction. Either way, the growth of programmation will favor efficiency and fairness.

An issue that will surely arise during the course of the shift is how far the monitoring and regulatory functions of government should be allowed to penetrate the internal activities of corporations. At present, a large corporation routinely sends the government copies of a few of its tapes and jealously guards the rest. When the government's computers are netted with the corporation's computers, however, the access protocols will be represented in software, and governmental monitoring will not be limited by considerations of inconvenience and cost. In fact, there will be no inconvenience at all—the programs will probably come from a computer manufacturer or software house with the monitoring functions built in—and the cost will be no more than the cost of the machine cycles, which will be figured at a round billion percent. Other than political philosophy, the only remaining bases for objection to such penetration of corporate activities will be a wish to be able to violate the law without getting caught and a lack of trust that confidentiality will be maintained.

Looking into the distant future, one can imagine that once governmental regulations have been decided upon and cast in the form of legislation as well as software, they may come to be regarded in the same way as physical laws are regarded now: irresistible, inviolable, inescapable, part of nature, invariably enforced, and not the kind of thing one complains about. But the situation will not move that far in the next generation, and the programmation of monitoring and regulation will be a heated issue throughout it.

Traffic control While the federal government has assumed responsibility for computer-based air traffic control, only a few cities are active in street traffic control, and their involvement is mainly as experimental customers of electronics and computer firms that are exploring the market for traffic-signal control systems. It is doubtful that street traffic problems can be solved satisfactorily through control of traffic signals. The role of the federal government, if any, will probably develop in relation to more basic changes in ground transportation.

Such changes could involve restrictions on the size and power of private automobiles, restrictions on where they can be driven, reconstruction of the worst roadway bottlenecks, and eventually a kind of traffic control system in which traffic control computers communicate with microcomputers in individual automobiles and direct them through the maze of city streets at almost constant speed and in almost perfect safety. This kind of cooperative control, based on two-way computer-to-computer communication, makes sense now in air traffic control. If developments in computer and communication technology should make it feasible for ground traffic control, it would represent one of the more massive interactions between computers and government.

Technology export   What should the attitude of the U.S. government be to the export of computer technology, of all the major technologies the one in which the lead of the United States over other nations is the greatest? As far as the national interest is concerned, exporting any part of computer technology that could help a potentially competitive nation either economically or militarily is likely to be costly in the long run. The argument that "if they can't buy it from us, they'll buy it from someone else or learn to make it themselves" has little weight when one is talking about the goose and not just the golden egg. From a national point of view, computer technology should be regarded as the main generator of future economic and military strength. Unless coupled with some other transaction that greatly favors the United States, export of advanced computers and computer technology is very likely to be harmful to its national interests.

From the point of view of computer technology itself, export is likely to have beneficial effects. By increasing the use and understanding of computers in other nations, it expands the computer field, increases competition in it, and fosters computer research and development in those nations as well as in the United States.

From the point of view of mankind—if only mankind had a point of view—the important thing would seem to be a wise rather than a rapid or intensive development of computer technology. Such crucial issues as security, privacy, preparedness, participation, and brittleness must be properly resolved before one can conclude that computerization and programmation are good for the individual and for society. Although I do not have total confidence in the ability of the United States to resolve those issues wisely, I think it is more likely than any other country to do so. That makes me doubt whether export of computer technology will do as much for mankind as a vigorous effort by the United States to figure out what kind of future it really wants and then to develop the technology needed to realize it.

Other issues and problems Among the many other issues connected to the regulatory functions of government are:

1. Patenting or copyrighting computer programs
2. Copyright law as it pertains to information stored in or used through computers or networks; whether royalties should be paid on information put into such systems or on information taken out of such systems; the concept of authorship when the author is a computer
3. Implications of networks and consoles in homes for the Office of Consumer Affairs: consumer complaints data bases and maintenance record data bases
4. Monitoring the environment
5. Government regulation of computer communications, pro and con
6. Government regulation of multinational corporations
7. Government action against alleged monopolistic practices in the computer field
8. Implications of data bases, computers, and networks for legislative oversight of executive functions

Computers and Fostering Functions

At present, the main involvement of computers in the fostering functions of government is conventional data processing. It may well be that for many years data processing will continue to account for most computer memory cycles in such areas as welfare and labor, but planning and modeling may become equally important. The potential involvement of computers in education and health, on the other hand, goes far beyond data processing. Areas like computer-based education, health monitoring, medical diagnosis, and aid to the aged, disabled, and immobilized could be revolutionized. In the commerce sector, the development of networking may create an unprecedented need for national and international standards and protocols.

Computer-based education Opportunity will surely knock a second time. In the early 1960s, Computer Assisted Instruction (CAI) appeared to many to be the wave of the future which would revolutionize the then-$35-billion-a-year education "business" within a decade. However, computers were still too expensive. The software did little more than ask questions and score answers; "page-turning programs" was the term used. And the legions of educators, entrenched in their labor-intensive domain, had not rebelled at all; they had remained largely unaware of the existence of the undermanned and poorly equipped invasion.

The CAI of the 1960s is unlikely to return as a significant movement, but a broader concept—what might be called knowledge-based education because knowledge bases are central to it—seems likely to present itself as another wave of the future within a decade or two. The new wave must await further advances in the technology of knowledge bases and the computer processing of natural language, as well as further gains in the cost-effectiveness of computer hardware. In due course, however, the technological prerequisites will be met for a major and fundamental attack on the still-deteriorating situation in the schools. The technological armamentarium will include devices and techniques to create a knowledge base for each field within the curriculum; knowledge-packaging programs that will convert cognitively structured knowledge into tutorial and exploratory interactions; interaction programs attuned to various ages and levels of mastery; consoles featuring speech input and output and graphical display; endless varieties of computer-based models, games, projects, experiments, seminars, journals, and competitions; and powerful programmed aids for human teachers. However, education will still be labor-intensive and short of funds for capital equipment. Government support will be required, which will raise again some of the old issues—government control; federal, state, or local responsibility; displacement of teachers by automation; public funds for private schools—that have inhibited federal initiatives in the field of education.

Will the promises of computer-based education be attractive enough to overcome the obstacles? Will they be dismissed by decision makers, opinion leaders, and a public unfamiliar with knowledge processing, or will almost everyone by that time have a basic understanding of the capabilities of computers and the main issues surrounding them? The problem is, essentially, how to get laymen to see computer-based education the way computer scientists do who are familiar with its potential and can envision the systems that could be created, given sustained support and dedicated effort. Computer-based education evokes two sets of images in people's minds, and the presence of the first makes it difficult to create the conditions for realizing the second. The first set includes "the dehumanizing effect of being taught by a machine"; "the bureaucrats behind the computers"; "facts instead of principles"; "computers cost millions"; and so on. The second set includes "initiative in the hands of the student—the entire world of knowledge waiting to be explored"; "education of the highest quality available to everyone within reach of a network"; "self-motivating, engrossing, compelling"; "a chance for every student to generalize from facts to principles and test the results"; "a computer is a $5 chip"; "it is the software that is expensive and difficult, but it has to be developed only once in order to be available to everybody."

Health monitoring and medical diagnosis   If and when every residence and every doctor's office are "on the net" and there is a microcomputer in every bathroom scale, it will be possible for an individual to build up a much more detailed medical record than is feasible at present. It will include daily values for each variable that can be measured as part of the morning routine, monthly values for each variable that can be measured automatically in the doctor's office, as well as yearly values for each variable that requires the doctor's personal attention. If, in addition, effective computer system and network security has been developed, sophisticated programs will be continually examining and analyzing the medical records of the entire population, discovering which patterns of values predict which kinds of trouble and detecting epidemics before they affect large numbers of people.

If the progressive "denaturalization" of our way of life continues, the threat of additives in the diet, exposure to synthetic chemicals, and so on could conceivably make it necessary to augment the individual medical record to include an item for almost every ingestion of or contact with food, drink, drugs, textiles, and living creatures. That would require identifying and keeping track of every package bought in the supermarket and every menu item in restaurants, as well as complete appointment schedules, attendance lists, and so on—a mind-boggling prospect. It is to be hoped that the future of pollution, contagion, allergy, and terrorism will not force us to any such science-fictional extreme, but it is by no means certain that we are not well along the way to it already. If we have to adopt such a system, the government will surely play a role in creating it and perhaps also in operating it.

Aid to the aged, disabled, and immobilized   In the near future it will be possible to equip a hearing aid with a digital processor that can transform sounds in ways not feasible with analog circuits, to customize the processor for a particular ear, and to optimize it dynamically for various listening situations. Reading machines for the blind are already in a fairly advanced stage of development, and the next decade could see them become affordable enough for wide use. Microcomputers may open the way to a whole new technology of prosthesis for manipulation and locomotion.

Another area that is obviously ripe for development is the monitoring of patients. Computerized devices are already in limited use for monitoring indicators like heart rate, but they could be applied to almost any significant condition. Automated monitoring also promises to be useful for babysitting and looking in on elderly people who can care for themselves except in emergencies. The monitoring computers might be sensitive to sounds caused by breathing or other movements, to speech, to the adjustment of light switches and faucets, and to prearranged "I am OK" signals—which the computers might prompt whenever they suspect trouble, at which time they would communicate with sources of help: relatives, friends, neighbors, special quick-response centers, or local police. With the aid of a network, the arrangements for calling for help could be quite sophisticated, the monitored situation could be checked out before anyone rushed to the scene of the alarm, and in many instances the whole problem could be taken care of remotely. Indeed, there is no real need to wait for a network before developing this notion, for quite a lot could be done with a telephone dialer, an intrinsically simple device though rather an expensive one in the absence of a mass market.

Suitably organized, networking will give immobilized people a chance to participate actively in on-line meetings, projects, and competitions, to avail themselves of essentially unlimited education and training, and to work—to be employed. For some, special consoles and special ways of interacting with computers will have to be devised, but for many immobilized people only a standard console and a network connection will be needed. Indeed, even present networks like the ARPANET* or Telenet could do great things for paraplegics in Veterans Administration hospitals: teleconferences, telegames, message services, learning to program and helping others learn—an "on-line" community in the best sense of that term.

Some of these notions, and others that they may suggest, may be developed even without governmental stimulation and support, but it seems unlikely that anything like their full potential will be realized in the absence of government involvement.

Network standards and protocols   If chaos is to be avoided in networking, it seems that one or the other of two approaches must be taken: (1) designing and building, preemptively, a single general-purpose network with a consistent and all-encompassing system of protocols or (2) developing, early, a "leading" system of network standards and making their enforcement a matter of international agreements and national laws. At the present time, the first approach seems very unlikely. The first half of the second approach is currently a focus of attention, with the National Bureau of Standards and UNESCO both hard at work on network standardization studies, but in at least six countries the development of actual networks is further along than the development of network standards. It can be argued, of course, that it is bad to standardize too early, and indeed the situation in networking may in this respect be like the situation in programming languages. But one of the most crucial differ-

---

* A research network of some 125 computers set up by the Defense Advanced Research Projects Agency of the Department of Defense.

ences between the technologies of the two scenarios I suggested is that while the many networks of Scenario 1 are incompatible, the subnetworks that comprise the Multinet of Scenario 2 are coherently interconnected. Network standardization in the interest of compatibility and coherence should become a matter of national priority.

Other issues and problems   Advances in computer technology may open up many other new opportunities for government to foster the well-being of individuals, organizations, and nations:

1. More numerous, more detailed, and more up-to-date statistics and indicators, made possible by programmated monitoring of commerce
2. New kinds of employment services, made possible by on-line interaction and networking, including precise matching of capabilities to needs and even the allocation of tasks requiring only an hour or two of work
3. An educational hobby program based on inexpensive but powerful and programmable pocket computers
4. Programmation and network distribution of government procurement notices (such as requests for bids and proposals) to open the door to wider and fairer competition for government business
5. Giving underdeveloped and developing countries access, via an international network, to informational resources that are very expensive to develop but very inexpensive to replicate and distribute

Computers and the Service Functions

Traditional American political philosophy, or so it seems if one watches television, calls for keeping government out of services like mail and transportation and leaving them to private enterprise. In avowedly socialist countries, on the other hand, these functions are clearly within the domain of government. Either way, there are problems in the service sector that require decisions by or on behalf of the entire society.

The future telephone system: basic multipurpose signal transmission and distribution   If a country were starting afresh now to build a general-purpose communication network, it would surely "go digital" for everything except television, and it would probably incorporate the technique called packet switching into the basic design of the system as an alternative to the technique called line switching that is used in all existing telephone systems. With such a communication network, the country would be ready to support intercomputer communications, computer-based message services, computerized commerce, computer-based home and plant security systems, and many other functions that will become important in the coming years if they are not precluded by the ineffectiveness or inefficiency of a basically analog, line-switched transmission and distribution system.

The problem is how to support new informational functions and services that cannot get started without digital transmission and packet switching and cannot pay for massive new construction until they have become well established. The situation is complicated by a ponderous investment in an analog, line-switched plant. The communication problem itself has two main aspects. The first has to do with communication among sites with concentrations of communicators and where local distribution is a relatively simple matter. The second has to do with communication among dispersed communicators, such as people in their homes, doctors in their offices, and merchants in their shops. Thus the overall communication problem is roughly analogous to the automobile and truck transportation problem, which also has long-haul and local-distribution aspects.

On both sides of the analogy, the first, or long-haul, aspect of the problem is the easier to solve. Satellites and waveguides, like autobahns and interstates, are expensive but efficient. They fulfill most of the needs of large organizations that interact mainly with one another and are able to locate at entrance-exits or put large antennae on their roofs.

A fundamentally different approach is required to solve the second aspect of the problem. Already having the right-of-way is an advantage, and it is much easier to modify existing facilities than to install an entirely new distribution system. Moreover, the demand for dispersed digital communication is not likely to develop rapidly. Dispersed digital communication will not be able to pay for new facilities on a month-by-month basis until demand is full-grown, and demand will not grow rapidly if digital service is poor or costly.

Under those conditions, it is not surprising that the Bell System is committed to an approach that combines an inefficient but simple quick fix with a program of gradual conversion from analog to digital. The quick fix superposes digital signal transmission upon channels optimized for analog voice communication. Insofar as packet switching is concerned, it provides only the lines and not the switches, leaving the latter to be the concern of the subscriber or an intermediary "value-added carrier," who leases the lines from Bell, interconnects them through his own packet-switching devices, and sells the packet-switched communication service. Nor is it surprising that IBM is exploring satellite communications, that Datran and Microwave Communications are going after niches in the long-haul market, and that no organization capable of having a significant effect in such a large arena is building an efficient, comprehensive network that will provide both long-haul transmission and local distribution, both analog and digital, and both line switching and packet switching. As a result, dispersed communication services are certain to be severely handicapped for many years, unless some external force intervenes.

Should the government become the external intervening force? Should it accept the basic communication grid as the street-roadway-highway-seaway-airway system of the informational future and subsidize it as it once did clipper ships and railroads-to-the-West and airmail routes, as Hitler did autobahns and Eisenhower interstates? Or should the government let the situation work itself out at its own deliberate pace?

Cable systems   We are now approaching the middle of the twenty-year period fixed for the definition and initial installation of a cable television system in the United States. It has been defined and is being installed as a collection of coaxial cable nets for the distribution (i.e., one-way transmission) of television programs. The manner in which the system is defined is of greater concern than its installation, for new lines will no doubt be installed later, after optical fibers have rendered coaxial cables obsolete. The definition of the system, which has the form of many local franchises, is of concern because it is one-way and limited to the distribution of entertainment. Despite some pressure here and there on franchise purchasers to plan for supplementary services, the heedless rush to grab up the franchises is locking the nation into its already well-established pattern of "spectator participation," which of course is nonparticipation. It is precluding future services that would require two-way connections between homes and cables in order to support two-way interaction. I have described some of the opportunities for selective and interactive participation that two-way cable, together with developments in computers, could open to the public in a chapter of *Public Television*.[1]

Without impairing its usefulness for television, the cable system could become the efficient local-distribution network needed to tie homes and small organizations into the national digital network of the future. Keeping that possibility open not only requires vision—it requires action now.

Computer-based message services   Perhaps the clearest result of ARPANET is that network message services offer significant advantages over mail. They include speed of delivery, convenient ways to address groups, independence of the physical location of recipients, and access to computer services in preparing and using messages. Message services quickly became and remained the most popular ARPANET services. They proved affordably inexpensive, even in the context of a low-volume experimental network. In a high-volume network, they should be considerably less expensive, overall, than typewritten mail.

Digital speech-compression techniques, recently developed, now make it possible to transmit speech over computer networks such as the ARPANET, store speech in computer data files, and distribute spoken messages in the same way as other computer data. Other techniques allow handprinting or handwriting, drawings, sketches, and fully pictorial images to be included in electronic messages. Moreover, such computer-based functions as indexing, abstracting, information retrieval, data management, and automatic acknowledgment of receipt are being incorporated into message services.

If the conventional postal services continue to become slower, less reliable, and more expensive, computer-based message services may begin even in this decade to displace them. Several companies are exploring or entering the computer-based message-service field. Within the government, which is a heavy user of digital (but not yet computer network) message services, the fact that the ARPANET is now operated by the Defense Communications Agency will give computer-based message services a broad exposure.

The issue of government involvement is prejudiced in this case: the government is subsidizing (though not operating) the post office, which requires fundamental improvement; it is also supporting the development of networking, which offers the only visible basis for fundamental improvement. Should the government stimulate the post office to create the appropriate contractor community and develop a computer-based message service, or should the initiative be left to private enterprise? Should the government have a computer-based message service of its own? For use in the defense sector only, or governmentwide? Those issues are simple and direct, but there is another one, less simple, that may be overlooked: What is needed is not just a message service, it is a system of services that includes data bases, documentation services, computing services, and others—in other words, a general-purpose network. Will the rush to exploit the message-service market spoil the chances of moving directly to a general-purpose network?

Other issues and problems   Perhaps the most critical issue raised by computers in the service sector of government is whether or not computers and networks will be made to provide a truly wide-band interface between the public and the government. Related issues include:

1. Whether or not speech input can be developed for the interface situation; that is, for the difficult case of conversations that are not strongly constrained either syntactically or semantically

2. Quick-response, adaptive scheduling of government-operated resources such as camping and picnic grounds

3. Programmed dissemination of government information; public access to records, schedules, agenda, bills, reports, statistics, archives, and so on, through computer information bases

4. Computer-monitored public transportation, which might let a person know to within a minute or two when his bus or streetcar or subway train will arrive at his particular stop

5. Computer-based libraries with interactive knowledge bases and question-answering systems, as well as document-retrieval capabilities

6. A new approach to the census, based on a continually updated National Roster and protection of privacy through programmed censorship of output, rather than aggregating the basic data to such an extent that few interesting conclusions can be drawn

7. A new level of government responsiveness, with computer-based services removing the limits imposed by the availability or knowledgeability of human employees

Computers and the Sustaining Functions

The sustaining function of government likely to be most affected by advances in computer technology, I think, is revenue collection. Some of the possibilities in that area were suggested in the two scenarios. An area that could be even more profoundly affected, although the likelihood is less, is the area of politics—which, while not properly a function of government, is inseparable from the process of representative government.

Computers and politics   It is technically possible to bring into being, during the remainder of this century, an informational environment that would give politics greater depth and dimension than it now has. That environment would be a network environment, with home information centers (which would of course include consoles as well as television sets) as widespread as television sets are now. The political process would essentially be a giant teleconference, and a campaign would be a months-long series of communications among candidates, propagandists, commentators, political action groups, and voters. Many of the communications would be television programs or "spots," but most would involve sending messages via the network or reading, appending to, or setting pointers in information bases. Some of the communications would be real-time, concurrently interactive. The voting records of candidates would be available on-line, and there would be programs to compare the records and display the results. Candidates and their followers would post favorable information about themselves and critical assertions about their opponents. Charges would be documented by pointing to supporting records. Under the watchful control of monitoring protocols, every insertion would be "signed," dated, and recorded in a publicly accessible audit trail. Because millions of people would be active participants in this process, almost every element of the accumulating information base would be examined and researched by several proponents, several opponents, and perhaps even a few independent defenders of honesty and truth. Nothing would be beyond question, and the question would go, along with whatever answers were forthcoming, into the accessible record. Interactive politics would function well only to the extent that the citizens were informed, but it would inform them as they had never been informed before.

Such an environment and such a process would undoubtedly open up new vistas for dirty tricks. However, by bringing millions of citizens into active participation through millions of channels, it would make it more difficult for anyone to control and subvert any large fraction of the total information flow. It would give the law of large numbers a chance to operate, and within its domain tricks would be more like vigorous expressions of the feelings of individual citizens—unless, of course, a government or a syndicate controlled and subverted the whole network. Then clandestine artificial-intelligence programs, searching through the data bases, altering files, fabricating records, and erasing their own audit trails, would bring a new meaning to "machine politics."

It is not likely that any agency of the U.S. government will deliberately develop anything approaching computer-based politics, because congressmen have such a reactionary attitude toward meddling with the traditional political process. However, the development of networking for other purposes may create the facilities required for highly participatory political interaction. This is yet another reason for emphasizing the importance of computer system and network security, since it would be absolutely essential to orderly and effective interactive politics; one might even say that the security would have to be Watertight.

Other issues and problems   The theme of government use of computers to control or repress the people deserves much more extensive examination, but the following notions will suggest some of the topics it might pursue:

1. Programmed instruction subverted to brainwashing in favor of a regime in power
2. Programmed monitoring and censorship, achieved with the aid of natural language understanding programs
3. An automatic system that appends the government's refutation to every article or program that is judged by the monitoring program to be critical of the government
4. Automated checking of adherence to government-prescribed schedules of activity and avoidance of government-proscribed activities
5. Automated compilation of sociometric association nets, showing who communicates with whom, who participates in what activities, who views which programs, and so on

Computers and the Metafunctions

The metafunctions of government are those that define the goals and agenda of the society and evaluate progress. Whether or not these are proper functions of government is a matter of political philosophy. To a large extent they are left to government by default, since other institutions lack the permanence and power to shape the twenty-five-year future. Political parties, large corporations, industry associations, foundations, and universities play metafunction roles but do not now seriously rival government in this area.

Computer-based planning and modeling   It seems likely that computer-based planning and modeling is about to offer a crucial test of the power of computers to influence government. In the United States, no major organized effort in planning or modeling is visible, but computers have overrun the Department of Defense and the intelligence agencies and have infiltrated several other departments, the White House, and the Congress. In several countries of western Europe and in Japan and the Soviet Union, *informatique* and cybernetics are the essential bases of ambitious national planning efforts. In the Soviet Union, indeed, there appears to be some kind of an effort, either a paper project or a real one some years ahead of its time, to create a 3,000-computer, nationwide network of computers and data bases for planning and management.

There is little prospect that any computer-based planning or modeling project will yield an overriding competitive advantage in the near term, but a sustained national effort might well break through to a new level of administrative effectiveness in ten or twenty years. The American approach, less concerted and less organized but with a greater degree of freedom and a stronger technological base, seems perhaps the more likely to produce results despite the inevitable disappointments of the interim. However, their deliberate intention to master the art will give some of the other countries a significant advantage if they do indeed persist.

A major obstacle to effective use of large-scale planning and modeling is the fact that it is not sufficient to have even the most sophisticated and detailed plan or model running in a computer if it is disconnected from the real world. Exploration can be carried out within simulated environments, of course, but without this connection it is impossible to achieve any validation. In the context of national planning or anything approaching that scale, it would require an extensive hierarchical system of models reaching out to the real environment and connecting to its sensors and effectors, not a complex program in a giant computer but a complex of programs in a network of computers. Some of the programs in some of the computers would constitute the model; others would be part of the real-world environment. One of the latter, for example, might operate an oil refinery on the basis of data received from sensors in the vats and stills of the refinery and in fuel storage tanks in remote parts of the country.

A national network   The network concept appears to be one of the essential keys to the future of computers, but networking is not yet a major focus of U.S. national policy. The ARPANET research and development program was forced to taper off without really attacking the problems of use by nonprogrammers and a network's potential impact on nonresearch organizations. The first commercial network, Telenet, is using protocols just different enough from those of the ARPANET to make interconnection difficult.* Six or seven other countries are planning or building networks** generally similar to the ARPANET but not sufficiently compatible with it to facilitate interconnection. Even so, the technology of interconnection is years ahead of policy pertinent to the topic.

In the spring of 1975, NBC News broadcast a series of special programs by Ford Rowan in which the ARPANET and its technology played a prominent role. Rowan reported that there was in operation a vast spy network, linking the White House with intelligence agencies and myriad data banks all over the country and that through this network, with the aid of AR-PANET Interface Message Processors, a presidential aide could read out the contents of any computer, even without its cooperation, by dialing it from his desk telephone. Alarmed by this story, several congressional committees immediately held hearings, delved into network technology, learned that computer spying was not nearly as easy as the broadcasts had suggested, and then dropped the whole thing—evidently without realizing that the true and actual capabilities of network technology were rapidly expanding the horizons of both creative interaction and repressive control.

The network concept is susceptible of development in either of two modes, one featuring cooperation, sharing, meetings of minds across space and time in a context of responsive programs and readily available information, the other characterized by supervision, regulation, constraint, and control. It is clear that the first can be realized only through a long, hard process of deliberate study, experiment, analysis, and development, whereas the second can merely evolve under the pressure of economic competition and the criterion of local gain. What is urgently needed, therefore, is a broad and sustained program aimed at formulating the concept in terms of the public interest and developing it accordingly. The study phase of such a program might be supported mainly by foundations, but it should include government. The implementation phase will necessarily involve government, at least as regulator, at most as organizer, developer, and operator.

An international network   Before the end of the century there will no doubt be one or many networks international in scope, but if international

---

* The interconnection of packet-switched networks has been facilitated by the unusually rapid development and formalization of standards, ISO X.25 for packet discipline within a network and X.7X for interconnection.

**Editors' note: Other American networks are now in the planning stage, by Satellite Business Systems, the Bell System, and Xerox.

networking is to be achieved in whole or in part through the interconnection of national or local networks, then the philosophy and protocols of internetting must be worked out at an early date.

If networks are going to be to the future what the high seas were to the past, then their control is going to be the focus of international competition. The United States should formulate its national interest in this area. An effort to preserve or extend its economic and cultural leadership among the nations of the world would seem to call for such early initiatives as establishing a packet-switched satellite network and inviting other nations to join in the development of network protocols and services. Genuine, non-self-serving interest in the health, education, and welfare of other peoples would seem to support almost exactly the same actions. Any initiative in international telecommunication is bound to confront the vested interests of national telecommunication authorities, particularly in western Europe, but there are large areas of the world that are not yet dominated by such entrenched and reactionary organizations.

There is a strong connection between the issue of international networking and the issue of computer technology export. If the United States were connected by suitable wide-band channels to countries that wanted American computing rather than computers to take apart and copy, it could export the computing without exporting the computers. In other words, it could sell the golden eggs and keep the goose.

Other issues and problems　Among the other issues and problems related to the metafunctions of government are:

1. The prospect of greatly augmented facilities for communication between individual citizens and their elected representatives
2. Organization by governments (but probably not by the U.S. government) of various international sports and games competitions in which computers might play a role in skill training, performance measurement, record keeping, and administration (and might be, for some of the games, the medium in which the games are played)
3. Increased efforts to explore and exploit the oceans, the interior of the earth, and the moon and neighboring planets
4. Increased efforts to communicate with extraterrestrial intelligences
5. The opportunity for the government to regain public trust by sponsoring research and development in unambiguously prosocial technology

General Issues and Problems Affecting Several Governmental Functions

Estrangement　The fact that large sectors of the public are distrustful of the federal government in general and several of its departments and agencies in particular affects the computer field in several important ways. Public sensitivity to threats to the privacy of information has increased, especially when they involve information about individuals contained in large and interconnected data bases. The sensitivity of the public seems to have been the reason for congressional opposition to a potentially governmentwide computer communication network (FEDNET). FEDNET was not well thought out, and it was right and proper for Congress to kill it; the trouble is that the decision to do so appears not to have been well thought out either, since it was based on the assumption that centralization of data and interconnection of data bases are bound to do more harm than good. The current tendency to oppose any scheme that involves the collection or sharing of large amounts of information about people hampers and could even preclude the development of the computer security technology required to protect privacy in an environment of controlled sharing. Thus the reaction against untrustworthy behavior on the part of government may perpetuate conditions under which there is safety only in efficiency.

The authors and supporters of the Mansfield amendment undertook to diminish the role of the Department of Defense in the support of basic research because they thought that defense had too much influence over the universities. That is of course a proper concern for the Congress; the problem is that the Mansfield amendment, together with the changes in attitude it signaled, reduced not only the Defense Department's support but the sum total of support for basic and widely applicable research, since it did not provide adequate alternative channels. Moreover, it diminished the participation of university people in the affairs of the defense sector. Whereas in the early 1960s university and think-tank people held many of the top-level positions in defense research and engineering, in the early 1970s almost all those positions were held by people from industry or from government laboratories. Over the same decade, the planning horizon moved closer, from ten or fifteen years to two or three.

Many individuals and some organizations in the research and development community are disinclined to work on military and intelligence problems. This is evidently related to their feeling that the Department of Defense and the intelligence agencies are monolithic organizations whose members are uniformly in favor of and committed to all the activities undertaken in the name of national security. In fact, of course, there is great diversity within those organizations, and no matter what one's philosophical, moral, or political position is, there are almost certain to be some members who agree with it and others who do not. By and large university laboratories are not doing research on intelligence problems and university people have little intellectual contact with information-oriented people in the intelligence community.* This estrangement has

---

* This is not exactly the question of university participation in classified research, for not all research on intelligence problems must be classified. The overall problem of the relation of universities to national security intelligence has many dimensions, of which only one is addressed here. The whole problem needs deliberate and unprejudiced study; the present situation is not a satisfactory or proper solution.

dire consequences for research in knowledge-based systems, data management, and image processing, because the intelligence agencies are the organizations that have the most challenging and most pressing problems in these fields. As a result, many university scientists are separating themselves from the frontiers of their fields of research and forgoing the opportunity to influence attitudes and events in a very important area of government.

What I have said here does not address the "moral" question posed by the fact that some intelligence computer problems are connected with code breaking and spying. Any discussion of that question would have to weigh the crucial role played by code breaking in World War II, about which many facts have now been declassified. However, it is worth observing that insofar as questions of code breaking and spying inhibit interaction between university people and intelligence people, informed discussion of the place of those functions in a democratic government is also inhibited—which can cripple the process of determining governmental philosophy and policy.

There has been a widespread reaction against the government's presuming to define the public and national interest and, indeed, against centralizing responsibility, authority, and the control of resources in order to serve that interest. The distrust of Washington does not directly affect computer technology, but indirectly it may do significant harm. Computer technology is most likely to be developed vigorously in a situation characterized by centralized planning, concentration of funds for support of research and development, and government initiatives in the functions I have been calling "meta." Computer research and development and advanced computer applications will be neglected if the federal government lets each new year's program flow out of the last and if it distributes most of its stimulus money to state or local governments.

An incomplete formula for dynamic development At the present time, computer technology enjoys the best of three worlds. An important part of the computer field, including much of its frontier, is highly pluralistic and entrepreneurial. Many small groups are literally as well as figuratively killing themselves in attempts to gain competitive advantage through advancing one or another facet of computer technology. At the same time, there is the giant, IBM, able to move the technology uphill when a massive push or a major redirection of effort is required. Finally, there are still some middle-sized companies—more than seven sizable "dwarfs" worldwide—to keep the giant working hard. This situation accounts for much of the dynamism of the computer industry.

Since it is in the interest of the government that computer technology continue to be dynamic, the government should be concerned about three facets of the situation. First, it should continue to recognize that at least in the computer field, competitive pluralism plus gigantism work better than regulated monopoly. Second, it should be wary of upsetting the dynamics of the industry by subdividing the giant, which is the main source of support (far exceeding the government itself) for computer research and development. And third, the government should aid the industry to overcome a degree of stagnation caused by the accumulated investment in old technology.

The third facet of concern is probably one of the most crucial factors. In the past, each computer manufacturer was forced by competition to bring out a revolutionary "new generation" of computing equipment every few years. Now there is a $200-billion investment in IBM/360 or IBM/370 computer systems and related business procedures, and any new generation has to be compatible with—and therefore not radically different from—the old one. In the large-scale and medium-scale computer fields, the market has turned from a stimulator of change to an inhibitor of change. Concurrently, the government has largely given up its role as stimulator. For this reason the otherwise magically effective formula for dynamic development is critically incomplete.

Hard software   Can the trend of programmation be allowed to continue without fundamental improvements in the way software is created and maintained? Will it be adequate merely to develop better programming languages, smarter programmers, and more advanced debugging aids? Or will it be necessary to develop forms of "automatic programming," like interactive specification of what programs are supposed to do, automatic translation from the specifications to machine executable (or interpretable) procedures, and logical proof of the correctness of the translation? Does the software art have to be transformed into a hard science?

As I have already pointed out, the present software situation in the defense sector is so bad that the demand is for a quick fix, not a ten-year project. And in the business and industrial sectors the tendency is to keep on using the software that finally works pretty well after a long period of on-the-job debugging. The software art cannot be transformed overnight yet, there is no specific mission that foresees a crucial need for hard software in 1990 and has funds to bring hard software into being. Thus an obvious future requirement of the government, the nation, and the world fails to command a concerted and sustained research and development effort. Research and development do go on, but uncoordinated, pluralistically supported and duplicatively executed, on-again, off-again.

A pluralistic and uncoordinated approach is fine for the most basic research, and in the software field it may invent or discover new basic concepts and perhaps even formulate the first fundamental theorem, but it will not by itself solve the software problem. Any realistic solution of that problem must include discipline, standards, and uniformity.

General methods for the creation of knowledge bases   Intelligent programs such as DENDRAL[2] and MACSYMA[3] have shown that in certain application areas it is possible to develop knowledge-based computer systems that rival or exceed human experts. They have shown, also, that dozens of man-years and millions of dollars may be required to develop a knowledge base for a field that might be one of ten thousand fields in which it would be desirable to have knowledge bases. And they have shown that most of the knowledge in a knowledge base is, at the level of present-day analysis, specific to its application field. It is evident, therefore, that more efficient or more general methods are required: interactive knowledge-base builders; programs that can read books and translate what they contain into computer-processible knowledge bases; educable computer systems that can learn, infer, and generalize.

Riding on the shoulders of programmation   Although some people have been put out of work by automation, the consensus in the United States appears to be that automation has created more jobs for people than it has destroyed; that by and large people have learned to perform the more complex, more demanding tasks posed by the more advanced technology. Nevertheless, the question of what the future will bring still looms large. Will people be able to use automation as a stepping-stone as it becomes programmation and encroaches upon functions now considered beyond its reach—clerical, secretarial, analytical, inferential? Is almost everyone capable of learning to master and enjoy a more abstract, more informational, more interactive world? Or would the on-line society mean self-fulfillment only for some and an electronic ghetto for the rest? Is it a proper metafunction of government to resolve these issues?

Substitution of information for matter and energy   Future development of computer networks could make feasible modes of living up to now limited to science fiction, modes in which not only reading, viewing, and listening but also many more active informational pursuits replace activities that consume large amounts of material and energy. People could do office work without commuting to offices, "teleconfer" without traveling to meetings, and shop without going to the store. Electronic message systems and network information bases could free printed communications from dependence on paper and therefore on transportation. And beyond those things lies the possibility of developing exciting new activities—ranging from electronic games to virtual painting and sculpture—in the purely informational media of interactive computing and networking. Government, the only likely source of support for such developments, might foster them to save material and energy resources, to keep people happy after such resources have run short, or to reawaken a population that had drifted off into a coma of passive spectating.

Government initiative in metafunctions The future of computer technology will be influenced strongly by the degree of initiative taken by government in its metafunctions. Probably the most critical of the metafunctions in this connection is planning. If computer-based planning begins to yield obvious and significant results, and it seems likely to me that it will, then the kinds of technology needed to increase the effectiveness of planning will be fostered, regenerating computer technology as a whole.

The conditions seem favorable for such a turn of events, despite the seeming indifference of Washington, because other countries are going in for computer-based planning (and monitoring of execution) more extensively than the United States, and because international military and economic competition is intense. Not only nations but large multinational corporations stand some chance of carrying computer-based planning to a point of critical effectiveness, so it is conceivable that something like a computer arms race could develop. If it did, it might greatly accelerate the advance of interactive modeling, data management, intelligent terminals, and networking.

Although planning is perhaps the most regenerative of the fields open to government initiative, several of the others invite government support on a larger scale. They include computerized commerce, automation of manufacturing, electronic funds transfer, computer-based message services, a national digital communications grid, a two-way coaxial-cable network, computer-based education, and a governmental, national, or international information network along the lines of the Multinet. An intensive effort in any of those areas by the United States or any one of several other countries would move computer technology swiftly in the general direction of Scenario 2. One can imagine even a man-on-the-moon-like program with a computer-NASA to plan, manage, and fund the necessary developments. That may sound like unreconstructed 1960s thinking, and perhaps it is, but pendulums swing both ways.

Brittleness of the socioeconomic system The word *brittleness* is intended to recall the great New England power failure of 1965 and to suggest that something analogous might happen to the whole socioeconomic system after a long period of ill-considered computerization. A brittle system is one that is not "fault-tolerant," that does not display "graceful degradation."

It is easy to see how computerization might cause brittleness. For example, in the interest of efficiency, an industry reduces the cost of inventory by tightening the feedback loop that matches the rate of production to fluctuating demand and thereby destroys the cushioning effect of inventory in local warehouses. The industry is then more vulnerable to disruptions in long-distance transportation. What is not easy to see—and what will probably not emerge from the interplay of forces in a free market—is an overall design that could achieve efficiency without brittleness. Government initiative may be required to ensure that this problem is understood before it is too late. Should the government support research on the behavior of very complex systems at a level more nearly commensurate with the socioeconomic system itself? Computer-based modeling offers an approach to the understanding of very complex systems, but as Shubik shows (see chapter 13), modeling is only an experimental tool to aid understanding; it is not a formula that cranks out easy answers to difficult questions.

Computer power to the people   If the cost of computer hardware continues to decrease according to anything like the halve-the-cost-every-two-years rule, toward the end of the century it will be possible for almost everyone in the affluent countries to use network information services extensively and to own a computer—not just a microcomputer built into a toaster, but a powerful general-purpose computer with a console, speech input and output, and fully pictorial graphic display. But cost is not the only bar to the extension of computer power to the people. Development of low-cost speech input (i.e., low-cost speech understanding) and realistic pictorial display seems prerequisite to widespread popular use of computers—unless all children are taught to type and to understand dynamic graphs and displays. Either way, it will surely require government initiatives to create the conditions under which the public at large can join the on-line community. Whether or not the public does come on-line is crucial, of course, to whether or not the government uses computers extensively in interacting with the public. Computer power to the people is essential to the realization of a future in which most citizens are informed about, and interested and involved in, the process of government.

Other issues and problems   Among the many other issues and problems pertaining to government in general, the following are those I most regret having to omit:

1. The exploitation of computers and networks by developing countries in order to hurdle over intermediate technologies and move quickly into automated production, computerized commerce, and other activities of the projected future

2. The pressure for quick results and the corollary attempt to exploit a not yet sufficiently developed technology, which tends to discredit it and delay its successful application

3. The fact that most decision makers and opinion leaders still think of computers in terms of conventional data processing and are not able to envision or assess their many capabilities and applications

4. The demise of the technological imperative

5. The schizoid public attitude toward technology

6. Centralized versus distributed data bases, from the viewpoints of security, privacy, efficiency, accessibility, updatability, gracefulness of degradation, and the psychology of responsibility

7. Separation or melding of the computer and communication industries

8. Multinational corporations as factors influencing the interaction of computers and national governments

9. Government involvement in the definition of the role of computers and networks in entertainment—and the impact of home entertainment/information centers on the relation between citizens and their government

10. Government involvement in the development and exploitation of artificial intelligence and robots

11. Government access to expertise in computers and communications

12. The possibility that another country or countries (e.g., Japan, the Soviet Union, an OPEC country) will overcome the lead of the United States in computer technology—and the effect of such a threat on the interaction between computers and government in the United States

CONCLUSIONS

The broadest and most obvious conclusion about the future interaction of computers and government is that it will depend critically upon how far computer technology advances in several of the directions I have identified and upon how much initiative government takes in shaping the socioeconomic system and the culture. Those two factors are connected with many others by manifold positive feedback loops. If both technological advance and government initiative remain strong through the next few years, it is possible that their mutual reinforcement will lead to a crescendo of programmation, networking, and informational interaction. If both factors are weak, on the other hand, though there may be a steady increase in the use and cost-effectiveness of data processing, there will probably be no truly revolutionary departure from the general pattern that now characterizes government use of computers. And if, as seems most likely, computer technology advances at some intermediate rate and government displays some middling amount of initiative through the rest of this decade and on into the next, the information revolution will not reach its point of inflection in this century, and at its end many of the issues I have discussed will still be simmering, or perhaps just coming to a vigorous boil. Indeed, it seems quite possible that a considerable part of the remainder of the century will be spent in indecisive contention over some of the more crucial issues and that the future of the system will not be defined unambiguously for another decade or two.

Basically, however, we are moving at an accelerating pace in the general direction of computerization and programmation. What is uncertain is not the general direction but the particular course and destination. What kind of computerization and programmation do we want? Integrated or fractionated? Secure or open to eavesdropping and theft? Reliable or forever breaking down? Designed to serve a specific national or public interest or to maximize the utility of various agencies and corporations? The trends of recent years have favored the second alternative of each of the pairs, but there is a feeling of renewed hope in the air that the public interest will find a way of dominating the decision processes that shape the future. That does not mean simply that everyone must vote on every question, for voting in the absence of understanding defines only the public attitude, not the public interest. It means that many public-spirited individuals must study, model, discuss, analyze, argue, write, criticize, and work out each issue and each problem until they reach consensus or determine that none can be reached—at which point there may be occasion for voting. It means that many public-spirited individuals must serve government—indeed, must *be* the government. And it means that decisions about the development and exploitation of computer technology must be made not only ''in the public interest'' but in the interest of giving the public itself the means to enter into the decision-making processes that will shape their future.

Finally, the renewed hope I referred to is more than a feeling in the air. As a few thousand people now know—the people who have been so fortunate as to have had the first rich experience in interactive computing and networking—it is a feeling one experiences at the console. The information revolution is bringing with it a key that may open the door to a new era of involvement and participation. The key is the self-motivating exhilaration that accompanies truly effective interaction with information and knowledge through a good console connected through a good network to a good computer.

NOTES

[1]
J. C. R. Licklider, *Public Television: A Program for Action*, Report of the Carnegie Commission on Educational Television (New York: Bantam Books, 1967), pp. 201–255.

[2]
Edward A. Feigenbaum, "The Art of Artificial Intelligence: Themes and Case Studies of Knowledge Engineering," in *Proceedings of the Fifth International Joint Conference on Artificial Intelligence*, Cambridge, MA, 1977, 2:1014–1029.

[3]
Joel Moses, "MACSYMA—The Fifth Year," Proceedings of EUROSAM 74, Royal Institute of Technology, Stockholm, SIGSAM Bulletin 8, no. 3 (August 1974): 105–110.

II
Trends in Traditional
Computer Uses

7
The Use of Computers for Business Functions

Victor A. Vyssotsky

What follows is the view of one manager in one large corporation, based on encounters with computers and with management, of how computers are likely to change business functions between now and the end of the century. I shall consider enterprises like corporations, government agencies, public school systems, hospitals, or any of a number of other institutions characterized by a staff of both professional and nonprofessional employees, managers, a hierarchical organization, a payroll, budgets, a large body of procedures, and an implicit or explicit product line of goods or services that the enterprise provides to its customers. Because they differ substantially from this model, I will not be concerned with small businesses or professionals in private practice. Nor do I include the impact of computers on the business functions of legislatures, committees, professional societies, and other such bodies, except as it may apply to large staffs acting on behalf of such institutions. Universities have a very special structure, different enough from the structure of a corporation to make it questionable whether the business functions of universities will follow the same trends as those of the enterprises I do consider.

I shall not consider the direct impact of computers on production or transportation of goods, nor will I consider how computers may affect the role and function of the enterprise as part of society.* I say nothing about privacy and confidentiality, because I cannot add to what has already been said on these topics. My intent is not to set forth what I think should happen or what I think could be made to happen. I am not primarily concerned in what follows with whether the trends I foresee will have beneficial or adverse effects on the overall economy, on the effectiveness of our institutions, or on the quality of our lives. Rather, I will examine how

---

* For the first of these topics, including process control, see chapter 3. For the second, see various chapters in part 3.

Victor A. Vyssotsky is executive director of the Circuit Provisioning Systems Division at Bell Laboratories. In his present position, he manages large software projects.

increased use of computers is likely to change the manner in which an enterprise operates from day to day and from month to month, in terms of what the people of the enterprise do and how their jobs may change.

As far as the future of computer technology itself is concerned, I expect the cost of electronics of the sort used in computers to continue to decline sharply compared to the cost of almost everything else. In particular, I assume a technology in which the cost of a mass-produced microprocessor, together with 10,000 characters of random-access memory, will drop well below the cost of the keyboard mechanism of a conventional cash register or electric office typewriter. I also assume that the cost-performance ratio of processors and main memories for large computers will improve by a factor of 100 by the end of the century, and that the largest machines will be perhaps 100 times as fast as those of today, at a comparable cost in real dollars.

The cost-performance ratio of such electromechanical devices as disc drives, tape drives, card readers, line printers, keyboards, plotters, and their successors is likely to improve relative to the consumer price index or the GNP deflator, but not nearly as rapidly as in electronics. Since the cost of transmitting information from place to place electronically will decline substantially relative to the cost of transmitting physical objects, I foresee a trend toward capturing information in electronic form as close to the original source as possible and minimizing the amount of translation back to paper or other nonelectronic form. In particular, inexpensive sensors will permit detailed data to be captured from production lines, retail establishments, and the like, with little manual effort. As a result, calculation costs will contribute less to the cost of "computing" in business than the cost of bulk storage of data and of getting data into and out of bulk storage or from one bulk storage medium to another. Sometime within the next twenty years we shall also have electronic (or electrochemical or electro-optical) display devices capable of displaying the equivalent of a printed page with comparable resolution and contrast, and whose cost, weight, bulk, power drain, and reliability will be no worse than those of a standard electric office typewriter.

Productivity in the business of designing, writing, testing and installing computer programs will increase faster than productivity in the overall economy, on the order of 10 percent a year for the remainder of the century. However, I do not expect comparable productivity increases in methods work, in application analysis, in application design, or in system testing and conversions; in these areas productivity will probably rise by only 2 or 3 percent a year. For this reason, I expect the spread of mechanization to be controlled more and more by the cost of methods work, of application analysis and design, and of the testing and conversion to live operation of a complete system of hardware, software, and procedures.

A significant fraction of college students, and increasingly many high school students, are being exposed to computers and to algorithmic methods. Toward the end of the century I expect that almost all students who go through the high school academic curriculum will learn something about algorithmic methods and computer programming. So whereas today perhaps only one-half of one percent of the work force knows anything about how to make a computer do something, I expect that by the year 2000, 20 percent of the work force will have a usable knowledge of computing. This certainly does not mean that 20 percent of the work force will be professional computer programmers, or even that they will be expert in the skills, any more than universal literacy implies a population composed of journalists and novelists. But it does mean that we shall see a time when a substantial fraction of the work force understands how computers work and can personally program simple applications. People will commonly be able to implement applications of modest scope, not requiring extensive systems design or methods work, without making a formal project of it.

By contrast, even in the year 2000 only a minority of senior managers of business functions will be personally conversant with computer technology to the extent of knowing, by hands-on experience, what is hard to do and what is easy to do with a computer. For a while we shall see an increasing amount of small-scale, "bootleg" mechanization of business functions, some of it wise, some ill-considered, where the people who are doing it simply don't tell top management about it. This will be accompanied by less than completely successful efforts by senior management to regain control of the situation; one can observe quite a bit of this happening today. As the fraction of managers familiar with the art begins to increase significantly, I would expect this phenomenon to dwindle.

Eliminating Paper

The most obvious aspect of clerical work affected by computers is the creation, filing, retrieval, copying, moving, and transformation of documents; this is what one thinks of as the traditional clerical function. The trend toward representing information in machine-readable form and processing it with machines dates back to Hollerith in the 1890s; more recently, there has been a move toward dispensing entirely with paper records and keeping and transmitting the information electronically, leading to what is sometimes called the "paperless office."

In order to examine the potential impact of this development, we must consider what clerks actually do. In fact they do many different things—fussing with paper is only one aspect of their work. In an enterprise of some size, one whose work force includes, say, 2,500 clerks, they do a variety of jobs, about 250 of which are distinct enough to be characterized by job descriptions. Sometimes only one clerk in the entire enterprise does a particular type of job. In a few cases fifty or more clerks do work that comes under a single job description, but even here the work performed by the clerks assigned to one type of job may vary significantly. What has happened is that mechanization has already made major inroads into the classical clerical function, which occupied dozens or hundreds of clerks doing homogeneous, routine, repetitive processing of paper.

Clerks in such an enterprise do handle a lot of paper. At a rough estimate, perhaps 15 to 20 percent of their time is spent creating records or transcribing them from manuscript to typed or machine-readable form. Perhaps another 15 or 20 percent is devoted to filing, indexing, searching, retrieving, copying, distributing, and delivering records of one sort or another. How clerks spend the rest of their time can be inferred from a typical brief job description, in this case for a tax clerk:

Controls, calculates, prepares, summarizes, and balances complex tax data. Prepares various wage and tax reports using knowledge of company accounting procedures. Analyzes employer and employee taxes, and reports findings to Payroll Department and government agencies. Prepares back-up data and maintains control sheets. Engages in discussion with employees and outside agencies. Prepares special studies, reports and correspondence. Processes group life insurance tax liability and relocation tax data.

This job involves frequent interaction with existing computer-based systems and a lot of paper shuffling. It also involves quite a bit of oral discussion, much of it loosely structured, and a fair amount of decision making about how to do what is needed in nonroutine situations.

The transition to a paperless office will mean that some clerical jobs such as mail distributor and copying machine operator will nearly disappear, as it becomes cheap and easy to recall documents from a computer and display them on a terminal with good resolution and contrast. Other jobs, such as correspondence filing clerk, will be drastically changed if they remain at all. Still others, such as stenographer, will stay recognizably the same but will involve the creation of computer-readable text rather than typed memoranda. And some clerical jobs, such as receptionist, photographic assistant, and conference registrar, will be affected only slightly. Overall, one would expect a reduction of the total clerical effort by perhaps 20 to 30 percent. However, even assuming that the hardware cost for a paperless office becomes insignificant compared to the cost of labor (probably a safe assumption), the clerical saving is not a clear gain. It is partially offset by the methods work, the analysis and computer programming, and the planning and replanning required to support mechanization. Thus the net saving to this enterprise from conversion of clerical work to paperless form is unlikely to be more than 15 percent of the current cost of clerical work. This is certainly worthwhile—for the enterprise I have been considering, the saving would come to perhaps $5,000,000 per year—but it's not a revolution.

If there is a revolutionary potential in the conversion from paper to electronic records, it is not in the elimination of routine paperwork but in the opportunity it creates to modify other aspects of business operation.

Knowledge Work

Much clerical work, most of the work of such professionals as engineers and accountants, and some of the work of managers consists of the application of specific factual knowledge gained through education and experience. This shows up quite clearly, for example, in the tax clerk's job description. If nearly all of the data to which this knowledge is applied is available in a computer data base, it is possible to write computer programs to aid or replace the efforts of the human knowledge worker, although trying to write such programs brings one rapidly around to the viewpoint succinctly stated by C. West Churchman, that "it is no easy matter to make the computer behave as a clerk would do."[1]

It almost always turns out that nobody knows, in detail, what a particular knowledge worker does. The worker's supervisor can usually make a pretty clear statement on the subject, but one often discovers after watching for a few hours that the actual job function has aspects that the supervisor did not state and does not normally think about. The worker himself is in no position to offer a complete description of how all possible combinations of circumstances are handled; he simply takes them as they come. And the job function typically involves the use of a lot of fuzzy facts and constraints, such as "Don't route shipments through Harrisburg if you can help it, because they tend to get delayed in the Harrisburg yards," or "The employee address data in payroll are more likely to be correct than the address data in personnel," or "We've had problems in the past with quality control of widgets made by this particular supplier, so we use this outfit only as a secondary source."

In spite of this, much knowledge work can be automated, and conversion to automation will continue at a steady rate. However, it usually turns out that what gets automated is not the function as it has been performed; to do that would usually be uneconomic, and in some cases utterly impractical. Instead, one looks for a cluster of functions, typically consisting of fractions of the current work of a number of people, which can be redesigned so that the computer can do something equivalent, although usually not identical. Once such a cluster of work has been identified and the computer application designed, one must also redesign the jobs of the people with whom the computer application will have to interface.

This sort of methods work, analysis, and design is very slow, very expensive, and carries a significant risk of calamity if something is overlooked. Furthermore, most of the easy applications (such as payroll) have already been mechanized. The incentive to push ahead with further efforts comes from two factors. First, rising wage rates, falling computer hardware costs, and changing skill mix and expectations in the labor force make it attractive to substitute computers for manual techniques in a growing number of applications. Second, and more important, although knowledge workers do things that are difficult or impossible to mechanize, computers can do some things that are difficult or impossible for people to do. For example, there are problems in routing telephone traffic, scheduling inter-city trucks, and the placement of back-plane wires in computers where the best methods of solution require so much computation as to be utterly impractical without a computer. But if it is to generate a usable solution, the computer must be provided with accurate and detailed data about telephone traffic or trucks and shipments or the particular set of options and engineering changes to be assembled into a particular computer. And data of sufficient accuracy are not usually available unless the upstream work functions that provide the data are themselves at least partially mechanized.

While I expect the mechanization of knowledge work to be the largest single change in business functions that will result from further use of computers, it will continue to be a very slow and expensive process and will proceed at a very uneven pace, depending on the enterprise. However, well before the end of the century, I would expect to see many major enterprises, such as telephone companies, airlines, and electronics manufacturers, in which the job of almost every knowledge worker will have been substantially changed by the advent of computers.

The economic impact of the conversion on enterprises as a whole will show up primarily as productivity increases that prevent unit costs from rising as rapidly as wage rates, rather than as actual reductions in costs or employment. Costs and employment typically will not drop, for a combination of two reasons. First, although demand for internal services within an enterprise is not particularly price-elastic in the short run, it tends to be very price-elastic over several years. Second, because knowledge work takes a long time to automate and is automated in small increments, there is plenty of time for the extra demand to materialize. A typical example of this phenomenon is the slow, steady progress in computer-aided design of electronics. Each advance is followed by an interval during which engineers discover that they can get more compact, complex, and efficient designs than they could before. The engineers take advantage of the new techniques, so the total effort devoted to detailed design does not diminish. Rather, the productivity gain shows up far downstream, in either reduced costs of manufacture or sales increases resulting from product improvements, or in both.

As an example of the potential impact of computers on knowledge work, let us consider how the job of the internal auditor may change. The internal auditor is concerned not merely with financial audits but with auditing conformance to all aspects of the enterprise's methods and procedures. Auditors look for indications of sloppiness, ignorance, honest errors, and deliberate evasions of controls, as well as for rip-offs and for inadequacies in the procedures themselves. They sometimes deal with real things (such as policyholders or salad oil or freight cars), but mostly they work with records. As these records become electronic records in a computer, the auditor's job changes. One aspect of this change that has received a lot of attention is the added difficulty of performing conventional audits when there is no paper audit trail, and there is sure to be a great deal of clever fraud before this problem is resolved. Much less attention has been paid to another aspect of the change, namely, the potential for converting auditing, at least in part, from an ex post facto, corrective function to an a priori, preventive function. I shall illustrate this latter aspect by an example.

Over the years many people in many enterprises have attempted to evade limits on expenditure delegation by breaking a large purchase order into a number of smaller orders, no one of which is expensive enough to require higher-level approval. Internal auditors are well acquainted with this gambit, and it is one of the things they watch for. If an enterprise becomes largely a paperless operation, the purchase requisitions will begin in the computer and stay in the computer. It then becomes possible to write a program that applies the same "relatedness" tests the auditors would apply, not just to a sample of purchase requisitions but to all purchase requisitions, and to do so as the requisitions are generated instead of afterward, so that if a particular purchase order triggers a "tilt," it is routed automatically to the next higher level of management for approval, along with copies of the previously placed orders to which it seems to relate. Hence the auditor's role has changed completely with respect to this particular problem. Where his present role is to seek and report evasions of the rule, in the future it becomes the specification and programming of checks to assure compliance. Many of the auditor's tasks can be similarly transformed, thus freeing him to attack the really difficult problems which today get short shrift for lack of time. Analogous considerations apply to the work of attorneys, of marketers, of designers, of accountants, of librarians, and of the many other knowledge specialists involved in keeping a large organization functioning.

There is a side effect involved in this sort of mechanization. Human knowledge workers are very efficient at spotting nonsense and doing something sensible anyway. A clerk will not usually process a purchase order to procure 10,000 three-ring binders at a total estimated price of $21.00. Regardless of his job description, the clerk will observe that something is wrong, find out the unit price of three-ring binders, and call the originator of the order to get things straightened out. Computer systems are notorious for their bad behavior in such situations. But computerized systems need not produce sporadic garbage. Rather, a big part of the cost of introducing a new computer function properly is the cost of validating all of the existing manual records as they are converted to computer form, providing editing and validating programs to check new data on arrival, supplying defensive checking in processing programs, and designing and implementing appropriate procedures for routing obvious nonsense back to an appropriately chosen human being.

These costs of introducing computers into knowledge work are incurred sooner or later in the course of mechanization, since the consequences of having a computer system that cranks out nonsense are too painful to be tolerated indefinitely. As the records of an enterprise are captured in electronic form and processed by computers they gradually come to contain fewer gross errors than they now do, and there will be a much higher degree of consistency between related records, but this is not because computers are more accurate than people. Rather, it is because computers are more likely than people to generate a large amount of nonsense from a small amount of nonsense, and computer output containing a large amount of nonsense can completely disrupt the work flow of the enterprise. Hence management will make a special effort to prevent the occurrence of gross errors.

Management

Some management information systems (MIS), as well as much of the literature on MIS, rest on a significant misconception. The assumption is made that computer systems will benefit the management of the enterprise primarily by providing more historical or projected data and by supplying data of greater accuracy in a more timely fashion directly to the line manager for use in managing. But the problem of creating a good management information system is not solved by providing more data to the manager more quickly and accurately. Rather, the chief problem seems to me to lie in the difficulty of designing systems that will let managers at various levels get the answers they need in a world that feels no compulsion to mold itself to the design of anybody's computer system.

Very few line managers want more data than they now get, whether historical or projected; most managers are inundated with data, and if they want more, it is usually there for the asking. So far as timeliness is concerned, there are certainly plenty of cases where the lag in data availability is frustrating to a manager, but in most of them the lag is due to problems that are hard to cure with a computer, particularly if the data must reflect the real world with reasonable accuracy. For example, in many situations, accurate inventory data are unobtainable without a rather good estimate of pilferage losses, and it usually takes time to find out how much of what has been stolen.

Furthermore, line managers are concerned with what has happened in the past primarily as a base for estimating the impact of some potential action (where doing nothing is one potential action). Here the manager must use projections that are at best of dubious validity and for which the timeliness and accuracy of data are often a subordinate factor. Suppose, for example, that one is considering whether to stop a half-completed $10,000,000 construction job. If the best available estimate of wind-down and cancellation costs is $1,000,000 ± $200,000, it makes little difference whether the amount of money expended through today is exactly $5,218,763 or $5,200,000 ± $100,000 projected from somewhat suspect data a week old. The uncertainty about cancellation charges is in any case largely inherent, since many of them will have to be negotiated. Even more important is the uncertainty about when a buyer for the half-completed building can be found and what such a hypothetical buyer may be willing to pay for it.

Furthermore, it is not unusual even for past costs to be somewhat uncertain because negotiations concerning billing are still under way. Such negotiations may not be complete for many months; on a project of some size, say $50,000,000, it is not at all uncommon to have a 1-percent uncertainty about cost at the time construction itself is finished. These uncertainties may not show up very clearly on the accounting records, but the responsible manager is usually well aware that only 90 percent of a particular bill has been paid owing to a dispute over what was asked for and what was provided. The remaining 10 percent of the bill will show somewhere on the books, but it is probably not easy to find unless one knows how and where to look for it.

In fact, managers now get as much data as they do for three reasons. First, line managers perform an informal audit function: "Why hasn't this engineering estimate been closed out yet?" "Why does the Orlando shop need so many maintenance spares?" "How come we sent five people to the trade show in Las Vegas, when we got by with three in Detroit?" Second, managers know that impending trouble usually shows up somewhere as a speck on the horizon, long before that trouble becomes apparent from collated statistics which have been homogenized sufficiently for neat summary, display, and projection. So the manager searches for problems that are just starting to show up, such as an equipment failure in Richmond that looks like one last month in Atlanta, which may portend a rash of failures unless the cause is identified and corrected promptly.

Third, the manager and supporting staff may doodle around, either on paper or mentally, breaking out and recombining items in an effort to spot patterns and trends and trying to see a meaning in them as they emerge. "If sales are going up in some of our stores and down in others, what's happening? Does this correlate with the gross economic trends in the store areas? With the size and location of our stores? With the merchandise mix and a change in patterns of local demand? With the strength of competition, and openings and closings of competitive stores? With the relative capabilities of local store managers? Or what? And what should we do about it?" The difference between a mediocre manager and a brilliant one lies in the ability to spot such trends, to draw good inferences, and to take effective action *before* the trends reach the level of statistical significance on summary reports.

However, even if managers are compulsive workers and voracious consumers of both narrative and statistical data, their time is limited. So the manager's typical reaction to discovering something interesting in the mass of available data is to ask somebody, "How come? What's this about? What else is happening that looks like this? What's being done about it? What are our options?" The real potential market for management information systems consists of the recipients of these questions.

To answer questions of this sort, it is very important to be able to get at raw or partially summarized data (which are likely to be somewhat specialized and idiosyncratic in form), to be able to rummage around in such data, and to be able to extract various fragments in various ways. Much less often is it important to have access to a global corporate data base or model that contains everything in a uniform but unrevealing fashion. This is why, even though they may be reluctant to admit it, division and plant managers commonly have their own record-keeping systems for projecting such things as work-in-progress inventory, subcontractors' accruals, and local sales results, instead of relying exclusively on corporate record-keeping systems.

Thus the real impact of MIS is not likely to be felt until we can create specialized data bases at reasonable cost, either separate from or appended to the corporate record structure, and until we can capture and manipulate this specialized data. In many cases it turns out that such data are most easily acquired as a by-product of a system designed primarily to support knowledge workers. The availability of these specialized data bases will improve the accuracy and timeliness of answers to managers' questions, not so much because the data is more voluminous, accurate, and timely, or even because of built-in modeling tools, but rather because the subordinates who generate the answers will be able to do a better and faster job of finding and correlating anomalies.

Until now, such an approach to MIS has been difficult to pursue because of the scarcity of people with the skills needed to create and operate these specialized systems. As high school and university education increases their number, such systems will become common, and the chief effect will be to heighten disparities of performance among managers in large organizations. The performance of a mediocre manager will not improve much, because his mediocrity consists in being unable to formulate the right questions or to choose the right action when given the answers. The performance of the brilliant manager will improve dramatically; such a manager can ask far more of the right questions than a staff of any reasonable size can answer by purely manual methods.

This divergence in managerial performance should start to show up within the next decade, and I expect that by the end of the century the structure of many large enterprises will have changed somewhat as a result. The bureaucratic structure that characterizes all large organizations is partly a reflection of managerial performance. The supply of really talented managers is far too small to permit any large enterprise to fill all its managerial needs with outstanding performers. Given that MIS will increase this disparity, the desirable and practical solution is to give outstanding managers more autonomy and more scope for the exercise of their talents.

By the end of the century this debureaucratization may well change the nature of many managerial jobs, except those at the very highest and the very lowest levels. The top-level manager already has great autonomy. Enterprises are structured on the assumption that the chief executive officer (CEO) is outstandingly capable. If the assumption proves false, the remedy is replacement, not extra rules. And it is far from obvious that any set of computerized tools can help the CEO make better strategic decisions. It is these decisions that make or break the enterprise; they are the ones the CEO is paid to make. The quality of the available information on which such decisions must be based is commonly so poor that extrapolation by pencil and paper will usually yield as much insight as there is to be had. It may be cheaper and more convenient to use a computer, but that doesn't affect the CEO very much.

At the lowest levels of management, we find three types of jobs. One type is the job filled by new, young managers who are learning their trade. Here rules are needed to keep their inexperience from getting them into trouble that they can't get themselves out of. The second type of job is not really managerial but professional. In many organizations the only mechanism for attracting and keeping needed professionals is to call them managers, but since such employees are not in fact managers, new managerial approaches will not greatly affect them. Finally, although jobs like shop foreman, transcription leader, or car pool supervisor will benefit from greater use of computers, the people who hold this type of job are in close enough contact with the people doing the work to get most of the input data they need by direct personal observation.

Debureaucratization will not be merely a matter of decentralization and delegation of authority; it will require changes in how responsibilities are allocated within the management structure. Much of the bureaucratic rigidity of a large enterprise results from the need to treat employees, customers, and suppliers in a consistent and equitable fashion. Within one enterprise, severance pay practices in Camden cannot be much different from those in Philadelphia. Nor can one afford to have the Milwaukee sales office pulling business away from the Chicago office by offering large rebates. Hence managers cannot be given license within the existing structure simply to do as they see fit. Instead, the enterprise will have to search for logical divisions of responsibility to provide maximum freedom of maneuver to capable managers without jeopardizing necessary uniformities. This is not a new problem, of course, but one that large enterprises have struggled with repeatedly without reaching a solution. The right answers seem to be specific to the particular enterprise, and they are very hard to discover. So the process of debureaucratization will proceed slowly and fitfully; some enterprises may not undertake it at all, preferring to cling to what has worked in the past.

External Interfaces

As most large enterprises mechanize their paperwork, it will also become profitable to convert the transmission of information between enterprises to electronic form. One possibility that is currently much discussed is electronic funds transfer; it is already beginning to be used to a minor extent and will surely become widespread. Whether or not its growth takes place within the existing banking structure is immaterial to my projection, since if the banks are unable or unwilling to provide it, other enterprises will.

Electronic funds transfer is only one example of what will occur. Many large corporations already provide tax data to the IRS on magnetic tape, and enterprises that need census data commonly receive it on tape. Interchanges of this sort will continue to spread; some such interchanges will occur via physical transportation of bulk media such as tapes, cartridges, and disc packs, while others will be via electronic transmission. One can already find examples of manufacturing design information being transmitted between corporations in computer form; the originating company develops it by computer-aided techniques, and the receiving company uses it as input to further computer processing, so neither company wants it on paper. Some billing and invoice information is already being transmitted via computer media, and such use will spread.

Electronic transmission of ordinary business correspondence will grow, although it may be slowed somewhat by the fondness for engraved letterheads and hand-inscribed signatures, which seems to be almost as deeply rooted as the legal profession's fondness for notary public seals. Nonetheless, it will gain acceptance, just as the typewriter gradually became as acceptable as manuscript for correspondence. Thus I expect that before the end of the century nearly all transmission of most types of information between large enterprises will be in machine-readable form, whether by bulk media or by electronic transmission.

It is less obvious how much of the communication of individuals and small organizations will take place via computers. Some of it surely will, because it will be to the advantage of both the large enterprises and those who correspond with them to mechanize their communication to some extent. Some of it surely will not; just as today even the most advanced enterprise will accept currency in lieu of a credit card if the customer insists, so in the future a typed or manuscript letter will continue to be accepted as a form of communication. And just as some people insist on paying cash, so also some people will insist on using a pen or a typewriter, rather than keying messages into computer terminals or otherwise communicating in machine-readable form. Some enterprises will press their customers to conform to the way the enterprise wishes to operate. For example, the amount of effort required to correlate a longhand letter of complaint about a magazine subscription with the computer record of the subscription is a significant fraction of the price of the subscription. Magazine publishers may eventually strengthen their current polite request that the customer send back a copy of the mailing label and say in effect, "If you don't provide us with your name and address in our machine-readable format, we probably can't respond to you at all."

However, the extent to which transactions and communications occur via computer is affected by all sorts of forces and inertias, which makes me reluctant to hazard any guesses as to how rapidly the interfaces between the business functions of large enterprises on the one hand and individuals and small organizations on the other will be mechanized. For example, it is remarkable that large enterprises have not all converted to machine-readable employee identification media. The potential of such a conversion to simplify problems like monitoring stockroom withdrawals, controlling access to restricted areas, limiting parking in reserved parking lots, identifying employees who make expensive telephone calls, simplifying the checkout of documents from company libraries and files, and many other uses is great. The added cost of the identification medium is small, suitable terminals to read it are readily available, and almost every large enterprise already has a computer system able to do the checking and record keeping, yet most large enterprises have not gone on to take this obvious step.

New Functions

The business functions of large organizations are not static and immutable. The concept of the personnel function as a separate, identifiable business function of the enterprise, which is universal today, was nearly unrecognized in 1900. We may reasonably wonder whether increasing use of computers will lead to an analogous recognition of activities within the enterprise with important separable functions, activities that today are embedded haphazardly in various parts of the organizational structure.

Two instances occur to me of activities likely to receive this sort of recognition. One is already recognized in many enterprises—the "methods and procedures" function. This will surely receive more attention in coming years. Faulty methods in a manual environment are an expensive irritant, but people soon develop "workarounds." Faulty methods in a mechanized system are far more serious, because it is far harder for people to devise effective "workarounds" in a mechanized environment.

In particular, if a necessary but unobvious capability is omitted from a mechanized system, some ordinary type of business transaction may turn out to be nearly impossible to perform. This problem has occurred in a number of enterprises, with consequences ranging from extra work and irate customers to near paralysis of the enterprise. Less calamitous but very costly is the failure to analyze properly how the introduction of a mechanized system will change people's jobs. The field is replete with anecdotes of mechanized systems that increased instead of reduced manual effort. Such problems can often be traced back to inadequate methods work and analysis during the initial design of the application. Although methods and procedures work still tends to be regarded with profound skepticism by many line managers, there is a growing consensus that it is a function for accountable professionals, not dispersed amateurs.

The other activity that I think may come to be regarded as a separable activity is the function of data administration. I have already remarked that computers are less adept than people at working with missing, erroneous, or inconsistent information. At present, each department owning a chunk of computerized data is responsible for keeping the data in good enough condition to be used. With increasing mechanization, this approach becomes inadequate for two reasons. First, as computer applications are interconnected and integrated, discrepancies in their data bases that do not affect any one of them separately may create difficulties in the integrated system. For example, if payroll and personnel have recorded an employee's name in different forms, both of which are correct, and if payroll keys primarily on Social Security numbers while personnel keys on employee identification numbers and the employee quits suddenly, the chances of producing a correct final paycheck on time are pretty good if the interface between payroll and personnel is manual, but not nearly so good if the interface is a transaction inside a computer.

Furthermore, even aside from the problem of integrating computer systems many large-scale mechanizations already have difficulty when the department that needs correct data is not the department that generates it and the generating department has no incentive of its own to make sure the data are right. As an example of this, consider an enterprise that manufactures equipment, leases it to customers, and provides maintenance as a part of the lease cost. It is obviously an advantage to such an enterprise to minimize field failures and field maintenance, so the enterprise has a group of reliability engineers. The field force, however, has an incentive not to make accurate reports on a certain class of problems, namely, those the field force itself triggered. Such failures tend to be reported as due to other causes, such as power surges. This inflates the recorded failure rates for what may in fact be completely adequate aspects of the design, while failing to reveal the design inadequacies that get the field force into trouble. Human reliability engineers are well aware of this and try to interpret the reported failure information accordingly, but it is hard to program an automated reliability analysis to do so. For this reason I foresee the gradual recognition of a new business function, data administration, with responsibility for setting uniform approaches to the acquisition, validation, and preservation of computerized information and for determining requirements and standards of responsibility for crucial types of data.

Possible Breakthroughs

I have so far ignored the potential impact of certain technical breakthroughs that might occur by the end of the century, although in my opinion not for at least the next ten or fifteen years. I will mention just some of these possibilities.

Optical and acoustic pattern recognition by machine has been making slow, steady, unspectacular progress since before the digital computer as we know it was invented. For example, a spoken digit recognizer was on display at the New York World's Fair in 1939. I expect that progress will continue to be slow, steady, and unspectacular. I do not think that in this century computers will be able in any economically practical sense to identify particular humans reliably from a video image, or to read unrestricted manuscript written by arbitrary, unknown individuals. Similarly, I do not expect correct transcription of voice utterances from an unrestricted vocabulary, even for a single speaker, although I do expect sufficiently accurate identification of utterances restricted to a small vocabulary, without restriction to a single speaker. If my assumptions are too conservative, there are all sorts of interesting modifications of business functions that may be feasible.

I'm never quite sure what is meant by artificial intelligence. If it means the ability of a computer to discover algorithms for solving problems that humans have not been able to discover algorithms for, I doubt that this will be achieved in an economically practical form in this century. If it is achieved, all of my projections are far too conservative. If, instead, artificial intelligence is taken to mean the use of computers as assistants to expedite and improve the process by which intelligent humans solve problems, it is here today, and that is what I have been writing about.

I have ignored the potential impact of certain possible hardware developments, such as a very large, very fast, very cheap random-access memory. It would have a considerable impact on business functions if one could get, say, a one-microsecond random-access memory of 10^{15} bits at a cost of a few million dollars. It seems to me technically plausible that such a memory could be developed for commercial availability within the next twenty years. However, the costs, risks, and time scale associated with such a development make me doubt that it will be done.

I have also ignored one potential development that could have great impact, and which seems to me quite likely to occur. We do not know today how to organize narrative data in a computer in such a fashion that it can be accessed as conveniently and flexibly as one can access information in a good library of moderate size. In particular, if the content of the data base changes with time, one would want to access the data base without knowing about details of content and structure and still be able to retrieve pertinent information. This is not a question of computer programming, nor is it primarily a problem of data structuring as data-processing people commonly think of data structures. Rather, it is a question of organization of information. I expect to see a lot of progess on this topic within the next ten years, but I cannot envision what form this progress will take, so I cannot extrapolate its impact on business functions.

Conclusions

There is little doubt that the business functions of large and medium-sized enterprises in the United States will be significantly changed by further growth in the use of computers. The jobs of the great majority of clerical, technical, professional, and managerial workers will be changed to some extent, and some of these jobs will be transformed beyond recognition. But the net effect on productivity may not be overwhelming. For some organizations, overall productivity may be doubled or tripled by the impact of data processing over the next twenty or twenty-five years. For others the net effect on productivity may be as little as 10 percent. To hazard a guess, the average effect for all these enterprises might be 50 percent in twenty years, or about 2 percent per year. Assuming that toward the end of the century the affected workers in these enterprises constitute 40 percent of a total U.S. work force of about 120 million, then computer assistance will allow those 50 million workers to do what would require 75 million workers with today's methods.

Such a shift might be considered revolutionary. But it will come in small steps, over a long period of time, and at a high cost, so it is unlikely to have an impact on the work force of the sort that the enclosure movement had on the English agricultural population. Rather, the effect on enterprises and employees alike is apt to show up as the ability to handle a steadily increasing load of work without a corresponding rise in the price of the goods and services that the enterprise produces.

EDITORS' POSTSCRIPT

Some would argue that the "automated office," in which all typewriters are replaced by computer consoles connected to duplicating devices, represents a more revolutionary development than Vyssotsky's predictions would imply. In particular, the reader may wish to contrast this article with the one by Licklider, which discusses the possible impact of information processing on government functions.

NOTE

1
C. West Churchman: "Management and Planning Problems," in *Computers and the Problems of Society,* ed. Harold Sackman (Montvale, N.J.: AFIPS Press, 1972).

8
Scientific Use of Computers

Sidney Fernbach

WHERE WE HAVE BEEN

Computers were originally devised by mathematical scientists to aid them in their work. It is not strange, therefore, that most of the earliest large computers were found in scientific establishments. The situation has been changing over the years—since it was recognized fairly early that computers have spread into every industry, large and small. It is the scientist, however, who still seems to set the pace for development in most aspects of computing. It is the peripheral area that is changing most significantly, and it is the scientist who is encouraging it. Rapid advances in technology accompanied by substantial drops in the cost of components make it possible to bring the latest technology to the point of early utilization.

Let us see how computers are used in the sciences today and what directions we will be taking in the near and medium-range future. The first computers built were designated for either scientific or business purposes. There were numerous reasons for this distinction, such as the use of decimal notation rather than binary; fixed-point versus floating-point; types and numbers of peripheral devices; performance requirements, and so on. Today one finds that these distinctions still exist but are not taken as seriously. General-purpose computing is widespread, and many features of both scientific and business computers have a variety of industrial uses. There is such a large assortment of computers available today that one can acquire special systems for special purposes or make use of relatively large systems for general purposes even if they are not the most suitable for the job at hand. It is mainly the scientific community that requires either specialized hardware and software or high-performance machines that allow frills normally lacking in other systems.

Sidney Fernbach is deputy associate director for scientific support at the Lawrence Livermore Laboratory. For many years, he was director of the computer center there and was responsible for its evolution into the largest concentration of computers for scientific computation in the United States.

The world of computers for some time was thought to be made up of large, medium, and small computers. Then came the minicomputer, which was smaller than small, and now the microprocessor, which is smaller still. Of course, there is also the hand-held calculator, which at the moment is not classified as a computer. The distinction between small, medium, and large can be made on the basis of speed or overall performance but is most easily done on the basis of price (which generally has been equated with performance at any given time).

While the scientific community has been the user of most of the large computers built, interestingly enough, it also uses most of the minicomputers (and now microcomputers). The small and medium range of computers tend to go into the commercial world. The large computer is used to solve very large systems of mathematical equations representing some physical phenomenon. The greatest need for such computers is in such fields as meteorology, seismology, nuclear physics, reactor physics, and quantum chemistry. Solving problems in these fields is considered to be "number crunching" in that the machines are for the most part dedicated to carrying out the basic arithmetic processes. Measures of performance can very easily be taken to be the number of floating-point operations carried out per unit of time. Problems being solved today on the highest-performance machines are two-space dimensional as a function of time. Three-space dimensional (3-D) problems are hardly being touched. This is because the length of time required to carry out a 3-D problem is inordinantly high. Turnaround time for productive use would be too long for practical purposes. For this reason, it is rare that one sees experimental runs of such problems. The scientist generally wants decent turnaround time, especially if he is engaged in real-time or experimental work. He will not run extensive sets of problems if each one takes as many as twenty hours to carry out, and some of today's problems have become so complex that hundreds of hours might be required to carry out a single run. This is the case for 3-D—hence the rare occurrences of extensive use of today's computers for solving this category of problems. We will need much better performance in number crunching before this type of problem solving becomes commonplace.

The intermediate and small computers are used by scientists for more mundane problem solving, and for relatively small problems, which these computers do fairly well, with reasonable turnaround times. Time-sharing systems are quite useful for the small jobs, because the user can even interact with the system doing his job and get his work done in real-time fashion. The scientist with the small jobs will generally use whatever system is most readily available to him.

Another area of computer use of tremendous importance to the scientist involves the laboratory. Experimental facilities need both control and the means for acquiring and analyzing large amounts of data. The minicomputer has turned out to be ideal for these purposes. The very earliest minis were built primarily for the scientist. Although they now are widely used for many other purposes, large numbers of them are acquired each year as tools for measuring and controlling experiments as well as for gathering and analyzing data. Sometimes these operate as stand-alone systems; sometimes they are tied into large systems as peripheral devices, as a control for large-scale storage of information or for more extensive data processing and analysis.

In government-sponsored research, one of the most active scientific organizations is the Department of Energy (DOE) (formerly the Energy Resources Development Administration and before that the Atomic Energy Commission). DOE is the second-largest computer-using agency of the largest computer consumer in the country, the U.S. government. If one plots the acquisition of computers for this one agency (fig. 8.1), one gets a very good impression of the scientific user community's habits. In the period 1970–1976 the number of minis has risen exceedingly rapidly, the number of large systems (defined as those costing more than one million dollars each) has increased very slowly, and the number of intermediate computers has grown in a seemingly controlled way. The perturbation seen developing after 1970 probably represents the fact that mini systems started to grow large enough to exceed the $50 thousand limit defining a minisystem.

Mini-computers are being placed into engineering, chemistry, and physics projects in large numbers and have become replacement for, or parts of, scientific instruments. Furthermore, they are providing the scientist with the opportunity to digest his own data, feed new information back into a system, and effect real-time changes in an experimental environment. He can get his results back in time to interact with his experiment manually, or if he wishes he can build the feedback into the control system automatically. With the advent of the microprocessor he may be able to do even better.

The scientist at present runs the gamut of computing—nothing is too small, nothing too large. It is the extremes that are most important to him. What does he want in the immediate and remote future, and what can he expect?

Computers seem still to be in their infancy. Monstrous machines such as Illiac IV, CDC STAR, TI-ASC (4x), and CRAY-1, the top performers today, are not necessarily prototypes of the machine we shall see twenty years from now. They may be more like the dinosaurs of old, to be followed eventually by the equivalent of mankind—streamlined brains. The microprocessor seems to be the forerunner of things to come.

The number of machines worldwide capable of processing more than

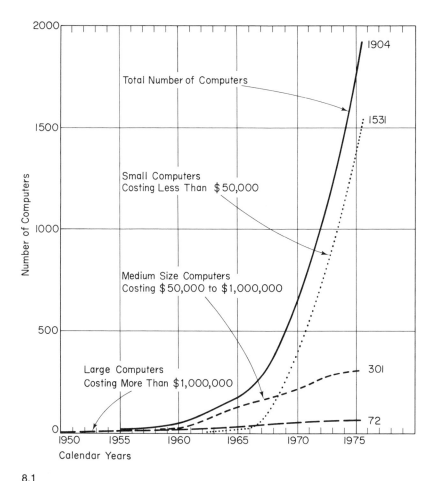

8.1
Number of Computers in AEC/ERDA, 1950–1976

several million floating-point operations per second is a good deal fewer than one hundred today. The architectural style of most of these systems is basically sequential; that is, they carry out computations one after the other, although there is enough parallelism built into each to optimize performance at reasonable cost. The top performers mentioned previously are few in number, for several reasons. First, they represent several architectural innovations; second, they are relatively new to the scene; and third, they are as yet unproved in performance. Furthermore, they do require a new approach to formulating problems. These are vector or truly parallel processors. In order to achieve high performance, the scientist's job must be formulated in such a way that the same operation may be carried out on a long string of operands or a well-specified sequence "simultaneously." Most scientists have not given much thought to such processing techniques and are not mentally prepared to deal with thought processes cutting across space in a parallel fashion. Those scientists who have used these machines have not yet learned to structure their problems properly, to debug them, and to optimize performance. One may raise the question of whether this is the way of the future. Cray Research's CRAY-1 computer, which is also a vector processor, uses advanced technology and architecture to achieve its performance levels. Its great virtue is that it allows for effective scalar processing as well as vector processing, so that the scientist can be in both the scalar and vector world at the same time. This may help make the transition to the vector world smoother.

We have come a long way in scalar processing in the twenty-five years of commercially available computing, a performance-level increase of approximately 5,000. Some small additional increase may be possible in the large scientific computer if wire lengths could be kept very short and if the system could be built into a tightly packed handful of chips. Hence, for the large systems the future must involve more parallelism. If there is a continuing need for number crunching, there will be a need for an architecture different from that provided in the past. Beside the vector processor built by Cray, the pipeline structure of the CDC and the TI machines, and the parallel processor of Burroughs, the multiprocessor has existed for some time but has not been exploited to the extent necessary to prove its value. Dual processors are in current use, but it seems they are not operating on the same problem concurrently in such a manner as to achieve the factor of two theoretically possible in overall performance. Not enough thought has gone into multiprocessing beyond the dual level. Which if any of these architectural styles will predominate in the next twenty years is difficult to foretell, but it is fair to say that there is enough demand for improving current performance levels to predict that the large computers will be around for a long time to come.

It is too much to expect the spectacular performance improvements experienced during the past twenty-five years. Initially, performance doubled each year, on the average. More recently, performance seems to be going up at the rate of a factor of two every three to four years. No doubt this will slow down even more. Dare we hope for a factor of 1,000 over the next twenty years, compared with the 10,000 of the last twenty-five years? To achieve such a number would require a great deal of learning: to think in terms of vectors, to segment problems, to devise high-level languages for vectorization, and even to find completely new techniques, unknown today. It is difficult to foresee such overall improvements in the large computer. Perhaps other alternatives will become available, allowing us to attack most of the large problems if not all.

At the opposite end of the computer spectrum, the minicomputer gets smaller with each passing year, its memory gets larger and faster, and the cost keeps decreasing despite inflationary factors. Today the mini available for thousands of dollars is considerably more powerful than the large computer available in the 1950s for hundreds of thousands of dollars. This trend toward smallness, greater effectiveness, and lower cost will continue until the mini on a chip (or two) becomes the state of the art.

There are numerous minicomputer manufacturers. Each mini has its own special features incorporated to provide more or less capability according to one's tastes or needs. Basically, minis are very much alike. The variations that are introduced from time to time to take advantage of the rapidly developing technology seem to be heading toward matching the performance levels of the medium or large computers of the past, thus providing equivalent capability at much lower cost. Earlier minicomputer word lengths were short, memory capacity relatively small, and peripheral equipment availability low. Today's mini no longer has such limitations, but in spite of their power and low cost, the additional peripheral devices that are being added tend to make them run into many tens of thousands or even hundreds of thousands of dollars. The revolutionary increase in computer CPU performance per dollar has not been as evident in the ancillary equipment needed to make up a system.

There is no doubt that the minicomputer will continue to be used heavily in the scientific laboratory, since its flexibility allows it to carry out a variety of tasks simultaneously. The growing availability and improving performance of microprocessors may change this somewhat, but even now the mini cost is low enough to make it the most versatile tool in the laboratory. It seems clear that every experiment will have one or more processors tied into it for control, data acquisition, and data analysis purposes. Every scientist's office will have a terminal, intelligent or otherwise, allowing him to communicate with the experiment or some other system where his data processing is being carried out. Currently, for example, the Lawrence Livermore Laboratory (LLL), with a total personnel count of 5,500 of which less than half are scientists, has well over 200 minicomputers installed. This represents more than one for every ten scientists. The University of California, as a whole, has several hundred minicomputers and fewer scientists. These are not atypical situations.

Now we are finding that microprocessors are taking the place of some of the minis and are also being used in other places where minis are too overpowering. Soon we will find the microprocessors far outnumber the minis. Some significant number of microprocessors per scientist will become the rule, since they can be used in very simple ways or combined in complex ways to represent the capability of a mini in accomplishing a given task. Even though the microprocessor is relatively new, LLL currently has 350 of them in use, and eventually it will become the mini on a chip. Hand-held calculators represent for the scientist a substitute for computers in many respects. Again, at LLL there are over 3,000 of these devices, many of which are programmable. Almost 800 were purchased in 1975 alone.

Where is technology leading us with respect to these tiny devices? Can we afford the costs of programming the multitude of mini and micro-processors, or even the programmable calculators? It should be remembered that the costs of software production have increased over the years to the point where they represent the most significant part of large computer installation costs. The cost of minicomputers may be insignificant compared to the cost of providing the software. There are hardly any cooperative efforts under way to provide common software for minisystems. With microsystems the situation may be much worse, primarily because of the extreme flexibility needed to put together special-purpose systems. This is a problem we must learn to solve.

WHERE WE ARE GOING

The topic of networks has been neglected so far. This is because the network provides the scientist access to a computer or computer system but little more. The situation with respect to networks, however, may and should change. The network properly conceived could provide the scientist with much more power than he now has, even if technology does not advance greatly beyond where we are today.

Today's networks consist of numerous terminals of various kinds communicating with various computers over local or remote communication lines. The processing of data is traditional; protocols vary from system to system; communication rates vary. The expansion of networking has hardly begun. However, a computer system is a network of sorts. It has a number of special parts that communicate with each other to carry out specific functions. Why should we not extend the concept of functional computation on a local basis, tying a number of functional boxes together into a network to carry out the required workload? Such a network could be configured to suit one's needs.

The general needs of the scientist involve a host of jobs large and small that he must carry out. He should have access to a computing facility from a local site, perhaps his office. His input could be vocal, some DO command, although vocal inputs will continue to be difficult to deal with for years to come. Unless they comprise simple instructions or commands, it seems unlikely they will become highly successful, but once a line of communication has been established with a computer system within a narrow context, vocal responses back and forth could reasonably be expected as a logical consequence of technological development. For example, if a scientist is making a series of numerical readings for input, they could very readily be in the form of oral communications.

In general the scientist has to think his problem through and put it into proper perspective so that the rational computer can attack it logically. It is not very likely that the scientist can rattle off a string of equations for solution and have the system attack them from scratch. He must interact in some convenient way. The use of written material must remain the predominant choice for input for years to come. This input could be on paper or cards or on chalkboard—anything that can be scanned, interpreted, and fed into the system. Lack of understanding or failure to read could be communicated back (even vocally) to clarify unreadable statements. Scanners or readers could be TV cameras. The written-medium material could also be collected pneumatically and brought to a central reader. There are many rather convenient, simple ways to collect information. No doubt the keyboard itself will be with us for a long time to come; the use of TV, however, should be expanded as a collaborative tool for the computer system.

What is this computer system? What I picture is networks made up of computers of all varieties. These can be local networks or local networks tied to any number of remote systems. In each there will be a set of functional boxes or computers dedicated to specific functions. One or more may do nothing but print, another plot, another create pictures on film, another retrieve information from a local data bank. In other words, instead of a large-scale general-purpose computer, I visualize a distributed system in which specific jobs are parceled out to specialists. Whenever a new specialty is needed, it is added to the system. If this can be done cost-effectively on a local basis, that is what should be done. If, on the other hand, such specialties already exist remotely and communication costs for the magnitude of use required are low enough, remote use of the special system can be provided. Each specialized computer, probably a minisystem, will be a very simple central processing unit (CPU) with sufficient circuitry to do its designated job. The program will be microcoded for the appropriate application. In this way the software could be packaged very neatly and be highly specialized—the minimal package to do the job. The high cost of large systems with frequent fixes or changes will be avoided. Additional facilities for each specialty could be plugged in when and where they were needed. Redundancy in case of failure of any unit could be provided to keep systems active twenty-four hours a day in a fail-soft manner, or even failure-free.

Thus far, we have considered functions normally thought of as being of the bookkeeping variety. What about the mathematical jobs for which the computer was first designed and developed? There is no reason to believe that relatively small computers are incapable of doing large jobs. Today's minis are superior to the first large computers, and the development of minis or small computers will continue at the same pace during the next twenty-five years as during the past twenty-five. Minis as capable as our large sequential machines will be developed. Even today, specialized minis exist that come within less than an order of magnitude of performance of our highest-level machines for special jobs. As a matter of fact, array processors being built today for specialized functions are capable of operating at speeds an order of magnitude greater than our highest-performing machine. There is no doubt that within the next few years we should be able to make small computers specifically microprogrammed to perform specialized mathematical jobs more cost-effective than the large general-purpose computer. Hence our network should contain highly specialized mathematical processors.

Somewhere in the network there will have to be an assignment and scheduler processor to determine where each incoming job should go. Mathematical tasks might have to be sorted and processed into the proper portion of the system. Jobs may be segmented and farmed out to different processors. To prepare for such eventualities, it seems clear that we must get on with the job of learning to use multiprocessors more effectively; we are just beginning to do so. Multiprocessing may become much more popular in the next five to ten years, thus providing us with the possibility of reaching into the future with greater confidence.

Symbolic processing has come a long way in the past ten years or so, and it is still progressing, although rather slowly. Here also is a sleeping giant of a prospect for the future. It seems unrealistic to believe that each scientist will forever have to take his primitive equations, break them down into discrete formulations for computers, provide the programs, debug, and so on. The same processes must be repeated thousands of times each day for roughly the same equations. Admittedly, the task of providing such a capability is difficult, but at the present time very few efforts are receiving proper support. We must dedicate more money, scientists, and systems to symbolic processing development if advances are to proceed at a faster rate in the next twenty-five years.

The computer has become the essential tool for the thinking scientist who has to carry out experiments to establish the validity of his theories. Thus far the computer has not contributed a great deal to original thought. The scientist experiences and learns to understand physical phenomena throughout his entire life, but his most active years for thought are relatively few. The experiences of large numbers of scientists can be put into the data banks of computer systems, and the computers then can be programmed to sort through all this information and come up with "original" ideas. With the incredible speed of the computer and the proper guidance of collaborative scientists, it should be possible to stimulate and accelerate thought processes and carry out the theoretical research necessary to establish new basic laws for the physical phenomena scientists are dedicated to interpreting and understanding. Having all such data in the computer system not only makes it possible to achieve major breakthroughs in scientific development but provides a most important mechanism for the scientific education of our young. With the computer the student should be able to trace through the hows and whys of a physical phenomenon until he is able to appreciate or understand the nature of the event.

Thus far I have provided for bookkeeping functions, data retrieval, problem solving in both numeric and analytic bases, and a reasoning system stocked with much of the scientific knowledge in the world. This latter system should not be restricted to science alone. Our educational facilities in general need to have the information in the Library of Congress at the fingertips of teachers and students. This could be the greatest educational tool in the world. What does it take to make such things feasible? There is no doubt that networks can be assembled to carry out specialized jobs or functions; it has already been done to a limited extent. Questions have been raised about the centralization of processors and data and about decentralization based on functions. No one scientist or group of scientists needs to have all the world's data at one site; nor must he have all the world's computer power at a local station. Even with the relatively high cost of communication, decentralized facilities are more feasible, more secure, and easier to implement. Perhaps there should be a national Library of Data to complement the Library of Congress which could house one or two of every bit of data. For every day of use there should be an appropriate dispersal of data, such that each scientific establishment can store what it must have readily available on a reasonable time basis. That data needed less frequently could be accessed from some not too remote site. Large storage media are becoming more readily available at a reasonable cost. The hopes for holographic memory devices that would permit much greater densities at low cost and much more rapid access than is currently possible have not been realized. It is to be hoped that within the next quarter of a century we will see such developments. Until such time, the progress toward large data base systems may be slowed somewhat.

It is not only the very large archival type of memory device that needs further development—primarily to bring the cost per unit of storage down to an exceedingly low level—but also the other hierarchical levels of memory that will be needed in distributed systems. Since the logic functions of a distributed system may be fairly simple, it is the memory and its management that provide the greatest costs and hence require the most attention. If memory costs could be reduced significantly, cost-effective management would not be so critical. Fortunately, numerous new technologies are being pursued that may result in the possibility of providing rather small CPUs with the very large memories that will be needed in future systems.

Conceptually, the system I have described may be seen as a matrix of switchable general function boxes along one dimension tied to each one of an array of specific function boxes along the other dimension. Thus, the general functions are carried out for each of the special function boxes and communicated back to them or other units as demanded. Each of the functional units will have its own memory and provide its own required processing. Some of the units may share common memories; others will have their own unique memories. Where necessary, there would be a common data base. This may be hierarchical in the sense that not all functional units need access to all data. Lines for communication to remote networks will also allow for interaction at the local sites. Where necessary, a local network may contain a large computer as one of its functional units, to be used for those problems that are still intractable for the smaller systems, for designing and debugging new functional units, and for experimentation with processes not functionally provided. This part of the system could be made available remotely so that other scientists lacking such systems locally could carry out their specialized work as well.

What can we project for the large computer at this time? It has been a fact of history that large computer development could not keep up with the growing need to solve problems on a larger and larger scale. The case can probably be made that there are some very large problems that are not easily segmented and that they will continue to outstrip the capability of the computer architect and manufacturer to keep up with their requirements. Hence, there will always be a need for the "supercomputer," not in large numbers but enough to satisfy the "experimental" needs of the theoretical scientist. Many problems seem to lend themselves to vectorization. Some computer scientists are spending a good deal of time studying vectorization processes, and more is needed. Unfortunately scientists have a tendency to seek alternate methods when the tools are not at hand to take advantage of new techniques, so we must make "parallel" processors readily available, encourage their use, and reward vectorization efforts. At the rate we are absorbing such systems into daily use, it will probably take ten years or more before we have a library adequate to start taking advantage of the capability afforded even by those systems now in existence or on the drawing boards. Even though costs for such systems are high today and will remain so for the next decade, LSI (large-scale integration) technology developments are coming along quite rapidly.

Costs will decrease on very large systems, making them affordable by large numbers of scientific institutions before the end of the century.

What about the scientist and his personalized computer? It has been shown that scientists over the years have acquired large numbers of minicomputers to be used primarily for their experimental research. Although many of these computers are tied into experiments, they also become available on a time-shared basis for other personal work the scientist may have to carry out. This, to him, may be more convenient than a terminal hooked into a central computer located elsewhere. With the reduced costs and greater capability of the modern mini, this is a very attractive prospect for the scientist to pursue in order to obtain the calculational capability he needs.

One problem with this approach is that the total software effort to program each mini for specialized jobs is very great. A second is that once programs are available a bookkeeping or library system must be set up to keep track of what is available. Documentation is very difficult if not costly. Unless the individual scientist has a very limited repertoire of programs, he may find himself hiring additional personnel or spending the majority of his own time carrying out computing functions. In this case, he may be better off gaining an understanding of and using a centralized facility.

There is an additional direction, however, that is being taken as a result of our revolution in technology. The microprocessor and hand-held calculators are making a tremendous impact on the scientist. For his own personal use, the calculator has great value. The programmable calculator even allows him to do jobs he would have saved for his mini- or terminal-based system. Here again, he must spend time programming, although the calculator capability is of course quite limited. It will not be long, however, before the calculator becomes the hand-held mini, greatly increasing its personal capability, since the scientist can carry the mini with him.

What about the programming requirement? It will be as severe as for the standard mini. The manufacturers of programmable calculators in many instances provide special canned programs, and when the mini on a chip becomes the standard, it will be necessary to make more canned programs available. I should like to suggest that these will be analogous to eight-track cartridge or cassette versions of recordings and that they will be sold at the corner drugstores that also carry the minis. There will no doubt be a great proliferation of competitive routines to do rather standard jobs. With the unusual job, the scientist will have the option of doing it himself or buying the services of a professional programmer. In the long run, it would be most desirable for the scientist to describe his job to the symbolic computer through his terminal and have the network system write the program for him, reproducing it in the medium he desires for implementing it in his mini.

Such a capability in the network does raise the question of the true need for the personalized mini. Indeed, the power to do a great deal more resides in the network, provided one is close to a terminal. Perhaps the personal mini will find its greatest use in the field, but at other times it may plug into a power source and telephone jack and become the terminal itself. Of course, one can conceive of a power pack supplying the needed power in the field and using radio or high-frequency communications from the mini terminal into a central computer system that may be available on call. In such a case output, if needed, could become a problem.

Output is currently a problem anyway, and the scientist does need to have improved methods for looking at his data or the results of calculations. Today most computer-generated output appears on paper, though there is a trend toward producing it on film through the use of computer output microfilm (COM) units. Film output requires developing, and after processing is complete it must be looked at through special lenses or viewers. Some more sophisticated users wishing to see their results multidimensionally use movie film or show animated pictorial representations of their data on high-precision cathode-ray tubes (CRT). The human eye is a great interpreter and integrator of data and is not easily supplanted by hardware. How then do we simplify output to make it presentable in the right form for the scientific user?

First of all, he must learn to ask the proper questions. The system must be designed to carry out any and all correlations, comparisons, and analyses necessary to provide him with minimum word responses. At the extremes, he should get yes or no responses that are readily displayed on a small hand-held keyboard device.

Second, we must develop our TV-supported computer output recording. The computer network system should be able to provide virtually any output that we currently place on CRT, paper, or movie film on TV tape. This information so recorded could then be transmitted to the local site for rerecording on a standard portable TV system for instant replay. No great advance is needed to accomplish such feats, although the hardware at the central facility will have to be well developed. We may wish to use laser recording in the first instance; but the problem in getting the data transmitted has already been solved, except for volume and cost. Although the computer profession is backward in providing multidimensional sight and sound as output, the techniques do exist and with time will be realized. Only recently, primarily because of the pressure of need, has the Federal Aviation Administration provided output warning signals in the form of flashing lights on the output CRT for alerting the controller that planes are approaching too closely to each other. Why they have not yet achieved color and sound signals that vary in intensity with danger is not clear. The techniques are there, the need is now—but results should appear over the next decade or two.

What are the inhibiting factors that may prevent us from achieving the computing world needed by the scientist? It does seem as if the technology is moving at the rate appropriate to providing hardware components for his system. But costs are still relatively high, and it is not clear that they will drop sufficiently to provide the tremendous array of storage and communications power needed. The greatest need, however, is for people power. It is a tremendous task to gather together into appropriate form the scientific data base for a working library. Even if a start were to be made immediately and we knew how to do it, it is doubtful that the task could be completed by the turn of the century.

Third, we must build more intelligence into our systems. One or two decades of effort in symbolic manipulation have not carried us very far. We can solve only rather trivial problems with the computer after all these years of effort. We must begin a much more extensive effort to build the capability that we have talked about since the advent of the digital computer. It can extend man's intellect, but to do so it must be programmed to interact with him in such a way that when he asks a trivial question it responds almost immediately, carrying on the dialogue. It must be able to carry out most mathematical processes using the standard, well-known techniques; it must be able to try new techniques and know when they fail and why they fail; and it must be capable of interacting with suggestions made by the scientist on the spur of the moment.

Today, we provide software packages to carry out mathematical or statistical tasks or the like. The individual user has to be well acquainted with the package to make effective use of it. The software is just sophisticated enough that the user can learn how to do what he wishes to do; at the same time, it permits the program to be extended to do something unusual. In other words, software systems themselves are in a very primitive state. Software engineering education (if that is what we need) is only now taking shape. Somehow I believe we need software science as well as software engineering; that is, development of new techniques of communication that will allow and encourage the symbiotic relationship between the person with the problem and the machine that can provide all the answers. Programmers are not well trained. The bases needed for good software development are not understood; the competitive spirit that tries to make trivial improvements in insignificant things inhibits creative thinking in providing better software design. We are simply still fumbling the ball in computer science education; we live in the past rather than the present, and we don't foresee the future. Unless something drastic is done now, we will not be there by the beginning of the next century.

Another problem area consists of the very large problem. Even if we do succeed in developing techniques for solving good-sized mathematical problems and providing appropriate software to conduct a reasonable user-computer relationship, there are still problems we encounter today and will continue to encounter that are intractable because of their immense size. First, we do not have the hardware to consider tackling these jobs; second, we don't know enough about the evolving architectures to decide which directions are most suitable; third, we do not have the proper formulations of the problems; fourth, we don't know the proper geometry or space in which to fit the problem; and finally, without all these there is little incentive to carry out any portion of the effort. We must find ways to support various architectural designs, support schools of study for particular applications of each, and generally move ahead in our attempts to solve larger and larger problems. To some extent such activities have been carried on under the auspices of agencies such as DOE and NOAA; but shrinking budgets, increasing competition for research dollars, the difficulties of the task, and the long-range nature of the effort tend to reduce interest in supporting the large computer and the accompanying mathematical formulations and software techniques. Without a major effort in very large scale problem solving using parallel/vector techniques, multiprocessing, or related schemes, the scientific world will simply delay the development of the understanding of such things as local meteorological phenomena, the impacts of climate control, and probably also the development of alternate sources of energy. Fortunately, it is possible to say that we are on the threshold of carrying out such tasks. What we need now is greater support to do those things we believe we must.

*III
Socioeconomic
Effects and
Expectations*

9
The Social Framework of the Information Society

Daniel Bell

The endless cycle of idea and action,
Endless invention, endless experiment,
Brings knowledge of motion, but not of stillness. . . .
Where is the Life we have lost in living?
Where is the wisdom we have lost in knowledge?
Where is the knowledge we have lost in information?
T. S. Eliot; Choruses from "The Rock"

INFORMATION AND TELECOMMUNICATIONS IN THE POSTINDUSTRIAL SOCIETY

In the coming century, the emergence of a new social framework based on telecommunications may be decisive for the way in which economic and social exchanges are conducted, the way knowledge is created and retrieved, and the character of the occupations and work in which men engage. This revolution in the organization and processing of information and knowledge, in which the computer plays a central role, has as its context the development of what I have called the postindustrial society.[1] Three dimensions of the postindustrial society are relevant to the discussion of telecommunications:

a. The change from a goods-producing to a service society
b. The centrality of the codification of theoretical knowledge for innovation in technology
c. The creation of a new "intellectual technology" as a key tool of systems analysis and decision theory

The change from a goods-producing to a service society can be indicated briefly. In the United States in 1970, sixty-five out of every 100

Daniel Bell is professor of sociology at Harvard University. He is widely known for his views on the postindustrial society—a term that he coined. In his numerous books and articles he has examined the interplay between technology and society and the way in which the infrastructures of transportation, energy, and communication tie societies together.

persons in the labor force were engaged in services, about 30 percent in the production of goods and construction and under 5 percent in agriculture. The word *services* of course covers a large multitude of activities. In preindustrial societies a sizable proportion of the labor force is engaged in household or domestic service. (In England until the 1870s the single largest occupational class was servants.) In an industrial society services are auxiliary to the production of goods, such as transportation (rail and truck), utilities (power and light), banking, and factoring. Postindustrial services are of a different kind. They are human services and professional services. The human services are teaching, health, and the large array of social services; professional services are those of systems analysis and design and the programming and processing of information. In the last two decades, the net new growth in employment has been entirely in the area of postindustrial services, and while the rate of growth has slowed (particularly because of the financial costs of education and the cutbacks in social services in urban communities), the general trend continues.

The axial principle of the postindustrial society, however, is the centrality of theoretical knowledge and its new role, when codified, as the director of social change. Every society has functioned on the basis of knowledge, but only in the last half century have we seen a fusion of science and engineering that has begun to transform the character of technology itself. As Cyril Stanley Smith, the distinguished metallurgist, has observed, "In only a small part of history has industry been helped by science. The development of a suitable science began when chemists put into rational order facts that had been discovered long before by people who enjoyed empirical diverse experiment."[2]

The industries that still dominate society—steel, auto, electricity, telephone, aviation—are all "nineteenth-century" industries (though steel began in the eighteenth century with the coking process of Abraham Darby, and aviation in the twentieth with the Wright Brothers) in that they were created by "talented tinkerers" who worked independently of or were ignorant of contemporary science. Alexander Graham Bell, who invented the telephone about one hundred years ago (though the actual fact is in some dispute), was an elocution teacher who was looking for some means to amplify sound in order to help the deaf. Bessemer, who created the open-hearth process (to win a prize offered by Napoleon III for a better means of casting cannon) did not know the scientific work of Henry Clifton Sorby on metallurgical processes. And Thomas Alva Edison, who was probably the most prolific and talented of these tinkerers (he invented, among other things, the electric light bulb, the phonograph, and the motion picture), was a mathematical illiterate who knew little and cared less about the theoretical equations of Clerk-Maxwell on electromagnetic properties.

Nineteenth-century inventing was trial-and-error empiricism, often guided by brilliant intuitions. But the nature of advanced technology is its intimate relation with science, where the primary interest is not in the product itself but in the diverse properties of materials together with the underlying principles of order that allow for combination, substitution, or transmutation. According to Cyril Smith, "All materials came to be seen in competition, with the emphasis only on the properties that were needed. Thereafter every new development in advanced technology—radar, nuclear reactors, jet aircraft, computers and satellite communications to name a few—has served to break the earlier close association of materials research with a single type of manufacture, and the modern materials engineer has emerged."

The nature of this change, in technology and in science, has been to enlarge the "field of relation" and the range of theory so as to permit a systematic synergism in the discovery and extension of new products and theories. A science, at bottom, is a set of axioms linked topologically to form a unified scheme. But as Bronowski has observed, "A new theory changes the system of axioms and sets up new connections at the joints which changes the topology. And when two sciences are linked to form one (electricity and magnetism, for instance, or evolution with genetics), the new network is richer in its articulation than the sum of its two parts."[3]

While modern science, like almost all human activities, has moved toward a greater degree of specialization in its pursuit of more detailed knowledge, the more important and crucial outcome of its association with technology is the integration of diverse fields or observations into single conceptual and theoretical frameworks offering much greater explanatory power. Norbert Wiener, in his autobiographical *I Am a Mathematician,* points out that his first mathematical papers were on Brownian motion and that at the same time electrical engineering work was being done on the so-called shot effects, or the movement of electric current through a wire. The two topics were unrelated; yet twenty years later the situation had changed dramatically.

In 1920 very little electrical apparatus was loaded to the point at which the shot effect became critical. However the later development—first of broadcasting and then of radar and television—brought the shot effect to the point where it became the immediate concern of every communications engineer. The shot effect was not only similar in origin to the Brownian movement, for it was a result of the discreteness of the universe, but had essentially the same mathematical theory. Thus, my work on the Brownian motion became some twenty years later a vital tool for the electrical engineer.[4]

Wiener's theory of cybernetics joins a variety of fields in the common framework of statistical information theory. "The development of ideas on the structure of synthetic polymers," Cyril Smith writes, "eventually came to bridge the gap between the nineteenth century chemist's molecule and the early twentieth-century crystal, so paving the way for the unified structural view of all materials which we see taking shape today."[5] The development of solid-state physics, which is the foundation of the electronic revolution, arose out of the work of metallurgists and physicists on the structure of conductor devices.

The methodological promise of the second half of the twentieth century is the management of organized complexity: the complexity of theories with a large number of variables and the complexity of large organizations and systems which involve the coordination of hundreds of thousands and even millions of persons. Since 1940 there has been a remarkable efflorescence of new fields and methods whose concern is with the problems of organized complexity: information theory, cybernetics, decision theory, game theory, utility theory, stochastic processes. From these have come specific techniques such as linear programming, statistical decision theory, Markov chain applications, Monte Carlo randomizing, and minimax strategies, which allow for sampling from large numbers, alterna-

Table 9.1
The Postindustrial Society: A Comparative Schema

	Preindustrial
Mode of Production	Extractive
Economic sector	**Primary** Agriculture Mining Fishing Timber Oil and gas
Transforming resource	**Natural power** Wind, water, draft animal, human muscle
Strategic resource	Raw materials
Technology	Craft
Skill base	Artisan, manual worker, farmer
Methodology	Commonsense, trial and error; experience
Time perspective	Orientation to the past
Design	Game against nature
Axial principle	Traditionalism

tive optimal outcomes of different choices, or definitions of rational action under conditions of uncertainty.

Since technology is the instrumental mode of rational action, I have called this new development "intellectual technology," for these methods seek to substitute an algorithm (i.e., decision rules) for intuitive judgments. These algorithms may be embodied in an automatic machine or a computer program, or a set of instructions based on some statistical or mathematical formula, and represent a "formalization" of judgments and their routine application to many varied situations. To the extent that intellectual technology is becoming predominant in the management of organizations and enterprises, one can say that it is as central a feature of postindustrial society as machine technology is in industrial society.

A Knowledge Theory of Value

If one compares the formal properties of postindustrial society with those of industrial and preindustrial society (see table 9.1), the crucial variables of the postindustrial society are information and knowledge.

Industrial	Postindustrial	
Fabrication	Processing; Recycling	
Secondary	Services	
Goods-producing		
Manufacturing	**Tertiary**	**Quarternary**
Durables	Transportation	Trade
Nondurables	Utilities	Finance
Heavy construction		Insurance
	Quinary	Real estate
	Health, education	
	Research, government,	
	Recreation	
Created energy	**Information**	
Electricity—oil, gas, coal, nuclear power	Computer and data-transmission systems	
Financial capital	Knowledge	
Machine technology	Intellectual technology	
Engineer, semiskilled worker	Scientist, technical and professional occupations	
Empiricism, experimentation	Abstract theory, models, simulations, decision theory, systems analysis	
Ad hoc adaptiveness, experimentation	Future orientation: forecasting and planning	
Game against fabricated future	Game between persons	
Economic growth	Codification of theoretical knowledge	

By information I mean data processing in the broadest sense; the storage, retrieval, and processing of data becomes the essential resource for all economic and social exchanges. These include:

a. Data processing of records: payrolls, government benefits (e.g., Social Security), bank clearances, credit clearances, and the like

b. Data processing for scheduling: airline reservations, production scheduling, inventory analysis, product-mix information, and the like

c. Data bases: characteristics of populations as shown by census data, market research, opinion surveys, election data, and the like

By knowledge, I mean an organized set of statements of fact or ideas, presenting a reasoned judgment or an experimental result, which is transmitted to others through some communication medium in some systematic form. Thus, I distinguish knowledge from news or entertainment. Knowledge consists of new judgments (textbook, teaching, and library and archive materials).

In the "production of knowledge," what is produced is an intellectual property, attached to a name or a group of names and certified by copyright or some other form of social recognition (like publication). This knowledge is paid for—in the time spent in writing and research, in the monetary compensation by the communications and educational media. The response of the market, along with administrative and political decisions of superiors or peers, judge the worth of the result and any further claim on social resources that might be made in its behalf. In this sense, knowledge is part of social overhead. More than that, when knowledge becomes involved in some systematic form in the applied transformation of resources (through invention or social design), then one can say that knowledge, not labor, is the source of value.

Economists, in their formal schemes to explain production and exchange, use as key variables "land, labor and capital," though institutionally minded economists such as Werner Sombart and Joseph Schumpeter added the notion of an acquisitive spirit or entrepreneurial initiative. The analytical mode used by economists, the "production function," sets forth the economic mix only as capital and labor—a system that lends itself easily to a labor theory of value, with surplus labor value as congealed capital, but neglects almost entirely the role of knowledge or of organizational innovation and management. Yet with the shortening of labor time and the diminution of the production worker (who in Marxist theory is the source of value, since most services are classified as nonproductive labor), it becomes clear that knowledge and its applications replace labor as the source of "added value" in the national product. In that sense, just as capital and labor have been the central variables of industrial society, so information and knowledge are the crucial variables of postindustrial society.

INTELLECTUAL FOUNDATIONS OF THE REVOLUTION IN COMMUNICATIONS

For Goethe, the basis of the human community was communication. Decades before other persons spoke of such projects, he envisaged a Panama Canal, a Suez Canal, and a canal between the Rhine and the Danube as the means by which the human community might become more closely intertwined. But it was the Canadian economic historian Harold Innis, more than any other person, who saw changes in the modes of communication, rather than production and property relations, as the key to transitions from one stage of society to another.

Western civilization has been profoundly influenced by communication . . . [and can be] divided into the following periods in relation to media of communication: clay, the stylus and cuneiform script from the beginnings of civilization in Mesopotamia; papyrus, the brush and hieroglyphics and hieratic to the Graeco-Roman period, and the reed pen and the alphabet to the retreat of the Empire from the west; parchment and pen to the tenth century of the dark ages; and overlapping with paper, the latter becoming more important with the invention of printing; paper and the brush in China, and paper and the pen in Europe before the invention of printing or the Renaissance; paper and the printing press under handicraft methods to the beginning of the nineteenth century, or from the Reformation to the French Revolution; paper produced by machinery and the application of power to the printing press since the beginning of the nineteenth century to paper manufactured from wood in the second half of the century; celluloid in the growth of the cinema; and finally the radio in the second quarter of the present century. In each period I have attempted to trace the implications of the media of communication for the character of knowledge and to suggest that a monopoly or an oligopoly of knowledge is built up to the point that equilibrium is disturbed.[6]

Innis was a technological determinist. He thought that the technology of communication was basic to all other technology, for if tool technology was an extension of man's physical powers, communication technology, as the extension of perception and knowledge, was the enlargement of consciousness. He argued not only that each stage of Western civilization was dominated by a particular medium of communication but that the rise of a new mode was invariably followed by cultural disturbances.[7]

One can say that the new media of communication today are television or the computer, or the variant modes of storage, retrieval, and transmission that will arise through the "fusing" of technologies. But the core of the present communications revolution is not a specific technology but the set of concepts represented by the term *information theory*.

The Statistics of Language

Information theory arose from the work of Claude Shannon on switching circuits to increase "channel capacity," the design for which he derived from the algebra of logic. The algebra of logic is an algebra of choice and deals with the range of choices in a determinate sequence of alternative possibilities in the routing of a message. The parlor game of "Twenty Questions" is often taken as a conventional illustration of how one narrows a range of possibilities by asking a series of yes or no questions. As Shannon points out in the article on information theory that he wrote for the *Encyclopaedia Britannica,* "The writing of English sentences can be thought of as a process of choice: choosing a first word from possible first words with various probabilities; then a second with probabilities depending on the first; etc. This kind of statistical process is called a stochastic process, and information sources are thought of, in information theory, as stochastic processes."

The information rate of written English can be translated into bits (*binary digits* 1 and 0), so that if each letter occurred with equal frequency, there would be 4.76 bits per letter. But since the frequencies are unequal (*E* is common, *Z, Q,* and *X* are not), the actual rate is one bit per letter. Technically, English is said to be 80 percent "redundant," a fact that one can immediately ascertain by "deciphering" a sentence from which various vowels or consonants have been deleted. By knowing the statistical structure of a language, one can derive a general formula that determines the rate at which information can be produced statistically and create huge savings in transmission time. But though transmission was the impetus to the formulation of information theory, the heart of the concept is the idea of coding. Messages have to go through "channels"; inevitably, they are distorted by "noise" and other forms of "resistance" that arise from the physical properties of the channel. What Shannon found was that it is possible to encode a message that can be accurately transmitted even if the channel of communication is faulty, so long as there is enough capacity in that channel.

Shannon's mathematical theory had immediate application to industry. The theoretical and statistical underpinnings seemed to confirm the more general theory of Wiener's *Cybernetics,* a work that had been commissioned by an obscure publisher in France after the war and became an immediate best-seller on its publication by Wiley in 1948. What Shannon's and Wiener's work seemed to promise was the move toward some general unified theory of physics and human behavior (at least in physiology, psychology, and linguistics) through the concept of information. As Shannon himself wrote in his *Britannica* essay,

A basic idea in communication theory is that information can be treated very much like a physical quantity such as mass or energy. . . .
The formula for the amount of information is identical in form with equations representing entropy in statistical mechanics, and suggests that there may be deep-lying connections between thermodynamics and in-

formation theory. Some scientists believe that a proper statement of the second law of thermodynamics requires a term relating to information. These connections with physics, however, do not have to be considered in the engineering and other applications of information theory.[8]

But this is a confusion of realms—compounded by the facile use of the word *entropy* to equate the degree of disorder or noise (i.e., the loss of accuracy) in communication with the loss of heat or energy in transformational activities in physics. As Wiener put it in his *Cybernetics,* resisting the easy comparisons of living with mechanical organisms, "Information is information, not matter or energy. No materialism which does not admit this can survive at the present day."[9]

However true it may be as a statistical concept that information is a quantity, in its broadest sense—to distinguish between information and fabrication—information is a pattern or design that rearranges data for instrumental purposes, while knowledge is the set of reasoned judgments that evaluates the adequacy of the pattern for the purposes for which the information is designed. Information is thus pattern recognition, subject to reorganization by the knower, in accordance with specified purposes. What is common to this and to all intellectual enterprises is the concept of relevant structure. This concept is what underlies the shift, in the works of Cyril Stanley Smith, from "matter to materials," from the classificatory and even combinational arrangements of elementary properties of matter that began with the pre-Socratics to our present-day understanding of the structural relations of the properties of materials.

These structural relations—in science, as in the economy—fall into two separate domains. The first is the transformation of matter and energy, from one material form into another. The second is the transformation of information from one pattern into another. As Anthony Oettinger puts it in an aphorism, "Without matter there is nothing; without energy matter is inert; and without information, matter and energy are disorganized, hence useless."

The Use of Models

Technological revolutions, even if intellectual in their foundations, become symbolized if not embodied in some tangible "thing," and in the postindustrial society that "thing" is the computer. If, as Paul Valery said, electricity was the agent that transformed the second half of the nineteenth century, in a similar vein the computer has been the "analytical engine" that has transformed the second half of the twentieth century. What electricity did—as the source of light, power, and communication—was to create the "mass society"; that is, to extend the range of social ties and the interaction between persons and so magnify what Durkheim called the social density of society. In that respect, the computer is a tool for managing the mass society, since it is the mechanism that orders and processes the transactions whose huge number has been mounting almost exponentially because of the increase in social interactions.

The major sociopolitical question facing the mass society is whether we can manage the economy effectively enough to achieve our social goals. The development of computers has allowed us to construct detailed models of the economy. Wassily Leontieff recently described the extraordinary expansion of the input-output system:

The first input-output tables describing the flow of goods and services between the different sectors of the American economy in census years 1919 through 1929 were published in 1936. They were based on a rather gross segregation of all economic activities in 44 sectors. Because of the lack of computing facilities, these had to be further grouped into only 10 sectors, for the purposes of actual analytic calculations.

The data base, the computing facilities, and the analytical techniques have advanced much further than could have been anticipated forty years ago. National input-output tables containing up to 700 distinct sectors are being compiled on a current basis, as are tables for individual, regional, state and metropolitan areas. Private enterprise has now entered the input-output business. For a fee one can now purchase a single row of a table showing the deliveries of a particular product, say, coated laminated fabrics or farming machine tools, not only to different industries but to individual plants within each industry segregated by zip code areas.[10]

Though it is clear that economists are able to model the economy and do computer simulations of alternative policies to test their consequences, it is much less clear whether such models allow us to manage the economy. The critical point is that the crucial decisions for any society are the political ones, and these are not derivative from economic factors.

Can one model a society? One immediate problem is that we do not have any persuasive theories of how a society hangs together, though paradoxically, because of our understanding of technology, we have a better idea of how societies change. One can only model a closed or finite system; the econometric models operate within a closed system. Yet society is increasingly open and indeterminate, and as men become more conscious of goals there is greater debate about decisions. Decisions on social policy become more and more a matter within the purview of the political system rather than of aggregate market decisions, and this, too, weakens our ability to model a society.

Beyond this there may be reasons intrinsic to the structure of "large numbers" that could prevent the computer from becoming the instrument for the modeling and prediction of any complex system. John von Neumann, one of the pioneers in the development of the theory of electronic computing, thought that the prediction of weather would be possible once computers became sophisticated enough to handle all the numerous interacting variables in the atmosphere. Yet as Tjalling Koopmans and others have pointed out, beyond a certain threshold introducing added complexity results in answers that are less and less reliable. Thus, the effort to optimize an objective by seeking for complete information may be self-defeating. The social world is not a Laplacean universe where one can plot, from the initial values, the determinate rates of change of other phenomena. If so many parts of the physical world now require us to deal with a calculus of possibility rather than determined regularities, this is even more true in a social world where men are less and less willing passively to accept existing arrangements but instead work actively to remake them. By letting us know the risks and probabilities, the computer has become a powerful tool for exploring the permutations and combinations of different choices and for calculating their consequences, the odds of success or failure. The computer does this by using a binary code that with high speed can answer a question with a yes or a no. What it cannot do, obviously, is to decide like a roulette wheel whether to stop on the yes or on the no.

The Economics of Information

Information is central to all economic transactions—indeed, perfect information is the indispensable condition for perfect competition in general equilibrium theory. Yet we have no economic theory of information, and the character of information, as distinct from the character of goods, poses some novel problems for economic theorists.

In a price and market economy, the condition for efficiency, or optimal use of resources, is complete information among buyers and sellers, so that one can obtain the "best" price for one's goods or services. But with the widening of markets and the reduction of distances by transportation and communication—which also enlarges the sphere of competition—efficiency increasingly demands not only a knowledge of contemporary alternatives but of the likely future ones as well, since political decisions or new technologies may radically alter prices. A political embargo may cut off the supplies of a resource. A tax cut or a tax rise will affect the level of spending. New technologies may sharply cut the price of a product (witness the extraordinary changes in two years in the price of small electronic calculators), leaving firms with large inventories or committed to older production techniques at a great disadvantage.

Information, as Kenneth Arrow puts it, reduces uncertainty.[11] The random-walk theory that one cannot "beat the stock market" is based on the assumption that stock prices reflect new information about companies so quickly that investors have little chance to earn better-than-average returns on their money. Therefore the wiser strategy is to place one's money in an index fund that reflects the average prices of the market as a whole. The job search in the labor market is enhanced by access to a wider pool of information. Accurate crop reporting controls the vagaries of the futures market in commodities. One can multiply the illustrations indefinitely.

But information is not a commodity, at least not in the way the term is used in neoclassical economics or understood in industrial society. Industrial commodities are produced in discrete, identifiable units, exchanged and sold, consumed and used up, like a loaf of bread or an automobile. One buys the product from a seller and takes physical possession of it; the exchange is governed by legal rules of contract. In the manufacture of industrial goods, one can set up a "production function" (i.e., the relative proportions of capital and labor to be employed) and determine the appropriate mix relative to the costs of each factor.

Information, or knowledge, even when it is sold, remains with the producer. It is a "collective good" in that once it has been created, it is by its nature available to all.[12] In fact, the character of science itself, as a cooperative venture of knowledge, depends on the open and complete transmission of all new experiments and discoveries to others in the field. Multiple discoveries of the same theory or experimental result or technique, which Robert Merton argues is a more dominant pattern in science than the image of the lonely genius or scholar, are one result of this openness and the rapid spread of knowledge.[13]

If knowledge is a collective good there is little incentive for any individual enterprise to pay for the search for such knowledge, unless it can obtain a proprietary advantage, such as a patent or a copyright. But increasingly, patents no longer guarantee exclusiveness, and many firms lose out in spending money on research only to find that a competitor (particularly one overseas) can quickly modify the product and circumvent the patent; similarly, the question of copyright becomes increasingly difficult to police when individuals or libraries can Xerox whatever pages they need from technical journals or books or when individuals and schools can tape music off the air or record a television performance on video discs. But more generally, the results of investing in information (i.e., doing research), are themselves uncertain. Because firms are averse to risk, they tend to undervalue such investments from the social point of view, and this leads to underinvestment in private research and development.

If there is less and less incentive for individual persons or private enterprises to produce knowledge without particular gain, then the need and effort falls increasingly on some social unit, be it university or government, to underwrite the costs. And since there is no ready market test (how does one estimate the value of basic research?), it is a challenge for economic theory to design a socially optimal policy of investment in knowledge (including how much money should be spent for basic research; what allocations should be made for education, and for what fields; in what areas of health do we obtain the "better returns"; and so on) and to determine how to "price" information and knowledge to users.[14]

The Merging of Technologies

Through the nineteenth and up to the midtwentieth century, communication could be divided roughly into two distinct realms. One was mail, newspapers, magazines, and books, printed on paper and delivered by physical transport or stored in libraries. The other was telegraph, telephone, radio, and television, coded message image or voice sent by radio signals or through cables from person to person. Technology, which once made for separate industries, is now erasing these distinctions, so that a variety of new alternatives are now available to information users, posing, for that very reason, a major set of policy decisions for the lawmakers of the country.

Inevitably, large vested interests are involved. Just as the substitution of oil for coal and energy and the competition of truck, pipeline, and railroad in transportation created vast economic dislocations in corporate power, occupational structures, trade unions, geographical concentrations, and the like, so the huge changes taking place in communications technology will affect the major industries that are involved in the communications arena.

Broadly, there are five major problem areas:

1. The meshing of the telephone and computer systems, of telecommunications and teleprocessing, into a single mode. A corollary problem is whether transmission will be primarily over telephone-controlled wires or whether there will be independent data-transmission systems. Equally, there is the question of the relative use of microwave relay, satellite transmission, and coaxial cables as transmission systems.

2. The substitution of electronic media for paper processing. This includes electronic banking to eliminate the use of checks; the electronic delivery of mail; the delivery of newspapers or magazines by facsimile rather than by physical transport; and the long-distance copying of documents.

3. The expansion of television through cable systems, to allow for multiple channels and specialized services, and the linkage to home terminals for direct response to the consumer or home from local or central stations. A corollary is the substitution of telecommunication for transportation through videophone, closed-circuit television, and the like.

4. The reorganization of information storage and retrieval systems based

on the computer to allow for interactive network communication in team research and direct retrieval from data banks to library or home terminals. 5. The expansion of the education system through computer-aided instruction, the use of satellite communications systems in rural areas, especially in the underdeveloped countries, and the use of video discs both for entertainment and instruction in the home.[15]

Technologically, telecommunications and teleprocessing are merging in a mode that Anthony Oettinger has called "compunications" (see fig. 9.1). As computers come increasingly to be used as switching devices in communications networks and electronic communications facilities become intrinsic elements in computer data-processing services, the distinction between processing and communication becomes indistinguishable. The major questions are legal and economic. Should the industry be regulated or competitive? Should it be dominated, in effect, by AT&T or by IBM?*

The entry of specialized carriers into the business field, undercutting AT&T prices, threatens its consumer rate structure as well, and would create large political upheavals. Yet the "computer" proponents have argued that technological innovation in the telephone field has been stodgy, whereas the energetic and bustling computer field has demonstrated its ability to innovate rapidly and reduce costs and prices, so that competition in transmission, in the end, would serve the country as a whole.

The questions I have been raising about the fusion of communications technologies—the rise of compunications—are not only technological and economic but, most important, political. Information is power. Control over communications services is a source of power. Access to communication is a condition of freedom. There are legal questions that derive directly from this. The electronic media, such as television, are regulated, with explicit rules about "fairness" in the presentation of views, access to reply to editorials, and the like. But ultimately the power is governmental. Decisions about the station's future lie with the Federal Communications Commission. The telephone industry is regulated on its rates and conditions of service. The computer industry is unregulated and operates in an open market. The print media are unregulated, and their rights on free speech are zealously guarded by the First Amendment and the courts.

---

* In 1976, AT&T introduced a bill in Congress to allow it to buy out its microwave competitors, and it wants Congress to require anyone plugging specialized services into its lines to buy a connecting device from the phone company. IBM has entered into a direct challenge to AT&T by setting up The Satellite Business Systems pany jointly with Aetna Insurance and Comsat General to operate a satellite communications service that would transmit the full range of "compunications" by 1981.

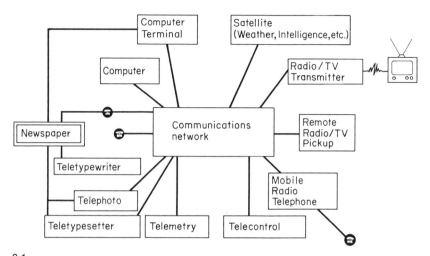

9.1
The Changing Telecommunications Network. As of 1974, the 144 million plain old telephones still predominated, but many other devices are now attached to a network that has become an infrastructure basic to most social functions, including many that reach directly into the home. As computers and computer terminals have become increasingly pervasive over the last two decades, the network has developed toward an integrated computer communications or "compunications" network. From Paul J. Berman and Anthony G. Oettinger, *The Medium and the Telephone: The Politics of Information Resources,* Working Paper 75–8, December 15, 1975, Harvard Program on Information Technologies and Public Policy, Cambridge, Mass.

Libraries have largely been private or locally controlled; now great data banks are being assembled by government agencies and by private corporations. Are they to be under government supervision or unregulated? All of these are major questions for the future of the free society and bear on the problem of a national information policy.

THE QUANTITATIVE DIMENSIONS OF THE INFORMATION SOCIETY

In 1940, Colin Clark, the Australian economist, wrote his path-breaking *Conditions of Economic Progress,* in which he divided economic activity into three sectors, primary (principally extractive), secondary (primarily manufacturing), and tertiary (services). Any economy is a mixture of all three sectors, but their relative weights are a function of the degree of productivity (output per capita) in each sector. Economic progress is defined as the rate of transfer of labor from one sector to another, as a function of differential productivity. As national incomes rise, the expansion of the manufacturing sector is followed by a greater demand for services and a further corresponding shift in the slope of employment. In this fashion, Clark was able to chart the rate of change from a preindustrial into an industrial society and then into a service society.

The difficulty remains the definition of services. In classical economics, beginning with Adam Smith, services were thought of as unproductive labor. Marx, accepting that distinction, had based one of his theories on the crisis of capitalism, that of the falling rate of profit, on the proposition that as a higher proportion of output shifted from "variable capital" (productive labor) to "constant capital" (machinery, for example), the rate of profit would fall since the base on which surplus value was produced would be shrinking (unless overcome by more intensive exploitation, such as lengthening the working day or speeding up the pace of work). As the notion that services were unproductive became increasingly dubious, economists were faced with a double problem of redefinition: first, determining which services were unproductive (e.g., domestic servants) and which were productive (e.g., education, by increasing the skill of labor, or medicine, by making persons healthier or prolonging working life); second, developing a more adequate set of distinctions within the services category. Some writers sought to restrict the tertiary sector to auxiliary blue-collar work, such as transportation, utilities, repair (e.g., auto mechanics), and personal services (laundry, barbers, and so on), and to define a *quaternary* sector made up essentially of the white-collar industries, such as banking, insurance, and real estate, and a *quinary* sector, made up of knowledge activities like scientific and technical research, education, and medicine. While such distinctions are useful for indicating the complexity of occupational distributions, with them one loses the thrust implicit in the original Colin Clark scheme, with its emphasis on differential productivity as the mechanism for the transition from one type of society to another.

Without pretending to be exhaustive, I have adopted a scheme for the postindustrial society of classifying economic sectors as extractive, fabrication, and information activities. The underlying sociological rationale is that it seeks to look at the character of work as a shaper of the character of individuals. The scheme is based on the distinction that some societies are primarily engaged in games against nature, others in games against fabricated nature (things), and others in games between persons. It also derives from the propositions I have put forward regarding the centrality of knowledge in the postindustrial society, the primacy of a knowledge theory of value as against a labor theory of value, and the growth of information processing within the traditional sectors, such as agriculture, manufacture, and services, which is beginning to transform the character of those sectors as well.

The Measurement of Knowledge

In 1958, Fritz Machlup, then at Princeton University, made the first efforts to measure the production and distribution of knowledge. The definition of knowledge was somewhat unsatisfactory, for Machlup rejected "an objective interpretation according to *what* is known," as against a subjective interpretation derived from what a knower designates as being known.[16] And Machlup worked from the standard national accounts, although in important details he varied from standard usages.[17]

Still, Machlup's painstaking work was crucial. In his accounting scheme, he grouped thirty industries into five major classes of knowledge production, processing, and distribution: (1) education, (2) research and development, (3) media of communication, (4) information machines, and (5) information services. The categories were broad. Education, for example, included education in the home, job, and church as well as in school. Communications media included all commercial printing, stationery, and office supplies. Information machines included musical instruments, signaling devices, and typewriters. Information services included monies spent for securities brokers, real-estate agents, and the like.

Machlup estimated that $136,436 million was spent for knowledge, or 29 percent of gross national product (GNP),[18] and that 31 percent of the labor force was engaged in that sector. Of equal importance, he estimated that between 1947 and 1958, the knowledge industries expanded at a compound growth rate of 10.6 percent a year, which was double that of the GNP itself during the same period. In 1963, Gilbert Burck, an editor of *Fortune,* replicated Machlup's estimates and calculated that in that year knowledge produced a value added of $159 billion, or 33 percent of the GNP.[19] Five years later, Professor Jacob Marschak, one of the most eminent economists in the United States, in computations made in 1968, said that the knowledge industries would approach 40 percent of the GNP in the 1970s.[20]

The last decade has in fact seen enormous growth in the "information economy," which includes various fields. In education, while the rate of growth of college education has slowed down, there has been a continuing increase in adult education which, in fact, has maintained its rise. In health, the expansion of health services continues, particularly with the multiplication of federal legislation. Information and data processing continue to rise, particularly as the volume of transactions and record keeping increases. Telecommunications finds its major area of growth in international communications, particularly with the launching of new satellites. Television is on the threshold of a number of major changes with the growth of both cable television and video discs.

Still, if one wanted to measure the actual economic magnitudes of the information economy, the difficulty is that there is no comprehensive conceptual scheme that can divide the sector logically into neatly distinct units, making it possible to measure the trends in each unit over time. A logical set of categories might consist of the following: knowledge (which would include situses such as education, research and development, libraries, and occupations that apply knowledge, such as lawyers, doctors, and accountants); entertainment (which would include motion pictures, television, the music industry); economic transactions and records (banking, insurance, brokerage); and infrastructure services (telecommunications, computers and programs, and so on).

Two somewhat different approaches have been adopted. Anthony Oettinger and his colleagues have taken the "information industries" from the Standard Industrial Classification used by the U.S. Census and listed their gross revenues in order to provide some crude baselines to measure changes. The difficulty here is that merging technologies and double counting defeat such efforts. The second approach, a more difficult and pioneering effort, is that of Marc Porat, which is to use the National Income Accounts to define a primary sector, the direct sale of information services (like education, banking, advertising) to consumers, and then to define a secondary sector—the planning, programming, and information activities of private and public bureaucracies in enterprises and government—and impute the value added by such activities to the national product and national income.

The Information Economy

Marc Porat has broken down the National Income Accounts for 1967 in order to see what portions may be attributable, directly and indirectly, to information activities. In doing this, he has used three measures to compute gross national product. One is "final demand" (which eliminates the intermediate transactions that would add up to double counting), the second is "value added," which is the actual value added by a specific industry or component of an industry to the product, and the third is the income or compensation received by those who create these goods and services. Theoretically, the totals of all three figures should be equal; in fact, for statistical reasons, in part owing to different methods of collection, the figures do not always dovetail exactly. But the virtue of using all three is that one can make different analytical distinctions. For my purposes, the most important measure is that of value added, for with it one can seek to determine the actual services provided by information activities and then check these figures against the income or compensations received by those engaged in providing the services.

Porat's work is the first empirical demonstration of the scope of information activities since Machlup, but it goes far beyond Machlup's work, not only because it uses finer categories and makes three different kinds of estimations, but also because it seeks to establish an input-output matrix that would permit, once the accounts were complete, an estimation of the impact on other parts of the economy of a change, say, from a "paper economy" to an "electronic transmission" economy or from books to video discs as modes of instruction, along with hundreds of similar questions. Here, however, I am interested primarily in Porat's findings on the value of information activities in the economy.[21]

Porat sets up a six-sector economy. There is a primary information sector which includes all industries that produce information machines or market information services as a commodity. (This includes the private sector, which contributes about 90 percent of the primary information products and services, and the government, which accounts for the remaining 10 percent.) There is a secondary information sector with two segments, the public bureaucracy and those private bureaucracies whose activities are not directly counted in the national accounts as information services—such as the planning, programming, scheduling, and marketing of goods or services—yet who are actually engaged in information and knowledge work. The value of these activities has to be imputed (for example, by factoring out the income or compensation of those persons within a manufacturing firm who are engaged in such work). The three remaining sectors consist of the private productive sector, producing goods; the public productive sectors (building roads, dams, and so on); and the household sector.

The primary information sector is the one that is most easily measurable, since it sells its products in a market. It includes industries and activities as diverse as computer manufacturing and services, telecommunications, printing, media, advertising, accounting, and education; it is the productive locus of an information-based economy.* In 1967, sales of information goods and services in the primary information sector to the four major sectors of final demand amounted to $174.6 billion, or 21.9 percent of

---

* Porat divides the sector into eight major classes of industries: (1) the knowledge production and inventive industries; (2) information distribution and communication industries; (3) risk-management industries, including components of finance and insurance; (4) search and coordination industries, including all market information and advertising vendors; (5) information processing and transmission services, both electronic and nonelectronic; (6) information goods industries, including information machines; (7) selected government activities that have direct market analogs in the primary information sector, including the Postal Service and education; and (8) support facilities such as office and education buildings.

These eight major groups are further subdivided into 116 industries, which can be located in the Standard Industrial Classification; the monetary figures can be located in the National Income Accounts.

GNP. In other words, seventeen cents of every consumer dollar represented direct purchase of information goods and services. If one looks at
the income side, in 1967 nearly 27 percent of all income originated with
information goods and services. The civilian government was the most
information-intensive—almost 43 percent of all federal, state, and local
wages were paid to federal primary information-creating personnel such
as Postal Service workers or education workers.

Strikingly, as Porat points out, over 43 percent of all corporate profits
originated with the primary information industries. All corporations in the
United States earned some $79.3 billion in profits in 1967; the primary
information industries earned $33.7 billion. After removing the govern-
ment's share of the primary information sector's national income ($37.2
billion), the information industries alone accounted for 21 percent of
national income but 42 percent of corporate profits. Each dollar of employee compensation generated thirty-four cents in profits, as against a
ratio in the overall economy of twenty-one cents—a difference that Porat
attributes to the large profits earned by the telephone and banking industries with their high profit-to-labor ratios. Calculating value added, about
25 percent of total GNP originated in the primary information industries. In
all, over $200 billion of the total GNP of $795.4 billion originated in information goods and services.

The most interesting and novel aspect of Porat's work is the definition
and measurement of the secondary information sector, a sector that Porat
derives from Galbraith's notion of the "technostructure." This is the section of an industry that is directly engaged in information work but whose
activities are not measured as such, for while the goods produced may be
sold in the market (and thus are reflected in the GNP as manufactured
goods like automobiles or transportation activities like airline flights), the
information components in those enterprises—the planning, scheduling,
and marketing activities in automobiles; the computerized reservation
processes in airline flights—are not counted directly in the GNP.

The secondary information sector expands for several reasons. One is
the inherent tendency for bureaucracies to grow, which while true is a
quite simple-minded explanation since there are always constraints of
costs. A second, more serious reason is the multiplication of technical
activities that comes with size, complexity, and advanced technology—
such as research, planning, quality control, marketing, and the like. And
third is the fact that firms integrate or coordinate to economize on information costs. Thus a group of independent, high-quality hotels in different
cities recently banded together to create a common reservation service as
a means of competing with the large hotel chains by saving on communications costs. In fact, as Porat points out, there are quasi-industries hidden within the secondary sector that under some circumstances could

become independent, primary (i.e., directly measurable) industries. One is the hypothetical "reservations industry." This "industry" sells its services to airlines, trains, hotels, theater box offices, and automobile rental companies through computerized data networks. In actual fact, each of the industries or firms maintains its own reservations systems, so the information costs are counted within the product cost. Yet if a single company created an efficient reservations network that it could sell to all these industries to replace the in-house services they maintain themselves, then these information activities would be measured in the "final demand" of GNP.

Other than these quasi-information industries, the bulk of the secondary information sector consists of planning and financial control, the administrative superstructure that organizes and manages the activities of firms or government agencies—in short, the private and public bureaucracies. In 1967, according to Porat, 21 percent of GNP originated in the secondary information sector—18.8 percent in the private bureaucracies and 2.4 percent in the public bureaucracies. Of the 168.1 billion in value added, some 83 percent ($139.4 billion) originated in compensation to information workers, some 3.5 percent ($5.8 billion) represented depreciation charges on information machines, and the balance was earned by proprietors performing information tasks. In sum, nearly 50 percent of GNP, and more than 50 percent of wages and salaries, derive from the production, processing, and distribution of information goods and services. It is in that sense that we have become an information economy.

The growth of the secondary sector is, of course, the growth of the bureaucratic society. In 1929, some 13 percent of the national income originated in the secondary sector, but by 1933 it had fallen to 9 percent. During the depression, the secondary sector shrank from 72 percent of the size of the primary information sector to 40 percent. But it is in the war and postwar years, with the expansion of government and the growth of corporate size, that the secondary information sector begins to swell, so that by 1974, about 25 percent of the national income could be attributed to the secondary information sector and about 29 percent of the national income to the primary sector.

The final necessary component is the change in the composition of the work force itself over time. From 1860 to about 1906, the largest single group in the work force was in agriculture. In the next period, until about 1954, the predominant group was industrial. Currently, the predominant group consists of information workers. By 1975, the information workers had surpassed the noninformation group as a whole. On the basis of income received, the crossover came earlier, since those in information occupations, on the average, earn a higher income. By 1967, some 53 percent of the total compensation was paid to information workers.

Figure 9.2 and tables 9.2 and 9.3 illustrate the change. In 1930, there were 12 million workers in the information sector, almost 10.5 million in agriculture, 18 million in industry, and 10 million in services. By 1970, there were 37 million in the information sector, less than 2.5 million in agriculture, 22.9 million in industry, and 17.5 million in services. In percentage terms, the labor force in the information sector today is over 46 percent; in agriculture, 3 percent; in industry 28.6 percent; and in services 21.9 percent.

What of the future? Extrapolations can be deceptive. The information sector has grown hugely in the last decade and a half, but that has been a result of both the rapid introduction of new technology in computers and telecommunications and the economic growth rate that financed it. In many sectors, such as education, public policy is the decisive variable. Although the cohort of younger people will begin to shrink—in absolute numbers it is still growing, but the rate is slowing rapidly—there is an evident desire on the part of many in the adult population to undertake continuing education. Thus many community colleges are finding themselves transformed into adult schools. Whether or not society can afford these costs or wants to pay them is a different question. But aside from issues of public policy the expansion of the information economy will largely depend on two developments. One is automation—in industry and in the white-collar occupations. The second is the growth of information and its retrieval—data bases, scientific information networks, and the explosion of international communications.

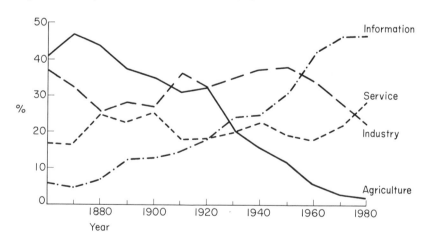

9.2

Four-Sector Aggregation of the U.S. Work Force, 1860–1980 (using median estimates of information workers)

Table 9.2
Four-Sector Aggregation of the U.S. Labor Force (Median Definition)

Experienced Civilian Work Force

Year	Information Sector	Agriculture Sector	Industry Sector	Service Sector	Total
1860	480,604	3,364,230	3,065,924	1,375,525	8,286,283
1870	601,018	5,884,971	4,006,789	2,028,438	12,521,216
1880	1,131,415	7,606,590	4,386,409	4,281,970	17,406,384
1890	2,821,500	8,464,500	6,393,883	5,074,149	22,754,032
1900	3,732,371	10,293,179	7,814,652	7,318,947	29,159,149
1910	5,930,193	12,377,785	14,447,382	7,044,592	39,799,952
1920	8,016,054	14,718,742	14,492,300	8,061,342	45,288,438
1930	12,508,959	10,415,623	18,023,113	10,109,284	51,056,979
1940	13,337,958	8,233,624	19,928,422	12,082,376	53,582,380
1950	17,815,978	6,883,446	22,154,285	10,990,378	57,844,087
1960	28,478,317	4,068,511	23,597,364	11,661,326	67,805,518
1970	37,167,513	2,466,883	22,925,095	17,511,639	80,071,130
1980[a]	44,650,721	2,012,157	21,558,824	27,595,297	95,816,999

Percentages

Year	Information Sector	Agriculture Sector	Industry Sector	Service Sector	Total
1860	5.8	40.6	37.0	16.6	100
1870	4.8	47.0	32.0	16.2	100
1880	6.5	43.7	25.2	24.6	100
1890	12.4	37.2	28.1	22.3	100
1900	12.8	35.3	26.8	25.1	100
1910	14.9	31.1	36.3	17.7	100
1920	17.7	32.5	32.0	17.8	100
1930	24.5	20.4	35.3	19.8	100
1940	24.9	15.4	37.2	22.5	100
1950	30.8	11.9	38.3	19.0	100
1960	42.0	6.0	34.8	17.2	100
1970	46.4	3.1	28.6	21.9	100
1980[a]	46.6	2.1	22.5	28.8	100

[a]Bureau of Labor Statistics projection

Table 9.3
Two-Sector Aggregation of the U.S. Labor Force

Experienced Civilian Work Force

	Inclusive Definition		Restrictive Definition		
Year	Information Workers	Non-information Workers	Information Workers	Non-information Workers	Total U.S. Labor Force
1860	580,040	7,706,243	372,883	7,913,400	8,286,283
1870	788,837	11,732,379	500,849	12,020,367	12,521,216
1880	1,340,292	16,066,092	887,726	16,518,658	17,406,384
1890	2,980,778	19,773,254	2,480,189	20,273,843	22,754,032
1900	4,286,395	24,872,754	3,120,029	26,039,120	29,159,149
1910	7,283,391	32,516,561	4,537,196	35,262,756	39,799,952
1920	9,963,456	35,324,982	6,023,362	39,265,076	45,288,438
1930	16,031,889	35,025,090	8,883,914	42,173,065	51,056,979
1940	16,470,313	37,112,067	9,883,428	43,698,952	53,582,380
1950	21,691,532	36,152,555	13,940,424	43,903,663	57,844,087
1960	30,851,510	36,954,008	19,256,767	48,548,751	67,805,518
1970	40,529,588	39,541,542	29,464,497	50,606,633	80,071,130
1980[a]	49,154,120	46,662,879	39,955,688	55,861,311	95,816,999
Percentages					
1860	7.0	93.0	4.5	95.5	100
1870	6.3	93.7	4.0	96.0	100
1880	7.7	92.3	5.1	94.9	100
1890	13.1	86.9	10.9	89.1	100
1900	14.7	85.3	10.7	89.3	100
1910	18.3	81.7	11.4	88.6	100
1920	22.0	78.0	13.3	86.7	100
1930	31.4	68.6	17.4	82.6	100
1940	30.7	69.3	18.4	81.6	100
1950	37.5	62.5	24.1	75.9	100
1960	45.5	54.5	28.4	71.6	100
1970	50.6	49.4	36.8	63.2	100
1980[a]	51.3	48.7	41.7	58.3	100

[a]Bureau of Labor Statistics projection

FUTURE PROBLEMS: THE RETRIEVAL OF INFORMATION

In his *Sartor Resartus,* Thomas Carlyle wrote ironically, "He who first shortened the labour of the Copyists by the device of movable type was disbanding hired Armies. . . ." He was, of course, referring to Johann Gutenberg (and praising him as well for "cashiering most Kings and Senates and creating a whole new Democratic world: he had invented the art of printing"). Yet such "technological" displacement, characteristically, had contradictory results. While old-fashioned calligraphers no longer could practice their skill and thus were relegated to the artisan scrap heap, more jobs were created by the increased demand for printed materials, and newer, less artistic but differently skilled men found employment.

And yet initially the pace of change was not so abrupt and rapid as to create wholesale turnovers in the print trade of the time. The printing press of the eighteenth century was little different than that used by Gutenberg three hundred years before. It was a wooden handpress on which a flat plate was laid upon a flat piece of paper with pressure created by the tightening of screws. Wood was eventually replaced by metal and the screw by a double lever, which allowed the speed of printing to be increased by half. By 1800 a radically new method of printing using a rotating cylinder—the basis of the modern press until the development of photographic technologies—was invented and with its greater speed began gradually to displace the flat press. The double rotary cylinder, developed for newspapers in the 1850s, made it possible to print two sides of a piece of paper at once. By 1893, the *New York World*'s octuple rotary press was printing 96,000 copies of eight pages in a single hour, whereas seventy years before the average was 2,500 pages an hour.[22]

Such developments, understandably, went hand in hand with complementary technologies. The linotype, developed by Mergenthaler in 1868, replaced monotype by selecting and casting type by keyboard, reducing composition costs by half while quintupling the speed of typesetting. The paper industry, which until the early nineteenth century was a time-consuming hand process using rags, was transformed in the middle of the century by the Fourdrinier process which mechanized the production of paper with the use of wire webs and cylinders. At the same time the development of wood pulp and a practical pulping process displaced rags, so that paper which had cost almost $350 a ton at mid-century had come down to $36 a ton by the end of the century. Each of these developments was sped by new sources of energy. Printing presses, originally turned by hand and briefly even by horse (in America at least), became powered by steam and then by electricity. Papermaking, dependent initially on waterpower, came to use hydraulic power accelerated by electric turbines.

But what is so striking is how long it took, from the time of Gutenberg, for all this to develop. It is only in the twentieth century that one finds the mass production of newspapers (with millions of copies of a single issue printed overnight), magazines (set and printed in widely dispersed places using common tapes), and books. And now, with the revolution in communications, all this will change. The information explosion is a set of reciprocal relations between the expansion of science, the hitching of that science to a new technology, and the growing demand for news, entertainment, and instrumental knowledge, all in the context of a rapidly increasing population, more literate and more educated, living in a vastly enlarged world that is now tied together, almost in real time, by cable, telephone, and international satellite, whose inhabitants are made aware of each other by the vivid pictorial imagery of television, and that has at its disposal large data banks of computerized information.

Given this huge explosion in news, statistical data, and information, it is almost impossible to provide any set of measurements to chart its growth. Yet there is one area—the growth of scientific information—where some reconstruction of historical trends has been carried out, and I will use that as a baseline for understanding the problems of the next twenty years.

The historical picture of the knowledge explosion was first formulated statistically by Derek de Solla Price in 1963, in his work *Little Science, Big Science*. The first two scientific journals appeared in the mid-seventeenth century, the *Journal des savants* in Paris and the *Philosophical Transactions of the Royal Society* in London. By the middle of the eighteenth century, there were only ten scientific journals, by 1800 about 100, by 1850 perhaps 1,000. Today? There are no exact statistics on the number of scientific journals being published in the world. Estimates range between 30,000 and 100,000, which itself is an indication of both the difficulty of definition and the difficulty of keeping track of new and disappearing journals. In 1963, Price estimated that 50,000 journals had been founded, of which 30,000 were still surviving. A UNESCO report in 1971 put the figure between 50,000 and 70,000. *Ulrich's International Periodicals Directory* (a standard library source) in 1971–72 listed 56,000 titles in 220 subjects, of which more than half were in the sciences, medicine, and technology; but these were only of periodicals in the Latin script and excluded most Slavic, Arabic, Oriental, and African languages.

Perhaps the most directly measurable indicators are university library holdings. The Johns Hopkins University in 1900 had 100,000 books and ranked tenth among American university libraries. By 1970, it had over 1½ million volumes, a growth of 3.9 percent per year, although it had dropped to twentieth place. In that same period, the eighty-five major American universities were doubling the number of books in their libraries every seventeen years, for an annual growth rate of 4.1 percent. (The difference between 3.9 and 4.1 percent may seem slight, yet it relegated the Johns Hopkins Library to the bottom of the second decile.)

A 1973 OECD survey of all the extant studies of the growth in scientific knowledge came to the following conclusions:

1. In all the case studies, growth follows a geometric progression, the curve being exponential.

2. However, the growth rates varied considerably, the lowest one being 3.5 percent yearly, the highest 14.4 percent.

3. The lowest growth rates are shown by the number of scientific periodicals published, covering a 300-year period, and the number of specialized bibliographical periodicals involved in indexing and abstracting over a 140-year period. In the case of scientific journals, the annual growth rate has been 3.5, 3.7, or 3.9 percent, depending whether the number published in 1972 is taken as 30,000, 50,000, or 100,000. The growth rate for indexing and abstracting organizations has been 5.5 percent a year. In 1972, there were 1,800 such services in science.

4. A recent series reporting the number of articles by engineers in civil engineering journals (from 3,000 pages of technical articles in three specialized periodicals in 1946 to 30,000 pages in forty-two specialized periodicals in 1966) shows growth rates of 12.3 percent a year.

5. The growth rate in the number of international scientific and technical congresses increased almost fourfold in twenty years, rising from 1,000 in 1950 to over 3,500 in 1968.[23]

The multiplication in the number of scientific reports and documents has naturally led to the conclusion that such progression cannot continue indefinitely, that at some point a slowdown would take place, probably in the form of a logistic curve that would symmetrically match the exponential rise of the ascent. The crucial question has been to identify the point of inflection where the reverse trend would begin. Derek de Solla Price argued in 1963 that "at some time, undetermined as yet but probably during the 1940s or 1950s, we passed through the mid-period in general logistic curve of science's body politic." In fact, he concluded, saturation may have already arrived.[24]

Yet as Anderla noted in his study for the OECD, "Today it is absolutely certain that these forecasts, repeated without number and echoed almost universally, have failed to materialize, at any rate so far." As evidence, he assembled the number of abstracts published between 1957 and 1971 for nineteen scientific disciplines and demonstrated that between 1957 and 1967 the output increased by nearly two and a half times, for an annual growth rate of 9.5 percent. Over the fourteen years from 1957 to 1971, the volume increased more than fourfold, for a growth rate of 10.6 percent, so that there was an escalation in growth rather than the predicted reverse.[25]

The major reason for this continued escalation is the tendency for science to generate more and more subspecialties, each of which creates its own journals and research reports system. At the same time, cross-disciplinary movements arise to bridge some of the subspecialties, extending the proliferation process even further.

What then of the future? The production of scientific literature is determined in the first instance by the projected rate of increase in the scientific population. It is calculated that in 1970 the scientific population represented about 2 percent of the total labor force. The rate of increase has been estimated variously at between 4.7 and 7.2 percent a year (a fifteen-year and a ten-year doubling time, respectively), although certain categories, such as computer scientists, have been increasing by more than 10 percent annually. Taking 1970 as a base, one can estimate the likely size of the scientific population in 1985 by making three assumptions: an unyielding exponential increase to the horizon year of 1985; a break occurring in 1980, with the logistic curve beginning to slow down at that time; or the point of inflection coming as early as 1975. Given these assumptions, the number of scientists, engineers, and other technicians in 1985 could account for a low of 3.8 percent to a high of 7.2 percent of the total labor force. If one takes the midpoints, between 4 percent and 5.7 percent of the total working population would be scientists and engineers in 1985.

In order to project the volume of information that is likely to be produced, we can take as a base a survey of the U.S. National Academy of Science which revealed that in the early 1970s about 2,000,000 scientific writings of all kinds were issued each year, or between 6,000 and 7,000 articles and reports each working day. For an internally consistent time series, the most reliable indicators are the statistics of abstracts of articles in the leading specialized reviews, which from 1957 to 1971 increased exponentially at a rate of more than 10 percent a year. As with the growth rates in the number of scientists, one can assume breaks in the logistic curves at 1975, 1980, or 1985 and then take a median figure. According to these computations, there is every indication that projections to within a year or two of the 1985 horizon might well lie within the index range of some 300 to 400. In other words, the number of scientific and technical abstracts would be three or four times the present number.

The End of the Alexandrian Library

Clearly, if the explosion in information continues, it cannot be handled by present means. If by 1985 the volume of information is four (low estimate) or seven times (high estimate) that of 1970, then some other ways must be found to organize this onslaught of babel. In one of these pleasant exercises that statisticians like to undertake, it is estimated that under present projections, the Yale University Library would need a permanent staff of 6,000 persons in the year 2040 to cope with the books and research reports that would be coming annually into the library. (Such projections recall earlier ones that if the U.S. telephone system had to handle the current volume of calls solely through operator-assisted methods, then every female in the labor force—a sexist remark obviously made before women's lib—would now be working for AT&T.)

Obviously, the information explosion can only be handled through the expansion of computerized and subsequently automated information systems. The major advance to date has been the computerization of abstracting and indexing services. Most of the printed abstract index bulletins in research libraries are prepared from computer tape. The Chemical Abstract Service (CAS), the largest in the field, is a case in point. Before computerization, it took the CAS about twenty months to produce an annual index; these are now available twice a year, while the unit costs for indexing have decreased from $18.50 to $10.54. Moreover, as the new substances are recorded in the Chemical Registry System—there are now 3,000,000 items in the files—it is possible to store, recreate, and display structure diagrams on video terminals from the computer-readable structure records stored in the system. A further development is the rise of computer-based searching services, drawn from the tape initially used to expedite the printing of indexes. Two American firms, the Systems Development Corporation and Lockheed Information Systems, provide on-line searching to over thirty bibliographic data bases. Together they provide immediate access to over 15 million citations, with an annual increase of approximately 3.5 million citations.[26]

The logic of all this is that the image of the Alexandrian Library—the single building like the Bibliothèque Nationale, the British Museum, or the Library of Congress—where all the world's recorded knowledge is housed in one building, may become a sad monument of the printed past. Data-based stores of information, especially in the scientific and technical field, will come from specialized information centers, transmitted through computer printouts, facsimile, or video display to the user, who will have consulted an index through on-line searching to locate items of interest and then order them on demand.

All this supposes two things. One, the creation of large-scale networks in which a national system is built through the linkage of specialized centers. And two, the automation of data banks so that basic scientific and technical data, from industrial patents to detailed medical information, can be retrieved directly from computers and transmitted to the user. But both suppositions raise two very different problems. One is the intellectual question raised by Winograd in chapter 4, the distinction between pro- gramming a data base, and constructing a program for use as a knowl- edge base. Retrieving some census items from a data base is a simple matter; but finding kindred and analogous conceptual terms—the han- dling of ideas—raises all the problems that were first encountered, and never successfully solved, in the effort to achieve sophisticated machine translation of languages.

As early as the pre-Socratics, when philosophy was first becoming self-conscious, there was an awareness of the ambiguities of language and the hope, as with the Pythagoreans, that certainty could be expressed through mathematical relations. Descartes, in creating his analytical geometry, thought he could substitute the "universal language of logic" for the messy imprecisions of ordinary language, as Spinoza felt he could create a "moral geometry" to deal with ethical questions. In each genera- tion that hope has arisen anew. In 1661 a Scotsman, George Dalgarno, published his *Ars Signorum* in which he proposed to group all human knowledge into seventeen sections (such as "politics" and "natural ob- jects") and to label each with a Latin consonant. Vowels would be used to label the subsections into which each section was to be divided, and the process of subdivision was to be continued with consonants and vowels alternating. In this way, any item of knowledge would have a specific reference and identification.[27]

In the twentieth century we have had the effort of Whitehead and Russell to formalize all logic using a mathematical notation, the effort of the logical positivists such as Carnap to construct (in theory) a language that would avoid the ambiguities of ordinary discourse and to propose (in practice) a verifiability principle that would specify which propositions were testable and could be held to "make sense," as against those that were (pejoratively) metaphysical, emotive, or theological and could not, given the nature of language, be "proved." And most recently, in the *Britannica 3*, Mortimer Adler has proposed a new scholastic ordering of knowledge, the *Propaedia*, that would guide encyclopedia users to interre- lated sets of relevant terms, as his earlier *Syntopicon* sought to be an intellectual index to the 101 major "ideas" of human thought.

The attempts to discipline human knowledge and create a vast and unified edifice, as Dalgarno and even Leibniz sought to do, were bound to fail. The effort to formalize knowledge or construct artificial languages has proved inadequate. The scholastic orderings of Mortimer Adler may help an individual to trace the bibliographic cross-relationships of ideas, but if the purpose of a library, or a knowledge-based computer program, is to help a historian to assemble evidence or a scholar to "reorder" ideas, then the ambiguity of language itself must be confronted. Terms necessarily vary in different contexts and lend themselves to different interpretations, and historical usages shift over time (consider the problem of defining an intellectual, or the nature of ideology), making the problem of designing a "knowledge" program quite different from designing an "information" program.

The process of creating new knowledge (reasoned judgments) proceeds by what Léon Walras, the great mathematical economist, called *tâtonnement,* trial-and-error tapping, by taking fragments of intellectual mosaics whose larger shapes cannot be predicted in advance and fitting them together in different ways or by regarding large conceptual structures from a new angle, which opens up wholly new prisms of selection and focus. A sophisticated reader, studying a philosophical text, may make use of the existing index at the back of the book, but if he is to absorb and use the ideas in a fruitful way, he has necessarily to create his own index by regrouping and recategorizing the terms that are employed. As John Dewey pointed out in *Art as Experience,* the nature of creativity is to rearrange perceptions, experiences, and ideas into new shapes and modes of consciousness. In this process, no mechanical ordering, no exhaustive set of permutations and combinations, can do the task. Descartes once thought that the geometer with a compass could draw a circle more exactly than an artist could freehand. But a perfect circle, or even a set of interlocking circles, is not art without some larger conceptual context that "redesigns" an older or different way of arranging shapes. Art, and thought, as modes of exploration, remain primarily heuristic.

A more mundane yet sociologically important problem is the lack of a national information policy on science and technical information, let alone on library resources generally. Should there be a national scientific and technical computer network? Should there be a government corporation or utility with direct responsibility to scientific and technical users or simply a major, governmentally organized data base (like the census) made available to commercial services that meet specific consumer needs? Such questions have been raised since the creation of the Office of Science Information within the National Science Foundation in 1958, and they have been asked over and over again in a number of governmental and National Academy of Science studies in subsequent years. No answers have been forthcoming; no policy exists. Yet if science information is the end product of the $35 billion annual investment that the nation makes in research and development and information, broadly defined, accounts for almost 50 percent of the gross national product, then some coherent national policy is in order.

THE POLICY QUESTIONS OF THE INFORMATION SOCIETY

My basic premise has been that knowledge and information are becoming the strategic resource and transforming agent of the postindustrial society. Inevitably, the onset of far-reaching social changes, especially when they proceed, as these do, through the medium of specific technologies, confronts a society with major policy questions. Here I can only schematically indicate some of the questions society will face in the next two decades.

The New Infrastructure

Every society is connected by diverse channels that permit trade and discourse between its members. These modes, or infrastructures, have usually been the responsibility of government—as builder, financier, maintainer, or regulator. The first infrastructure was transportation—roads, canals, railroads, airways—which breaks down the segmentation of society and allows for the movement of people and goods. Caravans and trade routes formed the social framework of older human societies. The second infrastructure has been the energy utilities—waterpower, steam pipes, gas, electricity, oil pipelines—for the transmission of power. By mobilizing technological rather than natural sources of energy and linking them into power grids, not only have we transformed the lives of cities through lighting, but we have provided power for the fabrication of goods and the use of consumer appliances. The third infrastructure has been communications—first the mails and newspapers, then telegraph and telephone, now radio and television—as media for the mounting explosion of messages, the bombardment of sensory experiences, and the increased degree of social and psychic interaction between persons that is now accelerating exponentially.

In the next two decades, there is little likelihood of any major developments in the first infrastructure, that of transportation. The adoption of the *Concorde* or other supersonic airplanes, if it comes, may halve the time for crossing the ocean, but the effect will be minor compared to the reduction in the time needed to cross the Atlantic in the last hundred years, from several weeks by steamship to six days by fast boat, to sixteen hours by propeller plane, to seven hours by jet. Mass transit in the cities, if it returns, is unlikely to replace the automobile or other modes of personal movement unless fuel prices rise so high as to overthrow the hedonistic way of life that has become entrenched in advanced industrial societies. The rising demand for personal transportation in the newer developing countries and increases in congestion may lead to new combinations of taxis, leasing, and motor utilities (in which one shares in a common pool). But much of the vaunted experimental innovations, such as monorails or automated elevated speedways or even hovercraft, have proved to be either uneconomic or technologically too complicated.

In the second infrastructure, energy, there are clearly major new developments requiring large capital expenditures, involving conservation (insulated housing), better extractive techniques for coal and its gasification, potential uses of nuclear energy, research in tapping solar sources of energy, and more efficient modes of electricity transmission, such as superconductivity. These efforts, if made, will stimulate a huge expansion in the areas of research and development (and of engineers and technically trained personnel), and, if successful, will establish new energy grids that will supply a steady source of renewable power and once again bring down the price of energy relative to other goods. But such changes, large as they may be, are primarily substitutes for existing energy sources and modes of transmission. They do not presage huge upheavals in the role energy plays in the society.

The really major social change of the next two decades will come in the third major infrastructure, as the merging technologies of telephone, computer, facsimile, cable television, and video discs lead to a vast reorganization in the modes of communication between persons; the transmission of data; the reduction if not the elimination of paper in transactions and exchanges; new modes of transmitting news, entertainment, and knowledge; and the reorganization of learning that may follow the expansion of computer-assisted instruction and the spread of video discs.

One may be skeptical, as I am, about extravagant claims regarding the quantum leaps in level of education that computer-assisted instruction and video discs will bring. Learning, as I think we have learned, is a function of both the ability to learn and the cultural milieu; any technology is only instrumental, and its impact depends upon other social and cultural factors. But in the realm of data transmission (especially in the world of business) and in the development of knowledge networks (particularly in science and research), what Anthony Oettinger has called compunications certainly will stimulate vast social changes.

This upheaval in telecommunications and knowledge poses two economic-political policy problems, one structural, the other intellectual. The structural question is what kind of technical-economic organization is best designed to be efficient, meet consumer (i.e., industrial, commercial, financial, scientific, library) use, and remain flexible enough to allow for continuing technological development. One proposal is for a single computer utility that would centralize and provide a single source for information and transmission of data for consumer use, either government-owned (as are the telephone and broadcasting systems in many European countries) or privately owned but government-regulated, like AT&T and the major broadcast networks in the United States. Among different versions of the computer utility idea, there is a proposal for diverse sources of information (i.e., different data banks operated publicly or privately) based on a single transmitting system (such as the present telephone quasi-monopoly) or, conversely, a centralized set of data bases with diverse means of transmission. Against these are the proposals for a completely unregulated, competitive market system, in which different "producers" would be free to set up diverse informational services and transmission would be through cable, microwave, or satellite communication operated by different combines, each competing for the business. These are the issues whose economic aspects Noll has addressed in chapter 12.

It has been argued that a single national computing service, interconnecting all user terminals from geographically dispersed data banks, would achieve vast economies of scale, and if run as a government utility (like TVA) would avoid the concentration of vast power in the hands of a single private enterprise. Against this, as Noll points out, computer systems sell not merely computational power or data processing but "information," and the large and varied needs of thousands of different kinds of users for different kinds of information—medical, technical, economic, marketing—would best be served by specific firms that would be responsive, in the way efficient markets can be, to the diverse needs of consumers. Others have argued that government control could be as dangerous, if not more so, than private concentration since it could be more easily misused for political purposes. And there is the further question of whether a competitive decentralized system would not be more flexible technologically, and more innovative, than a large monopoly system, either public or private. The record so far, in the instance of the computer versus the telephone, would indicate that technological innovation has come more rapidly and more responsively in an unregulated and competitive atmosphere than in the government-regulated sphere.

On the traditional grounds of economic efficiency and technological responsiveness, it seems to me that Noll makes a convincing case for the primacy of the market and for a market system. Yet he also points out that regulators tend to see prices as taxes to be levied according to some calculus of social worth, favoring one group over another, rather than seeing prices as signal-conveying information about costs that induce buyers to make economically efficient decisions. He is, I believe, right in his observation. Yet is the policy itself so wrong? Where markets are open and competitive, the allocation of resources does respond most efficiently to the preferences and demands of consumers, and this is the justifiable defense, theoretically, of the market as the arbiter of economic activity. Yet if in the institutional world income distribution is grossly distorted, or various social groups are discriminated against, then redress through subsidy may be one means of achieving equity, even if sometimes at the expense of efficiency. Second, there is the growing realization that markets do not often reflect the larger range of social costs that are generated in the process, and these may be unfairly distributed. As Arthur Okun has pointed out, the trade-off between efficiency and equity presents a real problem. The point is not to disguise the issue but to make it as explicit as possible, so that one knows the relative gains and losses in equity and efficiency that result from market and regulatory decisions.

The second policy problem posed by the upheaval in telecommunications is intellectual rather than structural and concerns the question of a national information policy, particularly the dissemination of science and technical information. The government is obviously committed to the furtherance of research and development. Increases in productivity depend increasingly on the more efficient distribution of necessary knowledge, but so far there is no unified government policy or an organized system to bring scientific and technical information to diverse users, to speed the process of innovation, and shorten the time of development and diffusion.

After Sputnik, there was a flurry of studies reviewing the problem. A report by William C. Baker of Bell Laboratories stated the unexceptionable principle that the flow of scientific information was necessary. A second report in 1962 by J. H. Crawford for the president's Office of Science and Technology recommended that each agency of government set up a specific office to produce scientific information, and these were created in the Department of Defense, the Atomic Energy Commission, and the National Aeronautic and Space Agency. In 1963, a report by Alvin Weinberg of the Oak Ridge National Laboratory argued that the government had the further responsibility to organize the dissemination of research information in order to avoid costly duplication of effort. The government did create a coordinating body called COASTI (Committee on Scientific and Technical Information) to implement this effort.

Yet the odd if not surprising fact is that little has been done. During the Nixon administration, COASTI, the Office of Science and Technology, and the Science Information Council were dismantled. Inevitably the number of hortatory studies multiplied. In 1969, the National Academy of Sciences and the National Academy of Engineering brought forth the SATCOM (Committee on Scientific and Technical Communication) report, which involved more than 200 scientists, calling for a national policymaking body to deal with information policy. In 1972 the Federal Council on Science and Technology and the National Science Foundation commissioned yet another report, by Dr. Martin Greenberger of Johns Hopkins University, which concluded, unsurprisingly, that the government was not well organized to deal with the problems of scientific and technical information facing the country.

It still is not. Meanwhile, the number of scientific papers and the volume of scientific information continue to rise. There is a growing trend toward cross-disciplinary information which the single-disciplinary systems (such as abstracting and indexing) are not equipped to handle. The proliferation of diverse types of material, stored in different ways from books, films, computer tapes, video tapes, and so on, makes it difficult to keep track of everything. And finally, the number of users continues to increase.

All trends pose a large variety of policy issues. Should there be, as Fernbach suggests in chapter 8, a national Library of Data, like the Library of Congress, to store all basic data and programs in giant memories? Should this library—if such a Library of Babel as Jorge Luis Borges envisaged ever comes about—also concern itself with the dissemination of data, as the government's Medlars system does for medical information, or should it be available for private companies, such as Lockheed or Systems Development Corporation or the *New York Times,* to provide specialized services for subscribers through proprietary communications and terminal systems?

The growth of shared communications systems and on-line terminals makes a national scientific and technical information network a tangible possibility. In chapter 17 Denicoff describes the development of the interactive computer network invented in 1968 by Dr. L. G. Roberts for the Advanced Research Projects Agency (ARPA), which was first employed by the Defense Communications Agency in 1976. Its most valued result, according to Denicoff, was the emergence of a "user community." The operational reality of such a community, he writes, is the proof of the gains we have made in scientific cooperation. In the same vein, Joseph Becker has argued that

a national scientific and technical information network implies the interconnection of discipline-oriented and mission-oriented information systems for remote use through standard communications. Unless cohesive development takes place, the separate systems will remain insulated from one another and from their users. But, if maximum communication can be established among them, the array can be converted into a national resource of immense value to America's scientific enterprise.[28]

H. G. Wells, in one of his megalomaniacal visions of the future, proposed a "world brain" that like a vast computer would bring together in one place all organized scientific knowledge and make it available through communication networks to the "new samurai," the coming scientific elite of the world. Is such a technological phantasmagoria feasible (as some computer scientists claim it is) or desirable (as others do), or is it simply one of those marvelously simple visions (like that of Sidney Webb) of tidily and neatly organized bundles of knowledge that can be separated and reassembled by pressing the right button? If the last, it is a deceptive vision, which misunderstands the way the mind actually works, and which makes the sociological error of assuming that some central knowledge system can function better than the decentralized, self-organizing system in which demand specifies the organizational and market response to the needs of the users. This is an issue that should remain open to extended debate, for it is too serious and too costly to be settled on purely ideological grounds.

And finally, on a more mundane level, there is the legal and economic question of what is an "intellectual property"—at least where the intellectual product is clearly defined (such as a book or a journal article), let alone where the boundaries are blurred, as in the instance of a computer program. How does one balance the rights of fair use as demanded by libraries against the economic rights of authors and publishers? As books become stored in computer memories and can be retrieved on tapes and printed by attached photocopying devices, who is to pay for what? Should Xerox and IBM receive financial returns while the intellectual producers gain only the psychic satisfaction of the widespread reproduction of their words?

The courts and the Congress have been struggling with these questions for years. Clearly no solution will completely satisfy those who press for the widest possible dissemination of intellectual material under some fair-use and information-need concept, or those who demand payment for any use of copyright material. But we need a clarification of the legal and philosophical issues at stake.

Social and Economic Transformations

The major determinant of policy issues, as I have indicated, is the question of what kind of infrastructure will be created out of the merging technologies of computers and communications. Inevitably this will give rise to more diffuse policy issues deriving from the economic and social transformations that may come in their wake. I will conclude by examining five central issues of this kind.

1. The location of cities   Historically, all cities were formed at the crossroads of overland caravan routes, at the strategic confluence of rivers, or at large, protected ports on seaways and oceans as entrepôts and trading centers. Almost all the major cities of the world have been located on rivers, lakes, and oceans since transportation—and particularly waterways for heavy barge loads—tied areas together in the first infrastructure.

In the industrial age, cities were located near major resource bases, such as coal and iron, as one sees in the English Midlands or the German Ruhr and most strikingly in the great industrial heartland of the United States, where the great iron-ore resources of the Mesabi Range in upper Minnesota were connected to the great coal regions in southern Illinois and western Pennsylvania through a network of lakes and rivers. In this way the great industrial cities of Chicago, Detroit, Cleveland, Buffalo, and Pittsburgh were intricately linked in one huge complex.

In the transition to a service economy, the metropolitan cities became the major financial centers and headquarters for the great enterprises. The histories of New York and London form striking parallels. Both began as port cities through which goods could be sent overseas or transported inland. New York was a large, ice-free port, protected by two great bays, yet connected through the Hudson River and the Erie Canal system to the midwestern Great Lakes complex. As trade increased, banking, factoring, and insurance arose as auxiliary services to commerce; later, with the rise of industry, they became nerve centers for financial and stock transactions. In its third phase, New York became a large headquarters city, where the major corporations located their head offices to take advantage of the external economies offered by the concentration of banking, legal, publishing, and communications services.

In economic geography, the resource base was the decisive locational factor up to the last forty years, when all this began to change. In the United States in the postwar years, the economic map of the country was reworked largely through politics, since the new large aircraft, space, and missile companies were created entirely by government contracts and the decisions to locate them in areas like the Pacific Northwest, southern California, and southwest Texas were made on political grounds. With the rise of air cargo, we have witnessed a phenomenon in which new "airplane cities," such as Dallas–Fort Worth, Houston, Denver, and Atlanta, rather than water and rail cities, serve as regional hubs for industrial and commercial spokes. And now, as the increasing spread (and cheapness) of telecommunications reduces the former external economies of physical proximity, we see the dispersal of corporate headquarters and major white-collar concentrations like the insurance industry from the decaying central cities to the suburbs. The location of research laboratories, new universities, and large hospital complexes is less dependent on the traditional factors of economic geography and more influenced by the nearness of educational facilities, easier life-styles, and political factors. Phenomena like the development of "Silicon Valley" in California—the ribbon of electronics and computer firms stretching from San Francisco to San Jose—and Route 128 around Boston were a response to the availability of university research facilities, plus more pleasant space for the smaller-sized physical plants and offices than the industrial areas could provide.

C. A. Doxiades has envisaged the growth of linear cities without the older focal piazzas and market centers of the classical European towns. B. F. Skinner has suggested that in an age of advanced communication, networks of towns will replace the large, increasingly ungovernable cities. The question of whether these apocalyptic visions will be realized is moot; the life and death of cities is a long historical process. But what is changing is the concept of "urbanism" itself. Thirty years ago Louis Wirth wrote a famous essay entitled "Urbanism as a Way of Life," in which he summed up the characteristics of urbanism as a highly interactive, heavily mobile, culturally and politically attentive mode, as against the older small-town and rural patterns centered on the church and the family. What is happening today is that the entire nation (if not large parts of the world) is becoming urbanized in the psychological sense, though increasingly more dispersed geographically.

The changes in the character and pattern of telecommunications poses problems of national land use, of the social costs of dispersions and concentrations, the management of the decay of old cities, and the control of the sprawl of new ones. Inevitably, the decisions will reflect the interplay of market and political forces, since neither one can be decisive in itself. But it is the exact mix of the two that remains as the interesting sociological question for the next decades.

2. The possibilities of national planning Leon Trotsky once said that a capitalist economy is one where each man thinks for himself and no one thinks for all. That a single "one" can think for "all" is probably impossible and, if so, would be monstrous, since the "one" would be some giant bureaucracy and the "all" a putative single interest equally applicable to all citizens in the society. As Alan Altshuler of MIT has remarked, "those who contend that comprehensive planning should play a large role in the future evolution of societies must argue that the common interests of society's members are their most important interests and constitute a large proportion of all their interests. They must assert that conflicts of interests in society are illusory, that they are about minor matters, or that they can be foreseen and resolved in advance by just arbiters [planners] who understand the total interests of all the parties."

In this respect, Altshuler is probably correct, yet such a view unduly restricts the meaning of planning in all its possible varieties. The different kinds of planning can be arrayed in a simple logical ladder:

a. Coordinated information Almost all major enterprises make five- and even ten-year plans (for product development, capital needs, manpower requirements, new plants) as a necessary component of their own planning. And various services, such as the McGraw-Hill survey of capital spending budgets or the federally financed University of Michigan surveys of consumer intentions, seek to provide more comprehensive information for firms about these trends to aid them in their planning. A national computerized information service, through the Bureau of the Census or some similar government body, could bring together all such relevant information—just as the various econometric models now in use make forecasts of the annual GNP and its major components, which become the basis of both governmental and private policies. To this extent, the idea of a coordinated information system is simply an extension of the planning process that is now so extensive in the corporate and governmental sectors.[29]

b. Modeling and simulation Using an input-output matrix, such as that developed by Wassily Leontieff, one could test alternative economic policies in order to weigh the effects of different government policies on different sectors of the economy. In a more radical version, the Russian economist Leonid Kantorovich has argued that a national computerized economic system, registering the different prices and allocations of items, could spot items that deviate from planned or targeted goals or the disproportionate use of resources in various sectors.

c. Indicative planning In this model, which is used by the French Commissariat du Plan, several thousand industry committees coordinate their plans regarding economic activities, and these plans become the basis of governmental decisions to stimulate or inhibit certain sectors, largely by easier credit facilities or credit restrictions.

d. National goals In this scheme, the government would stipulate certain major goals—the expansion of housing or levels of economic growth—and monitor the economy to see whether such goals were being achieved as a guide to which further measures (tax cuts, investment credits, credit allocations, preferred sections such as housing) might be necessary to achieve them.

e. Mobilized targets This is, in effect, a "war economy," such as that exemplified by the War Production Board in the United States during World War II or the British Ministry of Supply; in practice, it is the actual nature of Soviet "planning." In this system, certain key targets are specified (level of steel output, kind of machine tools, number of tanks and aircraft, and so on), and the government physically allocates, by a priority system, the key materials and manpower to designated factories. In this respect, the entire economy is not planned, but key sectors are controlled.

These different modes of planning range from direct controls and policing at one end to "simple" information coordination at the other. Which kind of planning society will adopt is a political question. Given the degree of interdependence and the spillover effects of various individual decisions, some larger degree of planning—analogous to the rise of environmental monitoring and regulation planning—than we now have is probably inevitable. The computer and the large-scale information systems that are being developed will make it feasible; but how one reconciles planning with various kinds of individual freedom is a very different and more difficult question.

3. Centralization and privacy Police and political surveillance of individuals is much more possible and pervasive because of sophisticated advances in the information process. In a survey of federal agencies' use of computerized data banks, former Senator Sam Ervin wrote in the preface to a report by the Senate Judiciary Committee's Subcommittee on Constitutional Rights: "The sub-committee has discovered numerous instances of agencies starting out with a worthy purpose but going so far beyond what was needed in the way of information that the individual's privacy and right to due process of law are threatened by the very existence of files. . . . The most significant finding is that there are immense numbers of government data banks, cluttered with diverse information on just about every citizen in the country. The 54 agencies surveyed were willing to report 858 [data banks] containing more than 1¼ billion records on individuals."

Government demand for information can be highly costly to enterprises and institutions. Derek Bok, the president of Harvard, reported that the demand of the governmental agency enforcing the affirmative action program for detailed information on every aspect of employment practices and the need to keep records of all job searches for applicants to teaching and other positions cost the university over a million dollars a year. What information is necessary and what is not is a difficult question to decide, particularly in the abstract. Yet the tendency of almost every bureaucracy, reflecting an aspect of Parkinson's Law, is to enlarge its demands on the principle that (a) "all" information might conceivably be necessary; and (b) it is easier to ask for everything than to make discriminations.

The simple point, for it is one of the oldest and most important truisms of politics, is that there is an inherent potential for abuse when any agency with power sets up bureaucratic rules and proceeds without restraint to enforce them. The other, equally simple point, is that control over information lends itself more readily to abuse—from withholding information at one end to unlawful disclosure at the other, both processes exemplified by Watergate—and that institutional restraints are necessary, particularly in the area of information, to check such abuses.

4. Elite and mass   Every society we have known has been divided, on one axis or another, into elite and mass. On a different axis, a society may be designated as open or closed. In the past, most societies have been elite and closed in that aristocracies have been hereditary. Even when there has been an examination system for choosing mandarins, as in Imperial China, the selection process has been limited to a small class of persons.

In the West the major elites have traditionally been landed and propertied elites. Even in an occupation like the military, which requires some technical skill, until about a hundred years ago (in Britain, for example) commissions could be purchased. The older ladders of social mobility were "the red and the black," the army and the church. Modern capitalist and industrial society began to break open those molds. In business, there was the rise of the entrepreneur, the engineer, and the manager. With the succeeding breakdown of "family capitalism," the managerial elites were no longer children of previous owners but men who earned their way up by technical competence. In government, there was the expansion of the administrative bureaucracy, in which top positions were achieved, as in France, through a rigorous selection system by rites of passage through the grandes écoles, or by patronage, as was usual in the United States.

Modern societies, in contrast with the past, have become more open societies, but at the same time, as knowledge and technical competence have become the requirement for elite positions, the selection process has fallen more and more onto the educational system as the sluice gates that determine who shall get ahead. The result has been increasing pressure on the educational system to provide "credentials" for those who want to move up the escalator of social mobility. In the postindustrial society, the technical elite is a knowledge elite. Such an elite has power within intellectual institutions—research organizations, hospital complexes, universities, and the like—but only influence in the larger world in which policy is made. Inasmuch as political questions become more and more intricately meshed with technical issues (from military technology to economic policy), the knowledge elites can define the problems, initiate new questions, and provide the technical bases for answers; but they do not have the power to say yes or no. That is a political power that belongs, inevitably, to the politician rather than to the scientist or economist. In this sense, the idea that the knowledge elite will become a new power elite seems to me to be exaggerated.

But what is equally true is that in contemporary society there is a growing egalitarianism fostered in large measure by sectors of the knowledge elite, especially the younger ones, and given the most vocal support by those in marginal positions and marginal occupations in the knowledge sector. Within institutions, this has taken the form of attacks on "authority" and "professionalism" as elitist and demands that all groups have some share in the decision-making power. In certain European universities, for example, even the nonprofessional staffs are given a voice and representation in university affairs, while on academic issues, from curriculum to tenure decisions, the three "estates" of students, junior faculty, and senior faculty have equal corporate rights. How far this egalitarianism will go remains to be seen.

The fear that a knowledge elite could become the technocratic rulers of the society is quite far-fetched and expresses more an ideological thrust by radical groups against the growing influence of technical personnel in decision making. Nor is it likely, at least in the foreseeable future, that the knowledge elites will become a cohesive "class" with common class interests, on the model of the bourgeoisie rising out of the ruins of feudalism to become the dominant class in industrial society. The knowledge class is too large and diffuse, and there seems little likelihood, either in economic or status terms, that a set of corporate interests could develop so as to fuse this stratum into a new class. What is more likely to happen, as I have argued previously, is that the different situses in which the knowledge elites are located will become the units of corporate action. One can identify functional situses, such as scientific, technological (applied skills like engineering, medicine, and economics), administrative, and cultural, as well as institutional situses, such as economic enterprises, government bureaus, universities, research organizations, social service complexes (like hospitals), and the military. The competition for monies and influence will be between these various situses, just as in the communist world the major political units are not classes but situses such as the party, the government machine, the central planners, factory managers, collective farms, research institutes, cultural organizations, and the like.

What one sees in contemporary society is the multiplication of constituencies and consequently the multiplication of elites; and the problem of coordinating these elites and their coalitions becomes increasingly complex.

5. International organization The problems of creating a new infrastructure for telecommunications (or compunications) on a national scale are magnified when the questions are projected on the international scene. Just as within the last thirty years the United States has become a "national society," so in the next thirty years we will have an international society—not as a political order, but at least within the space-time framework of communications. Here not only is the scale enormously larger, but more importantly there is no common political framework for legislating and organizing the creation of a worldwide infrastructure.

International telephone traffic, for example, has been growing by about 20 percent a year, and international communications is handled by Intelstat, an international commercial satellite organization with ninety-odd member countries. Yet Intelstat has been largely dependent on one American aerospace company (Hughes Aircraft) to build the satellites and on the American space agency to launch its satellites into orbit. The day-to-day financial and technical management of Intelstat has been in the hands of an American corporation, Comsat, whose ownership is distributed half among ordinary shareholders and half by the large communications companies, among which AT&T has a prominent voice. The question of such dominance is bound to become more and more of an international political issue in the next decades.

On a different level, the creation of worldwide knowledge data banks and services becomes an important issue as more and more countries and their scientific, technical, and medical organizations seek to share in the

enlarged computerized systems and on-line networks that are being developed in the advanced industrial societies.

And finally—although this is only a sampling of the international issues
that will play a role in the transformation of contemporary society—there is
the question of the spread of computers, specifically the sharing of advanced computer knowledge and the creation of international computer
data-transmission systems. In the period before World War I, steel production was the chief index of the strength of nations, and when Germany
began to overtake Great Britain and France as a steel producer, it was a
tangible sign of the growth of her economic and military power. A few
years ago, the Soviet Union overtook the United States in steel output, a
fact that received only passing mention in the back pages of the *New York
Times*. Yet the Soviet Union is far behind the United States in the production of computers and their degree of sophistication. The export of
computers—to the Soviet Union and to China—are still political, not commercial questions, for one of the chief uses of computers has been for
military planning, the design of military hardware, and most importantly
the creation of guided missiles and "smart" bombs.

Turning Points and Promises

I have been arguing that information and theoretical knowledge are the
strategic resources of the postindustrial society, just as the combination of
energy, resources, and machine technology were the transforming agencies of industrial society. In addition—is the claim extravagant?—they
represent turning points in modern history.

D. S. L. Cardwell has identified four major turning points in the rise of
scientific technology.[30] One was the era of invention at the close of the late
Middle Ages, signaled by the development of the clock and the printing
press. The second, the scientific revolution, was symbolized by Galileo,
with his emphasis on quantitative measurement and his technical analyses
of the strength of materials and the structure of machines (for example,
the square-cube law on the nature of size and growth). The third, the
industrial revolution of Newcomen and Watt, was the effort to realize a
Baconian program for the social benefits of science. The fourth is represented in the work of Carnot and Faraday, not only because it produced
new conceptions of thermodynamics and field theory but also because it
provided the bridge to a more integral relationship between science and
technology.

The new turning points are of two kinds. One lies in the changing
character of science. The transmutation of materials made possible by
knowledge of the underlying structure of the properties of matter and the
reorganization of information into different patterns through the use of the
new communication technologies, particularly the computer, are trans-

forming the social organization of science. On the one hand they create Big Science and on the other enhanced communication through on-line networks, cooperative ventures in the discovery of new knowledge and the experimental testing of results. Science as a "collective good" has become the major productive force in society.

The second turning point is the freeing of technology from its "imperative" character to become almost entirely instrumental. It was—and remains—a fear of humanists that technology would more and more "determine" social organization because the standardization of production or the interdependence of skills or the nature of engineering design forces the acceptance of one, and only one, "best" way of doing things—a theme that itself was fostered by prophets of the industrial age like Frederick W. Taylor. But the nature of modern technology frees location from resource site and opens the way to alternative modes of achieving individuality and variety within a vastly increased output of goods. This is the promise—the fateful question is whether that promise will be realized.

EDITORS' POSTSCRIPT

McCarthy's critique of Bell's essay rests on the argument that the new technology is not the main cause of change in our society today, given our reliance primarily on pre— rather than post—World War II inventions. In addition, the course projected for technology may veer off in unexpected directions. If, for example, firms and individuals keep progressively more of their records in computers, then automated paper handling may indeed reverse the growth trend forecast for the "knowledge industries." Further comments and discussion on Bell's views can be found in Weizenbaum's essay.

NOTES

1
For an elaboration of this concept, see my book, The Coming of Post-Industrial Society (New York: Basic Books, 1973). A paperback edition with a new introduction appeared in 1976 (New York: Harper & Row, Colophon Books).

2
Cyril Stanley Smith, "Metallurgy as a Human Experience," *Metallurgical Transactions A,* 64, no. 4 (April 1975):604. Professor Smith adds, "As an undergraduate (a half century ago) I had to decide whether to enroll as a ferrous or a non-ferrous metallurgist; I heard little about ceramics and nothing whatever about polymers. The curriculum, though refined in detail, had pretty much the same aim as the eighteenth century courses in the mining academy in Freiberg and the Ecole de Mines in Paris." (Ibid., p. 604.)

3
Jacob Bronowski, "Humanism and the Growth of Knowledge," in *The Philosophy of Karl Popper*, ed. Paul A. Schlipp (LaSalle, Ill.: Open Court Publishing Company, 1974), p. 628.

4

Norbert Wiener, *I Am a Mathematician* (Cambridge, Mass.: MIT Press, 1970), p. 40. (The book was first published in 1956 by Doubleday, New York.)

5

Smith, "Metallurgy as a Human Experience," pp. 620–621.

6

Harold A. Innis, "Minerva's Owl," in *The Bias of Communication* (Toronto: University of Toronto Press, 1951), p. 3, given as the presidential address to the Royal Society of Canada in 1947.

7

For example,

The use of clay favored a dominant role for the temples with an emphasis on priesthood and religion. Libraries were built up in Babylon and Nineveh to strengthen the power of monarchy. Papyrus and a simplified form of writing in the alphabet supported the growth of democratic organization, literature, and philosophy in Greece. Following Alexander empires returned with centers at Alexandria and elsewhere and libraries continued as sources of strength to monarchies. Rome extended the political organization of Greece in its emphasis on law and eventually on empire. Establishment of a new capital at Constantinople was followed by imperial organization on the oriental model particularly after official recognition of Christianity. Improvement of scripts and wider dissemination of knowledge enabled the Jews to survive by emphasis on the scriptures and the book. In turn Christianity exploited the advantages of parchment and the codex in the Bible. With access to paper the Mohammedans at Baghdad and later in Spain and Sicily provided a medium for the transmission of Greek science to the Western world. Greek science and paper with the encouragement of writing in the vernacular provided the wedge between the temporal and the spiritual power and destroyed the Holy Roman Empire. The decline of Constantinople meant a stimulus to Greek literature and philosophy as the decline of Mohammedanism had meant a stimulus to science. Printing brought renewed emphasis on the book and the rise of the Reformation. In turn new methods of communication weakened the worship of the book and opened the way for new ideologies. Monopolies or oligopolies of knowledge have been built up in relation to the demands of force chiefly on the defensive, but improved technology has strengthened the position of force on the offensive and compelled realignments favoring the vernacular. (Ibid., pp. 31–32.)

Marshall McLuhan, as is evident, was a disciple of Harold Innis (he wrote the introduction to the paperback edition of *The Bias of Communication*) and derived most of his major ideas from him. But McLuhan not only "hyped up" and vulgarized Innis's ideas, he also reversed the thrust of his argument, for Innis feared that the tendency of new media was to extend centralization and concentrate power while McLuhan, though propagating the notion of a "global village," argued that the newer media would encourage decentralization and participation.

8

Encyclopaedia Britannica, 1970 ed., s.v. "information theory."

9

Norbert Wiener, *Cybernetics* (New York: Wiley, 1948), p. 155.

10

Wassily Leontieff, "National Economic Planning: Methods and Problems," *Challenge*, July–August 1976, pp. 7–8.

Referring to the further consequences of this new capacity, Leontieff writes:

Such systematic information proves to be most useful in assessing structural—in this particular instance technological—relationships between the input requirements on the one hand, and the levels of output of various industries on the other. In the case of households these relationships would be between total consumers' outlay and spending on each particular type of goods. Stocks of equipment, buildings and inventories, their accumulation, their maintenance and their occasional reduction are described and analyzed in their mutual dependence with the flows of all kinds of goods and services throughout the entire system. Detailed, as contrasted with aggregative, description and analysis of economic structures and relationships can indeed provide a suitable framework for a concrete, instead of a purely symbolic description of alternative methods of production, and the realistic delineation of alternative paths of technological change. (Ibid., p. 8.)

11

Indeed information is merely the negative measure of uncertainty, so to speak. Let me say immediately that I am not going to propose a quantitative measure. In particular, the well-known Shannon measure which has been so useful in communications engineering is not in general appropriate for economic analysis, for it gives no weight to the value of the information. If beforehand a large manufacturer regards it as equally likely whether the price of his product will go up or down, then learning which is true conveys no more information, in the Shannon sense, than observing of the toss of a fair coin. (Kenneth J. Arrow, *Information and Economic Behavior*, ed. Federation of Swedish Industries [Stockholm: Federation of Swedish Industries, 1973].)

12

As Arrow remarks,

The presumption that free markets will lead to an efficient allocation of resources is not valid in this case. If nothing else, there are at least two salient characteristics of information which prevent it from being fully identified as one of the commodities represented in our abstract models of general equilibrium: (1) it is by definition indivisible in its use, and (2) it is very difficult to appropriate. (Ibid., p. 11.)

13

Robert K. Merton, "Singletons and Multiples in Science," in *The Sociology of Science,* the papers of Merton, ed. Norman W. Storer (Chicago: University of Chicago Press, 1973, pp. 343–370).

14

The problem is that economists have no direct measures of such "inputs" and treat them as "residuals," not accounted for by direct increases in the productivity of capital or labor. As Michael Spence writes,

The difficulty in measuring information has hampered research concerned with the effects of information on [economic] growth. It is common practice to estimate the effect of education and knowledge on growth in GNP by first estimating the impact of real factors like the increase in capital stock, the labor force, and so on. One then attributes the growth that is not explained in these real factors to increases in knowledge.

15

There is a huge and growing literature on all these questions. I have drawn largely on the reports of the Harvard Program on Information Technology and Public Policy for the material in this section.

16

See *The Production and Distribution of Knowledge in the United States* (Princeton: Princeton University Press, 1962). For a detailed discussion of Machlup's types of knowledge in comparison with those of Max Scheler and my own, see Bell, *The Coming of Post-Industrial Society,* pp. 174–177. Since, for me, the heart of the postindustrial society is the new ways in which knowledge becomes instrumental for science and social policy, I have attempted an "objective definition" that would allow a researcher to plot the growth and use of knowledge.

17

Marc Porat has reformulated the 1967 National Income Accounts to make them consistent with accepted practices, and despite some admitted deficiencies, he has hewed to the standard usages. As Porat points out,

Machlup's accounting scheme innovated rather liberally on the National Income Accounts and Practices whereas this study does not. . . . His work includes an admixture of "primary" and "secondary" type activities, whereas this study keeps them distinct. Third, a variant of *final demand* is used by Machlup as a measure of knowledge industry size, whereas this study uses primarily the value added approach but reports both sets of figures. . . .

"The Information Economy" (Ph.D. diss., Stanford University, 1976), 1:81–82.

18

Machlup's key data can be presented in tabular form:

Distribution of Proportion of Gross National Product Spent on Knowledge, 1958

Type of Knowledge and Source of Expenditures	Amount in Millions of Dollars	Percentage of Total
Education	60,194	44.1
Research and development	10,090	8.1
Communication media	38,369	28.1
Information machines	8,922	6.5
Information services (incomplete)	17,961	13.2
Totals	136,436	100.0
Expenditures made by:		
Government	37,968	27.8
Business	42,198	30.9
Consumers	56,270	41.3
Totals	136,436	100.0

Source: Fritz Machlup, *The Production and Distribution of Knowledge in the United States* (Princeton: Princeton University Press, 1962), pp. 360–361. Arranged in tabular form by permission.

19

Gilbert Burck, "Knowledge, the Biggest Growth Industry of Them All," *Fortune*, November 1964.

20

Jacob Marschak, "Economics of Inquiring, Communicating, Deciding," *American Economic Review* 58, no. 2 (1968), 1–8.

21

The statistics and tables here, except where noted, are taken from Porat, "The Information Economy," vol. 1. The page citations refer to that volume. The figures on trends in the work force are from a briefing packet that Mr. Porat had prepared for presentation at an OECD conference. I am grateful to him for making these materials available to me, and for his correspondence in clarifying some of my questions. His revised work is scheduled to be published by Basic Books.

22

I am indebted for this technological information to a research paper by Paul DiMaggio, a graduate student of sociology at Harvard.

23

Georges Anderla, *Information in 1985, A Forecasting Study of Information Needs and Resources* (Paris: OECD, 1973), pp. 15–16.

24

Little Science, Big Science (New York: Columbia University Press), p. 31. For a critical discussion of the use of logistic curves and some questions about Price's various starting points, see my *The Coming of Post-Industrial Society*, chap. 2, "The Measurement of Knowledge and Technology," pp. 177–185.

25

Anderla, *Information in 1985,* p. 21. The major specialist journals were: *Chemical Abstracts* and *Biological Abstracts* (which between them accounted for more than 550,000 items, more than half of the one million produced in 1971), *Engineering Index Monthly, Metals Abstracts, Physics Abstracts, Psychological Abstracts,* and a Geology Index Service.

26

The figures are taken from a paper by Lee Burchinal of the National Science Foundation, "National Scientific and Technical Information Systems," presented to an international conference in Tunis, April 26, 1976. I am grateful to Dr. Burchinal for the preprint.

27

Cited by Colin Cherry, "The Spreading Word of Science," *Times Literary Supplement,* March 22, 1974, p. 301.

28

Remarks made at the Science Information Policy Workshop, National Science Foundation, Washington, D.C., December 17, 1974.

29

One major difficulty is the inadequacy of our statistics. As Peter H. Schuck remarks, What is perhaps more disturbing, given the imminence of national economic planning, is the abject poverty of our economic statistical base, upon which a good theory must be grounded. In recent years the inadequacy and inaccuracy of a broad spectrum of economic indices—including the wholesale price index, the consumer price index, the unemployment rate, and business inventory levels—have become quite evident. The wholesale price index, for example, reflects only list prices rather than actual transaction prices (which are often lower) and uses anachronistic seasonal adjustment factors; yet it is considered a bellwether statistic in economic forecasting. ("National Economic Planning: A Slogan without Substance," *The Public Interest,* Fall 1976, p. 72.)

30

D. S. L. Cardwell, *Turning Points in Western Technology* (New York: Science History Publications, 1972).

10
The Consequences of Computers for Centralization and Decentralization

Herbert A. Simon

Today, the terms *centralization* and *decentralization* are heavily laden with value. In general, decentralization is the good thing and centralization the bad thing. Decentralization is commonly equated with autonomy, self-determination, or even self-actualization. Centralization is equated with bureaucracy (in the pejorative sense of that term) or with authoritarianism and is often named as a prime force in the dehumanization of organizations and the alienation of their members. If the reader shares these common attitudes toward centralization and decentralization, I shall ask him to hold them in suspension until I have inquired more closely into their meanings.

THE NATURE OF CENTRALIZATION AND DECENTRALIZATION

Picture a typical organization in hierarchical form with various decision-making functions being carried out at the nodes. Centralization is any transfer of such functions from a lower node to a higher one, decentralization any transfer from a higher node to a lower one. Centralization is always a relative matter, for decision making is never fully concentrated at the very top or at the very bottom of an organization. When we ask what effect computers will have on the centralization and decentralization of the institutions and organizations of our society, we are asking in what direction they will move the balance. It is perfectly possible, of course, for both movements to go on concurrently in an organization, some functions being passed upward at the same time that others are passed downward. Thus, in the 1950s, many production and marketing decisions in large

Herbert A. Simon is University Professor of Computer Science and Psychology at Carnegie-Mellon University. He is noted for his writing in many areas—political science, management, computer science, and psychology—and received the 1978 Nobel Prize in economics for his work on management decision making. He is also a winner of the Association for Computing Machinery's Turing Award for his pioneering work in artificial intelligence.

American corporations were being decentralized to product divisions at the same time that labor relations decisions were being centralized.

Functions of Centralization

There are three main motives for centralizing decision functions: to gain economies of scale, to coordinate interdependent activities, and to control lower-level activities in the interest of higher-level goals.

1. In decision making, economy of scale means mainly creating central units for handling certain classes of decisions expertly, where it would be too costly to distribute experts more widely through the organization—a classic application of Adam Smith's principle of the division of labor, although in this case the labor is mental, not physical.

2. The interdependencies that make coordination desirable are those that the economist calls externalities; that is, actions whose consequences fall on a part of the organization other than the one taking the decision. These external consequences may be undervalued or ignored if decisions are not centralized. It may be possible, however, so to design the reward system that a decentralized decision-making unit will be charged fully with the indirect consequences of its actions, in which case interdependence ceases to be a reason for centralization. Pricing mechanisms provide an important means for reconciling decentralization with interdependence whenever appropriate prices can be assigned to all of the relevant consequences of an action. On the other hand, prices that do not reflect important externalities can be a cause for divergence between decentralized decisions and higher-level goals, and hence a motive for centralization.

3. Even without interdependencies among units, some measure of centralization may be thought necessary in order to guarantee that the actions of individual organization units will reflect the goals of the whole organization. Successful decentralization assumes that lower-level administrators can be motivated to make their decisions in terms of higher-level goals.

Decision Premises

Making a decision involves weaving together many diverse premises—goal premises, constraints, side conditions, and factual assumptions based on data and theory—and deriving from them the choice of a course of action. Centralization need not involve transporting the whole decision process from one node in an organization to a higher one but may consist in establishing and communicating from the higher node one or more decision premises, with the injunction that they be employed in making the decision. One organization unit may provide another with objectives, with rules and constraints, or with facts. A single decision, then, may be manufactured out of a diversity of component materials that were themselves fabricated elsewhere in the organization.

It is important to view decision making as more than just the final signing on the dotted line. The decision-making process in an organization encompasses (1) determining what items will be on the agenda and receive attention; (2) inventing and designing alternative plans of action; (3) evaluating alternatives and making the choice; and (4) postauditing decisions and their consequences. If we take a longer view, we also have to include in the decision process all the varieties of investigation and research that build the organization's understanding of its environment and of the laws by which it operates. It is from this understanding that the invention of plans of action proceeds, as well as the estimation of decision consequences.

Decision making begins, then, with activities directed toward understanding the environment, proceeds through attending to selected aspects of the environment and the problems it presents, to devising courses of action, choosing among them, and reevaluating them by hindsight. For example, the energy shortage and rising energy prices may cause a company management to attend to the reliability of its energy supply and the efficiency of its use of energy. Means may be sought, discovered, and adopted for insulating buildings, reducing the energy requirements of manufacturing processes, or remodeling power plants to enable them to use alternative fuels. This whole stream of activities constitutes the decision-making process.

Decision premises do not only flow downward through the organization's channels of formal authority; they also flow upward and sideward. If the higher organizational levels provide authoritative instruction and information for decision making at the lower levels, the lower levels also provide much of the information that goes into higher-level decisions. In the unhappy history of the Vietnam War, no small part was played by the "body counts" and other local assessments of the battle situation that flowed upward to the top command in Saigon and thence to Washington. Whether this information was believed, or only partly believed, it provided a substantial part of the "facts" on which the decisions of war or peace were based. The information received by the top organizational levels is not always as bad, fortunately, as it was in this instance. In any event, it is typical of organizations that a large proportion of the facts for decision making at all levels originate either near the bottom or in specialized units outside the chain of command that perform one or another kind of expert or intelligence function (e.g., economic forecasters, market analysts, research and development departments).

Where decisions involve resource allocation, as they commonly do, much of the needed information can be encapsulated in the form of prices of inputs and outputs to each particular organization unit. Clearly the dissemination of this kind of information is not limited to any particular communication channels. Hence, where prices can be used to represent interactions, the decision-making process can be carried out in close proximity to the points where the decisions will be executed. Whether an increased communication flow to a decision center means more or less centralization of decision making depends, therefore, on whether the flow is from a lower level in order to inform decisions at a higher level, from a higher level to control decisions at a lower level, or from some expert source to a collateral point of decision making. Reduced autonomy for a high-level decision maker may imply a greater degree of decentralization (i.e., increased reliance on decentralized information sources) rather than centralization.

Perception of Autonomy

The premises of any particular decision may have their origins far back in time and may be stored in a variety of repositories—human memories, organization records, or books—before they are brought to bear on that decision. How centralized or decentralized we regard the decision as being will depend on whether we trace back these premises or consider only where they were stored at the time the decision was made. Herbert Kaufman, in his classic work, *The Forest Ranger*, describes a highly decentralized decision-making system in which the district ranger in the Forest Service exhibits great autonomy within his district. But Kaufman also shows how the forest ranger's training and indoctrination have instilled in his memory the decision premises—both goals and techniques—that give the organization confidence that he will work toward its objectives and will do so expertly and predictably. Thus, in this case and many others, autonomy in decision making goes hand in hand with the internalization of goals and the knowledge that make decentralization safe from the viewpoint of the higher levels of the organization.

From the standpoint of the autonomous decision maker's attitudes and motivation, it makes a great difference whether the premises on which he is acting have been received in the form of directives from other parts of the organization or whether they have come from his own memory, where they have long resided and become part of himself. But suppose one of his decisional premises comes neither from a directive nor from his memory, but from a reference book? Does he then view himself as acting autonomously, or under direction? Suppose it resides in a computer memory that he interrogates from a terminal? Is he acting autonomously, or is he being controlled by the computer?

His perception of his autonomy in these circumstances may depend on what motivated him to consult the book or computer memory in the first place. Was he instructed to do so by an organizational directive? Did his professional training teach him to turn to this source? What confidence does he have in the validity of the information? Clearly, autonomy resides in the mind of the decider and in his identification or nonidentification with the various parts of his informational environment. Any conclusions we draw about the implications of computers for centralization, and particularly its psychological consequences, must be carefully weighed in terms of the decision maker's attitudes toward the sources of information on which he draws and the extent to which he has internalized his recourse to those sources.

Feasibility of Centralization

Finally, the degree to which decisions are centralized or decentralized in an organization depends not only on the desirability of one or the other mode of operation but also on its feasibility. Any change in technology that makes it cheaper and easier either to centralize or to decentralize decisions will tip the balance in that direction.

COMPUTERS AND COMMUNICATION

An analysis of the consequences of computers for centralization and decentralization must take account of the electronic communications systems in which computers are embedded. It may even be that the communications systems, with or without computers, are of more import than the computers themselves.

Effects of Modern Communications Technology

Modern communications technology was introduced long before the computer. First the telegraph and cable, then the wireless, and then the telephone revolutionized communication at long distance. Already in the nineteenth century, the autonomy of ambassadors was greatly curtailed by the possibility of communicating almost instantaneously with the foreign ministry in the home capital. The same is true of overseas executives of corporations. On the other hand—and there almost always is another hand—the speeding up and cheapening of international communication and transportation greatly increased the volume of international transactions.

As a consequence of these countervailing trends, it is not obvious that the foreign representative of a governmental or business organization perceives himself as having less decision-making responsibility than his ancestors had. On the one hand, it is easier to instruct him. On the other hand, there is much more to instruct him about. Moreover, these communication links are two-way links; they enable the foreign representative to inform and advise the home office as readily as they enable the home office to inform and instruct him. As the costs of long-distance communication go down and the volume of information that can be transmitted increases, the opportunities for low-level inputs to high-level decisions are greatly enhanced. As I have already shown, this is a force toward greater decentralization.

These comments apply, of course, not only to international communications but also to communications within a single country, a single city, or even a single office building. Large volumes of information can flow electronically between any two points in an organization where it pays to install a broadband communication link, and the cost of such a link decreases each year.

The fact that information can be transmitted to a decision point does not mean that it can and will be used there. The world of modern communications is an information-rich world, in which the problem of absorbing information is generally perceived as more acute than the problem of generating or transmitting it. A decade ago, the U.S. State Department "modernized" its communications system by installing fast line printers to handle the traffic of messages from foreign embassies. Nothing was said about how the department staff would deal with the inundation of messages. Today, improvements in the efficiency of such a system would certainly encompass information filtering and information compression, as well as transmission.

Characteristics of the Computer

What can be done faster and better with a computer than without it? A computer can analyze the behavior of systems with many interacting variables—systems much too large to analyze without its help. It can store sizable bodies of information, indexed so as to meet a great variety of information needs. It can copy, input, and output information with great speed. And it can do all of these things not only with numerical data but with information in various forms, including natural-language texts and other nonnumerical information. Moreover, next year its descendants will be able to handle more information faster and cheaper than it can.

Modeling and Analyzing Interdependent Systems

The ability of the computer to model systems with many interdependent variables was exploited in one of its early management applications: making ordering, inventory, production, and shipping decisions for large, geographically dispersed manufacturing operations. These were decisions that had previously been made by factory and warehouse inventory managers and schedulers; hence the introduction of the computer has brought about a substantial centralization of these activities in many companies, where it has produced large reductions in average inventory holdings. It is undoubtedly the most striking example of computer-produced centralization, but it is perhaps not typical of the ways in which computers have been used.

A different use of computers to analyze complex systems of interdependent variables are the models of energy systems or combined energy and environmental systems that have been constructed in the past several years to help guide the formation of public policy. Here is another case where the power of the computer is needed to assemble a previously fragmented structure of numerous interacting mechanisms. But in instances like this it would be misleading to say that the computer brings about centralization. It would be more accurate to say that it allows a systematic, analytic approach to problems that previously were addressed in an unsystematic, almost chaotic way. It is not that energy policy was previously arrived at in a decentralized way; it is that there was no energy policy. The cause of centralization, if there has been any, is not the computer but the need to address the whole problem rather than isolated fragments of it. The computer enhances our ability to do this; it does not create the necessity for it.

Similarly, building a model of the economic and market environment of a corporation does not centralize management decision making so much as it allows top management to adopt an orderly, analytic approach to decisions it had already been making—but by seat-of-the-pants methods. Taking account of relevant variables that had previously been ignored is not to be confused with centralizing the locus of the decision process.

Two related fields of research, operations research and artificial intelligence, have built tools to enlarge the capabilities of computers for modeling complex systems and have devised more and more powerful analytic techniques for this purpose during the past thirty years. Of course these tools are applicable to a particular set of phenomena only to the extent that the phenomena themselves are understood. But the combination of research on systems analysis techniques with basic scientific research is permitting us each year to approach complex decision problems in business organizations and in the public domain with greater sophistication.

Information Storage and Retrieval

One form of centralization, although not necessarily of decision making, is the gathering of large bodies of information into central computer memories as the basis for information retrieval systems of one kind or another. An airlines reservations system is an interesting application of this sort, particularly because it involves remote access to the central memory over long distances. It can be seen that in this instance hardware centralization does not bring about any centralization of decision making. On the contrary, it allows each of the decentralized decision points to take actions independently, confident that automatic updating by the central memory will take care of all interactions among decisions.

An example of a different sort is the computerized systems for medical diagnosis that are just on the verge of moving from research and development into practical application. Let us suppose that a perfected version of such a system existed in some central location where it could be accessed from remote terminals. By an interactive procedure, information about the patient would be entered, say, from the local hospital. The system could request additional information or ask that additional tests be performed on the patient before arriving at a diagnosis. By any reasonable definition, such a system would represent a centralization of the decision-making process, even if its diagnoses were only advisory. But the important question is the psychological one: would the physician perceive the system as replacing him in his diagnostic function, or would he perceive it as a tool—like penicillin or an X-ray machine—to help him carry out his task? The answer to this question probably depends on the way the system is introduced and the institutional framework within which it is used. Physicians, after all, do not usually regard reference books as threatening automation of their functions, however good the answers or advice they may obtain by consulting them. The automated diagnostic system can simply be regarded as a more powerful and more easily consulted reference book—or it can be regarded as a "robot doctor." What it "really" is lies mainly in the mind of the physician.

TRENDS IN COMPUTER TECHNOLOGY

During the first twenty or so years that computers were on the scene, they had two characteristics that suggested their widespread use would inevitably move decision making toward centralization. The first was that the efficiency of computers increased rapidly with their size: a single large computer was substantially cheaper (perhaps by a factor of three) than ten small computers of the same aggregate computing power. The economics of scale seemed to argue for one or a few centrally located computers rather than many computers distributed through an organization. The second characteristic of early computer systems was that they could only be used by someone in physical proximity to them. Therefore, if the computers were geographically centralized, so would be their use.

In the past decade advances in technology have made drastic changes in these two characteristics, and the shift is still continuing. Minicomputers have been developed that for many purposes compete very well in efficiency with the largest computers. Economies of scale no longer provide a conclusive argument for centralization. Second, and perhaps even more important, with time sharing and remote access, many users in different locations can share the same central computer. (As the examples of the plane reservation system and the medical diagnosis system show, not only can processing capacity be shared, but also access to a memory bank.)

With the new and emerging computer technology of minicomputers, time sharing, and remote access, the decisions about where to locate components of the decision-making process can be pretty completely detached from decisions about the hardware configuration. Of course, long-line access to computers is not without cost, but the costs are relatively low today and still dropping, so that it is not at all unreasonable to look toward the development of nationwide networks. In fact, several experimental networks of this kind (in addition to special-purpose networks like the reservations systems) already exist.

THE IMPACT OF COMPUTERS ON ORGANIZATIONS

Although the computer revolution is far from having run its course, it has been under way for thirty years, and by now we have accumulated a considerable body of experience that should help us predict its direction. Its most visible consequence to date has been the automation of many clerical information-processing functions in accounting departments, insurance companies, and banks. This development, however important it may be from other standpoints, has no particular implications for centralization or decentralization.

Operations Research

Another consequence of the computer revolution is the centralization of middle-management decisions relating to inventory, production scheduling, and the like. At the same time, there has been a great expansion in the use of formal operations research models for making many kinds of middle-management decisions. At the outset, the introduction of such models probably caused some centralization of decision making in special operations research departments, but this was a transitory phase of a kind that often occurs when a new technology requiring specialized knowledge is introduced into an organization. As soon as knowledge of operations research techniques was diffused widely enough to become a part of the standard equipment of industrial engineers and other managers at middle levels, the decision-making responsibilities tended to return to their previous locations in the factory and departmental organizations. Middle managers now make some different kinds of decisions than they did traditionally, and use management-science tools in making many of them, but the management-science tools have become *their* tools and are not generally viewed as removing them from the decision process.

Strategic Planning

The spread in the use of complex models as an aid to decision making has not been limited to middle-management decisions. I have already mentioned the governmental use of models to aid in making decisions about energy and environmental policy. Increasingly, corporate planning at top management levels is being informed and assisted by a variety of computerized analytic techniques (systems analysis), including modeling of the firm itself and its economic environment.

The growing use of modeling as a component of strategy formulation and strategic planning has led to some expansion of corporate planning staffs and their counterparts in government agencies to carry out this function, producing new flows of information and advice from these staffs to top management. Again, it is difficult to interpret this development as an increase in centralization. What it principally means is that a considerable amount of managerial and technical effort all up and down the line, which previously was devoted to day-to-day decision making, is now devoted to the design of the decision process itself and to developing and maintaining the basic models and data bases required for strategic analysis. The change in managerial role is analogous to the change in supervisory role with the introduction of automated control into processing plants, where the main task of foremen and supervisors shifts from making operating decisions to maintaining and monitoring the performance of the automated decision system.

I should insert parenthetically, because there has been some confusion on this point, that the development of strategic planning systems and techniques has had relatively little to do with the development of so-called "management information systems" (MIS). Most of the MIS work has been aimed at computerizing existing internal accounting and production records systems and incorporating in them procedures (usually elaborate) for producing reports addressed to management at various levels. Experience with management information systems has generally been disappointing, mainly because insufficient thought was given to the nature of the management decisions they were to inform and because it was not realized that the important function of computers in organizations is not to multiply information but to analyze it so that it can be filtered, compressed, and diffused selectively. The systems that have been designed under the strategic planning label are generally more relevant for these purposes than are typical MIS systems.

The Qualitative Change in Decision Making

In summary, the very large impact that computers are having on business and governmental organizations cannot be described in terms of centralization and decentralization. What is occurring is a profound qualitative change in the decision-making process, which is being formalized, made explicit, and subjected to deliberate planning.

As decision processes become more explicit, and as their components are more and more embedded in computer programs, decisions and their underlying analyses become more and more transportable. If the method of analysis is explicit and the informational and other premises that enter into it can be specified, then it does not matter very much at what organizational locations the analysis is carried out. As a matter of fact, it becomes increasingly feasible to carry out alternative analyses, using different assumptions and even different decision frameworks and analytic techniques, and employ them all as inputs to the final decision process. With all sorts of organizational and extraorganizational sources providing inputs, the locus of decision making becomes even more diffuse than it has been in the past. The organizational hierarchy remains as a critical mechanism for monitoring the process, but an increasing part of the flow of decisional premises overlaps the boundaries of the formal hierarchy.

IMPLICATIONS FOR THE POLITICAL SYSTEM

Decentralization has entered the political rhetoric of our time in the discussion of two related questions about the organization of our governmental system. The first of these is the question of the relations among the different levels of government, national, state, and local. The second is the question of the participation of citizens in the governmental process. Although often discussed together, these really are separate issues which should be looked at individually.

Federal, State, and Local Relations

There is a long-standing myth abroad in America that local government is "closer to the grass roots" than state government and state government closer than the federal government. In the purely numerical sense that each person represents a larger fraction of the electorate of his city than of his state, and of his state than of the nation, the claim is undeniably true. But it does not follow from this arithmetic that each person has a greater influence on local decisions than on state decisions, or on state decisions than on national ones. It could be argued, in fact, that because it is easier to focus public attention on major national issues than on state or local ones, there is greater popular influence on national decisions than on the others—the Vietnam War and the impeachment of Nixon being cases in point. The principal mass media in this country, and particularly TV and the news magazines, attend largely to national affairs, attracting public attention to them to the relative neglect of what is going on at the state and local levels. While political participation is highly selective at all levels of government, it is probably most selective at the state and local levels.

As a matter of fact, the transfer of power from national to local government, a policy that has had wide popularity during the past few years and especially during the Nixon administration, is not motivated primarily by the desire for greater public participation in government decisions. Part of the support for the movement does come from advocates of participatory democracy, but a much larger part has had two other motives: (1) equalization of the disparate financial capacities of the states and cities to provide governmental services; and (2) the desire of a conservative administration faced by a liberal Congress to put power back in the hands of state and local governments believed to be more congenial than Congress to the administration's point of view.

That government in the United States has tended to become more centralized over the years cannot be doubted. It has become more centralized as activities throughout the nation, and particularly economic activities, have become more interdependent. A highly integrated economy with a highly mobile population cannot behave as though it were fifty independent states or three thousand independent counties. Any important trend toward decentralized decision making is unlikely to occur unless technical means can be found to deal with the real interdependencies that exist.

All of this is preliminary to putting two questions about computer technology: (1) Has the computer contributed, or is it contributing, to the movement toward centralization in American government? (2) Does the computer provide means for checking or reversing that movement? From what has just been said, it is reasonably clear that the answer to the first question must be no. The trend toward centralization long predated the computer, and is adequately explained by other causes. Nothing I have said about computer technology suggests a positive answer to the second question, either. However, there have been some claims, and even some experiments to verify them, alleging that the computer could become an important means for enabling citizens to participate more fully in public decisions. I should like to examine those claims next.

Participatory Democracy

A few years ago, a well-known physicist proposed putting a simple electronic voting device in all homes, so that a referendum could be held almost instantaneously on any issue. The same suggestion has been made by others, and an experiment along these lines appears to be under way at the present time in a West Coast community. Such a device would certainly go a long way toward solving one problem—that of ascertaining the state of opinion of any citizen on any issue at any time. (I hope provision would be made for a "no opinion" response!) The question is whether this is the problem that needs to be solved in order to enhance anything that could justifiably be called citizen participation.

The genius of democratic government is not arithmetic; it is informed consensus. Most questions of public policy do not begin life as dichotomies that can be decided by yes or no. Yet courses of action must be framed and decisions about them reached. Democratic institutions define a process for getting issues on the agenda, generating proposed courses of action, and modifying and amending those proposals until some measure achieves enough support to be enacted, but only in the most specious sense can we say that the chosen course represents the will of the majority. There is almost never a single action that is preferred by a majority over all alternative actions. There may, of course, be a majority preference for that action among all politically feasible actions—where "politically feasible" is defined by the decision process itself.

Different democratic systems define differently the processes for forming majorities. In many European democracies, the legislative body consists of members of numerous political parties, each having a more or less definable ideology and none commanding a majority. In such systems, the formation of coalitions among parties, a process in which each of them relinquishes some of its ideological purity, plays a central role in the formation of majorities. In the American system, with two amorphous political parties with almost unidentifiable ideologies, one of which is usually able to form a legislative majority, the formation of majorities is accomplished primarily through the process that creates and maintains the parties themselves.

This is not the place to enter into a lengthy discourse on political institutions, beyond demonstrating that they are not merely or mostly mechanisms for counting noses. To be sure, elections play a major role in our system and referenda a significant role in some states. But the question to be asked about elections and referenda is not whether the alternative finally chosen obtained a majority or plurality vote, but whether the process by which the decision was reached commanded consensus, whether the decision bore some reasonable relation to informed preferences, and whether—a point I wish to elaborate—the process was spacious enough to accommodate fact and reason along with all the other factors that enter into the formation of public opinion.

The political process, then, is not simply a mechanism for recording a majority of opinions already formed. It is a process for reaching decisions, often about complex matters of policy, in the light not only of already existing goals but also of the probable consequences of alternative courses of action. When we have legislative and public debate about measures to be taken to protect the environment, it is not that there are some people who are "for" the environment and others who are "against" it. There are deep disagreements, some about values, but most about the magnitude and seriousness of the consequences that would follow protection or failure to protect. Is the benefit to public health that will be gained by reducing the NOx emission standard for automobiles to 0.4 grams per mile substantial enough to justify the expenditure of several billions of dollars to achieve it? On many, if not most, questions of this kind, disagreement stems much less from conflicts of interest than from uncertainties about outcomes. Even where both are involved, we probably would regard it as an improvement in the democratic process if its participants could make more accurate estimates of where their interests lay.

Informing Public Opinion

If the computer has any implications for the effectiveness of democratic institutions, they have to do with the processes for forming and informing opinion rather than the processes for recording it. The computer enters as a tool that permits policy alternatives to be examined with a sophistication and explicitness that would otherwise be impossible.

Already one can begin to point to examples where the computer, used in conjunction with the tools of systems analysis, is beginning to play such a role. The debate on federal financing for the SST is one such example, the debate on the antiballistic missile is another. In both these cases, intelligent public debate was facilitated by analyses, some of them aided by computer, of what might result from choosing one alternative over another. With such analyses available, their assumptions explicit and open to examination and question, a layman could acquire not merely an opinion on the policy issue but an informed opinion.

Over the next decade, I think it is predictable that the computer is going to play an even more important role in helping us to understand the choices with which we are faced in matters relating to energy and the environment. The complexities here are an order of magnitude greater than in the SST or ABM decisions, and there is probably greater consensus about the values to be served by the decisions. But the computer is simply a tool in the process that enables us to calculate interactions better than we could without it. It will help us only to the extent that we have valid scientific theories of the systems whose behavior we are trying to model and predict. (It will help us too, of course, in developing and testing those theories.)

The effectiveness of democratic institutions, as well as people's confidence in them, depends in part on the soundness of the decision-making processes they use. Democracy does not require a town meeting in which every member of the public can participate directly in every decision. But it is enhanced by an open and explicit decision process that enables members of the public to judge on what premises the decisions rest and whether the decisions are informed by the best available facts and theories. In fact, such a decision process is a precondition to intelligent public participation of any kind. To the extent that computers can contribute to its growth, they can strengthen democratic institutions and help combat public feelings of helplessness and alienation.

CONCLUSION

I began by arguing that there are three main motives for centralizing the decision-making process: to gain economies of scale (expertness), to coordinate interdependent activities, and to control lower-level activities in the interest of higher-level goals. I went on to examine the implications of computer technology for centralization and decentralization in both management decision making and the formation of public policy. What remains is to show how the introduction of the computer affects the motives favoring centralization, hence tipping the balance in one direction or another.

The computer is making major contributions to raising the level of expertness in decision making on complex matters. It is doing this, however, not by concentrating the decision process at higher levels of management but by either (1) facilitating the construction and use of systems models that can incorporate expert knowledge about system structure and system behavior or (2) permitting the assembly of expert knowledge in large data banks that can be consulted readily from any organizational location provided with a terminal. It is a psychological question whether these sophisticated aids to decision making will be perceived as reducing the autonomy of executives or as enlarging and extending their capabilities. If care is taken in the ways in which computerized decision aids are introduced into organizations and employed in them, there is no reason why they should either be or appear to be centralizing mechanisms.

There probably exists a continuing long-term trend toward the centralization of decision making in both business and government as the matters about which decisions have to be made become more and more interdependent. It has perhaps been slowed but certainly not halted by the use of price and market mechanisms to reconcile interdependence with decentralization. It does not appear that computers have contributed to this trend. What they have contributed, through the modeling capabilities already mentioned, are powerful new means for decision makers to deal with problems involving large numbers of interacting variables. Decisions will not be more centralized as a result of the introduction of computers, but centralized decisions will be made in a far more sophisticated way, taking a fuller account of the real-world complications of the situation, than was possible before.

The use of computers in decision making has important implications for control over the goals to which administrative action and policy are directed, but these implications can as easily support broader as narrower participation in goal setting. What computers do in this respect is mainly to open the decision process to inspection. They objectify the process and make fully explicit the premises of fact and value that enter into it. As a result, the use of the computer will facilitate top management's control over decisions made elsewhere in the organization—in this way reconciling the notion of central control over goals with the notion of decentralization of the actual decision process.

More generally, the use of computers will permit multiple inputs into the decision process from a variety of sources, along with mutually independent alternate analyses of problems. In this way, computers will facilitate—and already have facilitated—a more extensive participation of both experts and laymen in debates on public policy, not by providing means for expressing uninformed opinions but in enabling opinions to be better informed.

Modern communications and computers have moved us from a world in which information was a scarce, valuable commodity, to be cherished and preserved, to a world so full of information that what is scarce is the capacity to attend to it. The computer has often been used incorrectly, as in many MIS systems, as a producer of information. Increasingly, we are learning to use it as a compactor of information, reducing the amount of data managers and policymakers must absorb and shouldering an important part of the burden of analysis that transforms a multitude of premises and predicted consequences into a decision to embark on a course of action.

Whether we employ computers to centralize decision making or to decentralize it is not determined by any inherent characteristics of the new technology. It is a choice for us to make whenever we design or modify our organizations. The technology does offer us a wide range of alternatives for fitting our decision-making systems to our requirements, whatever they may be.

REFERENCES

Kaufman, Herbert. *The Forest Ranger: A Study in Administrative Behavior.* Baltimore: Johns Hopkins Press, 1960.

Sackman, Harold, ed. *Computers and the Problems of Society.* Montvale, N.J.: AFIPS Press, 1972.

Sackman, Harold, and Barry W. Boehm, eds. *Planning Community Information Utilities.* Montvale, N.J.: AFIPS Press, 1972.

Simon, Herbert A. *The New Science of Management Decision.* 3d ed. Englewood Cliffs, N.J.: Prentice-Hall, 1977.

—— *Administrative Behavior.* 3d ed. New York: Free Press, 1976. Chaps. 13 and 14.

Whisler, Thomas L. *The Impact of Computers on Organizations.* New York: Praeger, 1970.

11

The Computer and World Affairs

Robert G. Gilpin

In assessing the impact of computers and other advanced scientific technologies on society, one must confront the general problem posed by social change. In effect one is asking, What is the role of technology and technological innovation in social change? Unless this problem is confronted directly, one cannot hope to deal with the more specific issue of the impact of computers on society. Without a conception of social change, and more particularly the role of technology in social change, it is a hopeless task to speculate about the international political implications of computers and data processing.

Unfortunately, the social sciences lack a conceptual framework for analyzing the process of social change, much less an acceptable theory. As Wilbur Moore observes in the latest edition of the *International Encyclopedia of the Social Sciences,* "Paradoxically, as the rate of social change has accelerated in the real world of experience, the scientific disciplines dealing with man's actions and products have tended to emphasize orderly interdependence and static continuity."[1] This is undoubtedly an overstatement; yet it is correct to say that the social sciences have paid scant attention to social change in general and the impact of technology in particular.

Marxist social scientists would disagree, of course, and would point out that they have a theory of social change that incorporates technological innovation as the key element. In its most crass formulation, Marxist theory sees a one-to-one correspondence between technological and social change. The replacement of waterpower by steam power led to the replacement of feudalism by capitalism.[2] Similarly, in the contemporary world the replacement of human labor by the computer and automation will lead inevitably to socialism.[3] Unfortunately, such gross oversimplifica-

Robert G. Gilpin is professor of politics and international affairs at the Woodrow Wilson School of Princeton University. His principal interests are in the field of science policy, especially the way in which science reshapes international relations.

tions do not help us very much, and one must look elsewhere for a useful perspective on the topic.

Among modern social scientists, the individual who was most sensitive to the social role of technology was William F. Ogburn. Ogburn was not a systematic thinker and did not develop a theory of social change, but his insights provide a useful tool for comprehending the impact of technology on society, the conception of social change I will set forth incorporates his ideas.[4]

A CONCEPTUAL FRAMEWORK FOR ANALYZING SOCIAL CHANGE

According to Ogburn, technological advance does not impinge directly upon society. That is to say, there is no one-to-one correspondence between technology and social structure such as Marxist theory implies. On the contrary, the ultimate effects of technology on society are indirect and are filtered through economic, social, and political institutions.

In general, technological advance has a differential impact on society through its effects on four areas: demographic structure, political organization, economic activities, and military techniques. In the first place, new technologies may alter the ratio of births to deaths and consequently the age distribution of society. Such a shift in demographic structure can have a profound effect on the family, the economy, and other institutions.

The impact of technological advance on political organization is largely owing to its effect on the ability of political centers to extend control over territory. As Kenneth Boulding has shown, the extent of control is a function of the loss-of-strength gradient of a political center, i.e., "the degree to which its military and political power diminishes as we move a unit distance away from its home base. . . ."[5] Although nontechnical factors may be of critical importance in determining the loss-of-strength gradient, a major factor in the extension of one political group's control over another and the growth of political organization has been advances in communications and transportation technology. By the same token, technological advances may also inhibit the formation of large political entities and lead to fragmentation. As the distinguished Canadian economic historian Harold Innis shows in his *Empire and Communications,* communications technology may be biased either way, in some cases encouraging political fragmentation and in others favoring centralization.[6]

In addition to its effects on the demographic structure and political organization of society, technological advance transforms society through its effect on the economy. For example, it may decrease the cost of transportation and communications and thus alter the location of economic activities. Or technological innovations may give rise to new products and production processes, which in turn change consumption patterns and the standard of living. Through its effect on economies of scale, comparative advantage, and economic efficiency, technological advance can recast the national and international division of labor.

The fourth major area affected by technological advance is military organization and technique. In part, this area cannot be clearly separated from the first three. Demographic, political, and economic changes profoundly affect military capabilities: improvements in communications and transportation have military as well as economic consequences. At the same time, changes in the technology of weapons themselves can transform domestic society as well as international relations.[7] Weapons innovations not only alter the international balance of power; they can disturb the relative strength of the offense and defense, thus influencing the propensity for war.

The second generalization concerning technology and social change suggested by Ogburn's approach is that the impact of a given technology tends to follow a sequence of several stages. The first stage is the technological innovation itself, which may be anything from a minor improvement in an existing technology, such as a new computer program, to the development of a revolutionary technology like the computer itself. The second stage is the immediate effect of the technology on social, political, economic, or military life. The third stage is the longer-term consequences for the demographic, political, economic, and military organization of society. Although Ogburn doesn't emphasize it, one could add a fourth stage: the political response, if any, to the innovation and its consequences.

This four-stage sequence can best be understood by considering two or three examples. The first, the discovery of antibiotics, demonstrates the far-reaching and unanticipated consequences of a simple technological innovation. The sequence begins with Alexander Fleming's accidental discovery of penicillin, the first in the now large family of so-called miracle drugs. The second stage, or the immediate consequence of the development of antibiotics, was the near conquest of infectious diseases. In combination with the improvement in sanitary conditions that has accompanied the rising standard of living in developed countries, the spread of antibiotics have had a more profound effect on the health of mankind than any other single development. The tertiary, or long-term, consequences of antibiotics derive from their effect on the birth and death rates. Both of these rates have declined, giving rise in the developed countries to a profound demographic shift toward an older population. This in turn has led to a shift in the incidence of different types of diseases—as one authority has put it, the development of an aged population with a high incidence of crippling illnesses, like heart disease, cancer, and stroke has meant a shift from mortality to morbidity.[8] The socioeconomic effect has been to separate the incidence of disease and the ability to pay. There is an increasingly large aged population requiring extended and costly medical treatment whose cost cannot be covered by the inadequate financial resources of this group. Finally, the set of consequences following from the innovation of antibiotics reaches its political consequences in the decision, through the agency of Medicare, to socialize the cost of medical treatment.

This is obviously a vast oversimplification of a complex process of social causation. Moreover, it smacks of technological determinism. It leaves out the social, political, and economic environment, which in itself can stimulate technological innovation and channel the consequences of technology in one direction rather than the other. This in fact is the last generalization to be made about the impact of technological advance on society: the analysis of technological innovation and its consequences must take into account the larger social and political context. The same technology may have vastly different effects on different societies. For example, the development of the railroad in the nineteenth century benefited the land powers, particularly the United States and Germany, at the expense of the sea powers. By undermining the then dominant position of Great Britain in international relations, the railroad had a profound impact on the distribution of power.

Given this set of relationships between technological advance and social change, what can one say about the impact of the computer and data processing on international relations? An analysis of this issue requires answering at least three sets of questions. First, what are the immediate effects of the computer and data processing on human capabilities? More particularly, what is their relevance for international relations? Second, what longer-term consequences, if any, will they have for demography, economic relations, and milliary power? And third, what is the larger political, economic, and social context for the transformation of international relations by the computer and data processing? Obviously, these issues cannot easily be separated, but I will attempt to do so.

In the simplest terms, the computer and data processing greatly enlarge man's capacity to store and manipulate vast amounts of data. In combination with other technologies, their implications for human capabilities are formidable indeed. In themselves, what the computer and data processing do is to decrease transaction costs and increase the substitution of electronic for human cybernation processes. These capacities vastly enlarge man's ability to extend his control over technical and human systems as well as to substitute machines for human physical and mental labor. It is from this perspective that one must analyze the impact of the computer and data processing on international relations.

In terms of the four areas of impact I have identified—demographic structure, political organization, economic activities, and military power—the computer revolution would appear to have little direct effect on demographic structure. It is obviously a major tool in demographic studies and may one day facilitate population policy. As such, it could have an influence on the power potential of nation-states, but this possibility has yet to be realized.

The impact of the computer and data processing on political organization is also unclear. One school of thought holds that the computer and other modern technologies have undercut the significance of the loss-of-strength gradient thesis that power diminishes with distance. Such, for example, was the argument of Albert Wohlstetter against those opponents of American intervention in Vietnam who argued that the United States had no business fighting a faraway war and was at a disadvantage relative to the regional powers.[9] Additionally, through the use of modern communications the president of the United States could actually direct military operations. However, other changes in military technology are of greater importance and have transformed the nature of warfare. For this reason, I will pass over the impact of the computer on political organization and concentrate on the two areas where the computer is having more profound effects on international relations, namely, economic and military affairs—although as I shall show, these economic and military changes have critically important implications for international politics.

THE COMPUTER AND ECONOMIC AFFAIRS

The impact of the computer and data processing on economic affairs and organization have been profound. The enormous potential the computer has for affecting economic life has in fact led to fascinating and in some cases wild speculation. At one extreme, Marcuse envisages the computer as ushering in the ideal of communist society, the total replacement of humans by machine labor.[10] More realistically, others identify the computer with the coming of postindustrial society; that is, the preeminence of the modern service sector with its emphasis on the production and utilization of scientific knowledge.[11] In a similar vein, Peter Drucker in *The Age of Discontinuity* foresees information processing as one of the key industries in the future evolution of advanced industrialized societies.[12]

These changes in the economic structure of the industrial societies will in themselves have a profound impact on the international division of labor and hence on world affairs. However, the full implications of the computer for international economic relations can only be appreciated by considering its effect on transaction costs. Together, the impact of the computer on industrial production and transaction costs promise to have revolutionary consequences for international relations.

The importance of transaction costs and the significance of major advances in the efficiency of doing business are generally unappreciated. Yet growth in productivity with respect to business transactions ranks as one of the most potent forces in the evolution of the modern world. One need only point out the invention of printing and the important role it played in the commercial revolution.[13] Substantial declines in transaction costs with their accompanying consequences provide a key to the rise and economic superiority of the West. They constitute in part a more realistic alternative to Marxist and radical-chic interpretations that explain the economic development of the West by the impoverishment and exploitation of the rest of the world, with gold and silver from the New World and the surplus labor of slaves and colonized natives supplying the primitive accumulation that financed Western capitalistic development.[14] The West, according to this view, used its military superiority to wrest wealth from the underdeveloped world. While it would be foolish to deny the fact or importance of colonial exploitation, more efficient economic transactions have been of much greater and more lasting importance in the economic and political supremacy of the West.

The importance of the lowering of transaction costs in the initial economic surge of the West is the theme of Douglass C. North and Robert Paul Thomas's *The Rise of the Western World*.[15] According to the North-Thomas thesis, the expansion of population, the rise of urban centers, and the emergence of a market economy dramatically increased the productivity of economic transactions in the developing Western European economies and fostered economic growth. In effect, the Marxists have historical causation running in the wrong direction. The factors that led to the rise of the West were internal to Europe and had their origins primarily in the nature of new economic institutions. As North and Thomas point out, it was increasing economic efficiency that led to the growth of Western military power and its extension overseas. While colonization of Asia and the New World fed wealth back into Europe, the process began with the increased efficiency of the European economy itself.

In the contemporary world the importance of the lowering of transaction costs is reflected in the emergence and global spread of the multinational corporation. Perhaps no single institution so embodies and symbolizes the economic superiority of the West. While numerous causes account for the overseas expansion of American, Japanese, and Western European corporations, a major factor has been a substantial lowering of transaction costs on a global scale.[16] Without dramatic improvements in communication and transportation, this type of corporate organization would be impossible. The jet airplane, satellite communications, and the computer have created the necessary technological means for the integration of the world economy by Western corporations, but economic integration could not have proceeded as far as it has without the underlying major decrease in the costs of conducting global business enterprise.

The decrease in transaction costs associated with the computer and electronic data processing has also been a major factor in the overseas expansion of American banks and the increasing integration of the world's financial system. As in the case of the global expansion of American corporations, domestic and international political factors are also responsible for this development. The computer could not have transformed international finance without the dominant position of the dollar in the world economy and the rise of Eurodollar (and Asian dollar) markets. A number of changes in American banking laws, particularly a 1966 amendment to the restrictive 1913 Edge Act, were also important factors in this financial revolution. In addition, diversification of banking activities and the need for funds stimulated American banks to go abroad. Together these political and economic changes created the necessary conditions for American banks to expand overseas. But the full potential of these developments were realizable only owing to the implications of the computer for banking operations.

The first thrust of American banking abroad took place in 1966 when American banks set up branches in London, the Bahamas, and the Cayman Islands to tap the Eurocurrency market and to funnel these funds back to the United States. The significance of this development lay in the fact that American banks became the first to recognize and treat Europe as a single banking market rather than a series of discrete and disconnected national markets. As in the case of American multinational corporations, American institutions were the first truly "European" entities and showed the way for their European rivals. In a similar case, though on a much smaller scale, American banks also began to set up foreign branches in Asia, particularly in Hong Kong and Singapore. By 1974, American branch banks abroad had expanded from 181 to 737; assets had grown from $7 billion to more than $155 billion. Of these branches, 333 were located in Europe, the Bahamas, and the Cayman Islands. There were 179 branch banks in Central and Latin America, 110 in the Pacific and Asia, 15 in the Middle East, and 2 in Africa. Though physically in Europe or Asia, they had become part of an interbank net integrating world financial markets.

A key element in this banking and financial structure is a five-year-old computer network called CHIPS (Clearing House Interbank Payments System) whose purpose is to process the complex of payments resulting from the vast expansion of international trade, investment, tourism, and other financial transactions. The creation of nine New York banks, this network handles the traffic of nearly sixty banks worldwide. It can process as many as 25,000 items per day and has handled daily transactions amounting to as much as $60 billion. Impressive as these capabilities are, CHIPS is to be replaced in the near future by a new computerized system nearing the implementation stage. This new system, SWIFT (Society for Worldwide Interbank Financial Telecommunications) will be faster than CHIPS and will link more than two hundred international banks, including thirty-five American banks.[17] Thus, although legal, economic, and political factors have created an environment conducive to the increasing integration of international banking and financial markets, the computer has made this revolution a reality.

As impressive as is this overseas expansion of American banking, the emergence of the multinational corporation is a far more impressive phenomenon. While definitions of the multinational corporation are numerous, it is sufficient to note its characteristics. In the first place, multinational corporations make direct investments in foreign countries. In contrast to portfolio investment, which involves the purchase of equities in a firm, direct investment involves the establishment of a foreign subsidiary or branch or the takeover of a foreign firm.[18] The goal of the investment is managerial control of a production unit in a foreign country.

Second, an MNC (multinational corporation) is characterized by a parent firm and a cluster of subsidiaries or branches in various countries with a common pool of managerial, financial, and technical resources. The parent firm operates the whole in terms of a coordinated global strategy. Purchasing, production, marketing, and research are organized and managed by the parent in order to achieve its long-term goal of corporate growth. Modern communications and computer networks integrate headquarters and subsidiaries into a unified global structure. Through vertical integration and centralization of decision making, the parent corporation seeks to perpetuate its monopoly position with respect to technology, access to capital, and so on.

The differences between portfolio investment, loans, and similar forms of capital export practiced by British and European capitalism in the last century, on the one hand, and the more recent American emphasis on direct investment, on the other, are of immense political importance. In the first case, the underlying motive is largely financial; that is, to obtain a higher return on investment capital; managerial control in general continues to rest with the borrower, and the liabilities incurred by debt borrowing can be liquidated through repayment. The motive for direct investment and the possession of foreign subsidiaries or branches is primarily the acquisition of markets and managerial control. A permanent position and source of income in the foreign economy are desired. As a consequence, even though mutual economic benefit may result, direct investment creates economic and political relations that are more enduring and significant.

Perhaps no one has characterized better the global implications of this development than the late Stephen Hymer, whose analysis of the rise of the multinational corporation suggested what would happen if economic forces were permitted to run their course. Fortunately or unfortunately, technological and economic forces do not simply run their course but are influenced and channeled by the larger sociopolitical environment. Nonetheless, though exaggerated in its implications, Hymer's analysis of the rise of the multinationals is important because of its identification of what he calls the two laws of development: the law of increasing firm size and the law of uneven development. The law of increasing firm size, Hymer argues, is the tendency since the industrial revolution for firms to increase in size "from the *workshop* to the *factory* to the *national corporation* to the *multi-divisional corporation* and now to the *multinational corporation.*"[19] The law of uneven development, he continues, is the tendency of the international economy to produce poverty as well as wealth, underdevelopment as well as development. Together, these two economic laws will produce the following consequences:

A regime of North Atlantic Multinational Corporations would tend to produce a hierarchical division of labor between geographical regions corresponding to the vertical division of labor within the firm. It would tend to centralize high-level decision-making occupations in a few key cities in the advanced countries, surrounded by a number of regional sub-capitals, and confine the rest of the world, i.e., to the status of towns and villages in a new Imperial system. Income, status, authority, and consumption patterns would radiate out from these centers along a declining curve, and the existing pattern of inequality and dependency would be perpetuated. The pattern would be complex, just as the structure of the corporation is complex, but the basic relationship between different countries would be one of superior and subordinate, head office and branch office.[20]

Precisely because the multinational corporation has, at least potentially, such dramatic implications for the organization of the world economy, it has become a source of intense controversy. In fact, few contemporary issues have generated so much heat and so little light. For its defenders, the multinational corporation is an exemplar of rational economic organization and, through its transfer of capital, technology, and management skills, the prime engine of economic growth in the contemporary world. The growing recognition of this fact, it is predicted, will lead to increasing global economic interdependence and the diminution of the power of nation-states over economic affairs. In the words of former Undersecretary of State George Ball, "While the structure of the multinational corporation is a modern concept, designed to meet the requirements of a modern age, the nation-state is a very old-fashioned idea and badly adapted to serve the needs of our present complex world."[21]

Critics of the multinational corporation, on the other hand, regard it as an instrument of economic domination and exploitation. Rather than a mechanism to diffuse technology and economic growth, it is regarded as the principal means by which the advanced capitalist economies have despoiled the less-developed economies. In effect, these critics argue, it is the development of the capitalist economies that has led to the underdevelopment of the Third World, a process in which the multinational corporation is said to have played a key role. What the Third World economies need, therefore, is a powerful state to counter the power of the multinational corporation. In the opinion of these critics, the arguments of George Ball and other defenders of the multinational corporation against the nation-state serves the interests of the corporation. As one Canadian nationalist has put it, "The international corporations have evidently declared ideological war on the 'antiquated' nation-states. . . . The charge that materialism, modernization and internationalism is the new liberal creed of corporate capitalism is a valid one. The implication is clear: the nation-state as a political unit of democratic decision-making must, in the interest of process, yield control to the new mercantile mini-power."[22]

One writer has characterized this debate by declaring that the fundamental conflict of our era is "between ethnocentric nationalism and geocentric technology."[23] In the early seventies the outcome of this struggle seemed to be weighted in favor of the multinational. Raymond Vernon in his influential *Sovereignty at Bay* came close to predicting ultimate success for the corporation.[24] Other writers were less guarded and announced the impending demise of the nation-state, at least as an economic unit.[25] But in 1973 a series of momentous events showed, to paraphrase Mark Twain, that the report of the death of nation-state was premature. The Arab-Israeli October war and the subsequent Arab petroleum boycott are regarded in retrospect as a major turning point, since for the first time host nation-states not only turned the tables on the multinational corporations but made them serve their interests. The role of computers in this development is sufficiently important to merit some attention. But first I will return to the argument between proponents and critics of the multinational corporation and consider the impact of the multinationals on the international distribution of power.

Contrary to the argument of its critics, the expansion of the multinational corporation has favored the development of the world economy. While one can cite cases of "excess" profits, exploitation, and detrimental effects on host economies, the major consequence of foreign investment has been to stimulate foreign economies through the transfer of capital, technology, and managerial skills. As a result, though foreign investment by multinational corporations reflects the superiority of the developed economies, its long-term effect has been to narrow the difference, altering the international distribution of industrial and hence political power to the disadvantage of the developed countries.

Ironically, it was Karl Marx, and more especially Lenin, who first appreciated the historical role played by foreign investment. In his remarkable essay, "The Future Results of British Rule in India," Marx went so far as to suggest that British imperialism was absolutely essential if the crust of custom were to be broken in India and India were to be set on the road to what we would call modernization.[26] Modern communications and particularly the railway, Marx argued, would become in India "the forerunner of modern industry."[27] Subsequently Lenin, in his polemic against capitalist imperialism, *Imperialism—The Highest Stage of Capitalism,* went a step further and argued that foreign investment by capitalist economies shifts the international distribution of power against them. "Capitalism itself," Lenin quotes Rudolf Hilferding as saying, "gradually procures for the vanquished the means and resources for their emancipation and they set out to achieve the same goal which once seemed highest to the European nations: the creation of a unified national state as a means to economic and cultural freedom."[28]

As an example of how the diffusion of Western technology affects the international distribution of power, I will examine the implications of the diffusion of the computer for the exercise of economic power. By economic power, I mean the capacity to inflict economic and political damage through the unilateral interruption of commercial intercourse.[29] In the contemporary world the exercise of such power has become at once more potent and more difficult. It has become more potent because of the increasing interdependence of modern economies; the scale of trading, financial, and investment transactions have made nations more dependent upon one another and hence more vulnerable, to displays of economic power. But by the same token, the diversity and complexity of trade relations in a highly interdependent world economy makes the exercise of such power more difficult. The ability of a nation to shift sources of supply or markets inhibits the ability of other nations to impose boycotts or other forms of economic pressure.

In this situation the possession of data-processing capabilities has become an important element of national economic power, because in order to exercise power, a nation must be able to process a vast amount of data. The classic case in point is the Arab petroleum boycott against the West following the October 1973 Arab-Israeli war.[30] Without sophisticated data-processing capabilities, the Arab oil producers could not have kept track of Western oil tankers, refinery output, and all the other information needed to enforce the embargo. Moreover, given the complexity of the oil industry and the potential for cheating by cartel members, it is doubtful if the Organization of Petroleum Exporting Countries (OPEC) would remain intact without the benefit of electronic data processing. At the least, it would be immeasurably more difficult for OPEC members to retain a high degree of confidence that other members were abiding by the rules set down by the cartel. There is no question that the diffusion of Western computer technology to oil-producing states by the oil multinationals has increased the economic power of these states.

In general, then, the decrease in transaction costs and the expansion of the multinational corporations are causing a major redistribution of world economic power and industrial capabilities. The problem this poses was recognized early in the nineteenth century by a now obscure English economist, Robert Torrens. According to Torrens, the diffusion of British industrial technology to the rest of the world would put Great Britain at a grave disadvantage. He warned that "as the several nations of the world advance in wealth and population, the commercial intercourse between them must gradually become less important and beneficial."[31] The argument that it was in Britain's long-term interest to keep her technology at home was expanded upon by John Hobson at the turn of the twentieth century. Like Lenin after him, Hobson argued that foreign investment was detrimental to the British economy. Through the transfer of capital and technology, Britain was industrializing her future competitors in world markets, and once industrialized, they would turn against her:

Thus fully equipped for future international development in all the necessary productive powers, such a nation may turn upon her civilizer, untrammelled by need of further industrial aid, undersell him in his own market, take away his other foreign markets and secure for herself what further developing work remains to be done in other undeveloped parts of the earth.[32]

The weakness of the Torrens thesis, as amplified by Hobson, is that it takes into account only the negative consequences for trade of the diffusion of technology, neglecting the fact that it has two opposed effects.[33] It is true that the spread of industry destroys markets as newly industrialized countries become able to meet their own needs for manufactured goods, but also creates markets, since developing economies will import capital goods and other products of advanced technology from the older industrialized countries. Additionally, as incomes in the newly industrialized country rise, there is a greater demand for imported as well as for domestically produced goods. Whether the market-destroying or market-creating tendency will predominate depends upon a number of factors: the flexibility of the older industrial economy and its capacity to readjust its exports; the extent of trade protectionism; rates of growth of various economies; and so on. Thus the precise effect of the spread of industrialism is an empirical question. In the case of the nineteenth century, however, Great Britain failed to make the necessary readjustments. This was a major cause of the ensuing intense commercial competition among the industrial economies and a contributing factor to the tensions that ultimately led to the First World War.

In the contemporary world a similar challenge faces the United States as the decline in transaction costs encourages the diffusion of American technology to foreign competitors who often have much lower labor costs. If, in addition, one accepts the compelling argument of Peter Drucker that the United States has largely exhausted the innovative potential of the industries upon which its economic supremacy has rested—steel, automobiles, petrochemicals—then a conflict in which the United States plays a role like Great Britain's in the nineteenth century may characterize the last quarter of the twentieth century.[34]

The escape from this potential conflict lies in the adaptability of the American economy and its ability to invent new industrial processes and products. It is from this perspective that one must view the impact of the computer on international relations. The computer and data processing, as Drucker argues, promises to be one of the great future growth industries for the United States.[35] Through the application of the computer to industrial production and the development of computer-related products, the United States can adapt its economy to the new realities of the world economy. These realities include the spread of American industrial technologies to low-cost foreign producers and the consequent need to apply computer automation to "low-technology areas" if the United States is to remain competitive. If American exploitation of the computer and its potential leads to the creation of a new international division of labor, the economic conflict toward which we appear to be heading might be averted.

THE COMPUTER AND MILITARY AFFAIRS

In 1966, Sir Solly Zuckerman, the scientific adviser to the British Ministry of Defence, surveyed the potential contributions of the then unfolding technological discoveries for the conduct of war and concluded that nothing on the horizon would make a "decisive change in the strategic balance between the great powers."[36] He immediately qualified this prediction, however. "There is one development of modern technology," Zuckerman wrote, "which, within the next ten years, could have a profound effect on the way that defense is controlled. I refer to computers."[37] The ability of computers to absorb, store, and process information, he held, could well have a profound effect on military operations and on the control of the military machine in general. Thus far, he argued, the computer had been incorporated into the working of particular weapons. In the future, it held forth the promise (or threat) of transforming the planning and conduct of war itself.

The impact of the computer on weapons and warfare has indeed been profound. It has touched every phase of military activities from logistics to weapons design. As Zuckerman suggests, its consequences for the nature and conduct of war have still to run their course. As war and the possibility

of war constitute the ultimate arbiter in the affairs of nations, the consequences of the computer and data processing for international relations
are likely to be far-reaching. Precisely what they will be in the final analysis, even whether they will be benign or malevolent, remains unclear, and
at this juncture one can only speculate.

The first glimmering of the computer's potential for military affairs came
during the debate over the development of thermonuclear weapons. In
October 1949, the Russians exploded their own atomic weapon and broke
the American monopoly. This startling event gave rise immediately to an
intense debate in scientific and official circles over the appropriate American response. On one side were ranged those scientists and officials who
believed that the United States had no recourse but to speed the development of a thermonuclear or hydrogen bomb. Ranged against them were
other scientists, principally led by Robert Oppenheimer, who believed
such a step toward even more destructive weapons would be the ultimate
folly.[38]

Underlying this debate were vastly different technical, strategic, and
political views.[39] But in addition there were fundamental philosophical
differences concerning the impact of technology on international relations
and man's capacity to control what his genius had created. The case of the
thermonuclear option was set forth brilliantly by John von Neumann in an
article entitled "Can We Survive Technology?"[40] The foremost consequence of the contemporary technological revolution, von Neumann argued, is that technology has largely replaced geography as the main
element in national power. The compression of time and space owing to
advances in communications and the destructiveness of modern weapons
have overturned traditional concepts of geopolitics. The advantage no
longer belongs to the nation that controls the sea, the heartland, or the
world island's rimland. The advantage in war and international politics
belongs to the nation that sets the pace in technological development. The
lead time that one nation has over another in the creation and application
of knowledge will be decisive.

In the energy-deficient prenuclear world, von Neumann continued, a
nation behind another in military technology could use space to purchase
time in which to catch up militarily. Traditionally, of course, this had been
the basis of American military policy. In the future, however, this strategy
would no longer be possible. The decisiveness of weapons of mass destruction had eliminated the option of buying time with space if a nation
fell behind its enemies. The only rational strategy had become that of
exploiting to the ultimate all technological options of potential military
consequence.

According to von Neumann, efforts to arrest technological development,
as advocated by Oppenheimer and his colleagues, were outright danger-

ous. In a world of decisive weaponry any attempts to control continued development of weapons places "a competitive premium on infringement." This is to say, in a world where nations through the exploitation of science are able to create revolutionary new weapons and where the offensive predominates over the defensive, a decisive military advantage flows to the nation that is first to possess such weapons. For this reason, any system to prohibit the development of new weapons would create a temptation to violate the control surreptitiously and thereby achieve a technological advantage that would tip the balance of power in one's favor. As a consequence, he reasoned, the only safe course for an open society such as the United States in competition with a closed society such as the Soviet Union is to forgo any effort to control technology. Developing the hydrogen bomb was the only safe course to follow.

The fundamental position of the opposing school was the imperative of bringing under rational control technological developments in general and the developing nuclear arms race in particular. In contrast to von Neumann's Faustian philosophy, these scientists believed that technology must and could be subjected to human control. If the genie could not be put back in the bottle, at least another genie could be created to control the first one. Moreover, they believed they had such a genie in the form of a new invention, the first electronic computer. With it, they believed, they could fashion a defense against the ultimate offensive weapon.

Throughout the early 1950s in a series of study projects (among them Project Vista, Project Charles, Project Hartwell) the group of scientists opposed to the development of the hydrogen bomb formulated an alternative set of policies for the United States.[41] Some of these policies, such as the development of tactical nuclear weapons and the reinvigoration of civil defense, are not directly relevant to the subject at hand. But one proposal is of critical importance. This was the idea of harnessing the computer and modern electronic systems to solve the problem of continental air defense, which led ultimately to the construction of a distant early warning line (DEW line) across the northern approaches to the North American continent.

The fundamental idea of these scientists was that the computer and rapid data processing would enable the United States to construct a nearly impenetrable defensive barrier. In combination with developments in radar and interceptor aircraft, the computer could drastically reduce American vulnerability to Soviet nuclear attack. If the Soviet Union could be denied access to American targets, it would have little incentive to initiate war against the United States or America's overseas allies. As we would say today, the Soviets would be deterred. But for these scientists continential air defense was the means to a larger goal. Their ultimate aim was that of reversing the spiraling nuclear arms race and of moving toward nuclear disarmament. An effective system of continental air defense, they believed, would enhance American freedom to negotiate a disarmament agreement with the Russians.

The importance of the DEW line is that it was the first albeit primitive attempt to deal with the problem posed by nuclear weapons through the implementation of the deterrence concept. It sought to forestall nuclear war by decreasing the incentive for nations to use nuclear weapons. The conception of deterrence on which it rested, however, was faulty and like DEW itself would be overtaken by future technological developments. By deterrence, these scientists (and the American military establishment as well) meant the prevention of an attack on American cities and America's overseas allies. As Soviet nuclear and air power grew, the concept of deterrence, which has become the fundamental principle of American military policy, would also change.

The new concept of deterrence grew out of a series of strategic studies begun in the early 1950s at the RAND Corporation in Santa Monica, California.[42] Shortly after the outbreak of the Korean War, the air force approached RAND and asked it to study the most effective and least costly way to build a series of air bases overseas. At that time it was assumed that the Korean War was the prelude to a major Soviet attack on western Europe, and if deterrence should fail, the air force wanted its bomber force positioned for a counterattack.

The assignment for carrying out what came to be known as the base study was delegated to a RAND research group headed by Albert Wohlstetter. At first Wohlstetter and his colleagues approached the problem as it had been presented to them by the air force: where and how to build air bases overseas in order to maximize America's offensive striking power against the Soviet Union. As they compared various alternatives and scenarios, however, the critical factor that emerged was whether one assumed the United States or the Soviet Union would strike first in a nuclear war and, even more important, whether or not the opposing nuclear force could survive the first blow.

Air force doctrine and the proposal for a series of overseas air bases were based on the assumption that the Soviet Union would strike first against western Europe and that American strategic air power would then retaliate against Soviet targets. The air force did not include in its calculations that the first Soviet strike might be directed against America's retaliatory force. From the air force perspective, basing American bombers abroad would enhance deterrence by increasing the offensive striking power of the Strategic Air Command. The air force had taken insufficient account of the fact that basing American planes would also increase their vulnerability to a Soviet first strike.

Wohlstetter and his colleagues came to the conclusion that the

Strategic Air Command would have deterrent value only if it could survive a Soviet first strike against it. In effect, the concept of deterrence came to mean the existence of a second-strike capability. The reduction of vulnerability to a preemptive first strike, they concluded, must be the key to America's military planning. Unless the United States Strategic Air Command were able to survive a Soviet first strike and retain the capacity to retaliate, deterrence would not succeed. Deterrence required the defense of America's retaliatory capabilities and not, as the advocates of the DEW line held, the defense of America's cities based on exploitation of the computer.

The irony of this tale, however, is that it was the computer that transformed weaponry in the direction advocated by the RAND researchers. Throughout the 1950s and early 1960s, efforts were undertaken to reduce the vulnerability of manned bombers. As Soviet bomber capabilities grew, the dangers inherent in a situation where both sides feared surprise attack became the nightmare of strategic thinkers. It was the advent of nearly invulnerable ballistic missiles, made possible by new generations of miniaturized computers, that finally ushered in the present era of relative stability based on mutual deterrence. Without this computer-induced revolution in weapons, détente and arms control could not exist in their present form.

Yet the relative success of strategic nuclear deterrence contains a paradox. Throughout history a basic relationship has seemed to hold between the destructiveness and the probability of war. As the destructiveness of war has increased, the probability it would occur has decreased. The sixteenth-century international lawyers who wanted to draw up a legal framework for war in order to tame it realized and agonized over this cruel relationship. Tolstoy, in the epilogue to *War and Peace*, cursed the humanitarians who would take the sting out of war. If men were to forsake war, he believed, they must not be spared its full and evil consequences. We are still haunted by this notion, out of which rises the fear that through their efforts to stabilize mutual deterrence and implement arms control measures, the United States and the Soviet Union are once again making the world safe for war. As the fear of unleashing total war recedes, the likelihood that one power or another will resort to limited war in order to secure an advantage increases, which suggests that we have not yet escaped from the historical relationship between the destructiveness and the probability of war.

Although there are few other generalizations one can make about war, one that seems to stand the test of time is the differential impact of offensive and defensive weapons on the propensity for war. Whereas weapons innovations that favor or at least appear to favor the offensive tend to encourage the outbreak of war, the ascendancy of defensive over offensive weapons tends to discourage war. The two great wars of the twentieth century were preceded by developments that at least appeared to favor the offensive. In the case of the First World War, it was the mobility provided by the railroad. Belief in the superiority of the offensive guided all military staffs in their preparations for war, though the introduction of the machine gun and trench warfare were to prove the superiority of the defensive.[43] Similarly, the Nazis' belief that they had fashioned an invincible offensive based on tactical aircraft and the tank was a major factor in unleashing the German war machine in 1939.

In an era of mutual nuclear deterrence and arms control at the strategic level, the balance between the defensive and the offensive at the level of conventional and tactical weapons will be a major determinant of international stability. If weapons developments tend to favor the offensive, as they have over the past half century, then strategic deterrence may usher in an era of limited warfare comparable to the situation that prevailed in the eighteenth century. If, on the other hand, the tide were to turn in favor of the defensive, then there would be a basis for hoping that political conflicts could be resolved peacefully. The inability of a potential aggressor to strike quickly and seize his objectives would be a major restraint on the exercise of force.

In assessing the future balance of offensive and defensive military power and its implications, one must appreciate that conventional weapons technology is undergoing revolutionary changes. The scientific and technological advances, particularly in electronics, that have transformed strategic warfare are beginning to produce an equivalent transformation of ground and sea warfare. Fortunately or unfortunately, the world is only at the beginning of this transition, though it has already begun to impinge upon military doctrine and operations. The terminology associated with the new weapons technology suggests their character: the automated or electronic battlefield; precision-guided munitions; "smart bombs"; surveillance and warning satellites, and so on.

In the two major conflicts of the past decade—Vietnam and the Arab-Israeli war of October 1973—these new weapons developments played a major role for the first time. In the Vietnam War, the American hope of "winding down" the war and creating an electronic fence around South Vietnam failed miserably. The dictum that in war morale counts twice as much as materiel was seen to be vindicated once again. But in the 1973 October war electronic weapons had a critical impact on the conduct and outcome of the fighting. For the first time, the two major offensive weapons of modern warfare—the tactical airplane and the tank—met their match. The impact of these advances in defensive weapons such as laser-guided bombs and electronic antitank weapons on Israel's past reliance on blitzkrieg tactics was summarized by one writer in the following terms:

Armor could not operate in dramatic offensive maneuvers. After their heavy initial losses, the Israeli armed forces reverted to working very closely with mechanized infantry and artillery and mortar units. . . . After two disastrous days on the Sinai front, the Israeli armored forces could no longer indulge in any charges of the Light Brigade.[44]

While Israel's reliance on the offensive has been blunted, by acquiring her own arsenal of electronic defensive weapons she has enhanced her security against the rapidly expanding Soviet-equipped Syrian armored force and the reequipped Egyptian tank army. As a consequence, these novel antitank weapons provide an element of stability among armies that deploy more tanks than were used by both sides in the Second World War. With all due respect to ex-Secretary of State Henry Kissinger and his shuttle diplomacy, the ensuing stalemate provided by defensive weapons is a major factor in the Israeli-Egyptian détente and the present (albeit uneasy) stability in that region.

The significance of this shift in the direction of the defensive may be appreciated if one considers its potential impact on the one military theater that more than any other could trigger a war between the United States and the Soviet Union, namely, Western Europe. The heart of the cold war has been the American-Soviet competition in central Europe. Without assessing the blame for this conflict, the military strategy of each side has been determined by its respective geopolitical position. The Soviet Union is a major land power controlling what Halford MacKinder called the heartland of the Eurasian continent.[45] It can easily employ its massive land armies against Western Europe. The United States, essentially a sea-air power, is separated from the main area of contention by an ocean expanse of three thousand miles. It has been able to check Soviet conventional superiority primarily through its nuclear deterrent. The major function of American forces in Europe has been to serve as a tripwire or trigger, but as the Soviet Union's own strategic retaliatory power has grown, the credibility of the American nuclear deterrent has weakened, while Soviet conventional power on the ground has remained intact.

As inconceivable as a ground war in central Europe may seem in an era of détente, it would be foolhardy to conclude that the potential for armed conflict has ceased to exist. A Soviet Union increasingly pressed by expanding Chinese power and fearful of a dynamic West Germany allied to the United States, for example, might well be tempted in the decades ahead to eliminate one or another of the dangers on her two fronts. If the Soviet Union felt that the United States was deterred from using its strategic retaliatory force and a rapid offensive action could eliminate the potential threat on her western front, such an action would not be beyond the bounds of rational calculation.

The inherent instability and danger in Western Europe resides in the fact that the offensive still reigns supreme at the level of conventional weapons. Contrary to a once-held belief, tactical nuclear weapons also favor the offensive rather than the defensive. But what is more critical is that one weapon presently dominates all others on the potential European battlefield, a factor that outweighs all other considerations to it. "In Europe today," as one military authority has written, "the tank is supreme. If it can be stopped, the ability to project force and to occupy territory no longer exist. No other means of projecting force seems practical."[46] Recognizing this, the Soviet Union maintains an overwhelming armor superiority on the European front, and the disposition of these forces suggests reliance on decisive striking power based on a blitzkrieg style of attack.

My purpose here is not to analyze the military problems of the NATO alliance but to suggest that in potential areas of military conflict technological advances may once again be shifting the balance in favor of the defensive. As Sir Solly Zuckerman has suggested, the revolutionary impact of the computer could push conventional warfare further in this direction. The application of the computer to early warning and command and control systems promises greatly to enhance the strength of the defense, and in combination with other recent developments, it could overturn the belief in the supremacy of the offensive that has been a major factor in twentieth-century warfare. If so, it would greatly reduce the propensity of the human race to settle its differences by violent means.

CONCLUSION

The economic and military changes associated with the impact of the computer and other advanced technologies on international relations suggest that the world is now entering an age where more is to be gained through economic cooperation and an international division of labor than through strife and conflict. Thus, in the opinion of Saburo Okita, president of the Japan Economic Research Center, the exercise of force for economic gain or to defend economic interests is an anachronism:

We are living in a century when such military action is no longer viable. To build up militarily just to protect overseas private property is rather absurd in terms of cost-benefit calculations. The best course for the Government in case of nationalization or seizure of overseas private Japanese assets is to compensate Japanese investors directly in Japan rather than to spend very large amounts of money to build up military strength.[47]

Such a charge, if true, was anticipated at the beginning of this century by that remarkable student of geopolitics, Halford MacKinder. In 1904, at the conclusion of the last and greatest phase of European expansionism, MacKinder observed that "the Columbian epoch" had ended.[48] For four hundred years, he noted, the European peoples had grown in wealth, population, and power; they had expanded their dominion over the entire globe; they had fought numerous wars of territorial division and redivision. Explorers had completed the outline map of the world; the Europeans had politically appropriated all but the most remote territories, China and Japan. Most significant of all, it had been a conquest involving relatively little cost to the Europeans and against negligible resistance. But now, he argued, it was finished; a new epoch was beginning. This new age, he predicted, would be different in that there was no longer any great, "empty" space to absorb the energies and surplus populations of the European peoples. The world, as ecologists today tell us, had become a closed system; the explosion of social forces accompanying growth could no longer be dissipated outward against weak and pliable peoples. Instead, MacKinder prophesied, national ambitions and expansionism would rebound back upon the European nations themselves as well as on their possessions throughout the globe. In the post-Columbian age, he predicted, the cost of territorial expansion and conflict would far outweigh any conceivable benefit. "Probably," MacKinder wrote, "some half-consciousness of this fact is at last diverting much of the attention of statesmen in all parts of the world from territorial expansion to the struggle for *relative efficiency*."[49]

Since MacKinder wrote these lines the world has experienced two costly and devastating world wars of territorial conquest and redivision. It is only today that MacKinder's prophecy that the struggle for economic efficiency rather than for territorial aggrandizement would become the central feature of international relations appears to be coming true. The advent of nuclear weapons and the technological revolution in warfare appear to have decreased the utility of the military instrument at the same time that world economic interdependence has enhanced the role of commercial and trade relations among nation-states. In short, commerce and the exercise of economic power have become a more fundamental—some would say *the* fundamental—determinant of international politics. The future, it is held, belongs to the centers of economic and commercial power.

One should not be overly sanguine, however, that economics have displaced force as the final arbiter of world politics. In judging the probable long-term success of such emergent commercial powers as Japan and Western Europe, I am reminded of a passage in Montesquieu's *Considerations on the Causes of the Greatness of the Romans and Their Decline* that occurs during his discussion of the success of the great commercial power of the Hellenistic world, Egypt, just before it was crushed by the Romans.

Commercial powers can continue in a state of mediocrity a long time, but their greatness is of short duration. They rise little by little, without anyone noticing, for they engage in no particular action that resounds and signals their power. But when things have come to the point where people cannot help but see what has happened, everyone seeks to deprive this nation of an advantage it has obtained, so to speak, only by surprise.[50]

Montesquieu's observation serves to remind us that we should be somewhat reserved with respect to the frequently heard argument that Western Europe and Japan in particular constitute a new type of world power, economic rather than military. Yet, if détente and mutual deterrence succeed, the argument that economic efficiency and commercial relations have supplanted, at least to an interdeterminant degree, the traditional pursuit of power through territorial conquest is worthy of serious consideration in any analysis of the contemporary world. As I have suggested, the computer revolution will have played a crucial part in bringing about this change in the conduct of international affairs.

EDITORS' POSTSCRIPT

Professor Gilpin's essay looks at the future on the basis of the past and present impact of the computer. As a result, it views the computer as one more cost-reducing technology, and it does not discuss the possible consequences of more far-reaching technical developments. If, for example, information networks and home computers become a dominant reality, then they may have a significant effect on demography through deurbanization—people will be able to work while enjoying the rural benefits of a clean environment and energy independence. In world affairs there is the possibility that totalitarian powers could exploit the computer to control travel and other individual activities, a purpose for which it is unfortunately well suited.

NOTES

1
Wilbur Moore, "Social Change," *International Encyclopedia of the Social Sciences* (New York: Free Press, 1973), 14:365.

2
See Preface to *A Contribution to the Critique of Political Economy*, in *The Marx-Engels Readers,* ed. Robert Tucker (New York: W. W. Norton, 1972).

3
This is essentially the view of Herbert Marcuse in *One-Dimensional Man* (Boston: Beacon Press, 1964).

4
For Ogburn's ideas, see *William F. Ogburn on Culture and Social Change: Selected Papers*, ed. Otis D. Duncan (Chicago: University of Chicago Press, 1964).

5
Kenneth Boulding, *Conflict and Defense—A General Theory* (New York: Harper & Row, 1962), p. 245.

6
Oxford: Clarendon Press, 1950. See also G. N. Clark, *Unifying the World* (New York: Harcourt Brace and Howe, 1920).

7
The influence of military organization and technique on social structure is treated by Stanislav Andreski, *Military Organization and Society* (London: Routledge, 1954).

8
Herman Somers, *Doctors, Patients, and Health Insurance* (New York: Doubleday, 1962).

9
Albert Wohlstetter, "Theory and Opposed-System Design," in Morton Kaplan, ed., *New Approaches to International Relations* (New York: St. Martin's Press, 1968), pp. 45–94.

10
One-Dimensional Man.

11
Daniel Bell, *The Coming of Post-Industrial Society* (New York: Basic Books, 1973).

12
New York: Harper & Row, 1968.

13
William McNeill, *The Shape of European History* (New York: Oxford University Press, 1974), p. 127.

14
For an analysis of these arguments, see J. H. Elliott, *The Old World and the New, 1492–1650* (Cambridge: Cambridge University Press, 1970).

15
Cambridge: Cambridge University Press, 1973.

16
The factors accounting for the rise of the multinational corporation are examined in my *U.S. Power and the Multinational Corporation—The Political Economy of Foreign Direct Investment* (New York: Basic Books, 1975).

17
This discussion on international banking is based on Deirdre Donnelly, "American International Banks," mimeo (1975).

18
For a more detailed discussion, see Gilpin, *U.S. Power and the Multinational Corporation.*

19
Stephen Hymer, "The Multinational Corporation and the Law of Uneven Development," in Jagdish H. Bhagwati, ed., *Economics and World Order* (New York: Macmillan, 1972), p. 113.

20
Ibid., p. 114.

21
George Ball, "The Promise of the Multinational Corporation," *Fortune*, June 1, 1967, p. 80.

22
Kari Levitt, "The Hinterland Economy," *Canadian Forum* 50 (July–August 1970): 163.

23
Sidney Rolfe, "Updating Adam Smith," *Interplay,* November 1968, p. 15.

24
New York: Basic Books, 1971.

25
See, for example, Harry Johnson, *International Economic Questions Facing Britain, the United States and Canada in the Seventies* (London: British–North American Research Association, 1970), p. 24.

26
Shlomo Avineri, ed., *Karl Marx on Colonialism and Modernization* (New York: Doubleday, 1969), pp. 132–139.

27
Ibid., p. 136.

28
V. I. Lenin, *Imperialism—The Highest Stage of Capitalism* (New York: International Publishers, 1939), p. 121.

29
This definition is from Albert O. Hirschman, *National Power and the Structure of Foreign Trade* (Berkeley: University of California Press, 1945), p. 16.

30
See "The Oil Crisis: In Perspective," *Daedalus*, Fall 1975.

31
Robert Torrens, *Essay on the Production of Wealth* (London: Longmans, Hurst, Rees, Orme, and Brown, 1921), p. 288.

32
John Hobson, *Imperialism: A Study* (1902; reprint ed., Ann Arbor: University of Michigan Press, 1965), p. 308.

33
See Albert O. Hirschman, "Effects of Industrialization on the Markets of Industrial Countries," in *The Progress of Underdeveloped Areas,* ed. Bert Hoselitz (Chicago: University of Chicago Press, 1952), pp. 270–271.

34
Drucker, *The Age of Discontinuity.*

35
Ibid.

36
Sir Solly Zuckerman, *Scientists and War—The Impact of Science on Military and Civil Affairs* (London: Hamish Hamilton, 1966), p. 88.

37
Ibid.

38
This debate is analyzed in my *American Scientists and Nuclear Weapons Policy* (Princeton: Princeton University Press, 1962).

39

See Herbert York, *The Advisors* (San Francisco: W. H. Freeman, 1976).

40

Fortune, June 1955, p. 152.

41

See Gilpin, *American Scientists*, pp. 114–115.

42

Bruce Smith, *The Rand Corporation* (Cambridge, Mass.: Harvard University Press, 1966).

43

See Stefan T. Possony and Etienne Mantoux, "DuPicq and Foch: The French School," in *Makers of Modern Strategy*, ed. Edward Mead Earle (Princeton: Princeton University Press, 1941), pp. 206–233.

44

Peter Wilson, "Battlefield Guided Weapons," *United States Naval Institute Proceedings*, February 1975, p. 19.

45

Democratic Ideals and Reality (New York: W. W. Norton, 1962). First published in 1919.

46

Steven Canby, "The Alliance and Europe: Part IV, Military Doctrine and Technology," *Adelphi Paper* 109 (London: International Institute for Strategic Studies, 1975), p. 2.

47

Quoted in John Sterbo, "Japanese Business: The Yen Is Mightier than the Sword," *New York Times Magazine*, October 29, 1972, p. 58.

48

Democratic Ideals and Reality, p. 241.

49

Ibid., p. 242.

50

Montesquieu, *Considerations in the Causes of the Greatness of the Romans and Their Decline* (New York: Free Press, 1965), p. 47.

12
Regulation and Computer Services

Roger G. Noll

Since the mid-1960s, proposals to regulate the computer services industry have surfaced periodically in the public-policy literature.[1] Proponents of regulation see several potential market failures in the provision of data-processing services through time-sharing systems attached to large, powerful computers through the communications network. Regulation is necessary, the proponents argue, to prevent the computer, computer services, and communications industries from exploiting these potential market failures to the detriment of the rest of society.

Regulation refers to a particular type of government policy in which a specialized agency is given the responsibility to control some important aspect of an industry through use of the administrative process for licensing, rule making, and case adjudication. The absence of regulation does not imply an absence of interventionist policy; alternatives to regulation include specialized taxes, subsidies, legislative definitions of property rights enforced by the courts through civil litigation, public ownership, and statutes that make illegal certain kinds of behavior, such as robbery or monopolistic practices.

There are three main rationales for the regulation of computer services. The first is that economies of scale and integration make the industry, at least in some services, a natural monopoly. The second is that computerized data banks threaten individual privacy. The third is that certain features of the communications and computer industries lead to "ruinous" or "unfair" competition that will result in monopoly or oligopoly even if economies of scale do not warrant such a development.

The three rationales lead to somewhat different regulatory proposals. The natural monopoly argument is used to support classic public utility regulation, in which the regulators control prices, profitability, and the expenditures of regulated firms, set technical standards intended to facilitate the development of compatible systems in interconnected areas, and

Roger G. Noll is professor of economics in the Program on Social Science at the California Institute of Technology.

award exclusive franchises to provide service in each market. The underlying idea is that these regulatory activities will enable society to capture the benefits of natural monopoly without giving firms monopolistic market power.

The privacy rationale applies to a wholly different regulatory process, one that does not regulate the economic aspects of the industry except indirectly but does control the nature of the service it offers. The principal policy instrument of this type of regulation is licensing: having the power to determine which firms and people are allowed to provide service and using this power to enforce operating standards. For example, the Federal Communications Commission theoretically awards and renews broadcast licenses on the basis of the type of service offered by the applicant, while states limit entry into various professions, ranging from medicine to hair styling, to those passing qualifying examinations or satisfying certain educational requirements.

The unfair competition rationale argues for a type of regulation that, while superficially similar to public utility regulation, is nevertheless quite different. Regulating competition involves controls on prices and profits, but the emphasis is on minimum (rather than maximum) limits. In addition, as with licensing, this form of regulation involves controlling the expansion of old firms and the entry of new ones, as in the case of route awards by the Civil Aeronautics Board and the Interstate Commerce Commission. Competitive entry is a continuing possibility in regulated competition but is impossible in a natural monopoly[2] and irrelevant when service quality is the only regulatory concern.

NATURAL MONOPOLY

In the mid-1960s, two related developments led some observers to conclude that the data-processing industry was likely to become a natural monopoly.[3] One was the development of ever larger, ever more powerful computers exhibiting scale economies to computational capacity. A rule of thumb emerged, known as Grosch's Law, which states that doubling the cost of a computing system purchases a fourfold improvement in computational power, as measured by processing speed, memory size, and rates of input and output.

The second development was the rapid spread of time-sharing computer services systems. Normally, time-sharing systems simply enable several geographically dispersed customers for computer services to capture scale economies by pooling their demand for data processing. But more elaborate extensions of the interconnection concept were immediately apparent. Computers could be linked to each other to pool computing capabilities, and geographically dispersed data banks, containing different kinds of information, could all be accessed by the same computer. A time-sharing terminal could be used for numerous informational purposes, ranging from normal data processing to delivery of mail. A single, national computing services system, interconnecting all terminals, processors, and data banks, would capture economies of scope; that is, it would offer each user the maximum flexibility in data-processing services as well as exploiting scale economies in hardware. The result would be the emergence of a dominant computer utility, resembling the Bell System or even functioning as a part of it.

Regulation of the computer services industry is said to have two advantages. First, it can prevent the computer utility from exploiting its monopoly position by setting prices that generate excessive profits. Second, regulators could hasten the development of the computer utility by setting technical standards and licensing equipment and communications links so that interconnection problems would be minimized.

Factors Working against Monopoly

Even if the factual premises regarding economies of scale and scope are accepted, the argument based on them does not constitute a valid rationale for regulating computer services because it ignores several potentially important countervailing influences.

The observation that computational capacity exhibits economies of scale does not necessarily support the conclusion that the computer services industry is likely to be a natural monopoly. The industry sells more than computational power; it sells information.[4] If the customers of the industry differ with respect to the kind of informational demands they place upon a computer system, scale economies in computational power may be worth sacrificing in order to reach other, more valuable objectives.[5] A firm that markets a single, homogeneous data-processing service capturing maximal scale economies in computational power may lose the business of a particular type of customer to a competitor producing a service that is more expensive but tailored to the informational demands of that class of user. If the first computer service firm tries to reclaim the business of the lost customer by diversifying the service it offers, it must incur increased managerial, coordination, terminal equipment, and software costs, which may offset the scale economies in computational power.

In the end, the computer services industry may exhibit either of two industry structures other than monopoly: a competitive industry in which firms exhibit neither economies nor diseconomies of scale, or Chamberlin's "monopolistic competition."[6] In the latter structure, each firm has unexploited scale economies. The service it sells differs from that offered by its competitors and is valuable enough to its customers to make them willing to forgo the possibility of paying a lower price for a service less suited to their informational needs.

A similar line of argument applies to the likelihood that economies of scope will yield a single, dominant computer utility. Accepting the proposition that users regard as desirable the ability to access numerous computers, data banks, and other information sources, the question remains whether the additional costs of a completely interconnected system are worth the candle. To the extent that total interconnection requires sacrificing some service diversity and accepting greater managerial, coordination, and software costs, a firm may find a less flexible, less interconnected system more cost-effective than the service provided by a computer utility.

Whether economies of scale and scope will naturally lead to a dominant computer utility is a question that turns on several empirical issues, only one of which is the existence and magnitude of the scale economies in computational power and the scope economies in a totally interconnected system. The former measures only one aspect of costs, while the latter refers to only one factor influencing demand. Other pertinent issues include the effect of firm size and diversity on all costs, not just computational power, and the extent to which customers for computer services have intense preferences for specialized services.

The cost issue has been addressed in Bower's extensive study of costs and profitability in the computer services industry, which examines purchases of computing systems by companies that serve their own informational requirements by establishing internal data-processing departments.[7] Bower finds scale economies only for relatively small firms and reports that large firms with internal data-processing departments are far more likely to expand computer service operations by adding new systems than by turning to systems with greater capacity. Bower concludes that the computer services industry is competitive and finds no reason to expect the industry to move toward a monopolistic market structure other than the possibility that one of the two corporate giants that supply the industry with vital inputs—IBM and AT&T—might adopt corporate policies that in the absence of effective antitrust or regulatory action could keep other firms from entering the market, even though a competitive market structure is economically warranted.

The best evidence on the demand issue is the history of competitive entry into telecommunications by specialized common carriers. The arguments against allowing specialized carriers to enter the telecommunications market were similar to the reasons for predicting the emergence of a computer utility, namely, that economies of scale and scope would make competition undesirable, and without regulatory protection not even viable. Yet in maximizing the extent to which these economies could be captured, the Bell System provided a menu of services that did not include the offerings that were most attractive to some types of users, particularly data-processing operations. What carried the issue for prospective competitors at the Federal Communications Commission was the failure of the Bell System to provide service tailored to the requirements of these users and the willingness of other firms to design long-distance telecommunications networks to meet these specialized demands.[8] For example, one type of service that is especially useful to data-processing systems is short-duration, high-reliability connections for rapidly transmitting bursts of data. The conventional telecommunications network, designed for switching and transmitting relatively slow telephonic and telegraphic messages, was unsuited to this task.

Although debate has raged for a decade on whether AT&T or its competitors can more cheaply offer these new computer-related telecommunications services, what is pertinent here is that the successful entry of specialized common carriers showed that an intense demand for particularized computer-related services does exist. This has been further demonstrated by the fact that AT&T responded to its competitors by offering new services with technical characteristics similar to theirs, in addition to cutting the price of the old services. If a single, homogeneous service were economically superior, price-cutting alone would have been enough to foreclose competitive entry.

The preceding arguments do not, of course, conclusively prove that a natural monopoly in computer services will not develop. The Bower study is based upon data from the infancy of the industry. Future innovations in computer hardware, communications, terminal equipment, software, system design, and other components used in producing information services may produce conditions favoring an industry with one or a very few firms. But even such developments would not necessarily call for public utility regulation of the surviving entity.

Whether a single firm has effective monopoly power depends upon whether close substitutes for the monopolist's service are available or could become so. A computer utility would always be limited in the extent to which it could extract monopoly profits by two alternative strategies available to its customers.[9] First, they can always install their own data-processing systems. Because of the rapidity with which technology is advancing in both communications and small computers, for most firms reliance on an in-house system is an acceptable second-best alternative which would severely constrain the monopolistic powers of a computer utility. Second, as long as communications regulatory policy and competition in computer hardware makes it possible to enter the business of providing interconnected computer service systems, the potential for monopolistic pricing by a single computer utility is further eroded. Finally, even if for some firms the services of a single, dominant system are so valuable that the possibility exists for monopoly pricing directed at them, antitrust policy should be adequate to prevent it. Because the computer utility would, for the first two reasons, be required to charge close to a competitive price to some users, ample evidence on discriminatory pricing should be easily assembled if the company attempts to target a few vulnerable users for especially high prices.

Ideal utility regulation would, of course, outperform the combination of potential competition and antitrust action. If a computer utility has any cost or service advantages, these factors will limit but not totally eliminate excess profits. Unfortunately, regulation in practice is a blunt instrument for dealing with this problem. Once regulation is imposed, competitive entry becomes far more difficult, as the past two decades have shown with respect to FCC decisions about specialized common carriers and "foreign attachments" to the switched telecommunications system.[10] In order to enter a regulated industry, a firm must first win approval from the regulators. This can be accomplished only through the cumbersome administrative process by which regulators are required to make decisions, with the possibility of further appeals to the judicial system. Participating in the regulatory process is expensive and time-consuming, and having to do so creates a significant barrier to entry. In addition, regulatory agencies are designed to have a conservative bias with respect to the structure of the regulated industry, since the burden of proof rests with those who propose changes.[11] Thus reliance on regulation to restrain monopolists requires abandoning some of the restraint provided by the possibility of competitive entry. Furthermore, because regulatory decisions are normally exempt from antitrust laws, if a regulated firm succeeds in obtaining approval for an anticompetitive practice, such as refusal to interconnect or price discrimination, the restraints imposed by the possibility of antitrust actions are also relaxed.

Regulation offers little in return for relaxing these natural limits on the monopolistic practices of a firm. Numerous empirical studies document the willingness of regulatory agencies to permit price discrimination by regulated firms. In part, this is because regulators have a tendency to see prices as taxes to be levied according to some calculus of the comparative social worth of various groups, rather than as signals conveying information about costs that induce buyers to make economically efficient decisions.[12] One conventionally applied principle of equitable taxation is ability to pay. When translated into regulatory policy, this tenet becomes value of service pricing; that is, those who are willing to pay the most for the service should be charged the highest price. But value of service measures, among other things, the degree of monopoly power a firm has over a customer. Hence value of service pricing results in a price structure closely resembling the one that would result from the normal price discrimination that a multiservice unregulated monopolist, free of potential competition and antitrust liability, would establish.

An additional factor limiting the ability of regulators to control monopoly is the informational advantage of regulated firms. An incumbent firm, if it is at all well managed, will always know more about the regulated industry—and especially about service costs—than either the regulatory agency, a group of customers, or a potential entrant. Even if a regulatory agency sought to prevent discriminatory prices, its ability to do so would be limited by its inevitable reliance on cost and demand information supplied by the firm. As a result, a regulated monopolist can use information strategically in adversary processes. One mechanism to achieve this end is to design the internal information systems of the firm in such a manner that only the data most likely to benefit the firm are collected and transmitted to the regulators. Another mechanism is to flood the regulatory authority with so much information that it exceeds the agency's ability to digest it.

As a result, regulatory agencies normally concentrate on a relatively few indexes of performance, such as the regulated firm's overall rate of return or the average change in prices over time, rather than on specific details of the price structure or the mix of services being offered. And even here, regulators do a poor job. In periods in which inflation is not a serious problem, so that normal technical progress produces continuing reductions in the nominal cost of providing service, there is no evidence that regulators have any effect on the profitability of regulated firms.[13] During inflationary times, agencies do limit profits, but primarily because their decision-making process is too slow to react expeditiously to changing conditions, rather than because of a specific policy objective. In the short run, at least, this lethargy can threaten the financial viability of regulated firms.[14]

In sum, the existence of a single firm does not establish the presence of monopolistic abuses and the desirability of regulation. On the contrary, if the technical and economic environment in which a firm operates subjects it to the threat of competition, imposing regulation is likely to make matters worse. Regulators are not likely to exercise more than loose control over a monopolist, but they are likely to increase the insulation of the single firm from the forces that limit its ability to engage in monopolistic abuses. This is not to say that regulation of natural monopoly is never justified. Local telephone-operating companies, for example, face only imperfect substitutes and no threat of competition for the provision of everyday switched telephone service, so that the undesirable effects of regulation are probably not very important in this case. Even crude regulatory controls, assuming that they are not excessively expensive to implement, could generate net benefits.[15] But in the computer services industry, competition is pervasive and likely to remain so, and competition is a more effective engine for efficiency than regulation.

PRIVACY

The concept of an individual right of privacy is an elusive one, and the debate about privacy is diffuse. The range of practices that have been discussed in the context of personal privacy includes such diverse items as selling addresses to direct-mail advertising companies, publishing accounts of bizarre sexual activities of famous personalities, and collecting political dossiers in the criminal records kept by law enforcement agencies. Although a major focus of the privacy debate since the mid-1960s has been the possibility of abuses in the use of computerized data banks, the problems pertaining to computers can only be understood in the broader context of the general issue of privacy.

Privacy as an Economic Resource

Although economists are prone to overemphasize the economic basis of seemingly noneconomic issues of social policy,[16] in the case of the debate about privacy some insight is gained by casting the issues in economic terms. The privacy debate concerns the appropriate legal definition of ownership and property rights in personal information; the economics of privacy are an interesting special case of the economics of information.[17]

   In principle, property rights to personal information could be allocated in a number of ways. Individuals could be given exclusive rights to information about themselves, preventing anyone, including government officials, from obtaining it without their approval. At the other extreme, all personal information could be public, to be provided on demand to whoever should request it. Realistically, American institutions are sure to establish property rights between these extremes; since normal government functions such as taxation, conscription, and education cannot be effectively performed unless the government has some coercive power over personal data.

   The definition of property rights to personal data matters partly because this information has economic value. Decision makers are called upon to make guesses about the likely behavior of an individual in a wide variety of circumstances. Which of several applicants will be the most productive employee? What is the likelihood that a speeding car is driven by an escaping felon? Will an applicant for a loan default on the payments? If a particular piece of personal information enables a decision maker to separate individuals into categories that correspond, on the average, to the sought-after characteristic, that piece of personal information will have economic value;[18] since possession of it increases the chance that a given decision will produce the intended result.

Normally, a free market in information has certain advantages in terms of economic efficiency. For example, if a piece of information enables creditors to separate high-risk from low-risk applicants for a loan or employers to categorize job applicants by their likely productivity, interest rates and wages will come closer to reflecting true economic values, thereby contributing to more efficient resource allocation. Unfortunately, the use of personal information does not always contribute to efficiency; it also raises several important issues of economic and social equity. A few examples will illustrate this point.

The most obvious equity issue is that the legal definition of the nature and ownership of the right to personal information affects the distribution of wealth in society. People can and do sell personal information about themselves if the price is sufficient to offset whatever value is attached to maintaining privacy. The spate of confessional biographies by Washington secretaries, an unanticipated Bicentennial diversion, was an obvious case in point. In principle, the market could work the other way. If a secretary possessed personal information about a fun-loving congressman, it is possible that the latter would pay the former an amount sufficient to maintain privacy.[19] Of course, such transactions are illegal, leading to an important asymmetry: if individuals do not have property rights in personal data about themselves, the privacy value of that information cannot influence its use for other purposes unless blackmail and extortion are legalized. Consequently, if the privacy of personal information is valued, legal allocation of the rights to personal information to someone other than its subject will lead to excessive use of it.

Another important element of the privacy issue arises from the costliness of enforcing rights to personal information. Once information is no longer completely private, the possibility exists for it to be used in ways not regarded as desirable by its subject. Even if individuals have the right to decide who will have access to personal information about them, whether or not they can exercise this right depends upon the effectiveness of the legal system. Most personal data, falling short of interesting scandal, has a comparatively low market value, yet the criminal and civil justice procedures used to enforce property rights are relatively expensive to deploy. As a result, a person would rarely find it worthwhile to make a criminal or civil complaint in order to enforce rights to personal information. Instead, the problem of enforceability would make individuals reluctant to provide personal data even for purposes of which they approve, for fear that unauthorized, unapproved uses may result.

A third source of concern about the use of personal information is related to the explicitly statistical purposes for which it is used. Separating individuals into categories according to some economically or socially important behavioral characteristic may still leave substantial interpersonal behavioral differences unexplained. If so, categorization, while contributing to economic efficiency, raises equity issues. Suppose, for example, a credit agency discovers that all people living on the west side of the tracks pay their bills on time but 10 percent of those living on the other side of the tracks default. In addition, suppose that twice as many people live on the east side as on the west side, and that among east siders one cannot tell in advance which are the 10 percent that are deadbeats. It is then economically efficient for the credit agency to lower the interest rate to west siders and increase it for east siders, since the latter are responsible for all the bad-debt costs of the company. But in taking such action, a majority of the population—60 percent—will face higher interest rates even though they are not any more prone than the favored west siders to fail to pay their debts. A society based on majority rule is quite likely to decide in this instance that the inequity of the use of this particular piece of personal data to separate credit customers more than offsets the efficiency gain. Of course, if the figures pertaining to east siders are reversed—only 10 percent are good risks—majority rule could produce the same result, except in this case the majority would be voting essentially to continue its credit subsidy from both west siders and the few honorable east siders. Whether demands for equity, efficiency, or subsidy drive the body politic on any particular privacy matter depends, of course, on the empirical realities of the division of citizens into socioeconomic categories (good risks and bad risks) and the imperfect signals (the personal data) used to assign people to one category or another.

The dilemmas of attempting to construct a legal definition of the right to privacy that serves the objectives of social equity and economic efficiency are not new, and they confounded legal scholars and public officials long before the rise of the computer services industry. The growth in the use of computers has not created these dilemmas, but certainly it has served to sharpen the issues.

Computers and Privacy

Computers pose a threat to personal privacy because they reduce the costs of storing and retrieving information. Since the early 1960s, data that were formerly stored on paper and in filing cabinets have been transferred to tapes and discs for use in computerized information systems.[20] In general, because computers lessen the cost of using personal information, the logical consequence of computerization is that more use will be made of this information; however, the specific aspects of data processing that computers have made cheaper have changed the emphasis as well as the amount of data use.

Not only have computers greatly reduced the cost of storing information, but because accessing data on computers does not entail physically separating it from its storage location, computerization has meant that data are misfiled or lost much less often. This reduces the expense of systems for maintaining and replacing information. Computers also reduce the cost of retrieving information from large files and of gaining access to files of other organizations. Prior to the development of time-shared computer systems, retrieval and delivery of data to the point of use was labor-intensive and time-consuming, even if facsimile transmission over communications lines was used to move data from the point of storage to the point of use. The one cost of information systems that has not been reduced through computerization has been the collection of new data. If anything, costs of collecting new information have been increased by requiring one more stage in entering data into storage—that it be transferred from hard copy to a computer storage system—and a more uniform format for ease of future reference. In fact, these requirements are sufficiently onerous that some types of data, such as detailed personal histories, have not been extensively computerized.[21]

Because computers affect costs unevenly at different stages of information processing, computerization has led to greater use of existing information, but not to a comparable increase in the collection of new information. With data easier to access and more reliable, decision makers find it worthwhile to reference them more frequently, and organizations find it more advantageous to share them across physical distances. Of course, if data are consulted often enough the reduced cost of storage and access will offset the increased cost of collection, so that computerization will cause some information to be collected that was not collected in the past; however, this is still likely to be less important than the more extensive use of data that have always been collected.

Westin and Baker have reached a similar conclusion but have stated it somewhat more strongly.[22] They conclude that computers have had essentially no effect on the type of personal information collected, based upon their study of the effect of computers on numerous, diverse systems. But their cases reveal only the early response of organizations to the introduction of computerization. In general, the more innovative uses of a new technology are likely to come later than the use of it to perform established functions more efficiently. The least innovative use is simply for an organization to transfer its existing information system to computers and exploit the lower access cost, by consulting the data more frequently. It requires some innovation, but not a great deal, for an organization to enter into more extensive sharing arrangements with other organizations possessing related information. What requires the greatest creativity is to uncover new uses of the powers of computerized information systems and the new information that these uses require. As time goes on, and users become more attuned to the potential of computers, the scope of data included in computerized files can be expected to increase, but in order to make the costs of collecting the new information worthwhile, the data must be used more frequently than was the case under the old methods.

Computerized data systems threaten to reduce privacy in two ways: (1) lower storage costs lead owners of data banks to keep historical information longer, and (2) the premium on frequent use of data extends the social and economic arenas in which data that are already collected are used. Both trends represent for the most part the addition of marginal uses of personal information, uses that were not worthwhile when the higher costs of traditional systems had to be paid, in response to the specific kinds of cost advantages that computerized systems offer. The most egregious invasions of privacy—collecting data about lifestyle and beliefs—may be serious problems, but they are not created by computerization. Computers do not reduce the relatively high costs of gathering such information, although they do significantly reduce the cost of using and sharing it once it is collected. Currently, only government finds collecting this kind of information in a systematic fashion worth the costs, and computers are unlikely to change matters. The threat posed by computers is that government will respond to the new cost incentives by making more use of such information and by offering to share it with private data systems, or even to sell it.

Unlike matters of personal behavior and belief, economic histories of individuals are valuable to the private sector and have been collected since long before the advent of computerized information systems. Here the threat of computers is that more decisions will be based upon the kind of thorough review of past performance currently conducted by credit institutions. One obvious candidate is the use of financial information by firms for advertising purposes, in which likely customers for a particular product could be identified by reviewing the history of past transactions and income.

One of the consequences of computerization is an increase in the consequentiality of any given decision. More extensive use over a longer period of time of a particular piece of a person's history increases the potential stake of the person in the decision that generated the information. To the extent that personal goals are consistent and behavior rational, increasing the consequentiality of decisions contributes to economic efficiency and, at least arguably, to social equity (a person is less easily deceived by another in the presence of data on past behavior). To the extent that the future consequences of present actions are fundamentally uncertain, that personal goals change over time, and that behavior is at least occasionally random or emotional, increasing the consequentiality of decisions can make them more stressful, make individuals more conservative and hesitant to take action, and reduce opportunities for personal growth and flexibility. For purely economic purposes, current and relatively recent behavior is likely to be deemed most valuable, so the threat of lengthening the period covered by computerized records is probably minimal. But as the McCarthy era illustrates, in the political and social arena historical information can be used in damaging ways against individuals, regardless of their recent actions.

These are only a few of the problems associated with the more extensive use of personal information that results from the economies of scope computerized systems provide. In essence these problems entail social diseconomies of scope that may give rise to public actions to limit the extent to which information resources can be pooled and exploited. Nevertheless, computers have not been responsible for invasions of privacy, and consequently effective controls on the use of computerized data banks will not end the misuse of personal information. Numerous organizations already collect data that are by any definition private, and they did so long before information systems were computerized.

Privacy, Computers, and Public Policy

Proponents of regulation see the effect of computers on privacy as giving rise to the need for a government agency to decide who shall have access, and for what use, to which data. Regulators would implicitly decide what constitutes an invasion of privacy and license data banks, data bank interconnections, and computer personnel only if they complied with the norms promulgated by the regulators.

The alternative to regulation is a body of law that makes privacy rights explicit. The ultimate source of the public-policy issue regarding privacy is the failure of legislatures and courts to develop such law, since with relatively few exceptions, the law recognizes no individual right of privacy.[23] Most of the relevant law places limits on the use of personal information but does not protect individuals from being required to provide it. Through common law the rights of privileged communications—with doctors, lawyers, spouses—are protected. The courts have also limited FBI dissemination of political information to local law enforcement agencies. Legislation has placed limits on the uses of certain types of information collected by the government, such as census responses and tax returns, and through the Fair Credit Reporting Act has provided new rights of notification and challenge to persons denied credit.[24] In addition, some government agencies have self-imposed regulations regarding the use of data they collect, notably the Social Security Administration.[25] Aside from these exceptions, most data, especially data collected by private individuals and corporations, are not subject to privacy restrictions. In fact, the Supreme Court has rejected the notion that personal information is valuable personal property, an opinion that whatever its legal merits is economic nonsense.[26] The courts have readily recognized the economic value of private information in business law by affording protection to trade secrets and corporate financial information but have failed to give legal recognition to the functional identity of corporate and personal privacy.

One avenue of legislative remedy for the failure of the courts to develop a common-law right of privacy is the creation of a regulatory agency to control the use of personal information. Such an agency would have a dual task. First, through rule-making procedures, it would create a body of law that would distinguish legitimate from illegitimate uses of personal information and establish standards for maintaining the security of sensitive data. Second, through case-by-case adjudicatory processes, it would allow information systems to be constructed and maintained only to the extent that they conformed to the normative standards developed by the agency. The enforcement mechanism would be licensing information systems and the people who manage them, coupled with the power to suspend or to fine licensees. The process would resemble the regulation of broadcasting by the Federal Communications Commission, aviation safety by the Federal Aviation Agency, nuclear reactor safety by the Nuclear Regulatory Commission, or occupational standards by virtually all states.

However, the disadvantages of licensing to control information systems are numerous, especially when the task is in the area of making judgments about standards of behavior for the regulated industry rather than dealing with purely technical matters. One source of difficulty arises from the dependence of the regulatory process on formal procedures satisfying the strictures of administrative law. Administrative rules of procedure have two important effects on regulatory agencies. They make agencies dependent on the evidence and arguments presented in formal adjudicatory proceedings, which normally makes agencies rather passive bodies. They also limit participation in the regulatory process through formal rules of standing and because participation itself is time-consuming and expensive. Consequently, individuals are rarely represented in the process, whereas well-organized groups with high stakes in the proceedings are always represented and are often the only force participating besides the agency itself. Such uneven representation leads to biased decisions.[27]

If rights of privacy are a serious public-policy issue, it is because the existing legal system fails to accord much in the way of protection of personal privacy. The controversial issues that a regulator would be called upon to resolve all involve conflicts between the value of personal information to large organizations and the individual's right to keep such information a private matter. Where regulation only involves resolving conflicts among powerful groups, its decision-making procedures need not introduce insurmountable difficulties; but the issues raised by the privacy debate are those with which regulators are least able to deal effectively, since they involve conflicts between powerful organizations with a major stake in the issue and a dispersed, heterogeneous group of unorganized individuals.

Based upon the history of licensing in other industries, creating a regulatory authority for computer data banks in order to protect individual privacy is likely to have as its primary effects the reduction of competition and the codification of privacy rights in a manner beneficial to data users, not the subjects of the data. For example, in the name of promoting localized service, the FCC has used its licensing power to limit the availability of television in most cities; the effect has been inflated profits in television and no significant local programming other than the nightly local news.[28] In the name of promoting high standards of professional conduct, numerous professions have been regulated by the states through the process of occupational licensing; the primary effect has been to limit entry into licensed professions, raising the income of licensed professionals in comparison with those in states without licensing or with those in the same state who have similar skills but are not licensed.[29] Even the mundane taxicab industry is subject to licensing, allegedly to provide safer, more regular service; however, the consequence is scarcity and monopolistic pricing.[30] The overwhelming evidence of economic research on licensing is that regardless of its initial purpose it degenerates into a vehicle for serving the interests of the licensed group. The best evidence supporting this conclusion is that government licenses to do business are sold for remarkably high amounts: over $20,000 for a taxi license in some cities and typically several million dollars for a license to operate a VHF television station. These figures represent the excess profits created by limited licenses. One can only conclude from this sorry record that licensing of information systems is likely to become a vehicle for protecting data processors against assertions of individual property rights and incidentally against competition.

The situation if anything is likely to be worse when regulators are called upon to control the collection and use of data by other governmental entities. Most obviously, presidential appointment powers can undermine the independence with which an agency judges the policies of executive bureaus. But even with full independence, regulators can be expected to exercise minimal control over other agencies. In addition to strong representation, governmental authorities also possess a political legitimacy that a private organization cannot claim. In dealing with regulatory agencies, courts rarely question the social wisdom of the agency's decisions; instead they focus on the procedural correctness of the decision-making process, as long as the agency can legitimately argue that its legislative mandate gives it authority to act on the issues in question.[31] Being adjudicatory bodies, regulatory agencies normally take this same stance with regard to other governmental entities. Since government is the primary source of the most outrageous abuses of private information, passivity with regard to other government actions is an especially troublesome weakness of regulation.[32]

Another inherent weakness in regulating the use of personal information is that the creation of a regulatory authority carries certain implicit presumptions about the nature of the problem of privacy. First, it presumes that decisions about limits on the use of personal information should be centralized rather than individual. Second, in assuming that the essence of the problem is a conflict of rights, it presumes that users of information have the right to use personal data.

To the extent that individuals value their privacy differently, uniform rules regarding the collection and use of information are inefficient, just as centralized decisions about occupational choice or consumption expenditures are bound to produce imperfect results for most individuals. Delegation of individual decision-making to allocate resources, whether personal information or anything else, makes sense only if some intrinsic characteristic of the resource makes decentralized decisions inefficient for other reasons, such as scale economies in processing information or pervasive third-party effects of transactions.[33] While it can be argued that government access to certain personal information is a component of legitimate collective actions, it is difficult to imagine a market imperfection relating to private uses of information that justifies establishing the right of private data systems to any personal information. Even in the most innocuous case of privacy invasion, the sale of mailing lists for advertising purposes, the market failure works the other way; that is, involuntary costs are imposed on the recipient of advertising (he must process the unexpected information and dispose of the medium that brings the message).[34]

Other than to define their ownership, the only sense in which maintaining the rights of privacy calls for collective action is in the enforcement of these rights. Because in most instances enforcement costs are high relative to the value of personal information, single actions to force compliance by actors committing multiple violations make sense. But this can be accomplished by writing explicit legislation with regard to the ownership of rights, the penalties for violating them, and the mechanism for policing adherence.

The simplest form of such legislation would be to assert that individuals have the power to determine what use shall be made of information about their personal affairs unless Congress acts specifically to use the coercive powers of government to collect such information. Information collected coercively could be limited in use to the purposes and bureaus specifically named in the enabling legislation; sharing of data by government agencies, whether within or between jurisdictions, would be prohibited without explicit legislative authorization. Legislation could also specify that information about private transactions could not be used without the approval of one of the parties and the notification of the others, with the latter having the right to add qualifying information. Each file found out of compliance could be made subject to a fine that would be low enough not to be onerous in the case of occasional errors but would be a strong disincentive to massive violations (perhaps a few dollars for each name in the file for which appropriate approvals and notifications were not included in the record). Enforcement would be by a federal inspection agency, operating much as customs officials and bank examiners do now.*

This proposal would at least force the principal conduit of political values in American society—the Congress—to consider in detail the problems of personal privacy in an information-rich society. Furthermore, the issues would be debated and decided in the relatively open forum of Congress rather than in the obscure hearing room of a regulatory agency. Congress would be called upon either to enact explicit legislation supporting the concept of a right to privacy along the lines of the preceding proposal or to make known in a definitive, public fashion that with few exceptions the right of personal privacy, whatever it means, is not worth protecting against the continued accretion and use of personal information by public and private organizations. The latter decision, whatever its social merit, is at least clear and honest. The creation of a regulatory authority to study and deal with the problem would essentially be an equivalent decision, but it would convey the wrong message. While the creation of a new regulatory authority would seem to indicate the government's intention to enumerate and enforce meaningful rights to privacy, it is all too likely that the users of computerized information systems would be the ones to determine the rights to personal information.

RUINOUS AND UNFAIR COMPETITION

A common rationale for imposing economic regulation on an industry is the assertion that competition is "ruinous" or "unfair." Although lip service is paid to the welfare of consumers by arguing that these failures of competition create fluctuations in price and the availability of service, the main focus of the argument is on the welfare of incumbent firms. The

---

* The agency would not engage in regulation, since it would determine neither the standards of behavior nor the punishment for noncompliance.

essence of regulated competition is to afford firms protection against economic losses. Trucking and trunk airlines are two especially important examples of this type of regulation.

The rationale based on ruinous competition takes two forms. One is that "high fixed costs" cause normal competitive prices to be insufficient to cover total costs. Fixed costs are costs that in the short run are not dependent upon total sales, the clearest example being production capacity. The second rationale is that "unpredictable fluctuations" in supply and demand make a business too risky. While this argument usually has been made in support of controls on agricultural commodities, it was also used by the airline industry in supporting the creation of the Civil Aeronautics Board. Finally, firms have argued that regulated (or unregulated) businesses have an "unfair advantage" over unregulated (or regulated) firms in support of the proposition that unregulated firms should be included under the regulatory umbrella. Trucks and barges were regulated in part because rails were already regulated; cable television is regulated because it threatened to undo the objectives of broadcast regulation. Some form of each of these arguments has been raised in the debate about regulation of computer service firms.

Ruinous Competition in Computer Services?

A substantial proportion of the costs of a computer service firm are independent of short-term variations in sales.[35] Computer hardware and software are long-term investments based upon a firm's expectation of the demand for its services. In addition, the computer service firm may write long-term contracts for procuring communications links to interconnect its system. Thus the computer services industry satisfies the premise of the high fixed cost argument to roughly the same degree as many other competitive industries that have been regulated on this basis.

In addition, the computer services industry is subject to considerable uncertainties on the supply side of the market. The principal inputs to the computer services industry are computer hardware, communications apparatus, and systems analysis, all of which are subject to unanticipated advances in knowledge. While the rapid technological progress in these areas has been relatively smooth when measured over long periods of time, like all technical advance it is subject to fits and starts. A poorly timed investment in the best current hardware and software can spell financial catastrophe when another major breakthrough takes place soon after, making the new investment obsolete overnight. Again, computer services appear to have characteristics that satisfy the premise of unpredictable fluctuations.

The next step in making the case for regulation is to relate the factual premises of ruinous conditions to the efficiency with which the market operates to satisfy consumer demand. The argument is that high fixed costs and supply uncertainties cause some firms to go bankrupt, leaving the market less competitive and imposing costs on the users, who must find another source for the services that had been provided by the bankrupted firm. That this argument is factitious is evident when one pauses to reflect on how and why the factual premises of ruinous competition could lead to bankruptcy for some firms. A firm goes bankrupt because its revenues fall short of its financial obligations. This happens because either demand is insufficient to justify all of the production capacity in the industry or the firm has higher costs than its competitors. In neither instance is any social purpose served by preventing competition from eliminating some firms. If the customers of the bankrupted firms were to encounter excessive costs in switching their business to someone else, the weak firms could survive by charging higher prices, thus saving their customers the costs of switching. If the bankruptcy of some firms were to cause the number of firms remaining in the industry to be too small to guarantee competitive pricing, it would still be unnecessary to save inefficient firms, for the remaining firms would not be able to charge prices exceeding those that would attract new firms into the industry, firms that would face the same costs as the bankrupted businesses. Furthermore, an attempt to charge monopoly prices after bankruptcy had produced an uncompetitive market would be a clear antitrust violation, subjecting the perpetrator to triple damages claims by the bankrupted entities. Using regulation to preserve high-cost firms produces the worst possible result: prices are set high enough by the regulators to preserve the firm that would otherwise not survive, even though such pricing in an unregulated market after bankruptcy had reduced competition would be susceptible to antitrust attack, and even though other firms could provide the same or better service at a more attractive price.

The historical record provides unambiguous proof that regulated competition inevitably leads to higher prices and inefficiency. The imposition of regulation in railroading was based in part on allegations of monopoly pricing on short-haul routes and in part on ruinous competition for long-haul business. Railroads often competed for shipments between major cities, but because they had different routes between cities they could charge monopoly rates between intermediate points. Immediately after the Interstate Commerce Commission began regulating the railroads, short-haul rates were reduced, but by a tiny amount compared to the increases in the rates on competitive routes.[36] Regulated trunk airlines charge prices that run from 20 to 100 percent higher than the competitive price.[37] Deregulation of certain types of truck shipments in the late 1950s caused reductions in prices of about 20 percent.[38] Were regulation of computer services not to produce a similar result, it would stand as the lone exception to the proposition that regulated competition leads to higher prices.

An even more devastating cost of regulated competition is its effect on innovation. Preserving inefficient firms entails eliminating some of the incentive to reduce costs, since innovative firms cannot capture the full advantage of a technical advance by lowering prices and capturing more business. In surface transportation, regulatory attempts to preserve markets for high-cost firms severely retarded such innovations as unit trains,[39] piggyback truck-rail shipping, and "Big John" hopper cars.[40] The kind of innovation promoted by regulated competition is higher-cost service that in the absence of changes in price can win customers from a competitor but that would not be undertaken if both price and quality of service were competitively determined, as is illustrated by piano bars, flight-scheduling conflicts, sandwich wars, and seat-spacing competition in the airline business.[41] Because technical progress has been so rapid and economically advantageous in computer services, this is an especially heavy price to pay for regulating the industry.

The presence of conditions satisfying the factual premises of the ruinous competition argument is cause for some concern that the computer services industry will one day seek and receive regulatory protection. To date, growth has been exceedingly rapid, so that the widespread excess capacity or wholesale, instantaneous punishment of less efficient firms has not yet occurred. Consequently, calls for regulatory protection by computer services firms have been rare.[42] But rapid exponential growth cannot persist indefinitely. When growth begins to slow some firms will be caught in the middle of excessively optimistic investment plans, while others will pay more dearly for less efficient operations as competition for customers becomes more intense. If short-term market conditions become bad enough that most firms incur financial losses during the weeding-out process, an industry demand for regulation can be expected.

Unfair Competition and Partial Regulation

While computer service firms have yet to demand extensive regulation of the industry, calls for limited regulatory protection from competition with communications common carriers have been made. One basis for these demands is that a regulated common carrier can subsidize its data-processing service, setting prices that fall short of costs. The purpose of this action, of course, is to extend the communications monopoly of the common carrier to the computer services business.

An unregulated monopolist would have no incentive to gain entrance to a competitive industry by charging predatory prices, because unless the monopolist possessed cost advantages, he could not succeed in keeping out competition over the long run, in which case the immediate losses from predatory pricing could never be recouped. Furthermore, any attempt to engage in such a strategy by raising prices after competitors failed would be subject to antitrust prosecution and triple damages. Regulated monopoly, on the other hand, does possess an incentive to monopolize a competitive market even at a loss in some circumstances. First, the firm must be effectively regulated to some degree; that is, it must be charging prices below the monopolistic profit-maximizing rate in some markets. Second, regulators must limit prices by insisting that profits be related to some measure of costs (e.g., a fixed percentage markup over total costs or a limit on profits as a percentage of capital investment). Third, firms must possess some leeway in setting prices and allocating costs among services, with most regulatory attention focused on overall measures of prices, profits, and costs. Under these assumptions, the regulated firm can increase total profits by expanding sales in the competitive market at a price that does not cover costs and raising prices in monopolized markets to recover the loss.

The communications common carriers do satisfy the conditions of the preceding argument. Local operating companies and domestic long-distance services provided by AT&T are regulated in this fashion, although since the late 1960s the FCC has devoted considerably more attention to the structure of prices and the allocation of costs within the Bell System. Furthermore, in the early 1960s AT&T apparently did provide subsidized services for bulk communications users in response to the FCC's decision to allow firms to build their own private long-distance facilities.[43]

Another reason the computer services industry fears unfair competition by communications common carriers is their dependence on communications services.[44] Communications common carriers that also offer data-processing services could discriminate in favor of their affiliates by making interconnection with the communications system expensive (such as by requiring expensive interfaces), by providing competing computer services firms with inferior communications services, or simply by causing delays in the process of procuring interconnection. The potential gain from this practice is that a communications firm could extend its monopoly to computer services by denying competitive entry.

Since the FCC adopted its procompetitive policies with respect to terminal devices, computer services, and specialized common carriers, interconnection problems have been a recurring difficulty. Most of these involve interconnection disputes between AT&T and either competing equipment manufacturers or specialized common carriers, but the computer services industry has also been involved in some controversies. The first such case involved a charge by Bunker Ramo that common carriers had discriminated against the former's stock quotation and transaction service.[45] The issue was resolved not by the FCC, which was still investigating the matter years after the complaint was filed, but by AT&T's offer to interconnect Bunker Ramo if the latter would abandon the 2 percent of its service that AT&T found most offensive. The case illustrates the power of the common carriers to enforce their own policies regardless of the policy objectives of the FCC. Since FCC proceedings are necessarily slow because of their procedural requirements, victories by competitors can be hollow if in the intervening decision period the denial of interconnection and the cost of participation in the regulatory process have bankrupted the potential competitor. Consequently, even if Bunker Ramo regarded its chances of winning its complaint as good, the protracted sacrifice of 98 percent of its computerized stock information business to retain the 2 percent that AT&T opposed would be unlikely to have been worthwhile.

Despite the occasional interconnection dispute at the computer communications interface, in comparison with problems involving terminal devices and specialized common carriers the computer services area is remarkably peaceful. The actions of AT&T, with regard to specialized common carriers particularly, have been a continuing concern at the FCC and are now a major issue in antitrust litigation against the Bell System. One major reason for the relative inactivity in the computer services area could be the consent decree that ended the antitrust action by the Department of Justice against AT&T.[46] The consent decree restricts AT&T from engaging in any business other than furnishing regulated communications services and supplying itself with equipment to accomplish that end. Since AT&T provides both local and long-distance communications service to nearly all of the country, the vast majority of computer services firms operate free of potential competition from AT&T except in the rare instances in which they provide services over AT&T lines that compete with services Bell can legally offer.

The period of inactivity over the interconnection issue with regard to computer services may well be approaching an end, for two reasons. First, as time progresses the distinction between communications and computer services is growing increasingly blurred, and even under the consent decree Bell may legally claim that an increasing share of the computer services business is within its domain. Second, pending antitrust litigation could undo the 1956 consent decree, in which case whatever is left of AT&T might be freed to enter the computer and computer services business. If so, the chances are high that the industry will see a replay of the interconnection disputes that accompanied the attempts at competitive entry in terminal devices and specialized common carriers.

The obvious solution to the problem of possible discriminatory actions by communications common carriers is first to keep these firms out of all but the common carrier business and second to allow firms to resell communications services acquired from common carriers. The former would prevent a communications firm from extending its monopoly into most present computer services, while the latter would provide some protection against price discrimination in the blurred region between communications and data processing. The disadvantage of such a prohibition is the possibility that it might prevent the most efficient firm from entering a market. However, in the case of computers and computer services, the common carriers do not appear particularly likely to fall into this category; nor, as I have already argued, does a natural monopoly in computer communications services appear to be materializing. Since keeping the common carriers out does guarantee real competition (not the regulated, fake competition practiced in other industries), this disadvantage is probably worth accepting.

In its decision in the computer inquiry, the FCC fell short of endorsing a truly competitive solution, although it did endorse unregulated competition in most of the computer services industry. While the commission did not force communications common carriers out of the data-processing business, it did rule that: (1) a common carrier can sell computer services only through a wholly separate corporate affiliate; and (2) a common carrier cannot buy service from its own affiliate. The latter ruling had little functional merit; it simply forced a common carrier to have two computer services operations, one for internal use and one for external sales, which might have forced the sacrifice of some scale economies but in any event offered no significant barrier to predatory behavior by the communications firm. Subsequently, the courts declared the second provision to be invalid.[47]

The first provision is also of marginal importance. It does not change whatever internal incentives the common carrier possesses to engage in predatory behavior in the computer services market. Common carriers would be just as likely to engage in preferential treatment for their own computer services operation and just as likely to use the regulatory process to impose costs and delays on potential entrants. Eventually the FCC probably could detect the consequences of monopolization by observing prices, costs, and profits among computer services firms, but systematic review of these data would be tantamount to imposing regulation on the industry. Thus, while the separations may ease the task of allocating costs among services under a future regulatory regime, there is no reason to believe that it offers any protection against attempts by a communications common carrier to extend its monopoly to computer services.

The other principal feature of the FCC decision in the computer inquiry was a definition of the boundary between communications and computer services. The FCC ruled that data transmission was a communications function and would be subject to common carrier regulation, including controls on entry. Purely computational services, even if they involved communications links among components of the computer system, were ruled to be outside the regulatory ambit. Hybrid services, in which communications and computer services were inextricably linked, would be reviewed on a case-by-case basis, with the FCC reserving the power to declare any particular service sufficiently close to communications to warrant regulation.

One rationale for this distinction was to protect the long-standing regulatory policy of preventing the resale of communications services, a policy that enables regulated firms to maintain price discrimination. In the absence of an antiresale policy, customers facing services with low prices would simply resell their connections to customers facing high prices. Another rationale was the policy of the FCC of allowing entry to a firm only if it promises to provide services that are not offered or offered only imperfectly by existing carriers. A persistent theme in all procompetitive decisions by the FCC since Carterfone was allowed entry into the communications equipment business,[48] whether they involved specialized common carriers, hybrid computer services, or cable television, has been that the justification for competitive entry is the presence of an unexploited market for a new service. Implicitly, of course, this denies the importance of potential entry for mundane services as an incentive for efficiency among incumbent firms. By leaving the question of entry open with regard to hybrid services, the FCC is in a position to judge whether a new service with a large communications component is new enough to justify violating the principle that circuits cannot be resold. In the Packet Communications case, for example, the FCC ruled that the data-transfer offering was a common carrier service; however, because the service would provide certain special features with respect to checking and correcting transmission errors, it also ruled that the firm offering it could enter the communications market, but only as a regulated common carrier.[49] Of course, because the 1934 Communications Act is understandably somewhat fuzzy about the proper treatment of 1970s technology, the FCC could have justified any ruling, from disallowing entry on the ground that the exclusive franchise belonged to the entrenched common carriers to declaring the service to be primarily data processing and consequently beyond the scope of communications regulation.[50]

The FCC policy with regard to computer services shows the beginnings of the kind of protectionist, regulated competition that has plagued the transportation sector and that the FCC has practiced with respect to television, Western Union, and the international record carriers. The FCC has begun to get itself into the business of dividing markets among computer services firms. In so doing, it has fallen into the trap of adopting a purely structural definition of competition: an industry with many firms is thought to be competitive. But if a firm is granted a niche in the industry that will be defended against competitive entry, functionally speaking the market is monopolized, with the FCC acting as the enforcer of a cartel.

While most of the computer services industry remains unregulated, the future debate in the FCC may well be over membership in a cartel of growing importance. Technology may take us more in the direction of hybrid services, in which case the FCC will regulate more of the industry. If so, potential competition will be a diminishing force for efficiency because of the FCC's proclivity for a finding that a service is new before granting someone the right to offer it. But even if technology does not worsen the problem, the FCC will be in danger of falling into the regulatory trap.[51] The Packet Communications case has brought a new service under the heading of activities that are primarily communications. Sooner or later, a service will be proposed that offers slightly more data processing and slightly less communications than the Packet offering. Were this service compared to AT&T's, the FCC might well conclude that it was primarily data processing and permit unregulated entry. But if history is any guide, the new service will be compared to Packet's and because of the greater resemblance, will either be declared as falling under communications and therefore regulated or as too similar to Packet's service to be permitted into the same markets.

Since the natural inclination of a firm is to look for ways to expand along existing lines, the problem of defining the boundaries of regulation has no easy solution. Currently, the FCC approaches the problem with two guiding principles: (1) the burden of proof is on the potential entrant to show that additional service should be offered, and (2) regulated common carriers should be on equal footing with other firms in competitive markets. Whatever the procedural or normative value of these principles, they inevitably lead to inefficient results. The resources of the entrenched common carriers make the regulatory game an unfair one, causing the regulator to retreat from a procompetitive policy or to protect the competitive entrant. This leads to an ever-widening role for regulation.

The alternative is to regard common carrier status as sufficient reward for reversing both principles, by (1) making the common carrier prove that it can provide a service more efficiently than a potential entrant and (2) keeping it out of competitive markets, particularly if the common carrier seeks to enter an already established market. Ancillary policies in keeping with these principles are: (3) allowing resale of communications services and (4) vigorously pursuing antitrust enforcement against whoever might seek to establish a monopoly. In addition, federal preemption of state regulation of workably competitive markets may also be necessary. State commissions are notably more anticompetitive than the FCC, in part because the magical separation process that divides interstate from intrastate costs for rate-making purposes favors local rates. The National Association of Regulatory Utility Commissioners, in petitioning for reconsideration of a procompetitive FCC ruling, put the matter as follows: "The only means of affording relief to local users, under existing technology and this age of inflation, is to generate excess earnings in interstate operations and to 'flow through' these earnings for the benefit of local users by allocating more of the cost of our national communications system to interstate operations."[52] Obviously, the state regulators see cost allocation and pricing as political issues and see the objective as minimizing the price of local telephone service. State regulators may also see the services at the communications computer interface as vehicles for providing subsidies to local telephone service and therefore subject them to regulation that sets monopolistic prices by limiting competitive entry.

The fundamental point is that regulators must take a firm position either for or against extensive reliance on competition and back up that position with policies that either allow true competition a chance to prove its value or permit maximal exploitation of whatever economic advantages might justify monopoly. Federal policy has ostensibly favored competition, but too hesitantly for it to have long-term viability. Because the computer services industry is competitive and performs well, it should be covered as little as possible by the regulatory umbrella of the communications industry, even if this means encroaching on the business of the common carriers. Otherwise, economic regulation of computer services by the FCC will occur gradually, without the public's fully realizing it or given an opportunity to consider the consequences.

CONCLUSIONS

None of the three rationales for regulation of computer services offers much justification for abandoning open competition in the industry. Yet the chances are good that the industry will become increasingly regulated during the coming years. Several forces are at work to bring about this result. Regulated communications common carriers are likely to covet an increasingly large share of the computer services pie. Failing effective prevention of predatory actions by these firms, the computer services industry is likely to see joining the regulatory fold as its preferred and perhaps sole means of survival. Even with strict controls on regulated carriers, the end of rapid growth in computer services will lead at least some firms to plead for protective regulation on the ground that competition is ruinous. Congress, to avoid the difficult job of writing effective legislation or perhaps even to give the appearance of reform without the substance, may impose regulation in any event to deal with privacy issues. In all cases, the result is likely to be reduced competition and an end to the industry's good record of cost reduction and service innovation.

All of the major governmental actors could reverse this trend: the FCC could be more daring in its communications regulatory policies, other government agencies could make serious reforms in the collection and use of government data, the courts could be less of an obstacle and more of an expedient for protecting personal rights of privacy and promoting competition in industries that are regulated or on the fringe of regulation, and the Antitrust Division could provide meaningful structural relief in both the AT&T and IBM antitrust cases. But at the center of the stage is Congress. Congress could write clear, comprehensive legislation defining the rights of privacy and establishing an effective enforcement mechanism. It could also respond to the legislation proposed by AT&T, which seeks to outlaw competition in communications services, by rewriting the sections of the Communications Act dealing with common carrier regulation to achieve the opposite end. Recently, the congressional careers of the chairmen of both the House and Senate Communications Subcommittees came to an end; perhaps the new leadership, without a stake in past policies, will undertake real reforms that will rely on competition to capture the full benefits of computer technology. [Since this article was written, Congress has been considering bills that attempt to implement major revisions of the Communications Act of 1934.]

NOTES

1
For example, see Martin Greenberger, ed., *Computers, Communications and the Public Interest* (Baltimore: Johns Hopkins University Press, 1971); Paul Baron, "The Future Computer Utility," *The Public Interest*, no. 8 (Summer 1967), pp. 75–87; and Arthur R. Miller, *The Assault on Privacy* (Ann Arbor: University of Michigan Press, 1971).

2
The exception to this generalization occurs when the incremental cost of service from the monopolist exceeds the average cost, but not by enough to offset scale economies captured by earlier expansion of service. If so, total costs may be minimized by granting an exclusive franchise, even though a monopolist cannot set prices such that entry will be foreclosed and all demand at those prices will be satisfied. At present, there is no empirical evidence that this theoretical possibility has practical importance. For a discussion of the theory, see John C. Panzar and Robert D. Willig, "Free Entry and the Sustainability of Natural Monopoly," Bell Laboratories Economic Discussion Paper no. 57 (Whippany, N.J., 1976).

3
For further elaboration, see Baron, "The Future Computer Utility," and John G. Kemeny, "Large Time-Sharing Networks," in Greenberger, *Computers, Communications and the Public Interest*.

4
See Herbert A. Simon, "Designing Organizations for an Information-Rich World," ibid.

5

See Richard S. Bower, "Market Change and the Computer Services Industry," *Bell Journal of Economics* 4, no. 2 (Autumn 1973): 539–90.

6

Edward H. Chamberlin, *The Theory of Monopolistic Competition* (Cambridge, Mass.: Harvard University Press, 1933).

7

"Market Change and the Computer Services Industry."

8

First Report and Order, Docket no. 18920 (Specialized Common Carriers), *FCC Reports*, 2d ser., 29: 886–887.

9

Limit pricing is developed more thoroughly in Joe S. Bain, *Barriers to New Competition* (Cambridge, Mass.: Harvard University Press, 1956).

10

Regulation by the FCC has already slowed several innovative entries in computer services simply by engaging in the process of determining whether the entrant is primarily offering a telecommunications service. See Manley R. Irwin, "The Computer Utility: Market Entry in Search of a Public Policy," *Journal of Industrial Economics* 17, no. 3 (July 1969): 239–252.

11

For more on the behavior of regulators, see Roger G. Noll, *Reforming Regulation* (Washington, D.C.: Brookings Institution, 1971), chap. 4.

12

For a more complete statement of this view, see Richard A. Posner, "Taxation by Regulation," *Bell Journal of Economics* 2, no. 1 (Spring 1971): 22–50.

13

See, for example, Paul W. MacAvoy, "The Formal Work-Product of the Federal Power Commissioners," *Bell Journal of Economics* 2, no. 1 (Spring 1971): 379–395, and Paul L. Joskow, "Inflation and Environmental Concern: Structural Change in the Process of Public Utility Price Regulation," *Journal of Law and Economics* 17, no. 2 (Autumn 1974): 291–327. For a survey of the literature on the effects of regulation, see Roger G. Noll, "Empirical Studies of Utility Regulation," Social Science Working Paper no. 135, California Institute of Technology (Pasadena, 1976).

14

See, for example, Paul L. Joskow and Paul W. MacAvoy, "Regulation and the Financial Condition of the Electric Power Companies," *American Economic Review: Papers and Proceedings* 65 (May 1975): 295–301.

15

Some believe that public ownership or competitive bidding for local franchises would produce an even better result. Public municipal utilities generally have lower prices than private firms; see Thomas Gale Moore, "The Effectiveness of Regulation of Utility Prices," *Southern Economic Journal* 36 (1969–70): 365–375. For a discussion of competitive bidding for monopoly franchises, see Harold Demsetz, "Why Regulate Utilities?" *Journal of Law and Economics* 11, no. 1 (April 1968): 55–66, and Oliver E. Williamson, "Franchise Bidding for Natural Monopoly—in General and with Respect to CATV," *Bell Journal of Economics* 7, no. 1 (Spring 1976): 73–104. One study provides evidence that at least for some electric utilities, the efficiency gains from monopolistic competition offset the gains from allowing a monopolist to capture scale economies; see Walter J. Primeaux, "A Reexamination of Monopoly Market Structure for Electric Utilities," in *Promoting Competition in Regulated Markets,* ed. Almarin Phillips (Washington, D.C.: Brookings Institution, 1975).

16

For a parody of this tendency, see Mohamed El-Hodiri, "The Economics of Sleeping," University of Kansas Department of Economics, mimeo (Lawrence, 1974), in which the celebrated First Law of Soporifics—that it makes sense to sleep for eight hours a day—is stated and proved as a theorem in mathematics.

17

The seminal paper on this important issue is George J. Stigler, "The Economics of Information," *Journal of Political Economy* 69, no. 3 (June 1961): 213–225.

18

For a thorough development of this argument and of the social problems associated with using information in this way, see A. Michael Spence, *Market Signalling* (Cambridge, Mass.: Harvard University Press, 1974). Much of the following discussions is derived from Spence's important contribution.

19

If both types of transactions are freely available, and if the value of the information does not depend upon the income of the secretary and the public figure, the ultimate outcome—publication or privacy—is unaffected by the allocation of rights to the information, although the allocation does affect the distribution of income by specifying who will capture the benefits from it. See Ronald Coase, "The Problem of Social Cost," *Journal of Law and Economics* 3 (October 1950): 1–44.

20

The best compendium of illustrations of the use of computers in information systems is Alan F. Westin and Michael A. Baker, *Databanks in a Free Society: Computers, Record-Keeping and Privacy* (New York; Quadrangle, 1972).

21

Ibid., pp. 244–245.

22

Ibid., pp. 254 ff.

23

For a review of the status of the right of privacy in law, see Arthur R. Miller, *The Assault on Privacy* (Ann Arbor: University of Michigan Press, 1971), pp. 169–210.

24

Westin and Baker, *Computers, Record-Keeping, and Privacy,* p. 241.

25

Ibid., pp. 36 ff.

26

Miller, *Assault on Privacy,* pp. 170 ff.

27

For a more thorough treatment of the problems of representation in regulatory proceedings, see Noll, *Reforming Regulation.*

28

Roger G. Noll, Merton J. Peck, and John J. McGowan, *Economic Aspects of Television Regulation* (Washington, D.C.: Brookings Institution, 1973), chap. 4.

29
George J. Stigler, "The Theory of Economic Regulation," *Bell Journal of Economics* 2, no. 1 (Spring 1971): 3–21.

30
Edmund W. Kitch, Marc Isaacson, and Daniel Kasper, "The Regulation of Taxicabs in Chicago," *Journal of Law and Economics* 14, no. 2 (October 1971): 285–350.

31
Kenneth Culp Davis, *Administrative Law Text* (St. Paul, Minn.: West Publishing, 1959), section 29.

32
Westin and Baker, realizing this problem, propose that each agency have a citizen advisory group concerned with privacy issues to monitor its uses of information (*Computers, Record-Keeping, and Privacy,* p. 351). Lacking authority and consequently real commitment, and being appointed by the agency, such a body seems unlikely to do more than threaten to expose the most egregious actions.

33
For more elaboration of this point in another context, see Nina Cornell, Roger Noll, and Barry Weingast, "Safety Regulation," in Charles Schultze and Henry Owen, *Setting National Priorities: The Coming Decade* (Washington, D.C.: Brookings Institution, 1976).

34
Simon, "Designing Organizations for an Information-Rich World," pp. 38–52.

35
For detailed analysis of the costs of computer services, see Bower, "Market Change and the Computer Services Industry."

36
Robert M. Spann and Edward W. Erickson, "The Economics of Railroading: The Beginning of Cartelization and Regulation," *Bell Journal of Economics* 1, no. 2 (Autumn 1970): 227–244.

37
Theodore E. Keeler, "Airline Regulation and Market Performance," *Bell Journal of Economics* 3, no. 2 (Autumn 1972): 399–425, and Michael E. Levine, "Is Regulation Necessary? California Air Transportation and National Regulatory Policy," *Yale Law Journal* 7 (1965): 1416–1447.

38
James R. Snitzler and Robert J. Byrne, *Interstate Trucking of Fresh and Frozen Poultry under Agricultural Exemption,* Marketing Research Report no. 224 (Washington, D.C.: U.S. Department of Agriculture, 1958), and the same authors' *Interstate Trucking of Frozen Fruits and Vegetables under Agricultural Exemption,* Marketing Research Report 316 (Washington, D.C.: U.S. Department of Agriculture, 1959).

39
Paul W. MacAvoy and James Sloss, *Regulation of Transport Innovation: The ICC and the Unit Coal Trains to the East Coast* (New York: Random House, 1967).

40
Aaron J. Gellman, "Surface Freight Transportation," in William Capron, ed., *Technological Change in Regulated Industries* (Washington, D.C.: Brookings Institution, 1971), pp. 166–196.

41

George W. Douglas and James C. Miller III, *Economic Regulation of Domestic Air Transport: Theory and Policy* (Washington, D.C.: Brookings Institution, 1974).

42

The FCC decision in the computer inquiry provides a synopsis of industry views. See *FCC Reports,* 2d ser. 28 (1971): 267–308.

43

FCC Reports 34 (1964): 1120.

44

Bower, "Market Change and the Computer Services Industry," p. 553, estimates that communications links account for 8 to 18 percent of total costs for most computer services firms.

45

Irwin, "The Computer Utility," pp. 240–243.

46

U.S. v. *Western Electric and AT&T,* consent judgment, January 24, 1956, U.S. District Court for New Jersey, 13 RR 2143; 1956 Trade Cases 71,134.

47

FCC Reports, 2d ser. 40 (1973): 293.

48

FCC Reports, 2d ser. 13 (1968): 420.

49

FCC Reports, 2d ser. 43 (1973): 922.

50

For a detailed defense of this proposition, see Paul J. Berman, "Computer or Communications? Allocation of Functions and the Role of the Federal Communications Commission," *Federal Communications Bar Journal* (1975), pp. 161–230.

51

James W. McKie, "Regulation and the Free Market: The Problem of Boundaries," *Bell Journal of Economics* 1, no. 1 (Spring 1970): 6–26.

52

FCC Reports, 2d ser. 31:1108.

13
Computers and Modeling

Martin Shubik

The process of model building involves the construction of abstract representations of organisms, organizations, and institutions. These representations are simplifications of reality that vary according to which is best suited to answer the question at hand. For example, one aggregate model of the economy might be constructed to answer questions concerning inflation, while a different model would be used to analyze the balance of trade.

Ours is a data-rich and information-poor society. The advent of the high-speed digital computer, communications satellites, hand calculators, and the myriad data-processing and communication devices of the last thirty years is vital to our way of life, but it cannot guarantee the survival and growth of modern, high-technology, mass societies that wish to preserve democratic and libertarian values.

In all societies, and organisms in general, quantitative change usually implies qualitative change. Although the body of science and technology and the population of the world have both grown exponentially in the last two hundred and fifty years, wisdom, perception, and other individual traits have not. The growth of vast populations consisting of individuals who are essentially no different from their ancestors is posing new problems for the organization of society. Yet while we are on the brink of seeing the development of intelligent machines, we are far from developing wise and skeptical machines. As modern communications systems become more sophisticated, they will depend heavily upon the models of man and society that serve to guide their calculations. Mass societies with fast-changing technology that wish to preserve democratic freedoms must be "choreographed" at a level of sophistication unknown to any previous society.

In a world with billions of individuals, it is possible to achieve control by statistical justice, by the invention of a few crude aggregate categories and

Martin Shubik is Seymour Knox Professor of Mathematical Institutional Economics at Yale University. He is a noted authority on economic games and modeling.

rules of thumb that rarely acknowledge individuality but are capable of providing the low-information mode of governance that is one of the important features of a repressive society. A system that lacks freedom and has little concern for individuality, no matter how technologically advanced, needs less information than one in which individual differences are important. For example, it is cheaper, quicker, and easier to punish those guilty of virtually anything if one does not intend to worry about the possibility of making an error and punishing the innocent. Simple rules, broad generalizations, simplistic laws, customs, or taboos enable mass societies to function, but the cost is measured in lack of individual freedom and lack of societal sophistication.

The growth of computerized data banks has evoked great concern about threats to personal freedom: Big Brother may be building up his secret files on the citizenry. This is a real and disturbing danger, but it is easy to draw the wrong inferences from it. The source of the danger does not lie in the technology itself but in societal control of it. Before the new advances in the construction of data banks and the transmission and processing of information, the choices for a mass society were anarchy or faceless, depersonalized control. With the new technology, the possibility of preserving and even extending the scope of individuality has grown.

The importance of the advent of the computer to the behavioral sciences is at least as great as were the invention of the telescope and microscope to astronomy and the biological sciences. The computer and mass data-gathering and processing systems provide a powerful viewing device for man to examine his own behavior as a social animal. The new methods of data analysis, simulation, computation, and gaming all multiply many times over our resources for studying models of man and society. Yet the assistance that can be rendered by the new technology is dependent upon the quality of the models that form the basis for our view of reality.

Science-fiction writing has the top generals and diplomats seated in their war room with computerized map displays showing the disposition and movement of military forces. Articles have been written describing a central planning display room for a beleaguered city mayor. In his headquarters supported by his operations research staff, the mayor surveys the maps indicating the relative importance of the various issues. By calling up from his executive console, he can be supplied with detailed information in answer to his "what if" questions. In another scenario, the vice-president of a corporate division hears that the national defense budget has been reduced by several billion dollars. He wishes to know what might be the impact on the subdivision of his firm that produces aircraft engines. He goes to his time-sharing system and calls up a macroeconomic model interfaced with a model of the defense industry, which in turn is broken into components showing the probable magnitude of various impacts on different firms.

Large computer models of corporations, cities, and major societal forces have been proposed and built in projects devoted to industrial dynamics, urban dynamics, and world dynamics. The efforts of the Club of Rome and several other groups of "world modelers" have been devoted to calling the attention of society as a whole to major future problems. The large simulations can be regarded as predictors of the future (unless we change our ways), or they can be regarded as "what if" exercises producing hypothetical scenarios. Phrased differently, it is easy to build a large-scale simulation of virtually anything; but it is hard to determine if the simulation provides a good model of any particular firm, city, country, or other organism.

THE ART OF MODELING

A model is an abstraction. It is the representation of some aspect of the world about us by a simplified entity which we can more easily comprehend and use to clarify our views about the real phenomenon. The acts of model building and analysis involve a retreat from reality in order to reach a deeper understanding of some aspects of reality.

The advent of the new computer and communications technology has enlarged the scope of model building and analysis. The growth of world population and the striving for personal freedom and better standards of living have made the need for more sophisticated models of man and his environment an absolute necessity. As I have suggested, while the new computer and communications systems are essential to this task, they alone do not provide all the means for our societies to solve their current problems. They need guidance in the form of appropriate models which make clear what are the important questions, what is the information needed, and how one obtains answers to the questions.

Much of what goes on in model building should be regarded as more of an art than a science. It is reported that Gertrude Stein on her deathbed tried out as her last line "What is the answer?" Realizing that this was not going to be particularly memorable, she then switched to "Well, then, what is the question?" Good model builders are first and foremost question seekers. The right question is intimately related to the purpose at hand. The basic research scientist may find generating questions the easiest of tasks because frequently he is his own client. He may wish to know the causes of some type of cancer or the reasons for the irregularities in the motion of the planet Mercury. But in general he does not have to answer his questions to meet any particular deadline, and he does not have to second-guess the reasons for asking a particular question or the way any answer is going to be used.

The applied scientist and the planner are less independent. They are part of an ongoing process, and they need to know if the questions that seem germane to them are seen as such by those who are going to use their advice. They have to consider purpose and relevance. It is one thing to develop a general theory of monetary inflation, but it is another to provide the president of the United States with a decent ad hoc model of economic activity, capable of providing answers to questions concerning current antiinflationary policy.

Modeling, especially when the models are to be used for planning and control, is part of an iterative process. The perception of what the questions might be comes first. The clarification of the questions and their relevance to the purpose at hand comes next, followed by the sketching out of the type of data needed to answer the questions. Tied in with considerations of what information is needed is a simple but critical act of perception: Will the asker of the question recognize an answer if it stares him in the face? "Is there going to be a storm soon?" is a question that can be answered with reasonable accuracy by someone who has observed a precipitous fall in barometric pressure. He does not even need to know the details of why pressure systems influence weather. He does however need to know what a barometer is, how to read it, and how to translate its reading into a prediction.

Given the questions, their relevance to the purpose at hand, and given an idea of the data requirements and the available time and resources, the model builder is in a position to construct his model. Possibly the basic source of all wisdom concerning the construction and use of models is that there is no such thing as an all-purpose model. The more general the set of questions posed to a specific model, the less likely it is that the model will provide sufficiently detailed answers. An all-purpose model tends to be a no-purpose model.

If the model builder and his associates know what they are after, they proceed to select from reality those facets they judge to be of prime importance in answering the questions at hand, disregarding those they do not. For example, if they are concerned with evaluating the impact of the supersonic jet on the environment and on international trade and travel, the effect on sales of tax-free liquor at airport stores may be a negligible one to the planners and thus left out of the model, although this particular factor could be crucial to someone wishing to open an airport store.

In general a different question calls for a different model. A feature of reality that is left out or aggregated in one model may require great detail in a model designed to answer a different question.

TYPES OF MODELS

There are four major categories of models meriting distinction. They are (1) verbal models, (2) analytic or mathematical models, (3) iconic, pictorial, or schematic representations of reality, and (4) digital simulations.

Verbal models   A verbal description of some aspect of our environment may be regarded as a model. It may purport to supply only a description; it may also provide an explanation of the events it describes. Thus works of history commonly map the causes of events, rather than merely chronicling them. Motley's *Rise of the Dutch Republic* or Mahan's *History of Sea Power* and many others even read like detective stories. The reader is not only told of the environment, the actors, and the actions, but motives are also suggested, and reasons for the unfolding of events are supplied. The briefs in a law case, the plot in a novel, the scenario and action in a play can all usefully be considered as verbal models. The essayist may not think of himself as a modeler in the way that an operations research expert or a mathematically trained behavioral scientist does. Yet some of the best scenarios for war games have been constructed by historians skilled in the writing of essays.

Ordinary language is simultaneously less precise and more flexible and subtle than computer languages or mathematics. It is possible to express nuances in meaning far more effectively with an essay than with a mathematical construct. A psychiatric model of man will be verbal. An analysis of Sino-Soviet relations will tend to be primarily verbal; the subject matter calls for the use of many adjectives and adverbs to express shades of meaning, none of which is easily captured by the language of mathematics.

However, verbal models, unlike computer simulations, are essentially static. Even if they describe events, the dynamics is "frozen." It is not usual for books to be rewritten and published in several variations by the author in the space of a few months, yet mathematical models and simulations are frequently recalculated or recomputed as conditions change.

When a phenomenon is complex, when it is difficult to sort out and describe the key variables, and when those variables that can be isolated do not easily lend themselves to measurement, an effort to build too formal a model can be disastrous. Premature mathematization or too hasty a resort to computer models may result in putting a straitjacket of false precision on our representation of a phenomenon. There may be those who believe that items such as patriotism, morale, or national well-being can be usefully measured by indexes ranging from 0 to 1. For most purposes, however, these concepts are best treated verbally.

Mathematical and logical models   At the other end of the spectrum from the essay writer is the mathematical model builder. He maps his perceptions of the real world onto a parsimonious set of symbols. If he can do so successfully, he then has the ability to extend his analysis to a depth that would be out of the question with verbal methods. For example, in studying an arms race we may be interested in the effect of a change in the rate of expenditure on one type of aircraft on the rate of change in the machine-tool requirements of the aircraft factories. Expressed in words, the last sentence is a tongue twister; yet mathematically the rates of change could be expressed easily as first and second derivatives.

Mathematical models may be regarded as formal logical constructs with no necessarily close relationship to any aspect of reality, although model builders who stress formalism run the danger of producing sterile mathematical exercises akin to those described by Hesse in *The Glass Bead Game*. Without delving into the philosophical niceties, an axiomatic approach to a topic such as consumer behavior or voter behavior involves the making of a small group of basic simplifying assumptions about individuals and their environment. Having in this way established the primitive elements of the system and the relations among them, we may explore their implications by mathematical and logical means alone. For example, we might wish to assume that the economy is populated by a set of idealized entities called consumers, each of whom is able to state his preferences when confronted with any choice and is always familiar with the resources at his disposal. We may then use this stark model of economic man to deduce the demand for goods and services in an economy, constructing mathematical, diagrammatic, or computer models of economic behavior.

Modern economics deals with many mathematical models of this kind, but the relevance of what can be deduced from them depends upon whether their basic assumptions were a reasonable representation of some aspect of reality. When the model builders no longer question their assumptions or are uninterested in the bond between the mathematical models and the world, then there is a danger that what started as a bold venture into the use of mathematical models to reach a greater understanding of society will become no more than a logical game or mathematical exercise.

A simple example of a two-person duel may serve as a brief example of the construction and analysis of a mathematical model. Suppose that two individuals fight a duel under the following conditions. Each has a revolver with a single bullet. Each has an estimate of the shooting accuracy of the other and how this accuracy varies with distance. They start the duel a certain distance apart; I will call this distance 1. Once they begin to walk toward each other, they can fire any time they wish.

Suppose that the mathematical modeler has been supplied with empirically derived information that the accuracy of the first duelist can be represented by the formula $p(x) = x^2$, where $0 \leqslant x \leqslant 1$ and $1 - x$ is the distance between the duelists. This states that when they start the duel $x = 0$; they are far enough apart that the first duelist has approximately no chance of hitting his opponent. This is expressed by $p(0) = 0$. Similarly, if the first duelist were to reach his opponent before firing, then at point-blank range he could hit him with certainty. Thus $p(1) = 1$. The accuracy of the second duelist can be represented by $q(x) = x$.

The question to be answered from an analysis of the model is, What is the optimum distance at which a duelist should fire? As the range closes, each must calculate the trade-off between raising the probability of hitting his opponent at the same time as the probability of being hit increases. The best distance at which the first duelist should fire is max min$[p(x), 1 - q(x)]$, where the second term is the probability that the first duelist will survive if the second fires. The optimum occurs when $p(x) = 1 - q(x)$, or $x = (-1 + \sqrt{5})/2$.

This equation derives from a branch of two-person game theory that deals with the study of duels. At the cost of greater complexity, we could consider duelists with several bullets, with silencers on their revolvers, or imagine one with a bulletproof vest and the other without. We might then replace one duelist with a tank of given specifications and the other with a different tank. This is the type of mathematical model we might wish to study for weapons evaluation. Once the amount of detail required becomes large, we might switch from a mathematical representation to a computer study or simulation.

Iconic or pictorial models Diagrams are more flexible and easier to construct than mathematical models; and they are frequently easier to follow than a verbal description of the phenomenon they represent. They can readily be changed and modified on a blackboard, and it is not through historical accident but through considerations of efficiency and cost that the blackboard has survived in modern teaching. The value of a device on which one can rapidly draw and modify diagrams is such that modern technology found it worthwhile to develop a light pencil to draw on a television screen attached to a computer in much the same way as chalk is used on a blackboard.

In teaching subjects such as economics, elementary diagrams play a critical role. In architecture and building, plans and blueprints control construction. In navigation and travel, maps are the main form for representing information. But simple diagrammatic models have probably found their widest use in statistical displays such as pie diagrams and bar charts, which constitute an art form in and of themselves and are a key ingredient of corporate reports, governmental budget displays, and magazine and newspaper articles. Because these simple diagrams convey a broad impression of an important political or budgetary issue to a large audience, the techniques of lying with statistics while not actually lying are well recognized. In the simple example that follows, the two pie diagrams show how a slight change in presentation can give a considerably different impression of the same statistical information.

The first two pie charts, equal in size, show the (hypothetical) proportion of traffic deaths not involving an automobile for the years 1920 and 1970. The second two pie charts show the same information in the division of the pie, but extra information is given by the size of the pies, which indicates the number of automobiles per thousand of population. A casual reader looking at the first pair of pie charts might easily conclude that automobile drivers had become more homicidal over the years, but after looking at the second pair, he would probably conclude that the growth in the number of automobiles per thousand of population was a major factor in the shift toward a higher percentage of traffic deaths involving automobiles.

Before turning from diagrams to detailed pictures, it must be noted that one of the triumphs of mathematics is that it enables individuals to visualize and calculate in many dimensions. It is hard enough for the average individual to draw models of three-dimensional objects in two dimensions; yet some mathematicians find no difficulty in drawing pictures of the projections of tesseracts, or four-dimensional cubes. However, the diagram is really at its best as a means of communication when two dimensions or at most three are all that are needed.

"A picture is worth a thousand words" is not merely a florid turn of phrase; it is a reasonably accurate indication of the minimum amount of information needed to be able to produce a comprehensive picture. Paintings and photographs differ in the degree of freedom given to the artist. The painter is less constrained than the photographer in producing his view or model of the subject, but even so neither a photograph nor a painting is identical with its subject, since they are both usually purposeful representations. Flattering the grand duke may be one operational purpose for using a picture as a model of the person. Capturing an expression

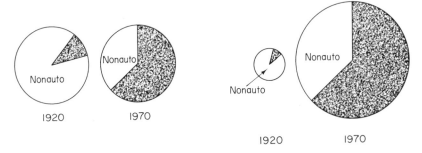

13.1
How to Lie with Statistics

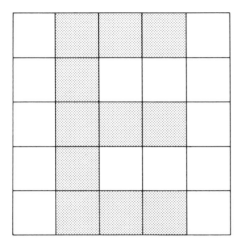

13.2
Grid with Letter E

that can scarcely be described in words is another. A more mundane reason is to be able to describe an individual so that someone could identify the portrait drawn from the description.

The elemental unit of information is the bit. It is the minimal amount of information required to recognize whether a system is in one of two states: yes-no or on-off. Suppose that we had a 5 × 5 grid, and suppose that a machine could turn a switch so that each cell in this grid was either black or white, dark or illuminated. How many recognizably different patterns could we generate? In each cell we have a choice of two states and there are twenty-five cells. Thus 2^{25} different patterns can be generated on this grid, or approximately 32,000,000. Even with this small a grid the number of patterns is enormous, and some of them would be recognizable to the individual as familiar symbols, as in the illustration, where the letter *E* is displayed. If we were to use a 200 × 200 grid and allow each cell to be shaded not merely black or white but with various shadings of gray or even different colors, we could still calculate the number of different patterns that would be feasible, and at this level of complexity it is possible to construct good recognizable portraits.

ANALOGUE SIMULATIONS AND SCALE MODELS

Madame Tussaud's waxworks presents full-size "lifelike" models of many individuals and scenes for the purpose of entertainment. Military war gamers have for many years used sand tables to illustrate tactical exercises, since scale models of hills, swamps, houses, churches, and so forth presumably add more realism to the exercise than two-dimensional maps. Specific scale models of items such as aircraft have been built for performance tests in wind tunnels. Disembodied automobile tires are rotated in place to simulate the wear from thousands of miles of road usage. Torrents of water are poured on windshield wipers operating on isolated windshields.

When a scale model or part is physically tested the presumption is usually that its performance under test conditions will be close enough to reality to predict the actual performance of the entity or system it represents. But it is one problem to build a model to test automobile tires and another to test complex physical or social systems. The value of the model is of course closely related to the purpose for which it is constructed. There is, for example, extensive model building in the fire industry, where appropriate models are needed to simulate the destruction of London during the Great Fire or the ruin of San Francisco in an earthquake. The purpose is to use make-believe to create a good semblance of a real event at a reasonable cost. In contrast, a scale model of San Francisco Bay and the mouth of the Sacramento River can be used to study actual flood, pollution, and silting conditions.

Finally, there are training devices, some not unlike those found in an amusement arcade, with which individuals can learn driving or piloting skills without an automobile or aircraft. The models may not be quite the same as reality, but such devices can provide training that is quicker, cheaper, and safer than could be obtained by the immediate use of an automobile or aircraft.

COMPUTER SIMULATION

The major trend in model building over the last twenty years has been toward large-scale, high-speed digital computer simulation and mathematical computation. The phenomenal advances in computational abilities and communications devices and systems have meant that it is now possible to construct models whose degree of complexity would have been completely beyond our power twenty years ago. When a mathematical model involves two or three equations or a handful of relations, as in the example already given of a duel, a solution can frequently be obtained using ingenuity, a pencil, and a scrap of paper. When however a mathematical model is meant to provide a reasonably close and complete representation of some aspect of reality, it may involve hundreds and in some instances thousands of equations. There are now mathematical models used for short-term weather forecasting that involve thousands of equations and mathematical models of transportation and inventorying systems that involve the use of linear programming and techniques of combinatorial analysis.

A simple example of a problem that is easy to state and understand but calls for a large amount of computation to solve is the traveling salesman problem. A salesman must visit all fifty state capitals. He can visit them in any order, but he wishes to minimize the number of miles he has to travel. How should be arrange his visits? Many important practical problems are of this kind. They involve decisions on where to produce various items, where to store them, and when to ship them to different points of demand.

A computer simulation is a representation of a system or organism by a set of computer instructions that create a model whose behavior can be displayed by running the program on a computer. The model's behavior is considered sufficiently close to that of the actual system that properties of its behavior can be inferred from the simulation.

Usually, before a system is modeled as a simulation, it has already been modeled in one or more ways. For example, one might start with a verbal description, which may then be translated into a mathematical model; the mathematical model may be modified and transformed into a set of flow diagrams, and these are turned into a computer simulation.

A flow diagram may be looked upon as a behavioral map describing what the computer must do. Say we wish to simulate the behavior of troops who are told, "Do not fire until you see the whites of their eyes." (Fig. 13.3) They begin to guard at "Start"; time is indexed to be 1 for the first period. The question is asked: "Do you see the whites of their eyes?" If the answer is no, the troops are instructed to go back on guard, time is indexed to 2, and the question is asked again. If the answer is yes, they are told to fire, after which event the simulation ends. A complex simulation may require hundreds of pages of flow diagrams, with each sector providing a detailed representation of some behavioral mechanism.

Simulations of human decision-making systems are modeled on different types of relations which can usefully be divided into three categories: accounting relations, behavioral relations, and control relations. For example, suppose we consider a simulation of the overall economy of the United States. Some relations in the model will amount to nothing more than balancing the books: all sales must equal all purchases. Other relations might model certain aspects of economic behavior, such as the propensity of an individual to spend or save a marginal hundred dollars. Yet other relations are constructed so that we can plug in different levels of taxation. We could run the simulation with several levels of taxation to study how sensitive is the behavior of the system to control through taxes.

How successful a large-scale simulation will be will closely depend on how clear and important are the questions being asked of it, how robust the model is when we examine variations of it, and how good a representation of reality it is for the purposes at hand.

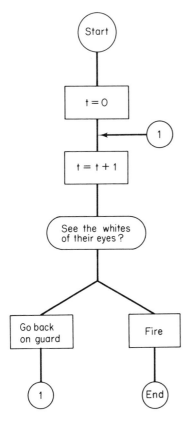

13.3
Flow Diagram: "Do Not Fire Until You See the Whites of Their Eyes."

TECHNIQUES OF MODELING

Along with all the various items he must consider, a good modeler has four overall concerns: intention, specification, control, and validation. Does he know what are the questions he wishes to answer with his model? Is he in a position to specify the model clearly and in a manner that is both relevant and parsimonious—reflecting the key features of actuality but not cluttered up with irrelevant detail? This type of detail is often introduced by those who fail to distinguish between superficial realism and fundamental causal patterns.

Control means first of all asking whether the data are available. Are the categories and measures clear, so that the modeler knows what data he is gathering and why? Even if he is sure of what he wants, can he obtain it with sufficient accuracy at an economic cost? Has he checked to see that his data base is consistent and complete?

Given that he knows his questions, has faith in the realism and relevance of the model, and believes in the accuracy and worth of the basic information, there still remains the problem of validation; that is, the use of criteria for judging whether the model has succeeded in answering specific questions. This is where statistical analysis becomes important.

Probably the largest and most widely used set of rules for model building in the United States are to be found in the generally accepted accounting principles used by the accounting profession as a guide in the preparation of financial documents and accounts. Accountants are often looked down upon as mere number pushers in contrast with economists, who are seen as thinkers and theorizers. But even if this caricature were accurate, since economists base much of their theorizing on data originally gathered by accountants, an understanding of the relevance, realism, and validity of an economic theory calls for a check of the accounting materials on which it is based.

The concepts of accounting include (1) objectivity, (2) consistency, (3) disclosure, (4) materiality, (5) conservatism, and (6) fairness. The first four apply to all model-building activity. The accountant's concern with disclosure shows an awareness that numerical displays alone may be misleading. There are occasions where they must be bolstered with explanatory statements.

The concepts of conservatism and fairness indicate that part of the implicit sociological assumptions of this profession is the understanding that its models of the state of business entities are going to be used by different parties for different purposes. For example, some might be better served by having the worth of assets reported as high and others as low. The conservative bias may serve only one group well, but if they all know that the bias is consistently conservative, then even though many groups use the same report for different purposes each may be able to readjust its own model accordingly.

Fairness, even more than conservatism, is addressed to the conflicting interests of different groups using the same reports. The accounting profession derives its criteria of fairness by reacting to the pressures of society: "Such fairness is to be determined in the light of the existing economic and political environment."

Assuming that all questions concerning purpose and who is going to use the models have been resolved, there remain five broad aspects of modeling that must be considered. They are Explicitness or specification, Aggregation, Symmetry, Consistency checking, and Sensitivity analysis.

Explicitness Good modeling calls for not merely knowing the questions to be answered but being able and willing to specify many of the features of the models. This is virtually the same as the process of specification. In specifying a model, decisions must be made concerning who are the major actors; what are the initial conditions; what are the basic variables; whether we have scales to measure the level of activities in the model, and so forth.

Even the choice of language becomes an important consideration in the specification of a model. If a professional wants to be able to reconstruct his ideas at a later date or communicate with a close colleague, he can use his or their special shorthand notations. Any language used by a group of specialists tends to become a highly coded means of communication which can be understood quickly and in depth by the few but may be virtually incomprehensible to others.

In building a model, it is important that the role of time be made clear. In many instances a static representation of the phenomenon is good enough for the purposes at hand. In others (such as the study of the depletion of natural resources) the essence of the problem is in the dynamics.

Another key distinction is whether competition or cooperation among the actors is sufficiently important that the strategic or "game" features of the model must be given special emphasis. Most problems in the physical sciences and many problems in operations research do not involve competition or collusion. In general it is not a useful assumption that several atomic particles are trying purposefully to damage each other or to form a self-help cartel. When the basic elements are economic or political units, this assumption may well be reasonable.

Aggregation   One of the most effective ways of misleading oneself and others is by using half-truths. Any model, being a simplification of the actual entity it is meant to portray, involves the omission of some aspects of reality and the aggregation of detail in regard to others. It is in this work that the main art of the model builder is concentrated. By leaving out key variables or by obliterating the behavior of parts of the system by aggregation, one can create models that are true as far as they go but may be extremely misleading.

The flexibility of large-scale computing systems invites the construction of large models. If it becomes easy to program detail, there is a tendency to add detail. The good modeler knows this is a delusion. Parsimony must be a critical guiding value in modeling, but parsimony must be pitted against relevance and the need for realism. In general, a model that appears to be sufficiently relevant and realistic to the professional is likely to appear overly simplified and impoverished to the layman.

Symmetry   The assumption of symmetry has many uses in scientific work in general. In particular, the use of symmetry is critical when we are modeling social, political, or economic systems. Many of our efforts to aggregate individuals into broad classes such as consumers or voters are based upon prior assumptions that for the purpose at hand two different individuals can be treated as though they were behaviorally the same. Considerations of fairness and equity may call for a similar approach.

If we can group individuals into large masses of behaviorally equivalent elements, then it becomes possible to devise special mathematical and computational methods devoted to predicting the overall development of mass behavior. At a somewhat more technical level, when a modeler is faced with a large system of equations representing the behavior of many individuals, he may be able to reduce the size of the system and simplify considerably by assuming symmetry in such a way that many equations are replaced by one.

Symmetry and aggregation techniques are related but are not the same. One of the major errors a modeler can commit is to fall into the fallacy of composition trap. A system consisting of many thousands of separate but identical individuals will not necessarily behave as if it consisted of one aggregated individual. For example, a stock market with thousands of small traders appears to provide liquidity for each trader, but if all of them moved together as one individual the liquidity would disappear.

Consistency checking When models or actual operating systems become large, the elemental task of checking to see if the system is complete and consistent becomes both important and difficult to perform. In U.S. law, for example, clear logical inconsistencies exist. Income is defined one way for income-tax purposes and another way for estate-tax purposes, and the definitions conflict.

The techniques for checking a model involve

(1) examining its equations for dimensionality checks;
(2) checking to see that it obeys the laws of conservation;
(3) checking for completeness and logical consistency; and
(4) checking for the presence or absence of time reversibility.

1. Consider the simple equation

$$d = \alpha x,$$

which may stand for the statement that traffic deaths d are some proportion α of the number x of automobiles in existence. A simple dimensional analysis will show that the number α cannot be a pure ratio:

Individuals $= \alpha$(automobiles)

Individuals $= \dfrac{\text{individuals}}{\text{automobiles}} = $ (automobiles).

If the number of deaths were only proportional to the number of automobiles, this would suggest that if the population increased tenfold traffic deaths would stay fixed, and if the population were reduced to next to zero, more people than exist would be killed by automobiles! A more reasonable hypothesis is that α is not a pure number but is measured in terms of the number of individuals per automobile. Performing checks such as this enables the modeler to see that certain equations cannot be correct even without going into a detailed analysis of their structure.

2. Checking for conservation seems to be so elementary as to be almost trite. But in several models of society it is virtually impossible to carry out, as it is not clear what quantities are to be conserved. Economists have over ten different definitions of the money supply (called M_1, M_2, M_3, and so forth). Depending upon how the money supply is defined, the conservation laws will vary. In political models the difficulties are even greater, since the modeler may wish to consider factors such as morale or patriotism. It may be that morale depends upon national solidarity and well-being, but how do we measure them?

The recognition of the use of the laws of conservation as a means for checking the consistency of models is one of the key features in accounting and the use of double-entry bookkeeping.

3. Checking for logical consistency and completeness has become both easier and more important with the use of computer models. Computer programs will either not run or will quickly print out nonsense if they are incomplete or inconsistent. Thus the discipline imposed by the construction of a running simulation goes a long way toward providing consistency and completeness checks. It must be noted, however, that a perfectly complete and consistent program can be a poor model of the phenomenon to be studied.

4. Should the program be capable of being run both forward and backward in time? Certain simple growth processes with no random elements appear to be indifferent to time's arrow, but this is not the case for processes involving random shocks. Scrambling the eggs appears to be easier than unscrambling them. In the combat between planners of different persuasions, the question is whether this also holds true of nationalizing and denationalizing industries or creating and destroying organizations in general.

SENSITIVITY ANALYSIS

Possibly the most important of all tests to which any model must be subjected is sensitivity analysis. How sensitive is the model to slight changes in parameters, to variations in initial conditions, modifications in behavioral relationships, or changes in the pattern of information? Depending upon our specific knowledge of the problem to be studied, we would expect a specific model to be more or less sensitive to changes in parameters or functional relations. There are three rough guidelines that can help us study sensitivity in some but not all models. They are (1) continuity, (2) direction, and (3) limiting mass behavior.

In most models, unless there is some good reason to suspect that one is approaching a breakpoint, a catastrophe or point of discontinuity, it is reasonable to expect that there will be a smooth or continuous change in the output of the simulation as some parameter is varied over a small range. If a great change is noted, either the model is wrong or a key point for study has been located.

Usually a sensitive modeler has a model of his model. He knows (or at least is more or less certain) in advance in what direction his model should move as certain inputs are varied. If the model does not behave as predicted, either it is unexpectedly subtle or it may be an indication that the model is inadequate.

In mechanics and in the study of human affairs, mass behavior may be considerably easier to describe and predict than the behavior of three or four individuals. Reasonably good models can be constructed and theories devised to explain the behavior of a single firm or consumer or of many, but in the intermediate zone between two and many, considerable specific detail is usually called for before a decipherable purpose or pattern emerges from the study of a model. An important test of an economic or other model of human behavior is whether a model that has been defined for an arbitrary number of participants shows regularities for individual or mass behavior.

Perhaps the hardest of all sensitivity analyses involves making slight changes in the basic assumption that an individual will either buy or sell a commodity at a point in time at a given price but will not do both. We might rule out the possibility that if an individual has 10 bushels of wheat and wants 20, he would obtain them by selling 5 bushels and buying 15. We could also build a slightly different model in which we do not rule out this possibility. In many circumstances it will turn out that behavior in the two models is identical, but there may be a minute set of instances where the individual wants to make a market appear to be more active than it really is by entering both as a buyer and a seller. This behavior is known as creating "wash sales" by buying from oneself.

Slight differences of the variety noted above can turn out to be critical in the applied use of large-scale models. For example, some apparently minor omission in the description of the properties of the terrain in an urban development model or a war game can totally change the conclusions to be drawn from an analysis.

MODELS, COMPUTERS, AND PLANNING

The uses of models in the sciences include detailed descriptions of subatomic particles, the anatomy of the double helix of DNA, and models of the formation of galaxies. At a more human scale, there are now many models devoted to the study of human behavior in society, business, and, unfortunately, war.

Power plants, hydroelectric dams, and the complex of grids used for the delivery of electrical power are controlled by on-line computer and communications systems surveying the whole network. The control of telephone switching circuits, railroad traffic, and airport traffic patterns are all based on elaborate models or simulations designed for a specific operating purpose. We take for granted the idea that one should be able to purchase an airline ticket routed through six cities on three different airlines in a matter of minutes, then change our minds and be rerouted in a few minutes more. The organization needed to verify credit, cash and clear bank checks, exchange stock certificates, or control traffic lights in response to the volume of traffic is enormous. It is obtained by constructing abstract representations of the actual systems that can be used to identify and monitor the key points of control.

Leaving aside the growth of the vast on-line control systems needed to provide individual service in a mass democratic society, there are a number of other major model-building and -using activities that have an important influence on the directions our society is taking. One of them, which is little noted but has considerable influence on national defense, is the use of models, games, and simulations in weapons evaluation, command, and control, the study of arms deployment, and many other military problems. A second, which has received much publicity, involves the use of simulations for the control of economic or socioeconomic processes.

There is a multimillion-dollar industry in the United States devoted to the construction of elaborate models of conflict. These models are used to test and predict the performance of weapons that have never been built and that in most cases never will be. Mythical battles are fought using new tactics and nonexistent weapons. At what point does science become science fiction, and when does science fiction become fantasy? It is not possible to answer this question with a general statement; it depends on specific details and on how effective and relevant the modeling is.

A newer and better-known use of models in the development of theory, in prediction, control, and in advocacy has been the development of economic and socioeconomic models. Since the advent of the Keynesian model of economic processes, there has been a proliferation of models used by their proponents to justify favored economic policies or to make predictions about the economy. There are planning-resource models using vast arrays of equations based on Leontieff's input-output analysis. There are large-scale macroeconomic models such as the Wharton model, which is used regularly to make economic predictions of employment, gross national product, and other factors. These models do not appear to have a record of prediction particularly worse or better than that of individual economists. Nevertheless, they do present an organized and coherent framework for looking at a great amount of economic information.

At a more ambitious level than the economic models, and somewhat more related to advocacy and the effort to influence societal attitudes in the formation of policy, are the global and social models. These are exemplified by Forrester's *Urban Dynamics* and the simulations built under the sponsorship of the Club of Rome illustrated in the book *Limits to Growth*. These books present models ranging up to several hundreds of equations showing possible patterns of urban growth and decay, the spread of pollution, the exhaustion of resources, and the explosion of world population.

Each model, as it is run as a computer simulation, produces a new hypothetical history. It is possible to learn from or moralize upon the histories produced. Most of the futures are possible, but whether or not they are probable is a matter that can be judged only after a close examination of their premises.

SYSTEMS, MODELING AND PROCESS

A modern mass society, in order to survive, must be able to control pollution, fight inflation, and provide justice and welfare to individuals, not aggregates. It must know how to control smoothly and without effort the myriad of little details that otherwise could overwhelm a free state. Large size, together with liberty and individuality, spells complexity and sophistication in communication and demands that human activities be coordinated and choreographed, a level that has not yet been achieved. The growth of activity in model building indicates that this need has been recognized, but a wish is not the same as its fulfillment. A clarion call to battle is not the battle itself. World models predicting prosperity or disaster must be looked upon as part of a new scientific and sociological morality play. They can be considered in the same way we might view Hogarth's *The Rake's Progress*—they warn of the dangers of the possible, they call upon us to consider our ways, but they do not necessarily provide adequate tools for prediction or control.

If our society is to survive, many bigger and more sophisticated models must be built. Computer and communications networks and systems models are to the twenty-first century as roads and administration were to Rome. There is every indication that we have or soon will have most of the communication and computational ability that we will need. The major shortage is in our ability to build relevant and dependable models of the phenomena we wish to control. Good model building calls for high skills in perception and ruthless constructive skepticism. Computer and communications networks have considerably enhanced the social value of the art of modeling, but the supply of master modelers may be a greater bottleneck than the supply of computer power. Teaching the art of constructing models may be in and of itself an important aspect of teaching, as Papert indicates in chapter 5.

Given our problems and given the new tools at our disposal, what is needed is the willingness to dare to model the complexities of economic and political life. But models or theories are not necessarily valuable or relevant because they lead to enormous computer programs. Their value lies in their ability to achieve the purposes for which they were constructed.

POSTSCRIPT

In the future the distinction between hardware and software will lessen. The easy distinctions between model, modeler, and machine will dissolve. The world views of historians, economists, engineers, psychiatrists, physicists, biologists, administrators, and mathematicians all differ, and these differences may well be manifested in a variety of specialized computer modeling systems designed to introspect and model in a manner characteristic of the field of inquiry.

Memory, size, speed of recall, and computation, along with the ability to observe and the potential length of life of a computer hardware-software modeling system open up the important possibility that we may be able to transfer specialized techniques of modeling and successful approaches to the arts and sciences to systems that will not merely solve problems passively but will be able to provide methods of diagnosis to locate new problems and be able to produce new models. While it may be many years before a "historian system" can interpret events better than a great historian, it may not be long before a medical or economic diagnosis system can perform better for some purposes than even the best diagnosticians.

The challenge we face is to start to model and build systems to produce as well as analyze models in many different disciplines. At the worst, if we fail to create model-creating and -diagnostic systems, we will have taught ourselves in considerable detail and in an operational manner where the fundamental difficulties in modeling lie.

In all probability, as we proceed, this approach will teach us more than we now know about perception and creativity and simultaneously enable us to embody these new insights in systems capable of utilizing them to produce new models of and for our civilization.

EDITORS' POSTSCRIPT

Professor McCarthy, in his critique of this essay, questions whether computer modeling is critical to the progress of our society. Would the lack of modeling cause a near-term or medium-term collapse of the economy? Taking a different view, others have claimed that highly parallel computer systems that offer thousandfold speed improvements over today's machines would have a dramatic impact on the art of modeling traffic systems, for example.

14
The Economics of Information

Kenneth J. Arrow

INFORMATION AND INDIVIDUAL DECISION MAKING: INFORMATION AS VALUE AND AS COST

The meaning of information is precisely a reduction in uncertainty. From the viewpoint of economics or decision theory, uncertainty is relevant because it concerns the consequences of decisions. An individual making a decision may be supposed to be choosing one among a set of feasible alternatives. In general, these alternatives are themselves plans extending in time, and he will want to choose the one that yields the most satisfying consequences. These may be profits in successive periods for a business firm, or they may be other satisfactions, such as consumption, power, bequests, or interesting challenges. It can be assumed that the individual compares the entire set of consequences deriving from each alternative in his decision set with those of the others and chooses the preferred one.

In conditions of uncertainty, the consequences of any given decision are not known. Instead, the set of consequences can be thought of as a function of the decision made and of a number of factors exogenous to the decision maker whose values are unknown to him. These factors, taken together, can be thought of as defining the state of the world, a description of the world sufficiently precise so that the consequences of any of the alternative possible decisions would be known if the state of the world were known.

Under uncertainty, the state of the world is not known. Ignorance may be modeled in different ways, but so far only the probability model has proved to be fruitful. Each possible value of the state of the world has a probability attached to it, a number that denotes the degree of credibility assigned to the occurrence of that value. These numbers add up in convenient ways.

Kenneth J. Arrow is James Bryant Conant University Professor at Harvard University. His interests are in the fields of general equilibrium theory and social choice. His research in these areas resulted in his being awarded the Nobel Prize for economics in 1972. Professor Arrow is considered to be one of the world's leading mathematical economists.

Perhaps most importantly, probability theory provides a useful way of characterizing learning, or the modification of perceptions through the acquisition of information.

Intuitively, a change in information is a change in the probability distribution of states of the world. If the individual is assumed to have a consistent set of probabilities, the changes in probability distributions have to be thought of as different conditional probability distributions from a fixed distribution over a larger set of variables. More specifically, it is necessary to recognize that in addition to the dimensions of the state of the world that directly affect the consequences of different decisions, there are other dimensions that do not directly affect consequences but that yield information about the distribution of the payoff-relevant dimensions. That is, the consequences of a given decision are not independent, in the sense of probability theory, of these other dimensions, which by analogy with communications engineering may be termed signals. Thus, prior to any observations, the individual is supposed to have a joint distribution over economically relevant states and signals. In the absence of any signal, a decision would be based on the marginal distribution of the relevant states. If a signal arrives or is acquired, the individual would use the distribution of relevant states conditional upon the observed value of the signal.

The probability theory relevant to decision making is, in the first instance, subjective. It is the ignorance or uncertainty of the individual decision maker that is relevant to his decisions. However, if different individuals have received common signals, each will use a distribution conditional on those signals; these distributions will in general be more alike than the unconditional distributions. If a group of individuals have had sufficient experiences in common, they may well have very similar conditional probability distributions, and hence the subjective viewpoint merges into an objective one.*

The choice among alternative decisions will then be a choice among probability distributions of consequences. An accepted formalism for expressing these choices is the expected-utility hypothesis, due originally to Daniel Bernoulli and Gabriel Cramer in the early eighteenth century and developed axiomatically by Frank Ramsey and independently by John von Neumann and Oskar Morgenstern. A real-valued utility function is defined over sets of consequences, indicating the individual's preferences, so that a higher utility is assigned to a preferred set of consequences; one probability distribution of consequences is preferred to another if the mathematical expectation of utility of consequences is higher if the first distribution

---

* The subjective probability model for uncertainty is not without deficiencies, but an examination of them would be the subject of another essay.

holds than if the second holds. Even if the consequences can be represented by a single number, such as profits, the utility might be a nonlinear function of that variable. In this case, the intuitive idea that individuals are prone to avoid risks would be represented by assuming that the utility function is a concave function of profits (i.e., its slope decreases as profits increase).

If the state of information (the set of signals received) is given and constant, then optimal choice is a problem of decision making under a given uncertainty, a situation that has been the subject of considerable analysis in the last thirty years. The problems of the economics of information proper arise when the probability distribution of states of the world is a variable. In the language adopted here, the signals received can vary. The existence of signals creates two important possibilities for the improvement of decision making. The first is taking advantage of the existence of signals. If the individual knows that a signal will be received before the decision has to be made, his optimal choice should be a function of the signal. We can think, alternatively but equivalently, of making the decision after the receipt of the signal and basing it on the probability distributions of consequences conditional on the signal, or of making the decision in advance for all possible values of the signal.

In this simple case, the analysis scarcely goes beyond that of decision making under uncertainty with given information, since for each given value of the signal, the conditional probability distribution is known. More complex are the situations in which the decision actually has several parts, some of which are made with less information than others. This situation is typical of investment choices. A sequence of decisions has to be made. The first decision is made before receiving any signals, for example, to start building a plant or to choose an inventory stock. By the end of next time period, some information has been acquired, for example on sales or production costs. At this point a decision has to be made on adding to the investment, but now it can be a function of the intervening signal. This process of successive decisions can be continued indefinitely.

What makes the analysis somewhat complex is that the first decision is made in the knowledge that future decisions will be based on more information. In many cases, this will lead to strategies that emphasize flexibility. If the initial commitment is of an irreversible nature (or reversible only at considerable cost), then the optimal strategy is likely to call for a low initial investment, to be increased if subsequent information so indicates. On the other hand, a larger initial investment can be optimal if it leads to a greater acquisition of information, as with a multiplicity of alternative research projects.

One aspect, then, of the economics of information is that of devising decision strategies that take account of varying information over time. But a second and even more distinctive feature is that the choice of which signals to receive itself becomes a decision variable. The individual decision maker may be thought of as adding communication channels. The scientist or researcher must choose which experiments to make; the businessman or even the part-time investor must decide which news sources to rely on; the student, and society as a whole on his behalf, must choose the schools to go to, the courses to take, the content and presentation of the courses offered, and the instructors to give them.

In general, of course, acquiring signals in and of itself confers a benefit; the value or utility expected from a decision function of a signal is greater than in the case of a fixed decision made independently of the signal. But against this must be offset the fundamental fact that information embodied in signals is costly; communication channels are not free goods. The acquisition of data by an individual requires time and effort on either his or someone else's part. This is true whether the information is to be newly wrested from nature or to be transferred from someone else already in possession of it. Developments in information-handling and communications technology have their impact on economic life through their effect on these costs. The amount of information that can be handled for a given cost has increased enormously and has contributed to the unprecedented growth in productivity of the last twenty-five years.

The possibility of reducing information costs is limited to the extent that the human being is an intrinsic part of the decision-making process. An individual's assimilation of information is limited by his information-processing capability. Any teacher knows the problem. This capability might be increased by training and by presenting information so as to minimize the difficulty of understanding. Costs may also be lowered by replacing the human being completely in some decisions, but this possibility is limited by the inherent superiority of human brains in complex decision problems.

To sum up, there is no generally acceptable formula for measuring either the costs or the benefits of information, although in many specific contexts there is no basic difficulty in formulating one or the other. In particular, the benefits are usually measurable, and costs of transmission of existing information are at least approximable, but the costs of acquiring information through research remain, as always, a guess based on experience rather than a formally specifiable value.

ORGANIZATION AS AN ECONOMY IN THE ACQUISITION OF INFORMATION

I have pointed out that the individual has a limited capacity for the acquisition of information. Among the ways of overcoming this bottleneck, the greatest innovation has been the social concept of an organization. When there are many individuals working together, each can absorb different bits of information; hence, the group as a whole can have much greater information-handling ability than any one member.

One of the most interesting economic characteristics of information is that its cost is independent of the scale on which it is used. A given piece of information costs the same to acquire, whether the decision to be based on it is large or small. Thus, the formula for a steel alloy has a given cost, though it may be used to make one ton or a hundred thousand tons. Therefore if by joining in an organization a number of individuals can acquire separate signals which can then be used by all of them, net benefits (benefits less costs of information) increase more than proportionately to the size of the organization.

Specialization in information gathering is one instance, in my view the most important instance, of the economic benefits of organization. The basic gain in all such cases is that a group working together can produce more in total than the sum of their products working individually. This surplus cannot be achieved if all individuals perform the same tasks, for then they might as well be working separately. It is achieved only by specialization of function, by a suitable sharing of duties. This is precisely the division of labor among individuals whose importance was so much stressed by Adam Smith.

Of all forms of division of labor, the division of information gathering is perhaps the most fundamental. Indeed, the chief gain from other forms of specialization is that the individual worker can acquire the skills for a particular task more effectively if the range of the task is restricted: in other words, the efficiency gain is owing to the lower cost of information permitted by specialization.

If there is one doctrine that all economists share, it is that summed up in the familiar slogan, "There is no such thing as a free lunch." Complex organizations have drawbacks to be set off against their efficiency gains. For one thing, an organization can be most easily designed when the information flow being handled is itself static in form. The signals being observed are indeed new in each period, but the structure remains unchanged; the signals concern the same kinds of facts. But an organization well designed to accommodate a flow of signals of a fixed form will in general be poorly adapted to accommodate to structural changes. Sclerosis of organizations may be as dangerous to health as sclerosis of the arteries.

Even apart from changes in structure, organizations have one necessary cost that offsets the gains in efficiency of information acquisition: the need for coordination. The greater efficiency of organizational behavior that results from having more observers can only be realized by transmitting the information from the initial observer to other participants. But it is of the essence of the economics of information that conveying information is costly. It may indeed be less expensive, in terms of resources used, to transmit information, once it is acquired, than to acquire it, so that the economies of organization are still present. Nevertheless, it is still desirable to economize on the transmission of information.

This elementary observation has profound implications for the nature of organization. In an optimally designed organization, the participants will have differing information. Each individual will transmit only part of the information he has; hence, after communication, each individual will be specialized in certain kinds of knowledge. It follows that it is optimal to specialize the decision making in conformity with this specialization in knowledge. There is a division of labor in action and decision corresponding to the division of labor in information gathering. Thus actions will necessarily have to be coordinated if they are to be effective. Of course, there are other reasons why decisions will be diffused and specialized and will need coordination. Differing abilities on the part of the members of an organization would call for specialization; as economists have long observed, it is the variation in comparative abilities at different tasks that is critical, rather than absolute differences.

The need for coordination has two basic causes: the various members (e.g., production units) are competing for a common pool of resources, financial and material; and different decisions complement or substitute for each other. For both reasons, the effectiveness of decisions made by one participant is influenced by the decisions of another. With limitations on the flow of information, the decisions themselves cannot be coordinated. That would require transferring all the information available, precisely what is to be avoided. It has been emphasized earlier that when information will be available, the individual should choose a decision function, a policy or strategy that determines what his actual decision should be for each possible signal he receives. Hence, ideally, in an organization there should be prior agreement on decision functions or strategies for all participants.

This picture of optimal organizational design when acquiring and transmitting informative signals is owing to Jacob Marschak and Roy Radner, who have given this approach the name of the *theory of teams*. To sum up, we start with a problem in which a group of individuals will receive benefits that depend on their choices among a number of actions as well as some unknown states of the world. A number of signals about the state of the world can be observed, though at a cost. The organization, or team, is designed to give each individual a set of signals to receive or acquire initially, a set of rules for communicating information based on these signals to other members of the team, and finally a set of actions over which he has control and a set of rules to determine which of these actions to undertake as a function of the information received, either initially or by transmission from others. The performance of the system as measured by the net benefits received depends then on the actions taken, the uncertain state of the world, and the costs of acquisition and transmission of information. The rules should be chosen so as to maximize the expected net benefits.

This summarily stated model permits an enormous number of variations. Thus the communication of information might take an iterative form. In the first round, rather gross signals might be sent, in which little of the detail originally acquired survives. The recipients may then ask for further details, their needs depending on signals received from other members of the team. As one example, some simple measures of profitability might be sent in the first instance, after which participants whose performance is relatively poor might be asked for greater detail. As another example, closer to the economists' central issue of resource allocation, the information transmitted might be in the form of claims to scarce resources. If the claims balance the resource availabilities, the process ends; if not, signals are sent by the resource managers indicating that claims should be increased or scaled down, according as aggregate claims fall short of or exceed availabilities, and this process continues until some balance is achieved.

The theoretical problems of designing organizations along these lines have barely begun to be analyzed. Even more interesting would be empirical studies of organizations to see to what extent they have been evolving toward theoretically optimal standards. At the moment, however, only qualitative insights have been achieved.

THE ECONOMIC SYSTEM AS AN ORGANIZATION

A familiar theme of economists, implicit even in the earliest work in the field and explicit since Léon Walras and Vilfredo Pareto at the end of the last century, is that the entire economic system of markets can be regarded as a large organization, with prices, purchases, and sales as signals communicated. This work arose partly in response to the challenge of socialism, though the idea is implicit in earlier thinking, such as Adam Smith's "invisible hand" and Jeremy Bentham's confrontation of utilitarian ethics with the free market system.

However, this remarkable conclusion, the result of a long line of theoretical discussion, holds true only under limited conditions. Consider an economic system in which there are two kinds of agents, households and firms. Households initially possess goods, especially but not exclusively labor power, which they may give up to others. They acquire other goods;

their satisfaction derives from the goods acquired or retained. Firms acquire inputs and transform them in accordance with their technologies into outputs. Compatibility of the choices made by the many firms and households requires that for each good the total produced or initially available should be at least as much as the amount used by firms and by households. A description of the goods used and supplied by each household and by each firm is termed an *allocation.*

Among the infinitely many possible allocations of resources conditioned by given technologies and given initial supplies, two categories are especially interesting. One is the class of allocations termed *Pareto optimal;* an allocation is Pareto optimal if there is not some other allocation that yields every individual in the economy a higher level of satisfaction. The other is the class of allocations termed *competitive equilibria;* they are those that would result from the operation of an idealized market system. More precisely, for any set of prices for all goods, suppose each firm chooses inputs and outputs to maximize profits at the given prices, and each household chooses sales of the goods it owns and purchases of other goods so as to maximize its satisfaction consistent with a budgetary rule that its expenditures not exceed its receipts. The resulting decisions will in general be incoherent, in that there will be some goods for which total amounts offered will differ from amounts demanded. But under general conditions there will be some set of prices at which supply and demand will be equated in every market. It can be shown that there is a close relation between these two concepts. Indeed, under suitable assumptions, a competitive equilibrium allocation is necessarily Pareto optimal, and conversely, any desired Pareto optimal allocation is a competitive equilibrium corresponding to some redistribution of the initial purchasing powers of the households.

These propositions are the basis for the general presumption that free markets are desirable. In particular they tend to support the view that any tendency of the market to produce an excessively unequal distribution of income should be met by appropriate measures of taxation and redistribution through payments to the poor rather than by subsidizing particular kinds of consumption. However, the assumptions that they rest on are neither so clearly valid in reality that they can be counted on as a basis for policy without further question nor so invalid that they are irrelevant. For present purposes, it is the logic of the propositions that is most interesting.

The competitive system can be viewed as an information and decision structure. Initially, each agent in the economy has a very limited perspective. The household knows only its initial holdings of goods (including labor power) and the satisfactions it could derive from different combinations of goods acquired and consumed. The firm knows only the technological alternatives for transforming inputs into outputs. The "communication" takes the form of prices. If the correct (equilibrium) prices are announced, then the individual agents can determine their purchases and sales so as to maximize profits or satisfactions. The prices are then, according to the pure theory, the only communication that needs to be made in addition to the information held initially by the agents. This makes the market system appear to be very efficient indeed; not only does it achieve as good an allocation as an omniscient planner could, but it clearly minimizes the amount of communication needed.

I have deliberately described the model so as to emphasize its information and communication structure. A firm need not receive the profits; all that matters is that it choose the set of inputs and outputs that would maximize profits. It is this informational interpretation that has been most stressed by the so-called "market socialists." Since the theorems that show the equivalence of competitive equilibria and Pareto optima seem to support the virtues of capitalism, one socialist school has replied that a socialist economy can achieve the same efficiency in resource allocation and communication. The households and firms need only follow the same decision rules that the competitive model predicts for a capitalist economy; neither households nor firms need actually own property or the rights to profits. The market socialists usually add that a real capitalist system is far from competitive, and therefore in fact performance will be superior under socialism.

A counterargument is that the market socialists take for granted that the decision and communication rules will be enforced. In a capitalist economy, it is argued, the agents carry out the rules of maximizing profits or satisfaction because in fact it is in their interest to do so. In the absence of self-interest, incentives for execution of the appropriate rules will be weak or absent.

If we confine ourselves to questions of efficiency, informational and otherwise, on the assumption that the optimal communication and decision rules will be followed, we have a very strong argument for the price system, whether under capitalism or under socialism. But there are serious qualifications. The system is efficient when the equilibrium prices have been found, but how can they be discovered? It is easy to verify that a set of prices is an equilibrium set; all that is necessary is that supply and demand for each good balances. In general, what is lacking is a process for getting to equilibrium.

Both in the real world and in the world of design of economic systems, successive approximations with information feedback are needed, but there are many possible approximation processes. The most common paradigm has been the price adjustment process. A given set of prices is announced, and the agents calculate demands and supplies as of those prices. These demands and supplies are summed over all agents. For each good, price is adjusted upward if aggregate demand exceeds aggregate supply, downward in the opposite case. This theoretical process mimics most closely the operations of an (idealized) market system. Notice that at each stage the information to be communicated is about as little as can be imagined; lists of demands and supplies from each agent, which are then subjected to the simplest of arithmetic transformations, addition.

Whether or not the process converges turns out to be problematical; it will under certain assumptions, but in their absence it may easily fail to do so. But even if it does, there is a serious problem with any process that converges only in the limit. Even if each step requires a minimal information cost, an infinite number of steps will require an infinite cost.

Processes other than price adjustment are equally possible and have been explored theoretically. But clearly any feasible process can require only a finite and indeed limited number of steps. It cannot achieve an allocation of resources that would be optimal in the absence of information costs. There is the need to explore the trade-offs among information transmitting costs per step, the number of steps, and the resource efficiency level achieved. These trade-offs will be seriously affected by changes in the technologies of communication and computing. It is noteworthy that large firms, whose internal coordination problems are small-scale replicas of those of entire economies, rely only slightly on the price system; centralized control with the aid of more or less efficient information systems is dominant.

THE PROBLEM OF INCENTIVES

In any organization, including an economy coordinated through markets, the members will have different interests. These differences may arise from opportunities for personal gain or simply from the desire for prestige or the avoidance of trouble. The members may not have incentives to make mutually optimal decisions or, what is more relevant to the present topic, to transmit correct information to each other. An important question is the possibility of designing incentive structures so as to motivate optimal information transmission.

Whether or not this can be done depends on a number of factors, one of which is the a priori information as to the motivating forces (utility functions) of the agents in the organization. It can be proved as a general theorem that no mechanism can be found that will achieve perfect incentives for all possible utility functions of the participants. On the other hand, if sufficient information is available on the possible utility functions of the participants, then in many cases it is possible to devise incentive mechanisms, payments depending on the announced information, that will induce truth telling or, more generally, optimal supply of information.

A simple example is the allocation of a single, indivisible object to that one of several individuals who values it most highly. If the individuals do not know each other's true values, an auction system may be misleading; the one with the highest valuation may bid low, guessing that others have a low valuation, but if he is mistaken he may not get the object. The auction bids will not be truthful revelations of information, or in this case valuations. Instead, however, we can have an auction with the rule that the highest bidder gets the object but pays only the amount bid by the second-highest bidder. A little reflection will show that no individual will have an incentive to bid anything but his true valuation, regardless of the valuations of others. Active research is going on just now to extend the range in which methods such as this can be applied.

Actual markets in the real world have adverse incentives. The problem is that initial information may differ among individuals even more than the pure competitive model just sketched allows for. In that model, individuals need know nothing of each other's production capabilities or tastes, but they are implicitly supposed to know the prices at which they could buy goods and the qualities of those goods. Neither of these may in fact be true. Finding out the prices of a large range of commodities is itself a costly enterprise, and knowledge of this fact by price setters is itself enough to create incentives for inefficient market behavior. If one individual has more information about the quality of a good than the second, the first may exploit the situation, and the second, distrusting him, may not take advantage of what is in fact a desirable trade.

In situations such as this, the market may take advantage of what would otherwise be extraneous signals. Thus a good part of the economic value of higher education may well be not the additional productivity the training actually imparts but the signal that the individual successfully completing it has superior ability. To the extent that individuals choose to embark on higher education just because employers believe it signals superior ability, the content of the signal itself is changed.

The economics of information contains whole ranges of topics, particularly those concerned with the demand for and supply of information as a commodity, that have not been touched on here. My intention has been simply to illustrate some of the salient problems of a subject that is intertwined with the most fundamental questions of economic organization.

EDITORS' POSTSCRIPT

Arrow argues that because information costs are the same independent of the scale upon which it is used, organizations that rely on information can derive economic benefits disproportionately large in relation to the size of the organization. It follows that if the forecasts of a vast information network are realized, there will be considerably more information available to organizations, probably at a lower cost. Accordingly, the computer revolution may affect organizations substantively, taking a primary role rather than the secondary role predicted for it in almost every essay in parts 2 and 3. Another major factor in the future evolution of information systems is the technology and cost of finding information of interest to an individual or organization. Thus being in the lobby of the Library of Congress, a few feet away from much of the world's written knowledge, is of almost no value to us unless we also have methods for locating and collecting all of the information relevant to our purpose. The same is true of a large information network, whose utility will largely be limited by the evolution of the technology for accessing information.

IV
Trends in the
Underlying
Technologies

15
Hardware
Prospects and
Limitations

Robert N. Noyce

The development of the computer has always been closely tied to the development of the active components from which the computer was assembled. The various generations of computers have been identified by the component technology used in their construction, from the first computer using vacuum tubes to those using germanium and silicon transistors, then small and medium integrated circuits, and now the appearance of the first machines utilizing large-scale integrated circuits, or LSI. Computer cost and performance have been dependent on the component technology.

An assessment of the prospects for computer hardware over the next two decades means assessing the prospects for component technology over a somewhat shorter period of time, as widespread computer applications do not come into being until perhaps five years after components are available. Since semiconductor technology has shown amazing versatility in satisfying the needs of the computer, I will limit myself to considering integrated circuits, which are now used everywhere in the typical computing system except in input-output mechanisms, and mass storage. Although other component technologies may come into use during this time, the development of semiconductor technology will set a lower bound on any new technology, if such technologies are to be used. Furthermore, since the development of semiconductor devices has a thirty-year history, it provides a base from which to extrapolate.

Cost reduction has been the major motivation for the continuing development of integrated circuit technology. Since the introduction of the integrated circuit, the cost per function has dropped by nearly a factor of two every year. Such cost reductions will continue until barriers are en-

Robert N. Noyce is chairman of the board of Intel Corporation. He has been involved with research and development activities in the forefront of the solid-state area. Among his pioneering contributions are the integrated circuit, on which he holds original patents, and Intel's promotion of the first microcomputer on a chip (the Intel 4004 and 8008), whose successors are revolutionizing computer applications.

countered, and as long as significant cost reduction can be achieved, the necessary research and development investment will be made. Performance and reliability will also improve as costs are reduced.

The following are the major topics I will consider:

1. Techniques by which progress has been made in the past.
2. An extrapolation of this progress to see whether the result is advantageous.
3. Fundamental barriers that may be encountered in the next fifteen years at the projected rates of advance in technology.
4. Practical limits that will be encountered.
5. The probable level of hardware technology that will be achieved, considering all these factors.

INTERCONNECTIONS ARE THE PROBLEM

Interconnections have been and are the major cost in computer hardware. Because of the physical size of these interconnections, delays are incurred in transmitting signals from origin to destination within the computer; because of their capacitance, a power loss is incurred every time a signal is imposed on the line, which means that the system must have high power drivers that would otherwise not be needed to drive the actual logic of the computer. And because the interconnections themselves act as antennae, they transmit to and pick up from other interconnections unwanted signals, or noise. As a result, there is an exploding design of increasing power, increasing noise, and increasing size, which requires higher power and leads to longer delays and higher costs. Yet current technology could contain the essential logic and memory of a large modern computer in 10 to 100 cm^3 of silicon chips! Interconnections also add to the apparent complexity of the large computer, resulting in maintenance and documentation problems as well as reliability problems whose severity increases with size. The integrated circuit is the component industry's solution to these problems.

Since cost has been the driving force behind the development of integrated circuits, let us examine where the costs of these components arise. The production costs are made up of two basic elements: the cost of the active element (today usually silicon) and assembly and test costs.

The silicon chip cost is dependent upon the processing cost per chip and the yield of good chips. There is a limit to the size of the silicon chip if it is to have a practical yield. A simple model would say that if a given size chip yielded only 10 percent good chips owing to random defects, then a chip twice as large would yield only 1 percent good chips. (Actually the situation is not this bad, since defects are not randomly distributed.) The cost for twice the function would then be twenty times as great (twice the processing cost, since twice the area of silicon is used, and ten times the cost owing to loss of yield). Clearly, if the cost of the active silicon is dominant, such a doubling of complexity would not be cost-effective; carried to an extreme, the single transistor is the most cost-effective.

The other major cost element borne by the component manufacturer is that of assembling and testing the devices. Assembly is the process of putting the tiny silicon active element in a housing that includes a mechanical transition from the microscopic interconnections included in the integrated circuit to the sizes normally encountered in electronic equipment; that is, lead separation of 10 microns to lead separation of 2,500 microns, or 2.5 mm respectively. As a first approximation, assembly costs are independent of the function included on the integrated circuit chip, although they will increase somewhat with the increasing number of electrical connections to large chips. Similarly, test costs increase much more slowly than the complexity of the chip being tested, although very sophisticated test equipment is required to achieve this result. Thus, the total cost per function will be made up of two elements, one increasing with complexity and taking the general form ae^{bN}, which represents the cost of the silicon chip, and another of the form c/N, which resprezents the cost of assembly and test where N is the number of functions included. This cost will have a minimum, as indicated in figure 15.1. As processes for manufacturing integrated circuits have been perfected and yields of good circuits have been improved, this minimum cost point has moved to circuits of higher complexity. It has been the strategy of the semiconductor

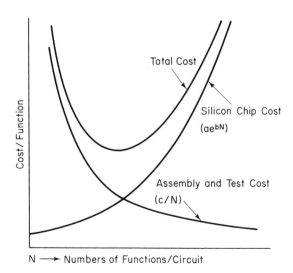

N ⟶ Numbers of Functions/Circuit

15.1
Cost/Function versus Circuit Complexity

device manufacturers to supply circuits that are near this minimum at any given time.

An examination of the integrated circuits offered by the industry as a function of time provides an approximation of how the minimum cost point has moved up with time, even though such products have been introduced in advance of what is shown as the lowest cost per function point. On this basis, the minimum cost/function point has been moving up in complexity, doubling every year since the introduction of the integrated circuit, as indicated in figure 15.2. If the present rates of increase of complexity were to continue, integrated circuits with 10^9 elements would be available in twenty years.

This increase in complexity has resulted in a cost savings in the subsequent assembly into computer hardware as well, since more of the total interconnections are made within the semiconductor components. Other advantages have also accrued. The interconnections within the silicon chip have proven to be more reliable than those at the next higher level, resulting in an increase in overall systems reliability. Because equipment can be made smaller, speeds can be improved and the costs of cabinets

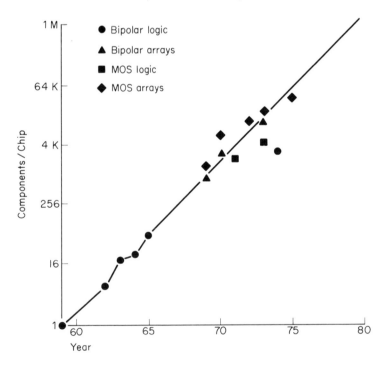

15.2
Circuit Complexity versus Time of Introduction

and cables reduced, along with total power and cooling requirements. Clearly there are limits to the complexity of integrated circuits. They may arise from our inability to improve the processing technology, as in the past, or from our inability either to design very complex circuits or to conceive of practical uses for them. Eventually more fundamental limitations will come into play.

Higher levels of integration have been achieved in three main ways:

1. By decreasing minimum dimensions, resulting in higher density circuit elements.

2. By decreasing defect density through improved processing techniques, allowing the practical production of circuits of larger area.

3. Through innovations in circuit forms, allowing higher functional density.

Line widths   The minimum average dimension used in integrated circuits (ICs) is shown in figure 15.3, plotted as a function of time. Production technology moved quickly from the pre-1960 dimension of 100 microns to the 10-micron range as photolithography was introduced as a method of defining the geometry of transistors. Steady improvement has been made since that time as equipment and methods have been improved. Recent production technology can utilize 4-micron widths, and laboratory work involves significantly smaller dimensions. These widths also define not only the size of interconnection patterns but also the source-drain spacing in MOS transistors and the emitter-base contact spacing in bipolar tran-

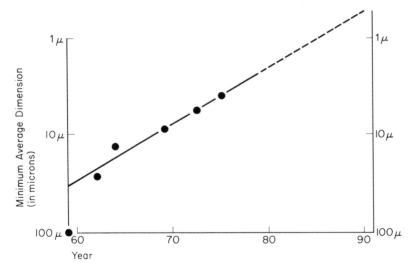

15.3
Minimum Average Dimension of Line Widths versus Time

sistors, which in turn are primary determinants of the performance of these transistors.

Defect density   The production of integrated circuits has always been a yield problem. Many circuits are made, the defective ones are thrown away, and the good ones are sold. Defects can arise from many sources. The photomasks used may have pinholes in dark areas or opaque specks in areas that should be clear. Severe defects in the basic silicon crystal can make the circuit inoperative. Dust in the photoprinting operation or in some other processing step that affects a critical spot in the circuit will cause failures. Errors in aligning successive photoengraving steps or lack of control over critical dimensions and impurity concentration will make the circuit inoperative. The correction and elimination of these defects is a difficult task and represents a major portion of the effort and expense of semiconductor device development and production. However, there is no indication that any fundamental limits exist. Progress continues at a rate that is advantageous and can be economically justified.

Progress in reducing defect densities can be seen from the history of silicon chip sizes of new products, as shown in figure 15.4. The absolute defect density is approximately the inverse of the chip size, since at higher defect densities the chip cost would be prohibitively high, while at lower defect densities higher levels of integration give a cost advantage.

New devices and circuits   Much of the progress has been accomplished as a result of new devices and new circuit forms. These are sometimes so intimately tied together that they are hard to separate. The introduction of MOS devices represented a breakthrough in the levels of integration that could be achieved. More recently, charge-coupled devices (CCDs) and integrated injection logic (I²L) have allowed higher levels of

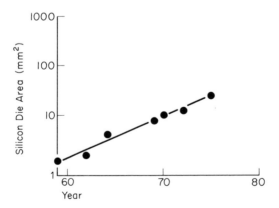

15.4
Silicon Die Area versus Time

integration to be achieved because of the higher density possible with these circuit forms. Although limitations come along with the advantages, these devices will find use in some applications.

Oxide isolation, rather than the more traditional p-n junction isolation, offers many advantages. Since it is an insulator, a layer of silicon dioxide can electrically isolate any combination of p-type and n-type silicon regions without the consideration of polarities or the possible transmission of minority carriers and transistor effect. A major reduction in the size of individual circuit elements, in some cases as much as 70 percent, is possible as a result, using the same minimum line widths. Oxide isolation reduces parasitic capacitance as well, resulting in performance improvement. The use of oxide isolation techniques is now becoming widespread in the industry, since it has such obvious advantages over more complex processing techniques.

The newer circuit forms appear to have approached the ultimate efficiency in packing density, although this may be simply because we have not yet conceived of the next improvement.

The cost reductions resulting from higher levels of integration have been remarkable. The individual diffused transistor sold for a price of approximately one dollar in 1961, a few years after its introduction. Today, a 1024-bit memory including over five thousand transistors sells for under two dollars a few years after its introduction, representing a cost reduction of about 3,000:1 in seventeen years. The resulting effect of equipment costs can be seen in the electronic calculator, which has been reduced in cost by a factor of 500:1 in the last eight years, creating a substantial new market unforeseen only ten years ago.

Performance has also improved as a result of smaller minimum dimensions and circuit innovation. The early integrated circuits had much lower performance than circuits made of the individual transistors. The first commercial integrated circuits, the direct-coupled transistor logic (DCTL) family, had gate delays of 100 ns. Successive development of DTL, TTL, Schottkey TTL, and ECL have decreased these switching delays to approximately 1 ns/gate today. Discrete transistors have been displaced in high-performance machines by faster integrated circuits. High-density LSI circuit technology is achieving similar improvements in speed, as figure 15.5 indicates.

As circuit complexity has increased, the reliability of the individual circuit has remained approximately constant, resulting in a drastic improvement of reliability on a per-function basis. Indeed, had the reliability not drastically improved, the large computers of today would not have been built: the mean time to failure would be so short as to make complex computations nearly impossible. Reliability improvement reduces the total cost of using the computer by reducing maintenance cost.

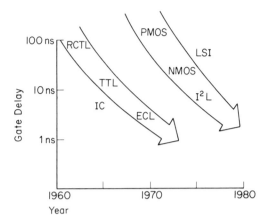

15.5
IC and LSI Performance versus Time

WHAT DOES THE FUTURE HOLD?

Extrapolating past results suggests that dimensions will continue to decrease, and density and chip size to increase. As a result, cost, performance, and reliability will improve.

As dimensions decrease, all of the device parameters move in a favorable direction. This can be seen by scaling device dimensions down and noting the changes in these parameters. As the device dimensions are reduced, we must not increase the electric fields in the devices, since transistors are designed to this limit now, and higher fields will result in avalanche or dielectric breakdown. (At lower voltages, quantum mechanical tunneling rather than breakdown will limit the fields to somewhat lower values.)

Since the dimensions are scaled with constant fields, the operating voltages vary as

$$V \propto x,$$

where x is the characteristic dimension of the device. Since the fields terminate in sheets of charge with finite thickness, the charge densities must increase to scale this thickness. Thus the impurity densities in the device vary inversely to x. Similarly, the mobile charge n must increase as $1/x$. The area A of the conducting path varies with x^2, so the current varies as

$$I \propto nA \propto x,$$

Since the field is constant, the characteristic impedance of the circuit is constant:

$$Z \propto \frac{V}{I} = \text{constant.}$$

We may look at circuit delay times from two points of view, carrier transit time and capacitance charging time. The transit time τ_t will be proportional to the distance to travel:

$$\tau_t \propto x$$

since the field is constant. Charging the collector or drain capacitance depends on the voltage, current, and capacitance. The capacitance C, varies as the dimensions, so

$$\tau_C = \frac{CV}{I} \propto x,$$

similar to the variation in transit time.

The power per circuit will be proportional to the product of current and voltages:

$$P \propto VI \propto x^2.$$

The power density is then

$$P/x^2 = \text{constant.}$$

Thus as dimensions are made smaller, all variables move in a favorable or at least not unfavorable direction. Speed increases, density increases, and power density does not increase. As density increases, the cost/function can be expected to decrease in proportion.

As figure 15.3 shows, a reduction in dimensions of a factor of two every five years, or a factor of eight in fifteen years, has been achieved. If such a reduction could be made in the next fifteen years, circuit densities would increase by sixty-four times and speeds would increase by a factor of eight while power remained constant. With such circuit densities, we could easily expect memories to reach the one million bit/chip level, with access times of 20 ns. Such a reduction in dimensions would reduce current internal gate delays of 1 to 10 ns to the 100 ps to 1 ns range, thus providing another motivation for higher levels of integration.

Propagation delays will begin to be significant if system dimensions are much longer than 10 cm. Extrapolating figure 15.4 over the next fifteen years, the chip area will reach about 600 mm², or a chip 2.5 cm on a side. Although signal delays within the chip owing to propagation times would not be a significant factor, delays propagating between chips would be significant. The combined density and chip size extrapolations would result in an increase of functional complexity of over 2,000. Costs would increase only slowly from those of today's complex integrated circuits, resulting in a cost reduction of 100:1 or even 1000:1. Clearly there is an incentive to try to achieve this result.

More effort than ever is now being expended to advance IC technology. Expenditures have risen from a level of $25 million per year twenty years ago to approximately ten times that today. Successful companies in the semiconductor industry expend 5 to 10 percent of sales dollars in developing new technology, and those sales dollars are growing at a rate twice that of the gross product of the developed countries. These expenditures will continue until some point of diminishing returns is encountered.

FUNDAMENTAL LIMITS

A comprehensive review and bibliography on the fundamental limits in digital electronics is presented by R. W. Keyes.[1] In this paper the author considers limits set by the laws of quantum mechanics and thermodynamics for information storage, limits set by the need to dissipate power to process information, limits set by fluctuations in semiconductors, and practical limits to the size reduction of semiconductor devices.

Voltage

The first fundamental limit that will be encountered as dimensions are reduced is a lower limit for voltage in transistor logic. Logic or memory circuits must be bistable in order to represent binary states. This implies that the circuits must be inherently nonlinear. Since electrons in semiconductors are distributed in energy, the operating voltage must be large compared to KT/q in order to satisfy this requirement. For practical circuits,

$$V \simeq 10 \, KT/q = 0.25 \text{ volts at } 300°K.$$

The signal voltages of common logic circuits could be reduced by a factor of approximately ten before encountering this limit. Since the circuit voltage levels scale with the dimensions of the transistors, a similar reduction in dimensions could be made.

The extrapolation of the dimensions in figure 15.3 suggests that a maximum reduction of 8:1 will be achieved in the next fifteen years. Thus the voltage limit will be approached, but it will not limit continued size reduction during this time.

Power

The scaling argument showed that power density remains constant as devices are properly scaled from current technology. Thus power limitations more severe than those now being accommodated are not encountered until the voltage limits are reached. However, it may be instructive to examine the power limits from another point of view.

Since for projected chip sizes the logic delays are longer than the on-chip signal propagation time, the major power dissipated for on-chip communication will be that lost in charging the interconnections. Therefore,

$$P = CV^2/\tau,$$

if a pulse of voltage V must be applied to the lines each τ seconds. As an example, assume that each communication line is active each cycle, approximate the capacitance of these lines by assuming they cover the entire surface, and scale the dielectric thickness 10:1 from today's technology. For 1-volt signals, these assumptions result in a power dissipation of

$$P = 4 \times 10^{-8}/\tau \text{ watts/cm}^2 \times \text{clock frequency.}$$

A maximum dissipation of 20 watts/cm² would put a lower limit on τ of

$$\tau \geq 2 \times 10^{-9} \text{ sec,} \qquad \text{clock} = 500 \text{ mc.}$$

Only half of the circuits would switch in a maximally efficient logic design, and normal logic may be far below this, relaxing this limit even further. In any event, this limit would not be approached until clock frequencies were increased by a factor of ten.

This analysis assumed no DC dissipation of power, a condition closely met by dynamic or CMOS circuits. For bipolar transistors, however, the DC power is significant and cannot be scaled in direct proportion to signal levels because of the necessary forward bias drop across the emitter base junction of 0.7 V. Thus power problems will be encountered with bipolar devices earlier than with MOS devices, in which no DC current flows across the input voltage drop.

In considering communication between the chips the situation is quite different, since the lines are no longer short and significant power is required for high-speed transmission. Assuming that a transmission line of impedance Z is used, the dissipation in each communication line will be

$$P \simeq V^2/Z.$$

Using values of $V = 1$ volt, $Z = 100\,\Omega$, yields

$$P = 10^{-2} \text{ watts.}$$

If the allowable dissipation were 20 watts/cm² and the duty cycle of the communication lines 100 percent, this would limit the off-chip communications to 2,000 lines/cm². Such a limit does not appear severe.

Other possible limitations have been considered. For example, with the dimensions expected, the statistical fluctuations in doping density begin to add some variation in transistor characteristics. However, none of these other effects appears to be limiting.

In sum, several of the fundamental limits to size will be approached but not reached during the next fifteen years.

PRACTICAL LIMITS

Since most production technologies use photolithography to define the circuits, the wavelength of light looms large as a limit to the dimensions that can be achieved. The resolution of the printed pattern is involved, but a more difficult problem is the reindexing of successive photolithographic steps necessary to build up the integrated circuit structure. Today's techniques require that the previously printed pattern be examined (either by human eye or automatic equipment) and be aligned with the new pattern to be printed. This examination is made using visible light, with the resolution that this implies. Realignment more accurate than about three wavelengths of light is not yet practical. The allowance for this amount of misalignment in the design of the circuit means that much smaller circuits cannot be produced by this technique.

One approach to avoiding this limitation is to remove the need for accurate alignment by using "self-aligned" techniques. For example, in the silicon gate technique used in MOS circuits, the gate itself and the source-drain spacing are defined in the same photolithographic step. The use of self-aligned techniques eliminates the allowance for misalignment of some masking steps from the design of the circuits and allows tighter packing densities.

Another approach is to develop new device forms in which the critical dimensions are defined by techniques other than photoengraving. An example is the "D-MOS" transistor, in which the source-drain spacing is defined by solid-state diffusion rather than by photolithography.

A third approach to eliminating resolution limitations is the use of electron beams rather than optical techniques. Indeed, the use of electron beams for the preparation of high-resolution photomasks is proposed now for use in industry. However, production use of electron-beam lithography in printing on the silicon wafers appears to be a decade away. The many problems of inspection and realignment techniques must be solved. In addition, production-worthy equipment must be developed. The economic payout of the use of the electron beam is not clear, particularly for the pioneer who would have to assume most of the burden of the technology development cost. For these reasons a more likely solution will be an immediate one, using the electron beam to prepare photomasks but using optical printing techniques on the silicon.

As stated earlier, there appears to be no fundamental limitation to the reduction of defect densities. The IC industry has proved very resourceful in the solution of these problems. Progress has been steady and seems to be determined by the amount of effort expended to perfect production processes. Since the economic payout is very high, we can expect the effort to continue, with results similar to those experienced in the past.

Innovation in circuit or device forms to improve densities seems to be reaching a limit, as devices are reaching an irreducible minimum, perhaps as a result of our inability to anticipate future innovation in new circuit forms. Possibilities for improvement may come from using three-dimensional forms rather than the present two-dimensional technology.

Redundancy in some form would allow much higher levels of integration than would otherwise be possible. As circuits become more complex, it appears that the overhead expense for achieving fault-tolerant circuits is a smaller proportion of the total. For example, error correction for an 8-bit word requires an additional 4 bits, whereas correction for a 64-bit word requires only 7 additional bits. A similar case can probably be made for logic. The relative cost of including redundancy is less in more complex systems. Today error correction is used in large memory systems to reduce failure rates. Partially good memory components are used in some systems by disabling faulty addresses. As new schemes are developed for the use of faulty circuits, the permissible chip sizes could expand greatly, allowing significant cost reduction with higher levels of integration.

FUTURE LEVELS OF HARDWARE TECHNOLOGY

Since the momentum of the drive is to higher levels of integration, I believe advances will continue. Minimum dimensions will continue to decrease but at a decreasing rate as optical limits are approached, reaching 2 microns in five years, and 1 micron in fifteen years (see fig. 15.6). Scaling arguments show that speed should then increase by 4 times by 1991. If defect densities are reduced as they have been in the past, chip sizes will increase by 3 times in five years, and 25 times in fifteen years (see fig. 15.7).

As a result of these factors, components providing 65 to 131 kilobits of memory with access time of 100 ns should appear in 1981, and the megabit memory chi (2^{20} bits) should appear ten years later. The use of redundancy could accelerate these times. Component costs should be comparable to those of today's memory components, or 10^{-3}¢ per bit.

For noniterated circuits such as control logic, the level of integration will be lower owing to inherent inefficiencies in packing random logic. However, the levels that could be achieved in five years would be approximately 25,000 gates and in ten years about 250,000 gates. These numbers exceed the gate count of today's medium and large processors, respectively. Internal gate delays of these systems would be comparable to those of today's high-speed computers. Leaving aside the amortization of design

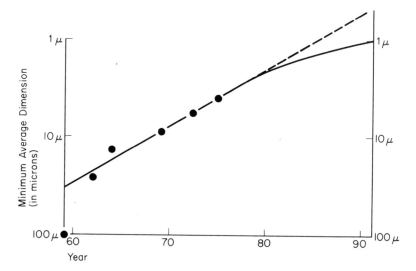

15.6
Fifteen-Year Projection for Minimum Average Dimensions

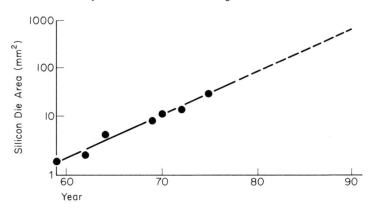

15.7
Fifteen-Year Projection for Silicon Die Areas

costs, such logic arrays could be produced for less than $100, or a cost of less than 0.4¢ per gate in five years and less than .04¢ per gate in fifteen years (see fig. 15.8).

A question still exists as to whether integration of logic circuits at such high levels will be attempted. The industry has already achieved the complexity needed for mass markets, such as the digital watch or the calculator, and the cost reduction that motivated these developments can only be achieved by volume production. The basic technology will be developed, however, to supply the demand for memory. Fortunately, perhaps, the designers and users of computers have an insatiable demand for memory, and the market is completely elastic at today's usage levels. The question, then, becomes one of the cost of designing high-complexity logic for a particular application. At high levels of integration, many more unique circuit designs are necessary than is the case for Boolean functions, which are limited. The market for each unique circuit becomes smaller, while the design costs become much higher.

The IC industry faced this problem with the introduction of LSI and found a solution in the concept of the microprocessor. The microprocessor was conceived as a method of supplying the many diverse requirements of random logic, thus allowing one, or a small number, of circuit designs to achieve high enough market penetration to justify its development. The true impact of the microprocessor is only now being felt, but already it is having a radical influence on our thinking about future computing systems. We may expect the capability of the microprocessor to improve dramatically in the future, if for no other reason than that it is feasible. The impact of the microprocessor will be seen first in smaller computing systems, such as terminals, controllers, and video games. As

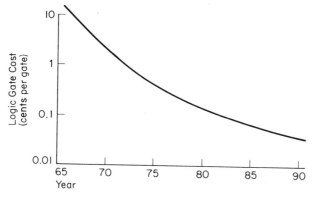

15.8
Logic Cost versus Time

its capabilities increase, the equivalent of today's processors will be built using this concept.

Several changes will probably occur in the computer industry as a result of the microprocessor. Economics will compel standardization on a small number of microprocessors, since as they are manufactured in volume costs will be reduced substantially. It now appears that identical microprocessors will generally be available from many sources. This will, of course, assure competitive prices, but it also opens the possibility that software sources will develop independent of the hardware manufacturers. The microprocessor will become another building block like a flip-flop or an adder for the construction of computing systems, and architecture is likely to change to take advantage of these very cost-effective building blocks. This development should favor increasing throughput by paralleling identical blocks, and networks of semi-independent processors should be more cost-effective than large time-shared machines. Structural changes will occur as well, since the microcomputer design must consider both the economics of component production and the economics of system use simultaneously. This suggests some amalgamation of the component and system producers or at least some mutual penetration of these industries.

The potential for developing inexpensive processing power is truly awesome. With low-cost processing available, many new tasks could be undertaken that are totally uneconomical today. Input-output devices could also benefit from the power available, since more powerful processing reduces the requirements of the simpler forms of information transfer to people, such as graphics or audio input and response. Our major challenge is likely to be defining the tasks to be accomplished with this technology and developing the software with which to accomplish those tasks.*

EDITORS' POSTSCRIPT

Noyce's projections seem entirely believable, especially since even the conservative estimates of other forecasters call for a change of two orders of magnitude in cost during the next twenty years. It is indeed remarkable that there is so much agreement about future hardware trends and so little agreement about the likely trends in software and applications. It should be noted that one area Noyce does not touch on is potential developments in our ability to manufacture small volumes of customized and sophisti-

---

* Having observed that near-term projections are usually too optimistic, I have overcompensated in the projections in this paper. Twenty-five-thousand-element microcomputers were introduced in 1978, and the 65-kilobit RAM was introduced during 1979.

cated integrated circuits in addition to the large-volume common-use circuits he discusses in his essay.

NOTE

1
R. W. Keyes, "Physical Limits in Digital Electronics," *Proceedings of the IEEE* 63 (May 1975): 740–767.

16
Computers and Communications   B. O. Evans

It was more than a decade after Faraday's experiments that Samuel F. B. Morse, exploiting the new electrical energy force, in 1844 sent the world's first telegram a distance of forty miles between a railroad station in Baltimore, Maryland, and the U.S. Supreme Court in Washington, D.C. Morse's "What hath God wrought!" message marked the beginning of electrical communications. When Alexander Graham Bell demonstrated his invention of the telephone in 1876, the reach and flexibility of communications took another important step. Two decades later Marconi sent the first message by his wireless telegraph, and radio telegraphy had its beginning. Innovation followed invention, and by the third decade of the twentieth century the telephone, telegraph, and radio were commonplace in most of the civilized world. Today communications facilities in all their variety are essential to business, social, educational, political, and military life.

Modern electronic computer systems grew from calculating devices that have a history dating from early Greek civilization. But lacking technology, progress was slow—often centuries passed between one step and the next. It was not until the seventeenth century that the mechanical digital calculator was invented by Pascal, and it was the mid-1800s before experiments with a mechanical device that could automatically calculate long sequences were carried out by Babbage.

The application of electrical energy to computation took almost a century after the invention of the telegraph, for it was late in the 1930s when H. H. Aiken of Harvard University and G. R. Stibitz of the Bell Telephone Laboratories developed an automatic electric calculator using electromechanical relays. Many electric accounting and calculating products followed.

World War II provided a catalyst for electronics; ideas and inventions flowed forth. Pioneers like Attanatsoff, Zuse, Mauchley, Eckert, and many

B. O. Evans is IBM vice-president for engineering, programming, and technology and ex-president of IBM's System Communications Division. Among his many accomplishments is the development of the highly successful IBM Series 360 computers.

Table 16.1
Market Estimates of Industrywide Consumption of Goods Shipped by U.S. and Foreign Manufacturers for the U.S. Market (in millions of dollars)

	1974	1975	Growth (%)
Electronic computer central processors			
Microcomputers	$ 20.0	$ 75.0	
Portable computers	—	3.0	
Minicomputers (less than $50,000)	600.0	775.0	
Small (up to $420,000)	900.0	1000.0	
Medium (up to $840,000)	1200.0	1000.0	
Medium, communication (up to $1,680,000)	1450.0	1000.0	
Large (up to $3,360,000)	1700.0	1300.0	
Giant (greater than $3,360,000)	1200.0	1100.0	
Subtotal	7070.0	6253.0	(−11.6)
Add-on memory	215.0	220.0	
Data storage (discs, flexible discs, drums, tape)	2475.0	2728.0	
Input-output peripherals (readers, punches, printers, OCR, etc.)	1364.0	1496.0	
Key entry (keypunch, key to tape, disc, cassette)	454.0	318.0	
Electronic computer centrals	11,578.0	11,015.0	(−4.9)
Data terminals (keyboard printers, CRT, intelligent, interactive graphic, audio, remote batch)	953.0	1037.0	
Point-of-sale systems (electronic cash registers/terminals, credit authorization terminals, electronic scales)	496.0	767.0	
Banking systems (automated terminals, cash dispensers, teller terminals)	28.0	63.0	
Industrial systems	70.0	75.0	
General-purpose and industry application terminals	1547.0	1942.0	25.5

Source: Reprinted from *Electronics,* January 8, 1976. Copyright © McGraw-Hill, Incorporated, 1976.

others contributed, but the biggest step came in 1946 at Princeton's Institute of Advanced Study when Dr. John von Neumann and his associates produced a new theory and architecture for electronic computation. Professor John Wilkes, returning to Cambridge University from the von Neumann group, in 1949 demonstrated a working model of the new theory and architecture—a stored program digital computer. Shortly thereafter the Institute of Advanced Study began to operate their stored program computer.

Early electronic computers were produced with a variety of components, including vacuum tubes, electromechanical relays, cathode-ray tubes, punched cards, and paper tape, later supplemented by magnetic tapes, magnetic core memories, and magnetic disc files. In the mid-1950s, the pace of electronic computer technology began to accelerate once more with the invention of the transistor, and since then it has literally exploded, from discrete transistors, capacitors, diodes, and resistors hand-assembled into single circuits to modern integrated process technology in which a few thousand circuits are contained on a single chip. In less than twenty years computer processing performance has advanced by a factor of more than 200 (fig. 16.1), the cost of multiplication has decreased by a factor of more than 100 (fig. 16.2), and magnetic disc storage capacity per dollar has improved by a factor of almost 100 (fig. 16-3).

The merger of communications and computers was brought about because the demand for computing power quickly outpaced the productivity of computer installations, since operational procedures were inefficient. Early users coded their own problems in each computer's unique instruction set, trying to deal with the idiosyncrasies of the computers' design— "113.5 milliseconds between the PRINT instruction and when the data need to be at the printer, so I'll try and squeeze in this table look-up subroutine. . . ." Such expensive and inefficient procedures quickly gave way to productivity-assisting tools, including standardized higher-level languages with compilers translating to each computer's unique structure. Innovations such as multiprogramming, multiprocessing, concurrent operation of input-output, and multiple input-output devices improved efficiency and throughput.

Within many enterprises the computer rooms were organized in such a way that intermediaries operated the systems, sometimes even coding the users' problems. The user often had to wait days for his response from the computer. Hence it was predestined that users would directly attach to computers through remote terminals, since the high speed of the computer allows it to respond simultaneously to multiple users.

The marriage of computers and communications through remote terminals is a natural union because computers and communications have

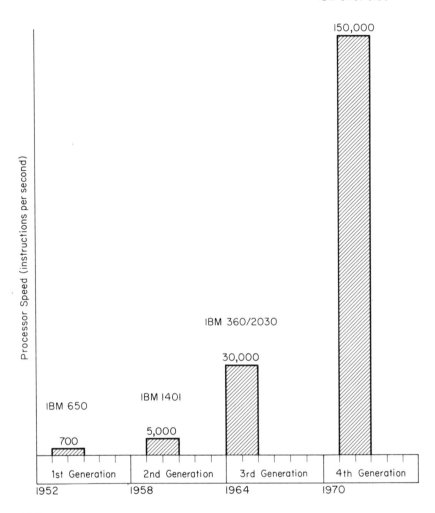

16.1
Processor Performance (in instructions per second). Source: IBM Corporation, material prepared for U.S. Department of Justice proceedings, September 5, 1974

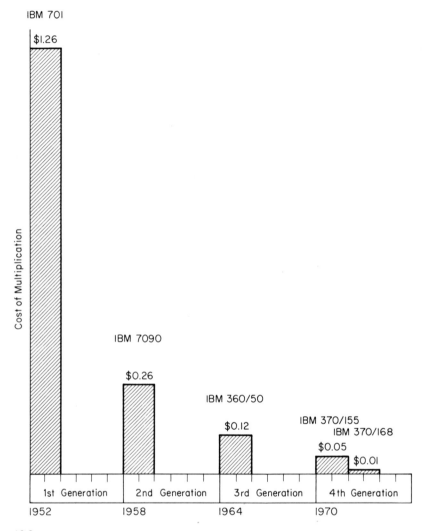

16.2
System Cost per 100,000 Multiplications. Source: IBM Corporation, material
prepared for U.S. Department of Justice proceedings, September 5, 1974

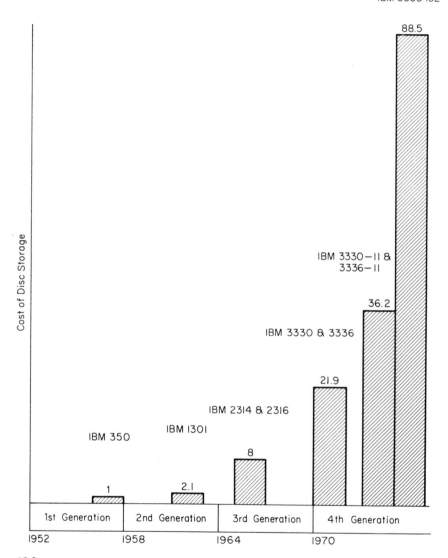

16.3
Magnetic Disc Storage Capacity per Dollar of Purchase Price. Source: IBM Corporation, material prepared for U.S. Department of Justice proceedings, September 5, 1974

much common technical and historical background. Both fields, besides their similar base in physics and electromagnetism, have been nurtured by the same inventions, technologies, and theories, such as Boole's algebra for describing and designing logic and switching functions; Erlang's traffic theory which today also reaches into computer architecture; the components of solid state physics; von Neumann's concept of stored program control, which now reaches into communications; information theory, developed for communications engineers concerned with achieving a maximum rate of information transmission over electrical channels, now an essential ingredient in computer architecture; and error detection and correction codes as well as data compression algorithms, now used throughout both communications and computers.[1]

The first linking of computers and communications was indirect. In the early 1950s transceivers operating independently of the computer transmitted punch card images from one unit to another, linked via low-speed communications lines. Soon thereafter transmission efficiency was improved by substituting magnetic-tape-to-magnetic-tape communication, but again inefficiencies triggered innovation, in this case because of the handling the media required between the computers and the off-line transmission devices. The direct connection between the user and computer did not occur until the advent of the key-driven terminal; the next major step in the evolution of computer communication systems. This step greatly assisted the response-time problem. By the late 1950s various terminals and input-output devices were on-line to the computers, remotely linked to central computers through many types of communications facilities.

By 1975 digital computers had become a major industry with worldwide revenues in excess of $25 billion for computer products and services. The 1969–1974 compound growth rate in the value of computer systems in use was 13 percent,[2] and it was predicted in 1972 that the number of computers with terminals attached would rise from 25 percent in 1970 to 70 percent by 1980 (see fig. 16.4). Indeed, in the three years after that estimate, terminals communicating with computers increased at an even faster rate (see table 16.1). Even with the struggling world economy of 1975, U.S. data terminals managed an estimated growth of 25.5 percent versus a decline of 4.9 percent for the other components of the digital computer system. Add to this the 1975 growth in Japan and Western Europe, and it is evident that terminals and communications are rapidly becoming a substantial percentage of computer systems, having reached approximately 18 percent of total computer systems sales in 1975. By 1980 terminal unit sales alone are expected to more than double (fig. 16.5) and will account for approximately 25 percent of computer systems hardware expenditures (fig. 16.6).

From the first simple terminals, the scope and range of terminals com-

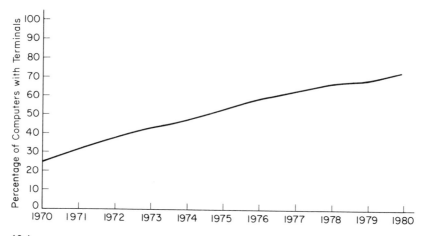

16.4
Percentage of Computers with Terminals, 1970–1980. Source: *Computerworld*, January 10, 1973

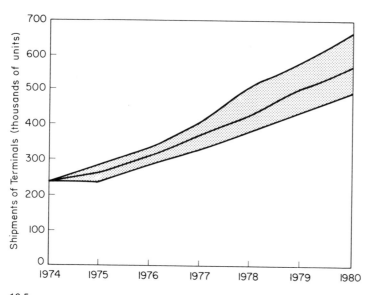

16.5
Estimated Growth of U.S. Terminals Market, 1974–1980. Source: Arthur D. Little, Inc., estimates, in *Datamation*, November 1975, p. 47. Reprinted with the permission of DATAMATION.® Copyright 1975 by Technical Publishing Company, Greenwich, Connecticut, 06830

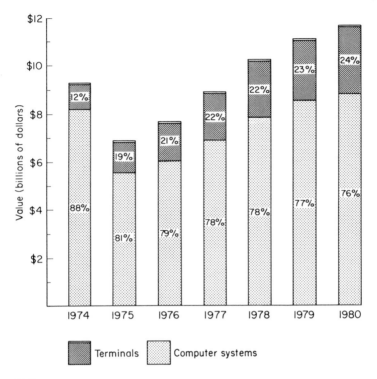

16.6
Computer Terminals as Percentage of Hardware Spending, 1974–1980. Source:
Arthur D. Little, Inc., estimates, in *Datamation,* November 1975, p. 49. Reprinted with
the permission of DATAMATION.® Copyright 1973 by Technical Publishing
Company, Greenwich, Connecticut, 06830

municating with computers has diversified and specialized in many directions. Arthur D. Little, Inc., has suggested a structuring of computer terminals into categories which I paraphrase here to illustrate the expansion of
terminals and communications applications.[3]

Simple keyboard printers   Alphanumeric keyboard with hard copy impact or nonimpact printing, including teletype and teletype-compatible
keyboard printers and keyboard displays operating in an asynchronous
transmission mode generally using ASCII code. Either unbuffered or buf-
fered up to a few lines for transmission efficiency. Can also include external data storage via paper tape, cassette, cartridges, or discette devices for
off-line recording and batched transmission.

Programmable keyboard printers   Same capabilities as simple keyboard printers, supplemented by a user-programmable processor for
tailoring the terminal to specific applications. Usually contains external
data storage for local data storage or off-line or batched transmission.

Portable   Functions similar to the simple keyboard printer packaged for carriage. An acoustic coupler is normally provided for connection to a conventional telephone handset.

Data entry   Keyboard-display terminals structured for data entry, including keyboarding, verification, editing, correction, reformatting, and supervisory functions. Either stand-alone or connected to a computer. Normally user-programmable, often utilizing remote communications.

On-line data entry/interactive display   Keyboard displays usually operating in synchronous transmission mode. Usually include cluster controllers for both local and remote interconnection and attached printers for hard copy output. Also usually available are disc files or discettes for local storage and increasing use of microprocessors for programmability.

Message switching   Telex transmission and message switching with store and forward facilities, usually including auxiliary storage facilities for audit and backup capability connectable to a wide variety of line disciplines.

Graphics   Display subsystem with keyboard and graphics input devices such as light pens, joysticks, styluses, and tablets for the display and manipulation of line images as well as alphanumeric functions.

Remote batch controllers   Cluster control subsystem with batch application input-output such as punch card readers and punches and printers. Usually include microprocessors and local data storage with extensive programmability.

Interactive systems controllers   Cluster control subsystem for interactive applications with communications to a host computer for master data base access and major processing. Generally include microprocessors and local data storage with extensive programmability.

Automated bank teller terminals   Customer-operated bank teller devices that accept coded identification cards and/or keyed input to permit a variety of automatic transactions including the dispensing and acceptance of cash.

Bank teller-assisting terminals   Teller-operated terminals that facilitate a variety of teller operations and capture appropriate data for master file and passbook updating.

Credit verification   Simple terminals that operate over either leased private line or dial-up communication facilities and read magnetic-striped credit cards or accept keyed account numbers, communicate with files of credit information, and report the level of credit purchase allowable. Usually include a one-line display. Some provide store name imprinting and sales receipts.

Point-of-sale terminals   Electronic cash registers operating on-line to a controlling in-store computer and/or a centralized host computer to assist salespersons' functions and capture sales data for cash, inventory, and

sales analysis. Frequently include price mark scanning devices, tag printing, and customer receipts.

Industrial data collection Factory data terminals, usually operated in
the plant production areas to collect production control, inventory, and
timekeeping information. Normally includes badge reader, punch card
reader, and manually operated data entry mechanisms as well as internally
generated data. On-line to an in-plant controller and/or a host computer
system.

Optical character recognition General-purpose devices capable of
machine recognition of either machine- or hand-printed numeric or alphanumeric information. Used typically in banking and remittance-
processing applications.

While there is functional overlap among many of these terminal and
controller types, there is little debate that terminals and communications
are the fastest-growing part of digital computer systems with significant
potential for new applications and services, a potential that is enhanced
with each advance in computer cost performance and function. Equally
important is that each terminal reflects an increased demand for processing power and data storage in subsystem controllers and/or electronic
computers. Thus terminals, communications, and digital computers are
synergistic.

PROBLEMS OF COMPUTER COMMUNICATIONS

Almost all of the communications common carrier facilities used for data
transmission today were originally designed for voice communications.
The world's telephone plant is undoubtedly the most complex single
system ever constructed, and for the most part it can be considered a
single system, since it is possible for more than 98 percent of the world's
more than 358 million telephones to interconnect. However, even though
these facilities can be utilized with reasonable efficiency for many data
applications, it is unrealistic to expect them to be ideal for applications
other than those for which they were designed.

In addition, even though data traffic is growing more rapidly than voice
traffic (see fig. 16.8), as of 1974 only 3 percent of AT&T's revenues were
from data communications. Adding to that the enormous costs that significantly changes in the communications plant would require, one must
speculate that data services within the present common carrier facilities
are likely to progress along evolutionary lines.

Today's common carrier network is built principally upon analog voice
channels of 4 KHz nominal bandwidth, suitable for transmitting either voice
or data up to several thousand bits per second. Using either frequency
division or time division multiplexing, voice-grade channels can be subdivided into a number of low-speed telegraph-grade channels. Frequency

division multiplexing is also used to combine multiple voice-grade channels into larger bandwidth blocks for transmission over long-distance carrier systems. A standard hierarchy of channels makes it possible to obtain broadband channels for data transmission or other purposes. These channels are normally equivalent in size to 12, 60, or 240 voice-grade channels. The largest part of the voice telephone network is currently based on analog signal handling using frequency division multiplexing. Although pure digital techniques are used in certain portions of the system, it is clear that analog facilities will remain predominant for many years.

The two major classes of common carrier services are private (leased) lines and switched services. Private line service gives the user dedicated lines in the common carrier system; while they pass through the switching centers, the necessary interconnections are permanently wired or assigned. Private line service is available in a wider variety of speeds and bandwidths than switched service, with transmission speeds such as 19.2 Kbps and 230.4 Kbps available only with private lines.

Private line characteristics are relatively stable since the same facilities are used for each connection. Variations do occur due to total system load, weather factors, and so on, but it is much simpler to compensate for changing characteristics with private lines than with switched calls, and it is possible to obtain line conditioning at an extra charge to extend the usable bandwidth and provide more ideal frequency characteristics. Thus the improved and more stable frequency characteristics of private lines make it feasible to transmit data at higher rates than over switched lines, especially since they avoid some of the impulse noise originating from switching equipment.

Switched service is available on telegraph-grade lines; for example, the standard dial network and the Western Union telex and TWX offerings in the United States. The circuits obtained when using switched services will vary in quality from call to call, and in some cases the variations can be quite pronounced, which makes it difficult to design transmission equipment that will operate satisfactorily over all circuits encountered. Either more narrow, compromised characteristics must be used in systems design, or expensive adaptive circuitry is required to adjust automatically to the changing line characteristics. In addition to the information-bearing signals, the switched system must exchange supervisory information for routing, "on hook" or "off hook" status information, network control information for seizing or disconnecting lines, and various types of ringing signals. Many of these signals are internal to the network and are of little concern to the user except as they affect the network's data-handling capabilities, connection setup time, and the permissible energy spectrum that can be transmitted.

Table 16.2 illustrates typical connection times for a direct-distance-dialed connection.

Table 16.2
Connect Time for Direct-Distance Dialed Calls

| Airline Distance (miles) | Connect Time (sec.) | |
	Mean	Standard Deviation
0–180	11.1	4.6
180–725	15.6	5.0
725–2900	17.6	6.6

Source: ©American Telephone and Telegraph Company 1971.

Thus where response time or higher-speed transmissions are important, dedicated communications facilities become necessary, and it becomes apparent that interconnected computer systems design faces many subtle complexities when interfacing the available communications facilities.

With respect to most transmission facilities, especially U.S. and Canadian, there are three main components—the local loop, short-haul transmission systems, and long-haul transmission systems. The local loop is generally a twisted pair of copper wires between users and the local central office. Design of local loops is influenced primarily by transmission requirements but additionally by economic parameters such as cost of right of way, installation costs, and future-service projections. Economic parameters pressure for large multipair cables channelized into as few routes as feasible. This results in at least some common routing for some local loops, which can have adverse consequences on a high-availability data-processing system that uses duplex paths to ensure availability, for redundant communication paths will not offer improved systems availability when an outage caused by a cut cable or a rainstorm-filled underground cable vault cripples several local loops simultaneously. Special arrangements to ensure separate redundant paths are sometimes possible, but in turn they are the most costly.

The short-haul system is restricted to spanning distances no greater than 50 to 250 miles. Open-wire pairs, coaxial cable, and microwave radio systems are used for different classes of most short-haul systems. Short-haul systems handle multiple voice-grade systems—typically 12 to 24 channels, with either frequency or time division multiplexing used to distinguish among the different channels. Analog amplifiers are used to boost the signal level each time it has traveled a certain distance, and since these amplifiers boost noise level as well, noise is introduced throughout the system. This becomes more limiting as transmission rates increase, reflecting the need for more comprehensive error detection, correction, and recovery capabilities in computer hardware and programming.

Digital communications facilities offer the promise of size reduction, lower power consumption, lower cost, increased reliability and flexibility, and improved local loop capacity. They are more compatible with electronic switching in both central and private exchanges as well as providing a more direct interface to computer terminal equipment. Digital facilities are being methodically expanded. The T-1 system and associated digital carrier systems signal one wave of the future for transmission of digital data. Two versions of T-1 are currently in use. In both T-1 carrier systems, 24 voice channels and system signaling information are time-division multiplexed into a I.544 Mbps bit stream of data. The newer systems do a better job of quantizing analog signals—62.667 bits per second per voice channel versus 56,000 bits per second for the older system. Both can accommodate I.544 Mbps of digital data. With T-1 systems a very low transmission error rate is obtained through the use of regenerative repeaters located approximately every mile. The new T-1 systems, as they become more widely available, will undoubtedly be the preferred media for transmission of data.

Long-haul carrier systems are designed to be extremely efficient. Thousands of voice channels are combined in a multiplexing hierarchy for transmission over coaxial cable or microwave channels. The voice channels are most commonly assembled into groups (12 voice channels in a 48 KHz bandwidth), supergroups (5 groups in a 240 KHz bandwidth), and mastergroups (10 supergroups in approximately a 2.4 MHz bandwidth). These systems typically span distances of 250 to 4,000 miles. Long-haul carrier systems are designed to exacting standards and usually contribute much less noise and distortion per unit per system than do short-haul systems. Most long-haul systems currently in use are analog in nature, using frequency division multiplex techniques. An exception is the digital T-2 system, with a capacity of four T-1 systems or 96 voice-grade channels and a range of approximately 500 miles. Echo suppressors are used to restrict the flow of energy to one direction in transmission systems 500 to 1,500 miles in length. To permit full duplex data transmission, the echo control system must be disabled, which is accomplished with a special signal from the data modem. In half duplex systems, where the channel is used first in one direction and then in the other, the echo suppressor activation and deactivation process consumes approximately 100 ms each time the transmission direction is reversed, often referred to as the turnaround time of the channel.

While there are many parameters and conditions within transmission facilities which add to the cost and sometimes reduce the performance of computer communications systems, international differences further compound interconnection problems. The data communications environment in each country is critical to development of data-processing applications, time-sharing services, and eventually international data-processing networks. However, the tariff structures for data, the attachment policies, and the regulatory environment vary from country to country. Figure 16.7 compares mid-1970 tariffs for leased telephone lines for data in terms of distance, excluding drop charges and modems. While absolute rates have since changed, the figure illustrates the widely varying structures that affect the implementaton of communications-based computer applications. In general, the U.S. tariff is lower for a 1200 bps half duplex line than those of the other countries shown. One conclusion is that a system in Germany or Japan utilizing leased facilities would have a larger percentage of communications costs, although both countries have since decreased long-distance charges and substantially increased local charges. An unusual situation occurs in Italy, where up to 150 km one finds the highest tariffs and fixed end-link charges. Interestingly, with the exception of Germany and Italy, the tariffs for leased telephone lines for data at 1200 bps are the same as a leased telephone line for voice. In the case of Germany, the tariff is increased for data, while the reverse is true for Italy.

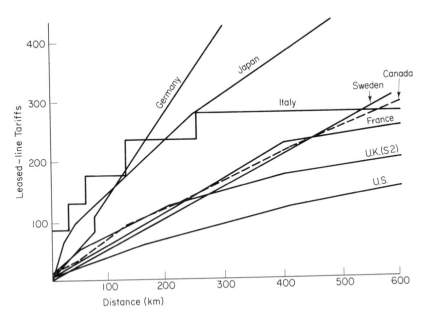

16.7
Tariffs for Leased Telephone Lines, 1970 (data at 1200 bps HDX). Source: G. J. Lissandrello, "World Data Communications as Seen by Data Processing," ACM/IEEE Second Symposium on System Design, October 20–22, 1971

With respect to the relationship between half and full duplex rates in the United States, full duplex is now the same as half duplex for interstate service but is approximately 25 percent higher than half duplex for intrastate service. In Germany, the full duplex tariff for 1200 bps is 1.17 times the half duplex rate; the same as half duplex in France, except in the case of high-quality lines, where there is an average increase for up to 600 kilometers of approximately 1.5 times the half duplex tariff. The U.K. tariffs are equal—half duplex is the same as full duplex.

With respect to break-even points, table 16.3 shows the crossover between the leased voice-grade and the public switched network, assuming that the public switched network is capable of 1200 bps transmissions. Here again the rate structure has since changed, but for comparative purposes, if applications in mid-1970 used the public switched network for approximately 1½ hours per day for 300 kilometers, it was just as economical to lease a line, whereas Germany and Sweden would require 4 hours of operation a day based on a 22-day work month. For 500 kilometers there were substantial differences, for in the United States an hour per day suggests leasing a dedicated line, but in Germany crossover is at 6 to 7 hours per day; France and Italy required 2 hours of operation a day at 500 kilometers to break even.

The break-even point between telex and leased telegraph is also shown in table 16.3. In the U.S. it is 11.9 hours per month for 500 kilometers, as opposed to a minimum of 38.9 hours in France. This means that in the U.S. if applications used TWX for more than a half hour per day the user could justify a leased line, whereas in France crossover would not occur until after 1.5 hours of use per day. In the U.S. there is small difference between telegraph and voice-grade data channel rates—$582 versus $525 per month for 500 km—while in Europe the communications system designer is more prone to use the switched network as well as remote multiplexers for the leased networks to capitalize on cost considerations. These differing tariff structures mean an optimal design using dedicated communications of a certain type in one country may be suboptimal elsewhere.

Attachment policies is another area in which the communication systems designer must be knowledgeable, since it deals with the various types of modems available. There are countries where the user can provide his own modulation-demodulation (modem) equipment to attach to the leased network and others where it is mandatory to use a carrier-supplied modem in the leased or switched network. The designer and manufacturer face a different situation in countries that do not allow the use of customer-supplied modems.

There are other policies that differ in certain countries and affect the

Table 16.3
Approximate Break-Even Point: Public Switched Network (PSN) and Telex versus Leased Voice-Grade and Leased Telegraph, 1970

PSN versus Leased Voice-Grade for 300 KM

Country	PSN (3 MIN.)	Leased	Equivalent Hours per Month of PSN
France	$0.98	$ 630/mo	32.2
Germany	$0.95	$1690/mo	89
Italy	$0.97	$1108/mo	60.9
Sweden	$0.38	$ 670/mo	88
U.K.	$0.42	$ 580/mo	69
U.S. (AT&T)	$0.70	$ 360/mo	25.7
U.S. (Western Union)	$0.60	$ 360/mo	33.3

Telex versus leased Telegraph for 500 KM

Country	Telex (3 MIN.)	Leased	Equivalent Hours of Telex
France	$0.54	$420/mo	38.9
Germany	$0.45	$750/mo	83.8
Italy	$0.64	$980/mo	76.5
Sweden	$0.27	$280/mo	51.9
U.K.	$0.26	$205/mo	39.4
U.S. (TWX)	$1.35	$320/mo	11.9

Source: G. J. Lissandrello, "World Data Communications as Seen by Data Processing," ACM/IEEE Second Symposium on System Design, October 20–22, 1971.

communications system designer. For example, acoustical coupling has not been allowed in many Latin American countries, Australia, Japan, Sweden, and Spain. Not only the specifications of the telephone network of a particular country but also the physical handsets that are used may present problems that limit the use of acoustical coupling devices in certain international systems. Similarly, in many countries the user is required to incorporate a carrier-provided terminal to operate on the telex network. (In the U.S., a user is allowed to interface the TWX network through a carrier-provided modem, while France allows a user to attach directly to the telex network.) Further, in certain countries the public switched network cannot be used for data, which means that communications systems designers are usually pressed to design systems around leased networks.

The communications common carriers continue to respond in many ways to computer requirements. For example, in the U.S.A. AT&T provides services such as Dataphone digital service, the T-1 carriers, and Data under Voice. Newcomers like the specialized carriers who have been constructing microwave radio networks linking major U.S. cities offer alternatives such as private line service for voice, teleprinter, data, and facsimile usage which have certain advantages, such as faster connect time, short billing increments, and abbreviated dialing, all benefiting the data user. Packet carriers are moving to provide nationwide communication services, using high-speed transmission and switching facilities leased from the established carriers and augmented by their own equipment and combining traffic from several users to gain in the economics of transmission in end-to-end networks. They generally charge by volume rather than miles or connect-time, and data is supplied from the computer system to the packed network in fixed format, which illustrates the growing attention given to data users. And the carriers should respond, for the growth rate of data traffic is strong. Statistics have been collected on telephone service since its beginning in 1876, and at an early date separate records were started for long-distance, business, and residential use and for revenues by type of service. These data show that both number of telephone instruments and total telephone conversations have been increasing at a constant rate of approximately 5 percent per year for many years. One projection made by AT&T in 1970 that still seems to stand the test of time is shown in figure 16.8. In net, voice is projected to grow steadily, written information via first class and air mail will also grow steadily, but video, record, and data transmission are expected to grow much more rapidly.

Thus between specialized communication carriers, the established common carriers, and the value-added networks there is rapidly growing competition, reduced rates, and improved communication services augmenting the needs of communication-based computer systems, all of which adds fuel to the fires of growth. Under the coordination of the International Consultative Committee for Telegraphy and Telephony (CCITT) the various carrier agencies are working to resolve standards and improve telecommunications with special attention to digital hierarchies.

Other Alternatives: LIT and CATV

Different media offer potential services for short-distance interconnection within computer systems. For example, light-interconnection technology (LIT) converts electrical signals to light using light-emitting diodes and provides for transmission over reliable and relatively economical groups of small-fiber optic bundles; light is reconverted to electrical signals with photodiodes. LIT has some intrinsic advantages, including nonmechanical

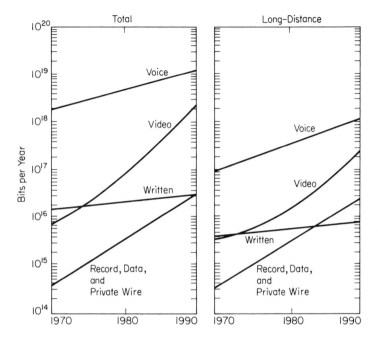

16.8
Potential Information Transfer Volume, 1979–1990. Source: American Telephone and Telegraph Company, 1970

signal connection, since interconnection is accomplished with light-emitting diodes and photodiodes, devices that are made in area arrays. Therefore, LIT has the ability to communicate directly with the large-scale integration chips in the computer subsystems, a characteristic that may have important potential. In addition, LIT offers potential for high density, in that the array LED (light-emitting diode) and photodiode chips, like any other LSI component, can be fabricated at very high density. Equally important, the light-carrying channels can be high-density without concern for cross-talk. LIT also offers electronic insulation, as it is not affected by ordinary electrical interferences and does not radiate energy that can be intercepted and decoded. Therefore, at least over short distances, and perhaps in environments where electronic noise or security are very important, light-interconnection technology should play a role in computer communications of the future.

In addition, potential sharing of CATV facilities will certainly be a consideration, for by the end of 1970, five million American households were connected to CATV. By the end of 1973, one household in eight was connected, and an estimated one in five households is in physical proximity to CATV. Industry sources predict 90 percent of U.S. households will be in proximity to CATV within the next ten years. While there may be difficulties in adapting computers to the varying CATV implementations, and while additional equipment is required for two-way digital transmission, these networks do offer substantial bandwidth, and given their growth, especially in the larger cities, CATV seems destined to play a role in computer applications, particularly where home services develop.

Communications Satellites

Despite the fact that communications carriers will be installing higher-speed digital services for many years to come, the principal geographic coverage will be the 4 KHz analog voice channels. This presents a serious hindrance to computer communications in that today many central processors run at internal arithmetic rates of one million or more instructions per second, and internal data transfer rates are more than a million characters per second. Yet the computer designer and user must face complex and widely varying terrestrial communication facilities, at the same time transmitting at no more than a few hundred or few thousand bits per second. Overcoming this speed mismatch requires very complex hardware and programming in order to slow down the internal rate for transmission, in addition to the complexities of designing and operating with the idiosyncrasies, differing parameters, and conditions of the terrestrial networks. At the receiving end just the opposite takes place—very complex hardware and programming to speed the transmission rate back up to the internal rate of the computers.

The great attraction of communications satellites that is most fascinating for both the computer designer and user is that they are capable of providing wide-band, switched, all-digital network service connecting the far-flung reaches of large geographical areas such as the contiguous United States. The significance of this is that the very high transmission rates promise a communication speed matching the computers, as well as service in which an enterprise does not require separate networks for voice, data, and image, as is generally the case today. Capacity can be added or transferred between classes of traffic and allocated dynamically. Moreover, services from communications satellites are largely distance-insensitive.

Although communications satellite technology is still in its early years, costs have come down steadily. A rule of thumb is that for low-speed point-to-point voice channels in high-density areas of the United States (fig. 16.9), if the transmission distance is more than approximately 1,000

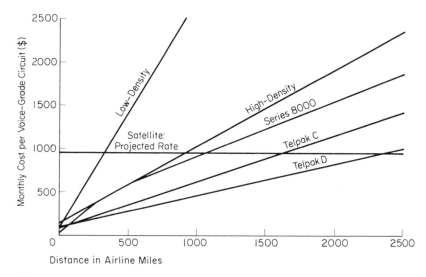

16.9
Point-to-Point Voice: U.S. Common Carrier Rates (1974) versus Projected Satellite
Rates. Source: CML Corporation

miles, it is generally more economical to transmit via satellite; for wide-
band that distance is substantially reduced (figs. 16.10 and 16.11).

Today's communications satellites operate in the 4–6 GHz frequency
region, thus sharing frequency with terrestrial microwave facilities, which
imposes limitations on radiated power and physical placement of the earth
stations. This, in turn, has cost consequences for the very large antennas
and sensitive receivers that are required. However, certain to be operated
soon commercially will be communications satellites using the reserved
frequencies where there is no regulated limit on power radiated, little
terrestrial frequency congestion, and therefore no serious geographic
restraints. With the greater power, one can envision smaller, less expensive earth stations on customer sites under the user's control and security.
Given the likelihood of technological advances and increased competition, by the early 1980s economic crossover for communications satellites
should be only a few hundred miles for communications up to 9,600 baud
and much less for wide-band transmissions.

There are functional advantages to communications satellites, such as
the broadcast characteristic where all stations in the antenna's earth
coverage will simultaneously receive the transmitted information, important to enterprises where multiple-destination messages are frequently

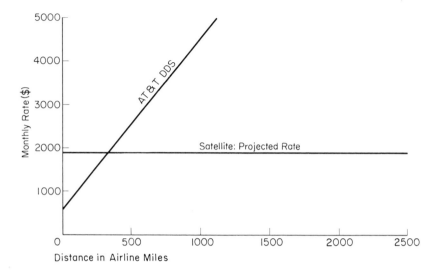

16.10
56 KBPS Data Point-to-Point: U.S. Common Carrier Rates (1974) versus Projected
Satellite Rates. Source: CML Corporation

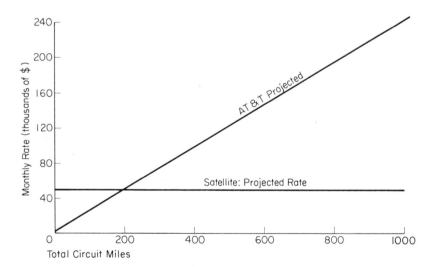

16.11
1.5 MPBS Five-Node Network: U.S. Common Carrier Rates (1974) versus Projected
Satellite Rates. Source: CML Corporation

used. Where encryption techniques are employed, selective authorization will be available, thus enhancing the security and privacy of satellite communications.

The characteristics of essential distance insensitivity and dynamic resource allocation should offer some marked reduction in complexity in certain types of computer communications networks, but communications satellites will not by any means significantly displace terrestrial facilities; indeed, they will complement each other. The economic impact of communications satellites on terrestrial communications facilities is many years from being understood, but in time they should strike a balance.

Communications satellites are not without their problems, such as the catastrophic effects that would occur if the orbital facility were lost. This possibility is guarded against by the employment of orbital and ground-ready spares. There is a potential problem particularly affecting the 12–14 GHz and higher-frequency transmissions where satellite transmission is attenuated beyond reception by intense rain droplets. This introduces complexities in the placement of satellite earth stations, especially in high-density rain environments and where real-time network operations require constantly available communications. The problem can be solved either by the placement of selected redundant earth stations, which has some cost implications, or by selective off-load to terrestrial communications facilities. There are the classical problems that arise if errors occur in the "fire hose" stream of data moving between the earth stations and the satellite, for if it takes too long to detect and correct them, the result can be chaos. However, application of forward error-correction techniques seems to assure that this situation will be under reasonable control. There is also a transit-time problem, since with the satellite in synchronous orbit at approximately 35,000 km, an interactive transaction requiring a round trip through the satellite will require approximately one-half second. That fixed delay could simplify some network programming when one considers the satellite approach versus the variable delays encountered in a multinode terrestrial path, but the half-second delay could temper satellite applications where fractional-second response time is essential.

Communications satellites present political problems as well, for today only the United States, Canada, the Soviet Union, Indonesia, the Arab consortium, and Japan are moving meaningfully toward the economical application of communications satellites. The major countries in Western Europe are moving more cautiously, in part because their smaller trans-country distances do not permit satellites to offer the economic benefits that are predicted for the larger countries. As the new technology reduces costs, the crossover distances will surely decrease, and it seems inevitable that in the 1980s satellite communication will be available in many developed countries in the world. Until this becomes true, however, computer developers will be faced with a dual task, designing systems using satellite communications where they are best suited and available but having to use terrestrial communications for the same application elsewhere in the world where satellites are not available—a situation that one can predict will cause compromises in the optimization of both designs.

Nonetheless, if on-line, operational, communications-based computer systems using terminals are the fastest-growing part of computer systems, the promise of memory-bus-to-memory-bus transmission at rates compatible with internal computer speeds, the rapidly improved cost-performance of communications satellites, and the prospect of wide-band, switched, all-digital service seem clearly to point to the day when not only computers will be interconnected into networks by communications satellites; in the 1980s, cluster controllers will be connected to computers via satellites, and perhaps in time terminals will be directly connected to cluster controllers via satellites.

Future opportunities for satellite communications extending beyond the voice and data environment are considerable. Consistent with the trend toward integrated voice and data networks, there exists a growing interest in developing communications applications for electronic mail, document distribution, and conferencing. The significance of this trend lies in value-added and cost-displaceable potential that can be impacted by an integrated satellite network solution. The high bandwidth capability offered by satellites will allow communication applications to emerge that require partial wide-band, 56KB to 224KB, to full wide-band, 1.5MB to 6MB. Examples are the convenience voice-grade line facsimile applications offer to high-volume, high-speed applications like intracompany mail, and the prospect of moving from the limited television-studio context of communications to general-purpose video conferencing, allowing large-group participation in an enterprise.

Assuming the rates now predicted are attained, communications satellites will have a profound effect on the architecture, application investment, and business direction of computers.

Computer Networking

Many enterprises have multiple divisions or subsidiaries and find each with interconnected computer-to-computer and computer-to-terminals systems (fig. 16.12). These enterprises, which are discovering redundant computer capacity at similar geographic locations, with load-sharing and improved availability potential untapped, would benefit if their division and subsidiary computation facilities were more optimally connected into an enterprisewide network. Moreover, there is an increasing trend within

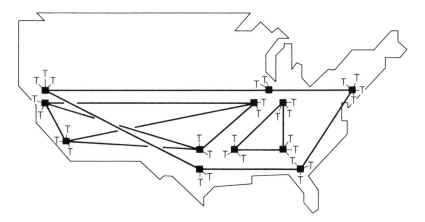

16.12
Unoptimized Communications Network

enterprises to split data bases for local control reasons or network cost optimization, although requirements for information exchange between distributed data bases increase the demand for computer networking. Frequently, the communications paths interconnecting the individual networks are optimized only for cost, so that the necessary alternate paths are sometimes lacking, or there is duplication of individual low-speed lines between the same locations. Since these multiple individual networks do not provide an optimal rate-traffic relationship, there is a natural trend toward optimizing both computer capacity and communication interconnection by enterprise-integrated networks (fig. 16.13). The computer industry is presently in the process of providing the control programming for such networks, but it must face complex questions such as terminal independence, systems recovery, network management, traffic routing, multiple-data-base access, data-base sharing, and security and privacy— although solutions to these problems seem within the reach of architecture and programming technology. The networking trend can be expected to accelerate and spread to medium-size enterprises; later, with the promise of reduced communication costs, networking should spread even to smaller enterprises.

Microcomputers and Minicomputers

It can be argued that the cost-performance of micro and minicomputers will erode the structures of contemporary computer systems, that with such "computational plenty" available stand-alone configurations will quickly usurp traditional applications, thus negating large central computer installations, networks, and multiapplication systems. The facts are that not enough is known of the interactions to be precise. But while micro

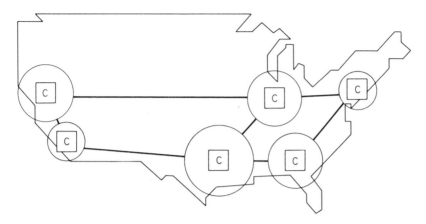

16.13
Optimized Communications Network

and minicomputers will unquestionably have an effect on traditional top-down computer systems configurations, it does not appear to be a question of one or the other. Contemporary computer systems have been steadily moving toward distributed intelligence, where processing is accomplished in both local and remote terminal controllers. Front-end processors handle simple transactions at a network node without having to transmit to the larger controls. In addition, whether computing is accomplished within mini, micro, or other larger computers, the operational needs of enterprises will more and more require interrogation of remote data bases as well as interchange of computational results and capacity. Hence, it seems clear that micro and minicomputers will not stunt the growth of communications in computing applications—indeed, the cost-performance of micro and minicomputers should strongly spur the growth in new applications, thus strengthening the computer communications relationship.

Finally, minicomputers are rapidly improving in capability and performance and moving into general-purpose applications, while general-purpose systems with their improving cost-performance and distributed intelligence are moving forward the capability and applications of minicomputers. This merging of functions should in itself have a synergistic effect on the growth of computer applications.

CONCLUSION: THE 1980S

The environment in 1985 should see a prevalence of high-bandwidth communication services, probably paced by communications satellites for off-premises communications and a variety of wideband interconnection offerings for on-premises communications. There should be pervasive computer power available, with a maturation of distributed intelligence and general-purpose networking. Data bases will be distributed throughout enterprise networks. Durable interfaces will increase across the computer industry, so that users will be able to mix or match from various vendors, and acceptance of standards should help accelerate computer use.

With the cost-performance made possible by large-scale integration, microprocessors will provide "intelligence" throughout the system, not only in terminals but in other input-output devices as well. People in general should be more comfortable with computer terminals, which will approach the telephone in familiarity, and the use of display terminals will, as expected, continue to grow at a significant compound rate. Portable terminals, with jacks to plug into data outlets, should become more widely used, and there should be accelerated use of self-service terminals. With wideband communications, image input-output and processing will become more widespread, and cryptography as well as refined personal identification techniques will safeguard image and character data against misuse. Data, image, and voice terminals will be mass-produced and be quite flexible in their application and adaptability, as manufacturers and users will select from a menu of subassembly alternatives to form the function and capacity required for each application (table 16.4).

Computer terminals will spread into varieties of applications for business, industry, government, education, and special applications. Terminals can be expected to be applied to, among other things, traditional billing, inventory control, remote job entry, accounts receivable and sales analysis, purchasing, and remittance processing. They will increasingly enter newer areas, such as mass data entry; portable data entry presentation preparation; discipline problem solving such as design automation; production procedures; engineering and scientific calculations; administrative automation, including internal mail, telephone logs, and action files; image data file processing, copying, and reproduction; and in-house publication, including text processing. In addition there are expanding varieties of business-specialized terminals, such as image processing in insurance; hospital services, including interconnection of pharmacy, laboratories, billing, and patient administration; generation of automated stock quotation, broker browsing, and on-line transaction systems; crime information systems; airline reservations, ticketing, boarding, and baggage management, and travel-agency interconnection; point-of-sale terminals moving electronic processing into medium and smaller stores; automatic tellers with cash accepters and dispensers, electronic funds transfer transaction terminals, postal window terminals, and electronic mail subsystems; multimedia terminals for education; plant floor subsystems for manufacturing and process industries; self-service gasoline vend-

Table 16.4
End-Use Terminal Primitives

In	Out	
X	X	Paper Tape
X	X	Card
X	X	Mag Card
X	X	Mag Tape
X	X	Stylus
X	X	Microfilm
X	X	Telephone Handset
X	X	Voice
X	X	Other Audio
X	X	Disc
X		Keyboard
X		Tablet
X		Wand
X		Optical Character Recognition
X		Magnetic Ink Character Recognition
X		Image Scanner
X		Sensor
X		Light Pen/Probe
X		Sound Pen
X		Template
X		Toggle Switch
	X	Discrete Light
	X	Printer
	X	Reproducer
	X	Process Signal
	X	TV
	X	Plotter
	X	Displays
		(A/N—Graphic—Image—Text)

ing terminals; dispatch, shipping, and warehouse control systems for surface transportation industries; energy optimization systems for utilities, and so on.

For home use, terminals have potential for catalog ordering, activity planning, home library and education, and family health, including histories, diagnosis, doctors' specialty lists, and emergency procedures; family recreation, including music selection and games; career guidance, tax records and returns; home safety and property maintenance, including house plan, retrieval, maintenance schedules, electrical and other physical facility layouts, and energy management; and budgeting and banking. In other public applications one can expect terminals to be used for post office automation, library operations, theater ticketing, sophisticated games, and restaurant management, among others.

In sum, terminals are the fastest-growing products in computer systems industry; this growth is predicted to accelerate, and the tie between communications and computers will grow more swiftly. New communications services, particularly those bringing more cost-effective wideband communications, will lead to further acceleration in the use of terminals and computers. Therefore, communications cost-performance and price flexibility will be one of the most important determinants of the continued growth of electronic computers.

EDITORS' POSTSCRIPT

Evans's essay does not discuss two questions that may turn out to be important during the next twenty years. First, will information networks be technically capable of handling queries and responses among geographically distributed and independent units which cannot "know," by virtue of the network's overall complexity, the informational capabilities of all such units in the network? Second, will information networks grow beyond their intracompany usefulness to form an interorganizational and interpersonal free market where buyers and sellers of information engage in meaningful transactions? It is difficult to answer such questions with a high degree of confidence at this time, because the field is still in its infancy and because we do not know how society will react to such a medium.

NOTES

1
K. Ganzhorn, World Telecommunications Conference, Geneva, October 10, 1975.
2
EDP Industry Report, April 30, 1975, p. 9.
3
Electronic News, supplement, March 8, 1976.

17
Sophisticated Software: The Road to Science and Utopia

Marvin Denicoff

The year is 1976, the twenty-fifth anniversary of an important milestone in the history of computing machines—the delivery of the first UNIVAC to the United States Census Bureau—and of the author's baptismal brush with the new big boy on the American industrial scene. From the vantage point of a junior committee member assessing the possible utility of a computer for handling Navy inventory control problems, I was privileged to learn from IBM in its pre-701 and 702 era that punch card machines would continue forever to be the most efficient and economical form of data processors. I was also privileged to learn, on alternate days from that very same source, that drawing-board designs, only one step away from production, would assure IBM the lead in the digital computer field. Patience was being counseled, packaged, and sold everywhere in those days. Everywhere but Univac, that is. At Sperry Rand, there was the confidence and excitement that come with the first sale to a bona fide customer. Full speed ahead was the order of the day in the Eckert-Mauchly-Hopper quarters of the corporation, even as the head shakers in the boardroom were sounding warnings that total government purchases might never be more than three or four machines. Independent of the validity of that forecast, RCA was determined to join the race by getting there, if not the fastest, then with the biggest. BIZMAC, the world's largest vacuum-tube machine, was being proffered by RCA in Camden, just across the river from my committee site in Philadelphia. Here too, as one watched the evolution from prototype design to prototype hand-crafted construction on the factory floor, patience was the watchword.

More than a quarter of a century after its beginning as a commercial venture, patience may still be the watchword in the computer industry. For

Marvin Denicoff is head of the Information Systems Division of the Office of Naval Research. In this position, he has been instrumental in defining, monitoring, and funding major research projects in computer science during the past two decades. Many of those research efforts, such as time-sharing and artificial intelligence, were cooperative efforts between ONR and ARPA, the Advanced Research Projects Agency of the Department of Defense.

the dreamers among us who saw in those earliest machines the initiation of a scientific and cultural revolution that would profoundly affect the American lifestyle, patience is indeed our watchword, if not our epitaph. Who does not recall the certainty with which we proclaimed that the world's champion chess player would someday be forced to say uncle to our computer's delighted cry of "Checkmate"? Not satisfied with victory at the game table, computers were going to write poetry and novels, would compose great music, and go on to choreograph folk dances and modern ballets. Even the field of painting would yield to the mechanical marvel. The promise was of a stylistic freedom and creativity that would wipe away forever those embarrassing artistic endeavors of the punch card machine era—block-lettered facsimiles of United States presidents and elaborately drawn Christmas cards. We did more than our fair share of muscle flexing on computers and the seven lively art forms. For a brief moment in time, the threat was real, or it seemed to be real, and the Norman Mailers, Dylan Thomases, and Pablo Picassos were put on their guard. To our delight, their attacks on even the possibility of mechanizing talent gave recognition and credibility to our posturing.

If not the cultural scene, then factory automation was a guaranteed setup for computers. The business world was to be another oyster. "Duck soup," said the just-born computer to the challenges of banking, accounting, inventory control and production scheduling, manpower planning, and payroll processing. Duck soup, all right, if you define duck soup as accomplishing the same old ends—turning out essentially the same reports and summary statistics faster and more economically than had ever before been possible. Whether faster and more economical add up to better is another question; indeed, translating speed and economy of information handling into a demonstrable, truly significant improvement in management decision making is a challenge that still taunts us.

To the question, What about the professions? we responded with a resounding yes. Partnerships were to be fused between computers and medical doctors, computers and lawyers, computers and architects, computers and city planners. It seemed clear in the decade of the fifties that these partnerships were to be, could be, ones of coequal intellectual participation, each party contributing to the knowledge and activity base of the other—man and machine involved in a synergistic relationship and sharing of responsibilities to the ultimate benefit of the total profession and to professionalism itself. The promise, as we saw it then, went beyond the passive role of supporting the professional's information storage and retrieval needs to the potential of active machine participation in such areas as medical diagnosis; not simply the digitization and recall of legal data, but assists to lawyers in evaluating courtroom testimony; and the leap would be made from reducing the architect's drafting burden to inspiring the cooperative design of houses, offices, bridges, and vehicles.

Not even the home environment was sacred or immune from our reveries. The woman of the house, before the women's liberation movement raised the state of our consciousness about role assignment in the American family, would be computer-aided in the daily functions of menu selection, cooking, and grocery budgeting. Computers would be available to balance Dad's checkbook and to assist him in the onerous task of preparing his tax forms. The entire family, mother, father, and offspring, would profit from the machine's capacity for allowing them immediate and varied access to the world's storehouse of entertainment—for bringing to them, on request (in whole or digested form) the total book, periodical, and newspaper contents of society's library resources.

Only in the field of scientific and mathematical computation did actual progress come close to matching expectations. For the rest, we are still struggling with the anticipation that we would someday be routinely programming computers and retrieving information from memory banks via natural-language, everyday English commands. The further hope that we might communicate with machines in spoken as well as written English is still a hope. Foreign-language translation, another sure bet of the 1950s, was to be as simple as the one, two, three, easy-as-pie inputting into memory of dictionary equivalents for words in the source and target languages. Surprisingly enough, many of us believed it until a man named Bar Hillel and others who followed him pointed out the enormous complexities of dealing with such factors as synonyms, similes, homonyms, and idiomatic and colloquial expressions. We went on to learn the lessons of context and the difficulty attendant upon distinguishing between narrative and allegory or comprehending the clever employment of metaphorical expression. The retreat from that yellow brick road to certain success was as bitter a pill as the computer industry had to swallow. We said way back then that computers would perform deductive search and that even subtle relationships across information elements could be recognized and acted upon. We were convinced that the large-file problem, even though we had not yet properly defined it, would bow to improvements in the technology of hardware design.

Looking back, such labels as naive and unrealistic seem properly descriptive of our forecasts for the computer as an instrument for profoundly altering the human condition. Unlike the development of electricity, the telephone, and the automobile, computers remain external and even foreign to the day-to-day interactions of mankind. With few exceptions, the only contact the average person has with modern computing machines is the rendering of monthly billing statements. This unwelcome association, complete with its universal reputation for proneness to errors and its unresponsiveness to complaints, results too often in a public mockery of automation and the media orchestration of cheering sections as yet one more department store or public utility shucks off its mechanical monster in favor of a return to "humanism."

While the pocket calculators pioneered by Hewlett Packard and Texas Instruments have become as common a household item as the television set, these machines (as they are currently designed) contribute little to the grandest ideal of the computing era—the expansion of man's intellectual and social well-being by facilitating his access to the world's storehouse of knowledge and entertainment and enhancing his interactions with his fellow humans. Even acknowledging the enormous contributions of computing to the efficiency and economy of information processing, it is undeniable that the larger societal goals of automation are still to be realized. However, neither the goals nor the hope of satisfying them have diminished with time. Rather, the technological advances of these first twenty-five years can be viewed as having provided a necessary foundation on which to build further progress, along with insights into the direction future progress will have to take.

TIME SHARING AND NETWORKING

Time-shared computer systems, a development of the 1960s, had the primary objectives of achieving data-processing economies through the concept of sharing the services of a large central computer over a multiplicity of users and of facilitating on-line, real-time cooperative interaction between people and computers. Inherent to the concept was the necessity for designing hardware and software capabilities to permit ease of communication and access to the computer for remote systems users. Among the features considered important to the success of time-sharing were the ability to: (1) allow remote interuser console communication for activities that ranged from on-line data summarizing to simulation and management game playing; (2) facilitate greater flexibility and immediacy in accomplishing program debugging operations; and (3) allow foreground-initiated jobs to be run as background without the necessity of the user's remaining at his console.

The world's first time-shared computer system was developed at MIT with the support of the Office of Naval Research and the Advanced Research Project Agency. This pioneer effort, between the years 1959 and 1962, resulted in the creation of a working model known as the Compatible Time-Sharing System (CTSS). It used IBM 7090 and 7094 hardware and demonstrated its capabilities on a representative data base and user community of MIT academic departments. In addition to its major accomplishment of proving the viability of the basic time-sharing concept, CTSS also served the purpose of underscoring limitations and providing insights into the requirements for future research activity. Both research results and shortcomings were reported at the Spring Joint Computer Conference in 1962.

During this same period, other time-sharing and remote-console efforts were being initiated. Among these were a system at Bolt, Beranek and Newman using Digital's PDP-1 computer, work at Carnegie Institute of Technology with the G20 computer, research at Berkeley with an IBM 7090, and activity at Rand Corporation with Johnniac. Credit for the development of the time-sharing concept at MIT belongs to many people and includes philosophical papers and lectures in 1959 by C. Strachey, H. M. Teager, and J. McCarthy. Institutionalization of efforts to move from philosophy to the creation of prototype designs came from Robert Fano.

The CTSS experiment provided a new set of goals and standards for yet-to-be-developed time-sharing systems. These included (1) improvement in reliability to a level where it was possible to run continuously seven days a week, twenty-four hours a day, a capability essential to realizing the goal of time-sharing centers that could function as large-scale computer utilities; (2) provision of a capability for automatic recovery of data in the event of loss or damage to files; (3) sophisticated control over user access to the system, to files, and to unique combinations of access and processing speeds through exploitation of multiprogramming and parallel processing techniques, which permit a single processor or combination of processors simultaneously to perform a multiplicity of logical operations; (5) automatic cost accounting and billing for use of computer time by the system's customers; (6) simplified language development to improve the use of time-sharing services by the nonprogrammer; (7) system flexibility, through modular design, to accommodate expansions in the number of users and/or central processors without the necessity for major revisions to the system software, and to permit automatic reconfiguration of the system's hardware/software assets tailored to individual user needs; and (8) incorporation of a "virtual memory" approach for users requiring a very large addressable memory—virtual memory consisting of a high-performance paging drum to provide such rapid and selective core and secondary storage interaction that "memory" effectively is constrained only by the totality of secondary storage (drums, discs, etc.) attached to the system.

The CTSS effort also revealed limitations of then-current computer hardware and underscored a requirement for specifying new architectures if the full potential of the time-sharing philosophy was ever to be realized.

In response to the goals developed by CTSS, in 1963 a decision was made to extend the time-sharing research project at MIT. This extension or expansion, called MULTICS (for Multiplexed Information and Computing Service), had the objective of explicitly defining all of the desirable features of an idealized time-sharing system as well as building a system that would simultaneously encompass all of these sought-after capabilities. Bell Labs joined forces with MIT as both a funding source, along with ARPA, and a participant in the research. Early attention was paid to specifying an appropriate hardware design, with the result that General Electric was able to produce a prototype machine for the MULTICS effort; this machine eventually evolving into GE's 645 commercial time-sharing system.

Armed with a powerful central computer capability and with a first-rate, well-organized research team, the MULTICS project made enormous strides in the years 1963 through 1968. It demonstrated a capacity for the simultaneous servicing of between forty and fifty users; it coupled computer graphics (CRT devices) with a high-speed digital processing capability to provide a versatile, interactive management tool; it developed computer languages to enable on-line interaction by users other than professional programmers; and it demonstrated a capacity for routine handling of a wide variety of higher-level and problem-oriented languages. MULTICS showed that the sharing of "canned" library routines for performing arithmetic and information-processible functions was both feasible and beneficial; it proved the possibility of significant improvements in programmer coding and debugging operations through time-shared, interactive programming; and it achieved acceptable levels of reliability.

Most important, MULTICS had evolved, over a brief five-year time span, from a highly experimental activity to a situation in which it was routinely satisfying the computational needs of a diverse community of users. The case for time-sharing had indeed been made. Proven customer utilization and satisfaction, as much as technological achievement, was responsible for spawning an industry of commercial time-sharing service centers that numbered more than forty in Washington, D.C., alone by the close of 1968. In addition to constituting a catalyst for moving a reluctant computer industry to face up to the inevitability of time-sharing, the MULTICS group produced literally hundreds of technical papers whose widespread distribution had a tremendous impact on research activity throughout the academic and business world. By the close of the 1960s, there was a general availability of computer systems tailored to time-sharing interests, such as IBM 360/67; GE 635 and 645; UNIVAC 1108; CDC 3600; SDS 940, and DEC PDP-10.

With all of the progress time-sharing had made, however, its early philosophers were somewhat disappointed that its success was being measured in purely economic terms. The case for improved decision making through data-base and algorithm integration was still to be made.

The dream of a computer utility benefiting the work and recreational life of the average citizen was still a dream.

To these still unrealized goals of time-sharing, a new concept, called networking, added one more vision—the hope that science itself would profit, that real improvements in scientific achievement could result from greater human-to-human computer communications among researchers working in similar problem areas. The structure for facilitating increased interscientist and inter–scientific community cooperation was to be a computer network. In 1968 networking was defined by its inventor, Dr. L. G. Roberts, then of ARPA, "as a set of autonomous, independent computer systems, interconnected so as to permit interactive resource sharing between any pairs of systems." Computer connectivity or linking, in the Roberts concept, was to be accomplished via interface message processors (IMPs) to be designed by Bolt, Beranek, and Newman (BBN) and wide-band leased circuits supplied by the telephone company. Dr. Roberts went on to describe the idea of an ARPA network, initially consisting of ARPA-sponsored university and think-tank research centers, which would employ the new technology to perform research for furthering network development as well as to demonstrate that the global cause of better science was enhanced by the networking philosophy. The technical goal of the ARPA network was generally put forth as that of enabling controlled remote accessing by every local user to all network resources (programs, software, algorithms, machine time) independent of the location of the desired resource in the network complex.

The year 1968 came to a close with the universal acceptance and commercial marketing of time-sharing systems. The new research challenge, as well as the inheritor of the leftover dreams for time-sharing, was, of course, to be networking. In a larger sense, the ARPA concept was a natural and logical extension of the original time-sharing concept. The fundamental technology essential to constructing a resource-sharing computer network was inherent in the process of splicing two time-sharing systems together as remote users of each other. An experiment of this kind was successfully made in 1966 between the TX-2 computer at Lincoln Lab and the Q-32 computer at SDC. A really useful resource-sharing computer network, however, would await the development of a completely new communications service. ARPA, with the early design assistance of personnel from SRI (Stanford Research Institute), UCLA, the University of Utah, Lincoln Labs, and BBN, specified the characteristics of the needed communications service, with the result that along with the development of IMPs at BBN, the possibility of a test of the Roberts network concept became a reality.

The first implementation of the ARPA network concept came about in 1968–1969. It involved computers at four sites: an XDS 940 (Stanford

Research Institute), an IBM 360/75 (University of California, Santa Barbara), an XDS SIGMA-7 (UCLA), and a DEC PDP-10 (University of Utah). From this beginning configuration, the ARPA network developed by 1975 to a system of fifty host computers with thirty-eight sites in the continental United States and Hawaii, and with connections to Norway and England. The fifty host machines were connected through twenty-five information message processors. The computers in the system included IBM 360 and 370 series machines, PDP 10s and 11s, the Honeywell H645, the Burroughs B6700, and the CDC 6600. Users of the network numbered in the thousands, and it grew from servicing a scientific community to the provision of hands-on network experience for the Defense Department (DOD) and other government agency personnel in such fields as logistics, command and control, manpower management, financial and office management, and vehicle design.

The year 1976 began with the announcement that management and maintenance responsibilities for the ARPA network were being transferred to the Defense Communications Agency (DCA). The experimental concept of 1968 was now ready for operational employment. Considerable progress had been made during this period of transition from research to near operational status. Network expansion and utilization had increased dramatically, both in terms of numbers and types of users and host sites and in terms of the traffic flow itself. Responsiveness goals had been satisfied—0.5 second transit time from one node to any other for a 1,000 bit (or less) block of information. The system had proved itself to be highly reliable, reliability having been achieved through such technological advances as providing at least two transmission paths between any two nodes, ruggedizing the IMP against external environmental conditions, and introducing sophisticated error-checking codes.

A less tangible, but equally important value of the ARPA network was that it allowed examination of alternative ways of distributing information-processing costs between the resources of computation and communication. The network provided a mechanism for cost-effectiveness experimentation for optimizing the organization and distribution of sites and IMPs. It yielded important insights on the billing and management functions in a networking environment and established a model computer-aided education and help facility for neophyte network users. The most exciting accomplishment of the network, however, and one of its most valued assets was the emergence of a "user community." In the reality of that community—cooperatively sharing its data, its algorithms, and its ideas, discussing and resolving issues of software design, language choice, and protocols—was the hard evidence that linking computer resources could and did result in improved human-to-human communication. Nevertheless, more time and additional network experience in other community situations are needed to evaluate the observed gains in human cooperativeness. The challenge is to demonstrate that the improvement is a universal, inherent product of networking rather than a unique circumstance associated with the adventuresome nature of the experiment itself.

As in the case of time-sharing, acceptance of the ARPA network philosophy was expressed through imitation. By 1976 more than ten commercial firms were marketing networking services. Other DOD organizations and non-DOD government agencies were broadcasting their plans for network designs and developments tailored to their specialized requirements.

Along with the general euphoria about the status of networking, research attention should continue to be focused on improving a network's capability for serving the large-data-base user and for preventing congestion under conditions of heavy loading. Techniques should be created for optimal distribution of a computing load over the resources of the network and for automatically reassigning jobs to machines in relation to changes or surges in the workload. More work would have to be done on understanding the fundamental characteristics of jobs to facilitate their logical assignment to host machines. Researchers will have to explore questions of job buffering and possibilities for the complementary introduction of jobs into the work stream for maximal exploitation of network resources. Most urgent of all, the network research community will be faced with the task of designing systems that represent some ideal interconnection of maxicomputers, minis, and microprocessors, and with developing algorithms for deciding on the location and update rules for the data bases involved.

ARTIFICIAL INTELLIGENCE

No aspect of computer science has shown more promise or created greater controversy than the field of artificial intelligence (AI). The guarantee of controversy, if not direct public concern, was inherent in the basic goal of AI research: to endow machines or robots with those characteristics that are called intelligence when exhibited by people.

The field, as a formal research activity under the banner of computer science, dates its origin to a 1956 Dartmouth Summer Institute meeting. Participants included professors Marvin Minsky (MIT), John McCarthy (Dartmouth, MIT, now at Stanford University), and Alan Newell (Carnegie-Mellon). These men representing the disciplines of mathematics, applied logic, and psychology, gave the new activity its name and set forth some of its goals and the mechanisms for realizing them. Their thinking was conditioned by the growing involvement between the years 1954 and 1956 of the best minds in computing, applied to such endeavors as mechanized chess and game playing, theorem proving, and language translation. They were influenced by the work in perceptronics or learning machines and by ongoing research in pattern recognition. Funding support from NASA and ARPA came in 1962. NASA interests included fundamental research for creating automated devices and techniques in support of astronauts exploring the moon surface. ARPA described its support in terms of the potential that robots held for supplementing or replacing men in the performance of useful or necessary tasks in hazardous or hostile environments.

By 1965 four major centers of AI research were established in the United States: Carnegie-Mellon University, MIT, Stanford University, and SRI. Their specific objective was to create robots (devices and concepts) that manifested humanlike capabilities of vision, mobility, hand manipulation, and reasoning. In the case of vision, researchers substituted a television camera and a computer for the human eye and brain. Early effort centered on the domain of polyhedra, and the research took the form of creating a capability for recognizing all of the objects in a child's world of toy blocks. The field of computational geometry was developed and sharpened to distinguish objects (blocks) scattered across the floor in spite of difficulties presented by such obstacles as shadows and occlusions. More recent work, aimed at achieving a closer approximation of human-level "seeing" abilities, has shifted from concentration on the blocks domain to research on the question of understanding the image arrays of such real-world scenes as a museum or office situation or an outdoor environment. As an example of progress along these lines, one researcher demonstrated how symbolic segment descriptions could be combined with modifiers to produce a descriptive base solid enough to differentiate among two dozen historically interesting Greek vases. But whether the scene is outdoors, in an office, or of archeological interest, the newest approach to machine vision is to perceive or identify objects related to such factors as shape, color, texture, location, function, and appearance with other objects. Understanding context, the totality of the scene, is now recognized as crucial to identifying individual items within the scene. Good progress has also been made toward the goal of bringing vision into practical use. At MIT, the central core of a minirobot vision system has been completed, and a number of successful applications programs have been devised: an inspection program tests wristwatches by following the hands visually; another inspection program checks finished circuit boards for improperly soldered connections; a program for preparing an NC (for *numerically controlled* machine tools) tape locates the proper coordinates for drilling holes in the center of printed circuit pads.

Research activity in machine vision was complemented by work in mobility and manipulation—endowing machines or robots with capabilities for generalized movement and with the dexterity humans have in their hands and fingers. At MIT, early progress in the design of manipulators was displayed in the automatical construction of children's houses or towers from an assemblage of randomly scattered toy blocks. More recent results have taken the form of a mechanical hand capable of assembling a seven-piece radial bearing with one-mil tolerances. Force feedback was the key to this success.

Complementary to this interest in sophisticated manipulation has been the development of a new, higher-level language for mechanical assembly. Stanford University participation in hand, eye, and robotics research dating back to 1962 resulted in a 1972 demonstration of computer programs and manipulators for the fully mechanical assembly of a simple automotive water pump. SRI's work in the area of robot mobility centered on building a robot device that could create a map of a room in which it was placed, pinpointing the location of such obstacles as chairs, desks, and tables so that it could move to specified destinations within the room and avoid furniture pieces in its natural path. By 1974, fundamental results in robot vision and manipulation were attractive enough to permit their application to industrial automation. Stanford University and SRI continued to do basic work contributory to factory automation and were joined in this activity by commercial firms with more directed objectives.

For computers to be able to reason—to understand and act upon commands or dialogues communicated to them in everyday written English—was from the first one of the principal and far-reaching goals of AI. Research in this area, including efforts at MIT, Stanford, SRI, and Bolt, Beranek, and Newman, ranged from projects to permit machine comprehension of single-person commands in a neuter domain to the understanding of multiperson dialogues involving the psychological nuances of human-to-human communication. In terms of a complexity measure, the upper end of the natural-language understanding scale is concerned with machine representations of knowledge about the total human social framework—the knowledge base essential to computer encoding and treatment of narrative related to people's purposes, beliefs, and intentions. One researcher put forth the notion of computer programs that could demonstrate commonsense reasoning abilities in responding to questions about simple narratives or stories. Another researcher, facing up to the most difficult aspects of language comprehension, described his objective as creating computer programs to deal with the human employment of language to convey both conscious and unconscious intentions of flattery, exaggeration, deceit, emphasis, and spite.

While natural-language understanding was considered a desirable feature from the inception of the computer era, pre-AI attacks on the problem were largely restricted to such simpleminded mechanisms as the use and matching of key words and phrases or the design of parsing algorithms to get to the deeper meaning of sentences through syntactic analysis. Over the first ten years of its life, AI introduced into this realm the concept of storing knowledge rather than words, the development of a special notation to process complex narrative, and the idea that semantic modeling was as important as grammar and that building "context" was crucial to language comprehension.

A milestone in the development of computerized natural-language systems came in 1971 with the publication of an MIT doctoral thesis by Terry Winograd. Dr. Winograd, working in the environment of MIT's robotics project, built a highly interactive question-and-answer capability (see chapter 4). The Winograd system uses semantic information and context to understand discourse and to disambiguate sentences. It combines a complete syntactic analysis of each sentence with a "heuristic understander" that uses different kinds of information about a sentence, other parts of the discourse, and general information about the world in deciding what the sentence means. It is based on the belief that a computer cannot deal reasonably with language unless it can "understand" the subject it is discussing. The program is given a detailed model of the knowledge needed by a simple robot having only a hand and an eye. Through the program, the human can employ straightforward and grammatically complex English sentences to direct the robot to manipulate toy blocks of various colors and geometric shapes. He can instruct the robot (computer) about physical properties of the blocks, and he can provide it with all the information it will require to make decisions on the logic and sequencing of actions (block movements and organizations) essential to building such structures as a toy bridge or a toy house. In addition to knowing the properties of the blocks, the program has a simple model of its own mentality. It can remember and discuss its plans and actions as well as carry them out. It enters into a dialogue with a person, responding to English sentences with actions and English replies and asking for clarification when its heuristic programs cannot understand a sentence through use of context and physical knowledge.

The Winograd achievement was afforded immediate recognition and universal praise. It represented without question the most powerful system yet developed to cope with natural-language understanding. The early rush to copy and to extend this work initially ignored limitations that mitigated against generalizing its application to all domains. The Winograd world was, after all, a world of children's blocks. Inherent characteristics of this universe included the neat geometry of the objects in it, the restricted nature of its vocabulary, and the neuter nature of the discourse it called for, which avoided treating the psychological complexities of interpersonal dialogues. The Winograd methodology could not, without additional theoretical development, be used for machine understanding of narratives requiring knowledge and interpretation of human behavior in complex, real-world situations.

If Winograd's triumph did not solve all of our natural-language problems, it quickly became a fundamental underpinning for advanced work in simplifying computer programming methodology and in computer-based inferencing and commonsense reasoning. A recent, directly practical application of a Winograd-like methodology has been the design of question-and-answer systems about Navy aircraft carrier employment by David Waltz of the University of Illinois and Richard Fikes and Marshall Pease of SRI. Even given the limitations of Winograd's work, these applications have usefully improved computer handling of planning and status dialogues on aviation maintenance and inventory control operations.

Going beyond Winograd's research to enable machine representation of knowledge about human psychological and social conditioning became one of the more actively pursued AI topics from 1973 on. Marvin Minsky's 1974 paper, "A Framework for Representing Knowledge" was an important philosophical response to this quest. Minsky proposed the organization of knowledge into chunks called FRAMES, each frame being a data-structure representation of stereotyped situations like visiting a person's home, going to the office, or attending a child's birthday party. Minsky also described the idea of a "frame system" consisting of collections of related frames and put forth the possibility of machine interpretation of multiperson, complex narratives through internal recognition of close or near fits to extant frames or the initiation of machine-to-man dialogues seeking more information if the man's initial input does not satisfy the frame's point of reference about events in terms of their admissibility or sequencing. A form of "reasoning" is accomplished by the employment of heuristics to discriminate between ideal frame matches, acceptable or minor variations from the textbook case, and the need for merging, hopscotching, or creating new frames to get at the meaning or truth of a narrative. If this concept of frames was not brand-new, Minsky at the very least had added structure, formalism, computability, and feasibility to the art and science of reasoning by analogy.

Along with this activity in natural-language text processing, ARPA, in 1973, launched a five-year program on the problem of "continuous speech understanding" by computer. Three separate projects or contracts were initiated, each contract group having the objective of developing a complete speech understanding system. BBN chose the domain of moon rocks; a coalition between SRI and SDC (System Development Corporation) tackled the problem of computer response to verbal questions about the ARPA network; Carnegie-Mellon University built its system to address verbal dialogues on chess playing. To all of the complexities associated with English text processing, speech understanding adds the enormous difficulties of dealing with the variation in human voices and accents, the problem of intonation, the absence of grammatical and semantic control, and disconnections and discontinuities in speech patterns.

The AI community currently anticipates some changes in the course of its research occasioned by its achievements, the virtual disappearance of NASA as a funder of basic research, and an ARPA push for practical results. The work in robotics is being supplanted by industrial automation efforts. Research in natural-language understanding and machine representation of knowledge continues. New directions include developing computer-based "expert consultants" for managers, office workers, and for technicians and professionals.

Throughout its fifteen-year history, AI has proven itself to be a storm center of intellectual fervor and debate. Its detractors simultaneously chastise it for having bragged so much and accomplished so little and whisper darkly of the imminent danger that AI results will hasten the rise of an Orwellian society. Its supporters and practitioners, including some of the most creative minds in computer science, remind us that twenty years is too brief a time for final judgments. Few fields of science have set such challenging goals or attempted to address more rigorously the fundamental hope that society's improvement can result from the modeling of man's dexterity and his reasoning abilities.

SOFTWARE DEVELOPMENT

Although some members of our computer society equate research success or propaganda about research success with significant operational advances, there is much evidence to the contrary. We have only to examine the operational world to confirm the suspicion that the technology transfer lag is considerable. Worse still, the technology is not always there to be transferred.

Because hardware and software are not standardized, we cannot readily exchange either computer programs or data across computational sites. We are continually in the position of reinventing the wheel, paying the price of duplicating our programming efforts at many organizations and paying the larger, less tangible price of management decision inconsistencies and general inefficiency because we cannot, in real time, communicate data across functionally related but geographically separated activities. Because of doubts about our ability to protect our files, we have been cautious about the sharing of data in a multilevel network environment. The lack of performance measurement capabilities leads to doubts about the initial procurement of hardware and software and about the cost-effectiveness of adding or deleting particular pieces of equipment or software to an existing computational environment. Without a useful technique of measurement, we are open to the accusation that our growth is both undirected and unstructured. Most important of all, existing computer systems have not been effective in dealing with the large data base problem, one that is conditioned not simply by file size alone but by such concomitant factors as the existence of a multiplicity of files that must be joined together in real time to affect particular decisions. In such a situation both file update and retrieval requirements will be voluminous and complex, and interrogation interests will vary by managerial levels and include a natural-language interface requirement. The error content of our data bases is large and worrisome; too little is known either about the classification of errors or the impact of errors on decisions.

Many requirements can be deduced from this menu of deficiencies. The first is to accomplish cost reductions through such mechanisms as increasing programmer, program, language, and computational efficiency. The second is to deal with the error problem, because errors have a negative impact on both costs and decision effectiveness and more than anything else destroy user confidence in automated systems. The third and most important requirement is to provide cost-effective measures of the systems we procure and modify for use in our problem environments.

Turning first to the most critical requirement—developing measures of performance—advancement has been slower than is healthy for a field that aspires to being considered a scientific discipline. Research has concerned itself with efforts to quantify the performance power of a given computing system for a given set of tasks or problems and with developing a meaningful and useful scheme or structure for defining problems. Progress has been made in addressing the virtual memory phenomenon of paging in terms of optimizing page sizes and paging algorithms. Techniques are under development for evaluating such performance criteria as vulnerability, response time, and throughput for alternative network configurations. Queuing models are being designed as a possible tool for analyzing the performance of computer systems. Far from covering this area in its entirety, we are at the earliest beginnings of research in performance measurement. We pay lip service to "life-cycle costing" but know little about how to measure it. In evaluating a system, little is understood about relationships and trade-offs among such factors as performance, maintainability, portability, costs, ease of programming, or use. We are just beginning to address concerns such as (1) translating a given workload requirement into a computer performance specification; (2) proving that a delivered system lives up to its specifications; (3) evaluating the impact of projected hardware or soft modifications on future performance; (4) tailoring network configurations for specified user situations;

and (5) the most difficult, complex, and necessary objective of all—being able to demonstrate the relationship between increases in computing power and evidence of improvement in the management decision process.

Performance measurement, in terms of our capabilities both for assessing internal operating efficiency and for relating computing power to costs and managerial payoff, is absolutely essential to the "computing is a science" objective. There must be far greater emphasis than has existed in the past on the careful design of experiments with statistically sound performance criteria and measures. This concern stems from the complexities and disappointments of evaluating progress when these factors are either ignored or given only cursory attention. A few examples of such difficulties will suffice. A past research project in "interactive programming" floundered because of flaws in the design of an experiment. The researchers did not account for programmer quality and training as a factor in productivity or accommodation. They did not discriminate among or measure the importance of such goals as writing faster programs; writing error-free programs; completing more programs; writing more efficient code; and improving operating efficiency during running time. Understanding these objectives and their relationships is a research task in its own right, and the research endeavor avoids them at great risk. A second case of a design flaw in the performance measurement of software techniques is found in the structured programming area. In this case, a well-advertised proof of the effectiveness of structured programming was contaminated by the later revelation that the structured programming team were Ph.D.-level programmers while the competing methodology was represented by personnel without advanced degrees.

For computing to realize the status of a science, much work remains to be done in the field of experimental design, in systematically identifying the significant internal and external properties of quality software and the relationships between these properties and the languages, tools, and techniques of the software life cycle. Research attention must be directed at arriving at an understanding of the complex cost-effectiveness interdependencies across the total spectrum of hardware/software devices and techniques and the relationship between computer systems and alternative notions of output and decision needs. How else are we going to choose among competing tools and programming methodologies or among proposed standards for documentation and languages? How are we going to discriminate between the trivial and the profound, between short-range and life-cycle cost considerations?

Promising steps toward the goal of achieving software cost reductions through increasing programmer, program, language, and computational efficiency include the areas of improving program writing and evaluation and the futuristic possibility of designing automatic programming systems and knowledge-based storage and retrieval systems. By the mid 1970s the search for more efficient program writing had yielded such programming design philosophies as "top-down programming," with its concept of a chief or lead programmer orchestrating a team effort. It also produced the idea of composite analysis and its product of relatable program modules, as well as the notion of structured programming or the structured walk-through, in which a formal structure is imposed on the total design effort before the coding begins. Depending on the source, these approaches are either profound innovations or obvious, time-honored conventions that obtain in any well-managed programming environment. If the would-be employer or user of these philosophies has difficulty in discriminating among them, the designers of these same cures for the programming blahs has even greater difficulty in demonstrating the relative efficiency of one approach versus another.

While all of these programming concepts have intriguing possibilities, there remains the problem of building a formal structure for such procedures as performing the top-down process of selecting the modules, mapping modules into page segments, creating representative skeleton programs, choosing the programmer team, and distributing the work load among the members of the team. Serious attention to this issue of managing the programming process would also address such questions as the relationship between programmer quality and the requirement of recognizing what is important in a large program and what is decomposable into modules. If programmer quality or experience is an essential element of structured programming, we will want to investigate the shape of the learning curve.

In the area of "proving the correctness of programs," the research community is inclined to look at the problem of eliminating bugs from the perspective of designing programming languages that facilitate both the writing of correct programs and the proof of correctness. The concern with after-the-fact program-proving methodologies stems from its relationship to the general problem of proving algorithms equivalent. A leading researcher has made the case that these are indeed similar problems and that there does not exist any finite set of axioms from which proofs can be elaborated to cover all possible cases of algorithm equivalence. He goes on to describe the complexities of proving programs not only on hypothetical machines but on specific machines with specific operating systems. The size and scope of such programs might break down under their own weight. Everyone in this field speaks pessimistically about the problem of debugging in contexts in which tens or hundreds of people are working together on the programming of very large systems. Unfortunately, this is very often the case. At least there is universal awareness of the complexity and importance of this problem, even if there is little hope for significant early accomplishment. Where progress has been made, it has been tied to a unique context or situation. Research activity at Berkeley provided Fortran programmers with "aids" for catching the most common and most dangerous program errors. This work includes a characterization of types of program bugs, specifies a context for the occurrence of specific kinds of bugs, and provides formal procedures for identifying and correcting them.

To deal with a monster of its own creation, the proliferation of assembly, higher-level, and problem-oriented languages as well as the disorganized growth of hardware and software, the computer industry has come up with two approaches: first, a continuing effort to develop and impose standards and second, research directed at creating mechanisms for survival in a nonstandardized computing environment. Facing up to the inevitability of existence in a nonstandardized world for the forseeable future, research investments over the past ten years have been directed at reducing the burden of that situation. The earliest efforts in this area, unconstrained by knowledge of or appreciation of the hardware/software/language/operating system growth pattern, spoke earnestly of developing an automatic, universal file and language converter, the clear and direct objective being that of achieving automatic conversion or translation from any conceivable source language to any specified target language. Disappointments in this push for a universal conversion tool yielded to more modest 1970s efforts at developing a data description language and a processor for the automatic conversion of data-base formats from a source file to any specified target file. This effort, conducted both by University of Pennsylvania and University of Michigan researchers, opened the door to the routine communication of data across nonstandardized computing centers and management organizations. If successful in an operational context, and that has still to be accomplished, it will relieve the tremendous reprogramming costs of accommodating file formatting requirements for changeovers of computers, operating systems, or languages.

The general situation in software development can be improved through better management and increased utilization of existing technology throughout the software life cycle. Benefits can also be realized by uncovering and eliminating those modes of current software practice to which some of the problems can be traced. In the long run, however, research must avoid responding only to external symptoms that are precipitated in large part by present-day approaches. Unfortunately, today's software is not based on the theoretical foundations and practical disciplines that are traditional in the established branches of engineering. No doubt, many of the problems that occur during the software development, acquisition, operation, and maintenance cycles are in part symptomatic of this lack of knowledge of the fundamental nature of computer software and its life-cycle process.

LARGE FILE SYSTEMS

The nonnumeric large file problem, most characteristic of civilian and military logistics, management, financial, and personnel and data-processing environments, is the problem area most poorly addressed by current computer technology. The requirement here, barely touched upon by research activity up to 1970, is the development of techniques to improve search and running-time efficiency; to design software that faces up to security issues in a highly interactive network environment; to accomplish a major breakthrough by moving away from systems that produce calendar-oriented, voluminous output; and to move vigorously toward the goal of real-time interaction between decision makers and stored data. In spite of almost twenty years of heralding the arrival of on-line computing, our current systems are largely batch-oriented; output is voluminous and calendar-directed; management by exception seldom occurs; there is very little direct, on-line manager interaction with computers.

Large data base research activity, initiated by the Office of Naval Research (ONR) in 1972, set out to develop a body of techniques for correcting these deficiencies. More important, the ONR program had the larger goal of moving computation from its current state of constituting a passive capability—all that data sitting there in storage waiting to be asked questions that are seldom or never asked. The 1972 objective was to push strongly in the direction of activist systems capable of carrying on extensive English-language dialogues, with an automated capacity for comprehending relationships across data, for making inferences, and for using that facility to take initiatives, in real time, to alert managers to the impending occurrence of critical events. Knowledge systems used to anticipate and prevent crisis, not computers used to reconstruct the history of past disasters, is the ultimate large data base research objective.

Large file system research has two major aspects, one being the design of software to facilitate the managerial data retrieval process, the other being the creation of mechanisms to improve managerial–data base interaction. From the software design perspective, the program includes such elements as privacy and selective access control capabilities; procedures for automatic reconfiguration of files across storage media; the inclusion of smoothing algorithms to control the reconfiguration process; the routine creation of "utility files" containing summary data; data structuring to facilitate inferential search; the capability for providing statements about the accuracy or relevance of output; and the incorporation of knowledge-representation methodologies to create a context for interpreting the meanings of interrogations arriving from diverse sources. From the user perspective, the research includes real-time interrogation; on-line modeling capabilities; a text-reading, text-summarizing, and message-prioritization capability; the development of a natural-language front end to enable direct contact with computers by high-level managers—this interaction ranging from "one-liners" to sophisticated on-line browsing and simulation—and building a capability for anticipating crisis situations through the setting and monitoring of automatic alarms or triggers.

Research results to 1976 were impressive, if not conclusive. SRI, working in the domain of aircraft maintenance and supply, has developed a "process modeling technique," or a way of computationally describing the maintenance operations and personnel interactions associated with aircraft employment. The model treats both the subject of goal structures and associated information elements and provides a rational context for responding to questions on maintenance and supply activity. SRI has also made progress in designing an alert capability and in developing a utility file concept, utility files being a 10 or 15 percent selection from the full file readily available to respond rapidly to frequently asked questions or high-priority questions. The utility file idea, by itself, promises a major improvement in output response.

University of Illinois researchers, working in the same aviation maintenance and supply environment, have created a natural-language system for English sentence communication. In this case, the natural-language capability has been specifically tailored to process questions and generate answers for a data base containing detailed, dynamic records of aircraft maintenance and flight information. Questions may range from fairly simple ones about the availability of spare parts to more complex interrogations concerned with the readiness status of groups of aircraft. The Illinois-designed system "understands" questions by matching requests with pre-stored request patterns. It is also capable of dealing with commonsense issues. Illinois has created a technique for recognizing and rejecting "unreasonable" or "nonsensical" requests without the necessity of incurring the cost of searching the data base for answers. In this area of natural or English interaction, deliberate effort was applied to reducing or tailoring the "total language understanding" objective to one of demonstrating a limited but utilitarian language capability in a particular operational environment. Putting aside the futuristic interest in making a computer response to the full range of human discourse possible, Illinois established a constrained aviation maintenance and supply linguistics world with such properties as a limited vocabulary, single, unambiguous meanings for specific words and phrases, a unique context; and a neuter domain that avoids psychological nuances.

Progress toward the goal of facilitating the on-line design and modification of large-scale decision making systems has been made at MIT. The work here, directed primarily at providing an interactive design and simulation capability for the nonprogrammer managerial community, represents the marriage of two university departments, with the Sloan School contributing expertise in the areas of operations research and logistics and the Laboratory for Computer Science prowess in the fields of artificial intelligence and natural language. To date, the research, initiated in 1973, has focused on the domain of production and inventory control. The ultimate aim within this problem environment is to create a total interactive decision system that includes a questionnaire for obtaining user descriptions of the general and unique properties of the user's business world, an internal machine source library of applicable production/inventory algorithms and programs, decision tables, optimizing routines, an editor, and an output generator.

The MIT approach to designing a questionnaire and to the automatic production of applications programs represents, from a theoretical standpoint, some advances over past industrial efforts in this field. First, the MIT approach limits the questionnaire context to a particular field—production/inventory systems for example—and achieves depth by exploring user requirements within this narrower scope. The system allows a user to specify requirements or procedures not directly included in the questionnaire. It provides for feedback in the form of on-line simulation—a "what if I make this choice?" kind of activity. It makes provisions for the inclusion of highly sophisticated decision models in the program library and for the incorporation of optimizing routines in the final program preparation. Promising even if somewhat primitive versions of these capabilities were demonstrated in 1976.

Large data base research at the University of Pennsylvania during the 1970s has included efforts to improve the automation of library functions as well as projects to build advanced data base management systems and to incorporate alert or alarm capabilities in decision-supporting systems.

In the library field, progress took the form of designing prototype capabilities for automating the functions of indexing, classifying, organizing, and retrieving textual data. Mechanization of the indexing and classification functions, perhaps the most labor-intensive operation in current library practice, was shown significantly to increase the availability of useful retrieval terms while improving the precision of recall. A working model of the computerized indexing/classification system, complete with relevant software, demonstrated improvement in the user's capability for interrogation and on-line browsing. This improvement was realized through the creation of a treelike hierarchy out of the computer-selected index terms, with upward movement in the tree broadening the scope of knowledge by providing more generic terms and downward movement sharpening the focus through the provision of increasingly specific terms. Futuristic systems of this kind will incorporate natural-language front ends for simplified user interaction. Given such tools, a user, only generally aware of what he wants, can have his vision expanded or his interests made more specific by controlled movement up, down, or even sideways in the data-chain hierarchy. Commercial systems similar to the Pennsylvania design began to be available in the mid 1970s and have found applications in medical and legal text document services.

Responding to the objective of reducing search time, Pennsylvania developed a data base management system that dynamically restructures files over the various storage media based on internal statistical monitoring of the interrogation stream. This technique promises significant improvement in search efficiency for all managers and also offers cost savings through elimination or assignment to tape of little-used data.

University of Pennsylvania research, along with comparable developments at SRI, concentrated primarily on the alerting phenomenon. To underscore once again the need for a triggering capability, one only has to examine the passive nature of the best available computer systems on the market today. Their vast potential for response—even with optimum storage and search algorithms—has very much a dormant orientation. Only to the degree that the right questions are asked by the right person at precisely the right point in time does this passive interactive capability support the decision maker's requirements. For management support systems of the future, the research community is designing a concept in which statistical threshold or alarm conditions, initially assigned by knowledgeable managers, are continually monitored by machine analysis for the incoming data stream. Satisfaction of a predesignated threshold situation is made known to the interested user through the device of terminal printouts augmented by flashing lights, the sounding of bells or buzzers, or the computer generation of human-sounding speech vocalizing the typewritten words, or calling out a warning signal. Demonstrations of "alerting" were beginning to be made by 1975 for such special cases as a significant rise in an equipment failure rate or an early warning that an assigned budget was in danger of being exceeded. As preliminary as these alerting systems were in 1976, they had already begun to show possibilities for a primitive form of intelligence. This came through the creation of a feedback mechanism that on request could inform the user about algorithms and data supporting the sounding of the alarm and could report (by memory search) on previous actions taken by other managers faced with the same alert situation.

While progress in the area of large data base systems has been considerable, the research community does not yet claim to have solved important problems. In fact it is keenly aware of the limitations of its accomplishments relative to the overall goals of the large file system. The work on alerting will suffice as one example of perceived limitations. Research has not begun to take on the large issues of recognizing inconsistencies or even contradictions across alarm thresholds set independently by many managers. We do not yet know how to introduce a smoothing methodology to avoid the inertia or cry-wolf syndrome that results from overalerting. Most urgent of all, we have not begun to understand how to build systems that establish their own alarms through automatic analysis of data and machine definition of crisis situations. These questions and many other large system problems represent significant challenges for the remainder of this decade and on into the 1980s. Possibilities for the enrichment and acceleration of research in this field were highlighted by ARPA's announcement in 1976 that it would begin to fund a program in very large data bases. Together with the extensive Office of Naval Research efforts, the ARPA support offers great hope for further advances.

CONCLUSION

By the midpoint of the 1970s, we were simultaneously bursting with pride at our achievements while lamenting our failure to gain the status of science for this creature that continued on as it started, half engineering discipline, half art form. It all came so fast. In what seems like an instant of time, the card systems of the 1940s became the tape storage systems of the 1950s. Our more enthusiastic programmers had no sooner learned how to create musical compositions by clever manipulation of tape stops than the stirring sounds of "Anchors Away" dissolved into the silent whirl of rotating discs and drums. Within a single decade, we saw the replacement of vacuum tubes by transistors. LSI technology promised us almost unlimited computing power on the head of the proverbial pin or chip. The concept of parallel computation was a proven reality, as was the advent of multiprocessor capabilities. Mass-memory researchers, doomed to frustration in their relentless search for new media to realize the ultimate, undefinable limits of low-cost, high-volume storage, produced their share of interesting candidates in the 1960s and 1970s. Chemistry offered such possibilities as photochromic storage through aniline chemical compounds. Physicists demonstrated the storage potential of microwave spin echo resonance phenomena. Glass delay lines were available to enhance associative search. We had begun to exploit the laser. In the field of software, we developed more than two hundred programming languages. Assembly language coding was succeeded by higher-order languages (HOLs) and problem-oriented languages (POLs). It was as if our goal was to produce a coding mechanism suitable for every taste and every situation. Certainly programming was easier, even if we could not claim or prove it was more efficient.

Time-sharing and networking have been among the most exciting and enthusiastically embraced developments of the 1970s computing era. Together, they afforded the promise of economic savings through the sharing of computer resources and data bases. More important, these concepts, shrinking the size of the universe through microwave and satellite computer-to-computer communication, held the potential for realizing the long sought after dream of real-time integration of information and decision processes. If by 1976 networking had not yet demonstrated it could guarantee a measured improvement in military, business, or scientific decision making, there was hard evidence of its acceptance in all of these communities. The ARPA network experiment had proven the possibility of facilities sharing to a worldwide academic and military establishment. For the commercial sector, the GE Mark III network system, among others, was providing proof that network participation was indeed a viable alternative to independent computer ownership and operation. By 1976, the GE System was servicing network users in 21 countries and 500 cities. Network resources in general could claim thousands if not tens of thousands of satisfied customers. The availability of host computer terminals, 1.3 million in the United States alone, is another indicator of network acceptance.

However, enthusiasm about the future growth, size and direction of time-sharing and networking was somewhat tempered by the tidelike introduction of mini and microcomputers. Suddenly, all was not as clear as it seemed to be. The small data base user, offered the option of a mini versus a host computer port as the answer to his computational needs, was frequently confused by the rhetoric supporting these options. Still-to-be-resolved organizational questions represented an even larger concern. Both the providers and users of networking services continued to be indecisive about issues of centralization versus decentralization of computer resources and data bases. Almost everyone agreed that the answer lay in some ideal combination of interrelated maxis, minis, and microprocessors, but none had the optimal linking formula in his hip pocket. This search for optimization was further constrained by a technological explosion in mini and microcomputer pricing and performance which threatened any hard decisions in this area with the taint of instantaneous obsolescence.

Yet one more tempering influence came from the sociologists and early computer visionaries. Many of these people had come full circle, from outright advocacy of networking or the computer utility as a mechanism that could change and benefit the fundamental life-style of the average citizen to near paranoia about the inherent dangers that networking represented to efforts to prevent the nightmare of a 1984 society. Attitudinal flip-flops were a common legacy of the 1970s American political scene. So while time-sharing and networking had left the laboratory to take their place in the operational world, still more research—of both a technical and social nature—would be a requirement of the end of the decade, if not the century.

In the total computing field of the 1970s, one thing was certain. Hardware costs were going down, down, down. Machines—central processors and memories—were truly less expensive than they had ever been and getting cheaper and more reliable by the year, if not the month. The accountants had calculated a software-to-hardware cost ratio of 3 to 1 in 1975 and were forecasting an "alarming" 8- or 10-to-1 ratio by 1980. Granted that there is little agreement on the interpretation of these statistics, there is no question that computer software is the focal point for future research. Certainly software research and its implementation, whether it takes the form of optimal accommodation to available hardware or goes the route of direct merger with the hardware by embedding such entities as compilers on the chips themselves, represents an activity to be carefully watched and worried over for some time to come.

Artificial intelligence, affording the possibility of machines that could approximate man's capacities for vision, physical dexterity, language understanding, and commonsense reasoning has achieved interesting if not quite utilitarian results in all of these areas. Clearly, the major continuing thrust of AI will be the extension and directed employment of its growing arsenal of innovative techniques. For AI researchers and the computer science community as a whole, responding to the higher-level goals of automation will require expansion of basic research activity as well as exploitation of past results. Certainly further theoretical development is crucial to the objectives both of putting computation on a firmer scientific basis and of realizing the long-promised dream of coupling man and machine in a highly creative, mutually instructive relationship.

The hard truth is that while much has been accomplished, much more is still to be done. Along with the computer revolution which followed so quickly upon that first delivery of a Univac I in 1950 has come a mature awareness of the scope and complexity of the technological and social barriers to achieving a more universal, more profound impact on the public's total life style. Contributing to mankind's fundamental well-being and creativity remains the ultimate challenge if computers are ever to earn every man's respect, let alone his grudging gratitude.

EDITORS' POSTSCRIPT

This essay places relatively greater weight on university research as opposed to industrial research, since that is the area in which Denicoff has had the greatest influence and experience. Denicoff does not cover achievements in many programming language developments or theoretical computer science, issues that are discussed by Perlis in chapter 19.

18
Computer Science and the Representation of Knowledge

Marvin L. Minsky

PARTS AND WHOLES

This essay discusses some problems and promises that arise from the prospect of artificial intelligence. Our culture has no precedent for the strange gifts that computer science offers or threatens to impose upon us. I will describe a little of the history of the subject, some of its present directions, and some of its future problems.

Computer science makes it possible to manipulate ideas as though they were things. Computer programs, systems, and techniques are treated like materials; they are bought and sold and rented. Already there is a public software market, and we expect this to evolve into markets for "understanding" and "intelligence." There is nothing new in the idea that knowledge can be manipulated like a material; we could always rearrange the pages of a book. Indeed, most early computer programs—the kinds usually written in such primitive languages as FORTRAN, BASIC, APL, or ALGOL[a] are made up of smaller pieces that can be put together and taken apart, just as the parts of a house or a car. But in the advanced programs of recent years we find unfamiliar new kinds of structures. They are assembled from preexisting parts the way physical things are. The new

a. The commercial and applied computation worlds call FORTRAN, ALGOL, APL, and BASIC "high-level languages." By modern standards, though, they are really implementations of very early ideas from the 1950s about automatic programming, motivated more by arithmetic than by symbolic requirements. The languages used in AI programs reflect later generations of development, both in control structure and in data structure representation.

One of the driving forces in developing the new languages is to make available for general use concepts like those in note b.

Marvin L. Minsky is Donner Professor of Science at MIT. He is considered one of the founders of artificial intelligence and for many years headed MIT's Artificial Intelligence Laboratory, one of the nation's leading laboratories for research in this field. He is a recipient of the Association for Computing Machinery's Turing Award.

"control structures" involve concepts that are substantially new to science.[b]

Is the whole equal to the sum of its parts? We often find two computer programs, each of which is part of the other. The everyday distinction between part and whole is simply inadequate to describe such situations; see my essay, "Matter, Mind and Models."* But with our new tools for describing processes, many problems that long baffled psychologists can be attacked. For in many ways, the modern theory of computation is the long-awaited science of the relations between parts and wholes; that is, of the ways in which local properties of things and processes interact to create global structures and behaviors.

Programs are reproducible without cost, or rather, at costs that do not depend on their value or on how difficult it was to create them. This is not completely novel: the copyright system developed in response to the analogous problem that came with the invention of printing. But programs can have active as well as passive knowledge, and the commonsense economics of things do not apply; we need a new economics for this. Dertouzos (see chapter 3) argues that the potentially radical economics of

b. New concepts grow from older ones so stealthily that one wonders if any are ever really new. I believe, however, that the concepts of computer science are so novel as to change qualitatively the prospect of understanding how minds work. In the past our reservoir of ways to describe complex processes was too feeble, I think, to deal with human mental processes and their development. (It remains to be seen, of course, whether we now have enough such ideas.) Let me cite, only by name, a few new concepts, familiar to AI programmers and cognitive psychologists, which have no substantial technical counterparts in traditional psychology or philosophy:

symbol table	subroutine	calling sequence
dispatch table	breakpoint	time-sharing
memory protect	trace	functional argument
property list	data type	format matching
hash coding	microprogram	pushdown stack
interpreter	production	garbage collector
list structure	syntax-directed	priority interrupt
content address	paging	indirect address
call-by-name	exec program	pure procedure

There are actually several hundred such terms, each standing for some clear and well-developed conceptual model, in contrast to the handful of quasi-mechanical concepts from mechanics, hydraulics, and Newtonian dynamics at the root of earlier thinking about thinking. Concepts like these are surely important in the functioning of nervous systems, but we should note that very little is actually yet understood about how brains work. In fact, there is no established (or even generally believed) theory of how information is stored in and retrieved from human memory.

* Full citations are in the references at the end of the chapter.

semi-intelligent automation may evolve in an orderly way. It is less clear how the economics of machine intelligence could develop smoothly.[c]

Finally, even the "quality" of knowledge-based computational structures is not fixed. At a certain point, we can expect such systems to

c. There are many different scenarios in science fiction about how real artificial intelligence might make its public appearance. These scenarios include slow evolution of increasing machine competence; a breakthrough in theoretical design leading to a rapid construction of a smart, reliable machine in David Gerrold's Harlie; the same but leading to an apparently sound machine with unsuspected malicious motivations in Arthur C. Clarke's HAL, in 2001, A Space Odyssey; and a completely unexpected reorganization of a large computer with benign humanlike intelligence in Robert Heinlein's Mike, in The Moon Is a Harsh Mistress. In John T. Sladek's The Reproductive System we find an intelligent machine with no apparent human motivations; in Frank Herbert's Dune we find only veiled references to some unspecified historical disaster resulting in the proscription, "Thou shalt not build a machine in the image of a man"—and intelligent machines play no role in this future. Machines with specifically beneficial intentions may come to carry them out with inhumanly rigid and, finally, tyrannical precision, as in David Jones's Colossus and Jack Williamson's With Folded Hands and The Humanoids. Isaac Asimov's robot stories are concerned with the problem of specifying constraints to guarantee benign intelligent computers. The "three laws of robotics," incorporated into the basic hardware, entail all the difficult problems of any formal ethical system. Unfortunately, he does not give full details of how the machines work.

Many issues interact in these thoughtful stories: the nature of sanity, the corruptive effect of power, the conflict of logic with sympathy, the communication with an alien thought system. Few are really especially concerned with computers. The problem of giving power to a computer you do not understand perfectly is only the extreme form of a constant and familiar ethical problem: how can you trust what another person—or even you yourself—will do. In any case, I am inclined to fear most the HAL scenario. The first AI systems of large capability will have many layers of poorly understood control structure and obscurely encoded "knowledge." There are serious problems about such a machine's goal structure: if it cannot edit its high-level intentions, it may not be smart enough to be useful, but if it can, how can the designers anticipate the machine it evolves into? In a word, I would expect the first self-improving AI machines to become "psychotic" in many ways, and it may take generations of theories and experiments to "stabilize" them. The problem could become serious if economic incentives to use the unreliable early systems are large—unfortunately there are too many ways a dumb system with a huge data base can be useful.

Should we be worried that insane computers may "take over"? Weizenbaum worries that people may be inhibited about trying to avert technological disasters because of the belief that such developments are almost inevitable—even if some scientists decline to pursue a dangerous activity, someone else is bound to continue. This is a real and serious problem in certain areas, such as some kinds of genetics research in which a single, poorly understood experiment could initiate a self-reproducing chain reaction in which a variant cell infects an entire population. I think perhaps the issue that bothers Weizenbaum is more a concern about social ideology than that of computers and public safety. Concern about whether or not a psychiatrist must be human or not seems, at least to me, less an issue than the questions others (such as Szasz) raise about patients' freedom: have we any right to change another's personality because we believe him "sick" or "defective"? One become self-improving. Again our present technical, pragmatic and economic intuitions are insufficient.[d]

Much of this essay is as much about the psychology of humans as about the psychology of machines. There are still many people who feel that those subjects are so preposterously different that this must be justified. Many of the notes touch on that issue.[e]

---

changes another's personality (and one's own) even by the simplest conversation; the ethics of absolutes seem always easier than the ethics of degrees, but the problems do not go away.

d. There is no paradox in a program's generating another program better than itself, because it is easy to design a program that will produce all possible programs. (See Minsky, *Computation*.) There certainly is a problem of time, if one adopts the monkeys-at-a-typewriter strategy. But AI research appears to be developing much more efficient, less silly program-improving methods. One problem, of course, is in telling when the new program really is "better"; this depends on formulating goals in acceptable ways. There are also interesting problems about whether a computer—or a person—could understand all about its own workings. I discussed this in "Matter, Mind, and Models."

I think it is important for outsiders to not be fooled by "commonsense" arguments like, "A program cannot do anything not planned by its programmer" or "A computer does only what it is told." Applied to self-modifying programs whose structure is evolving, this is a little like saying, "A child will do only what it is told." One can still certainly write restricted and unimaginative computer programs, but the stereotype that programs in general are straightforward and intelligible is an obsolete conception inherited from an earlier notion of what a computer is.

e. Outside the world of artificial intelligence and modern cognitive psychology but elsewhere within our general culture, the idea that a computer program might serve as a model for human thought still seems absurd. According to the stereotype of computers and their programs, computers are nothing but very fast calculators, and their programs are nothing but sequences of inflexible, rule-bound, predetermined actions which can have only comically "logical," either-or kinds of reasons for their decisions. Since they must make a one-track, mechanical, context-insensitive commitment to what has been decided, obviously they completely lack any profound source of originality and creativity, to say nothing of spontaneity; equally clear, they are incapable of empathy or intuition.

These, if valid, would indeed be fatal limitations, although I am not trying to suggest that (say, because of new discoveries) the old "computer metaphor" of thought has now become scientifically respectable. The situation is more complex than that. The computer metaphor has itself become much richer in a variety of dimensions. The control structure of programs has evolved from simple, serial, step-by-step branched sequences to elaborate structures more suggestive of social and organizational assemblies than of mathematical or bookkeeping rituals. The representation of knowledge in programs has moved from lists and files to complex, active structures that control their own applications. Along with lower-level "factual" knowledge there is higher-level knowledge about how to apply the former. And if programs can edit and develop other programs, then programs can grow and learn. This invalidates most features of the stereotype. In particular, the predictability elements and the step-by-step control ideas no longer apply. In any case, the computer metaphor should not be dismissed, as many antitechnologists like to do,

OLD AND NEW CONCEPTS OF KNOWLEDGE AND INTELLIGENCE

In our culture's traditional view, intelligence is seen as a general capacity or quality of thought. We talk of "powerful minds" or "good brains." This generalized quality is imagined to permeate all intellectual activities, but people find it hard to make useful and concrete assertions about it.[f] It is natural, in this traditional view, to ask questions like, How can we measure intelligence?[g] as though it were a solid or liquid to be weighed or measured, a definite albeit elusive substance.

Computer science has introduced many new ways to *describe* pro-

---

by confusing it with the image of inflexible, rule-obeying simplicity. The new ideas include ways to understand the internal relations of the machinery itself, the processes that go on within it, and the all-important "represenations" that conscious or even preconscious organisms must almost certainly use to make processes evolve.

f. In this essay I talk a lot about "intelligence," and many readers may feel that this is not the real issue. Traditionally, affective or emotional matters are believed to be harder to understand than intellectual activities, further outside the range of subjects accessible to scientific analysis. I can see no sound basis for this. If anything, it appears to me that on the whole emotions are better understood (by ordinary people as well as professionals) than affectively neutral cognitive activities. Perhaps the popular belief reflects a more arguable (but still dubious) deeper fear that understanding such matters might pose more difficult social problems and responsibilities.

I think most people believe "neutral" cognitive activities are based mainly on simple "logic," while emotional activities use infinitely more complex nonlogical, intuitive principles, plus some sort of more direct interaction with basic reality. I see matters as tilted the other way. I doubt that commonsense reasoning uses much logic at all—it seems to me based more on analogies and stereotypes derived from earlier personal experiences than from analytical processing. To push the argument further, I could point out that emotional states probably have more ancient evolutionary roots, so one might expect them to have more predictable, innately determined structures. As for the results of intellectual development after infancy, one would expect to find structures largely dominated by cultural heritage and individual learning experiences. These might well be more complex, obscure, and untidy. In any case, I would suppose that both involve the same general sorts of symbolic processes.

g. If we reject the concept of a definable quality or substance called intelligence, we can still ask what is the meaning of a score on an intelligence test, such as an IQ score? Clearly, a high performance shows that the subject can quickly solve a variety of problems or puzzles—the particular test is composed, of course, of a particular variety of problems, and the scoring procedure reflects the ranking of proposed solutions in the view of the test designer. In my view, a high performance would indicate that the subject has in fact accumulated the knowledge and procedures necessary for "solving the problems without much thought," and assuming that this takes a few years, the performance shows that the subject probably had acquired a certain variety and power of procedure-building processes some years earlier. Thus, the IQ score reflects not a generalized quality of the subject's mind at the moment but the successful exploitation of his knowledge-building systems of

cesses, and these make us feel much less compelled simply to "measure" them. Paradoxically, computer science was inspired by a demand for vast, quantitative calculations, but its unexpected process-describing capacities marked instead the birth of a "science of the qualitative." Describing processes has always been a goal of mathematics, but it never worked very well in dealing with complicated situations. One might, cynically, characterize mathematics as the "science of the nearly linear" and consider computer science to be the science that deals with the rest. But there is no point in arguing much about this, since one could just as well consider either mathematics or computer science to be a branch of the other.

Our new ideas about computational control processes have inevitably led to new views about minds, and today I see a striking contrast between these old and new views of intelligence. In the new view, the general quality of intelligence emerges, again somewhat paradoxically, from the exploitation of certain special skills—namely, the "self-programming" techniques one uses to build other skills. These self-programming activities are not directly observable; this might be why their role has been so long unrecognized. But how does an impression of general ability emerge from the operation of special skills? I can present here only a rough sketch of my point of view, like a portrait that gives only a suggestion of the personality behind it.

To be intelligent, among other things, is to be able to solve hard problems quickly. An expert solves problems that others think hard with little time or apparent effort. Commonsense says that this must be because he "knows how to solve them."[h] In this sense, being intelligent is not an activity of the moment; one must have accumulated, perhaps over a span of years, the knowledge (procedures) needed for the performance. And to do that, in turn, one must have learned to use the mechanisms for acquiring that knowledge.

---

some years before. As in any "evolutionary" discussion, judgments about the absolute quality of such systems are usually of little value, as contrasted with discussions of the details of the ways in which the behavior in question interacts with the subject's ecological or cultural situation.

h. We thus argue that moment-to-moment thinking does not require enormous computations. As Frank Lloyd Wright put it, "An expert is a man who has stopped thinking—he knows." In any case, one can imagine several alternatives. One is to look for a fieldlike physical principle that can do the computation. The gestalt conception is of this sort; it asserts that to solve a problem, all one has to do is to look at it the right way. The psychologists of the early 20th-century gestalt school studied such problems as how one separates visual figures from their backgrounds. Given the precomputational constraints on the kinds of machines one could then imagine, the problems seemed so difficult that they were led either to seek the solution within the physics theories of the time or to search for new holistic,

But if intelligence depends mainly on predeveloped procedures, we must ask how those procedures are learned.[i] Each person must develop techniques. For example, he must be able to recall and select (decide which old memories or procedures he should try to use in the current situation), monitor (check to see if the proposed procedure is working properly), diagnose (describe a failure clearly enough to suggest what sort of repair is needed), treat (apply "debugging knowledge" in order to suggest what changes to make), and remember (place something in memory that will make things work better "next time"). How could one possibly learn how to do such things? One must acquire programs for detecting, classifying, and remedying bugs in one's own processes. Of course, once we have some of these, we can apply them not only to other activities but to extend our self-programming ability itself. Such a bootstrap process is, I think, the only plausible explanation of intellectual growth.

---

essentially instantaneous physical mechanisms. Neither search led to much success. Today, computation-based models like those of Guzman, Waltz, and Marr seem to show that problems like these can be handled without such radical approaches.

Another idea is that intelligent activity does indeed involve enormous computations and that these actually take place in the subconscious, some sort of enormous computer in which vast calculations are done in some unknown but highly parallel and perhaps holistic manner. Technically, the need for such processes is simply not established. When it comes to guessing how much computation is absolutely required to do a certain job, even professional scientists' intuitions are notoriously unsound. The new mathematical science called the theory of computational complexity has produced numerous examples showing that such opinions were far off the mark, usually in the direction that much smaller computations could suffice. (See Borodin; Minsky, "Form and Content in Computer Science.")

In any case we have to explain how people can often quickly retrieve knowledge or memories appropriate to the current situation. Does this reflect the use of a vast parallel search calculation or memory-matching operation? I would not be at all surprised to find something like this in the brain, but I don't think it would remain useful after infancy without a substantial collection of new procedures for building meaningful interconnection structures among the memory contents. But if that is allowed, there really is no decisive theoretical reason to suppose that the retrieval computation must be terribly complex. Something like hash coding (see Knuth and Amble; Minsky and Papert) might well suffice, given that memory can be arranged into tree structures. The power of partition must not be overlooked: a thousand items can be selected by ten binary decisions, or by just three decimal choices. I am not suggesting that things work this way, only that one should review imagined needs for bizarre mechanisms in the light of careful complexity analyses. Unhappily, complexity theory is still too young to be of real help in most practical matters. And there is plenty of room for speculation about innovative hardware organizations for memory theories (see Fahlman).

i. Obviously, some programs must be "innate," part of the genetic endowment. These innate programs, interacting with experience, cause other procedures to be constructed, and the process evolves. The chain of predetermined causality be-

Is there a paradox about the idea of a machine programming itself? Is there a problem about a program's being smarter than its programmer—especially when it is its *own* programmer? Can a program work "correctly" while it is being changed? Can a machine—or for that matter any other entity—understand all about how its own mechanisms work? Do the classical paradoxes—Russell's paradox, or the liar's paradox, or Godel's theorem—somehow interdict the soundness of what I am proposing?[j] It would take too much space to give all the reasons, but my conclusion is that there are no serious logical problems in these areas. To be sure, when the traditional paradoxes of logic are exported into computation, one gets new phenomena. The liar's paradox—"This statement is false"—causes disaster in a mathematical logic. In a program the result might be more like that in a person: first one thinks it true, then false, then true, but after a while a smart program could just postpone the issue as a problem to be faced at a later time.

---

comes progressively weaker as the effects of environmental contingencies accumulate. No one knows much about how intellectual development depends on learning from one's individual experience and culture; it is clear that substimulated, culture-deprived, or language-deprived infants are severely handicapped, but the details are poorly understood. In any case, at some point each individual must develop procedures that are substantially beyond his genetic endowment, and at this point he must become his own programmer. Obviously, the better an innate structure a system has at the start, the easier it is for it to develop further. Many workers have strong views about the extent and quality of innate human endowment, but these are based on too little technical knowledge about the limitations and trade-offs involved. A central technical goal of AI is to discover the general limitations of self-organizing systems.

j. There is no paradox in giving a machine access to a complete description of itself; there are some problems in making it able to answer questions like, Why did you do that? But these are not simple logical difficulties; they force us to decide what kind of explanation is acceptable. There are serious logical problems in answering questions like, Are you capable of X?, and these problems are even more complex than logicians realize; they tend to think in terms of theorems like that of Godel, while I maintain that machines built for AI purposes will not satisfy the logician's beloved requisite of consistency. An intelligent machine could have an opinion but be wrong.

Can a machine understand how it works? Some philosophers might focus on the self-referential aspect of that question, but I don't think it is relevant. We should ask instead, What machines can understand other machines of the same order of complexity? Then we see issues like time, labor, and detail. Any smart entity can understand simple block diagrams, so any smart machine ought to be able to understand a simplified model of itself. Can it understand a detailed model of itself? Well, the word *understand* almost implies (at least to me) some sort of schematization—a getting at the basic principles rather than attending equally to all details, however small. In that sense, *understanding* means understanding an idealized model of something rather than the thing itself. I discuss this further in "Matter, Mind and Models."

Other issues have to be faced on a practical level. Are our informal ideas about finding and fixing bugs, of specifying and implementing improvements, really convertible to definite, technical implementations?

We do not yet know much about this. But it is clear that while it is related to serious philosophical problems of the past, in the new computational setting the problem of a logical vicious circle disappears. The paradoxes of self-referential statements stem from trying to describe in a single static instant something that changes and develops over time. A knowledge-using process should be envisioned as a spiral, seen from the outside as passing through stages of increasing sophistication. In each stage the quality of the special self-programming skill becomes manifested as a broader quality of the applied skills that appear in later stages.[k]

RESEARCH IN ARTIFICIAL INTELLIGENCE

Computer science has such intimate relations with so many other subjects that it is hard to see it as a thing in itself. Like mathematics, it forces itself on other areas yet has a life of its own. In my view, computer science is an almost entirely new subject, which may grow as large as physics and mathematics combined. Like them, it has applied and pure aspects. The more theoretical side of computer science can be seen as a branch of mathematics, but computer science can also be seen as more inclusive, for while mathematics does not undertake to explain how people "do" mathematics, computer science does—at least in one of its aspects. (See note f.)

The scientists who work in the field called artificial intelligence (AI) try to develop theories about the specific knowledge needed to solve problems and about the processes that use more general knowledge to put specific knowledge to use. Clearly, this field shares its goals with other sciences. With computer science we try to understand ways in which information-using processes act and interact. With philosophy we share problems about mind, thought, reason, and feeling. With linguistics we are concerned with relations among objects, symbols, words, and meanings. And with psychology, we have to deal not only with perception, memory, and such matters but also with theories of ego structure and personality coherence.

It is unwise to define the boundaries of a growing science. AI grew out

k. Are these the stages described by Piaget in the intellectual development of children? I would guess not. The phenomena that Piaget discusses are, on the whole, objectively observable; they demonstrate the acquisition and mastery of various intellectual skills. So the procedure-developing skills that I am proposing presumably antedate the appearance of the behaviors that they eventually contribute to. (This idea of computational development seems to have originated with Papert.)

of the cybernetics of the 1940s with the hope that the limitations of that methodology might be overcome by the new ideas coming from computation—particularly the recognition that programs themselves, rather than their applications, were objects of scientific interest. In the course of this work over two decades, computer programs were written to illustrate the evolving theories. These programs exhibited a great variety of behaviors suggestive of such mental activities as pursuing goals, reasoning by analogy, distinguishing meaningful figures from backgrounds, resolving ambiguities by contextual cues, learning from limited examples and experience, planning ahead, understanding one's own capabilities, and so forth. I say suggestive because I don't want to imply that any of these experimental models exactly captures the ordinary meaning of those concepts. Like any other science, this one has evolved through a series of changes in points of view and technical capabilities. There is no general agreement about which current theory is best.

Early Cybernetics

The era of cybernetics was a premature anticipation of the richness of computer science. The cybernetic period seems to me to have been a search for simple, powerful, general principles upon which to base a theory of intelligence. Among the ideas it explored were the following.

Negative feedback The psychological concept of goal was identified with the mechanism of setting up a generalized servomechanism to reduce the difference between an input goal parameter and an observed system parameter. This idea was exploited in various mathematical directions, but the secret of intelligence was not to be found in "optimal control" or similar knowledge-free theories. Nonetheless, the difference-reduction concept, reformulated in terms of a symbolic description of differences, finally became a key concept in artificial intelligence in the General Problem Solver system of Newell and Simon.

Pattern recognition The search for abstraction or invariance developed slowly, I think, because of the error of identifying the thing with itself; that is, attempting to match image against image, rather than description against description. The issues raised in this exploration—how a global or gestalt characteristic of a situation is discerned from an ensemble of local features—slowly evolved into a very rich collection of theories of description and representation, so rich, in fact, that the subject is still difficult to survey and criticize.

Stochastic learning The secret of creativity[1] was sought in the area of

1. I do not believe in a "faculty of creativity" as a special entity or component of mind; I see the word as concerning certain social judgments about novelty and about differences between individual thought-systems. That is not to deny that

controlled random search, both in models of learning and in models of problem solving. This paradigm of "requisite variety"—"If you don't know what to do, try exploring the neighborhood; if that doesn't work, flail about more violently"—has slowly been replaced in AI methodology by "If you don't know what to do, try something that will help you understand the situation better." The "stochastic learning models" of that era's mathematical psychology did not lead anywhere, nor did experiments on "programmed evolution" or "random neural networks." A somewhat later approach based on "perceptrons," which were self-adjusting learning devices, seemed more promising but subsequently died out.

Heuristic Search

The most productive approach, in this period, was called heuristic tree search. To solve a problem, one describes it so that finding the solution is like finding an apple in a tree. The tree consists of places called forks that correspond roughly to partial solutions or subproblems of the main problem. From each fork stem several branches, each indicating the use of a method to solve a subproblem or adding some detail to a partial solution. Finding an apple is solving the entire problem; a problem is "hard" if there are very few apples on the tree; that is, if most branches come to no good.[m]

There are different tree-searching strategies. "Breadth-first" searches explore carefully all branches near one's current location; "depth-first" searches make long, thin exploratory ventures far into unknown territory. Neither works well for hard problems because the trees are so inexhaustibly huge. Are there general problem-solving principles that work well for all sorts of problems? Probably not, unless knowledge specific to the problem area is used. But even a little specific knowledge makes possible "symbolic negative feedback," in a process that works to minimize disparities between what one has and what one wants. "Forward chaining" makes modifications in the current situation to move it toward the goal, while "backward chaining" modifies the imaginary goal, step by step, to

there are distinctive experiences or processes involved in solving hard problems, constructing new ways of seeing and representing things, and judging (and misjudging) when an idea is extraordinarily effective.

m. Sometimes one has only to solve one branch ("OR forks"), but in other cases they must all be solved ("AND forks"). To decide what to do when there is a choice, one needs knowledge about the comparative difficulties and values of the different branches, so a microeconomic analysis becomes necessary. Without such knowledge there are no good strategies. For hard problems, one has to consider not only the intrinsic economic problems but also the management of one's own total resources. A program to handle such problems would thus need a limited sort of self-awareness.

reach the initial condition. (Then the resulting string of actions must be executed in reverse.) Which is better depends on the detailed structure of the problem space.[n]

AI research has moved beyond these simple formal strategies in recent years. It is better to work on a higher level, analyze the goals (real problems usually have more than one goal, and the conflicts must be resolved), reformulate the problem in terms of the constraints that must be satisfied, and use knowledge-based processes to do this. See Hewitt "How to Use What You Know," and Waltz.

The most sustained and successful early attempt in this area was that of Newell and Simon, whose GPS system became a paradigm of the attempt to separate general principles of search strategies from details of particular problems. Their system sometimes showed a lifelike vitality in pursuing goals, but since it could not see very far ahead, it often gave up because of a transient disappointment. While only addition of knowledge-based planning concepts can make up for the limitations of local search strategies, the fundamental ideas from that period continue to be important in more advanced systems.

Separation of Specific and General Knowledge

In any scientific endeavor, one tries to separate elements into independent compartments. In linguistics such a tendency tried to keep syntax and semantics apart; this was a powerful technique in the early stages, but eventually a more comprehensive theory was needed to relate the two. Similarly, the early years of AI saw forceful attempts to separate specific knowledge from universal logical principles, learning from performing, and general administrative techniques from domain-specific content.

Can one expect to find a fixed, universal logic, applicable to all kinds of knowledge? Many such attempts have been (and still are being) made. But the price of fixed logic is high: all one's beliefs and knowledge must be made self-consistent, and I maintain this is essentially impossible to achieve. In any case, I feel that all serious attempts to produce a fixed yet adequate logic of commonsense have failed and will continue to fail, because one cannot separate general intelligence from expertise in specific areas—in particular, about how to become more intelligent. A

n. No direct exploration of the search space can ever solve really complex problems. When in trouble, one has to replace the complicated space by a simpler one: simplify the problem, remove distracting details, leave only essential features. This is "planning," or constructing a "planning space." Once the simplified problem is solved, one tries to extend the simplified solution to deal with the real situation by restoring the details.

number of books, notably Nilsson's and Slagle's, describe the various theories that came out of that era.[o]

Problem Solving, Skill, and Expertise

In 1961, James Slagle completed a program that was pretty good at solving college-level problems in integral calculus. This program behaved in many respects like a skilled but not very experienced student. Indeed, it seemed puzzling that a program constructed with so little regard for psychological validity should seem so humanoid in behavior. Only later did we realize to how large an extent a search-space exploration may be dominated by the structure of the problem, especially when inexperienced solvers are involved. In that respect, beginners are more alike than experts. But Slagle's program could solve only formal mathematical problems; it could not handle informal, verbal formulations. A few years later, Daniel Bobrow developed a program that could solve a variety of word problems in high-school algebra. The emphasis here, of course, was on the problem of understanding natural language; the mathematical problems were quite subsidiary.

AI research has shown a curious pattern of regression toward infancy. In 1961 we see a program for college calculus problems, in 1964 a program for high-school algebra, and in the early 1970s we see the machines playing with blocks in a parody of the preschool child.[p] This regression

o. The concept of logic seems very ancient. The basic idea is that one can discern certain general laws of reason that apply to any situation. These laws, once called syllogisms, evolved into the rules of logical inference formulated by the logicians of this and the last century. The rules of inference are separate from the "facts" and "propositions"—specific knowledge about the real world—on which the logical system operates, and the hope is to separate "knowledge" from "reason" in the same way. However, this enterprise has serious and I think fatal problems. The more facts one knows, the more new facts one can correctly deduce or infer. But if there is even one single inconsistency, then one can deduce anything, however absurd. Logic knows no way to admit anything less than ultimate perfection. (The difference between foolproof logical deduction, and less certain guesses and inferences is not the important issue here. The problem is one of finding something softer and more reasonable than "consistency.")

Another problem is that much of our knowledge is about how and when to use other knowledge. Although in principle some systems of logic are perhaps capable of including such statements as axioms, none of them is engineered to attend to them as rules of inference. Many people have worked to achieve this, but it is my impression that the more realistic such attempts become and the more successful they are, the smaller the final role of the original attempt to use logic, and the end result is the same kinds of informal structures actually to be desired.

p. While there is some truth to the regression story, Slagle's program was preceded by Gelernter and Rochester's geometry program, and followed by a better calculus program. But the main point is valid, I think. An expert is someone who knows what reflects a real phenomenon. It was much easier to simulate "expert" knowledge than to make good theories for childlike, commonsense reasoning. Why? Because commonsense reasoning, while often logically quite shallow, involves the manipulation of a greater variety of representations of different kinds of knowledge. In the early stages of computer science, we could handle only one representation at a time.

Of course, this regression was not uniform. In the later 1960s a really advanced descendant of Slagle's program was constructed by Moses, Engelman, and others, using the most advanced known mathematics for the subject and yielding performance of really expert quality.

Evans's Analogy Program

By the early 1960s, the idea that computer programs could be made to exhibit some intellectual qualities had become accepted. But perhaps because all of the interesting examples—mathematical solvers, chess and checker game players, and other puzzle-solving systems—had formal, precisely defined structures, most critics were ready to conclude that the computers were already showing fundamental intellectual limitations. All these mathematical demonstrations were, they said, just what one would expect of a computer, but we certainly would not see computers showing intuitions, using analogies and metaphors, or operating effectively in vague, ill-defined problem areas.

In 1964 Thomas Evans completed a program that proposed solutions to geometric analogy IQ test problems and achieved performances resembling those of teen-agers—although, of course, only in this restricted microworld. The exercise showed skeptics that computer programs could indeed operate in poorly defined, qualitative areas. Or to put it another way, it showed something about a situation traditionally considered qualitative and ill-defined: that with careful analysis it might be handled by a quite well-defined procedure. What was needed was to find and embed within the procedure sets of preferences and ways to look at things that could approximate human judgments. We do not have to find "exactly what people do"; there might be even more of a difference between different people, or different moments of a single person, than between Evans's model and a particular person at a particular moment. (See note i.)

Evans's program shows more than that a computer can be made to

---

to do without floundering around because he has a knowledge organization that accurately selects what procedures to use and what further knowledge to apply to them. This is easier to represent in a program than the procedure of the nonexpert, who must make do by finding, somehow, what to do from a huge base of everyday, commonsense knowledge. Everyone knows how much easier it is to organize his special subject files than to make sense of a large "miscellaneous" collection of one-of-a-kind items.

recognize a simple analogy to pass an IQ test. For in analogy lies the secret of really useful learning, a way to apply something learned in one situation to a problem in a quite different area. A decade passed before the beginnings of deeper applications of this technique. I think this was primarily because to use reasoning by analogy, one must also have the technology for using two different representations of knowledge at the same time, and this technology was slow in developing. Now that we know more about representing different kinds of knowledge, programs that use reasoning by analogy are at last being attempted.

Figure versus Ground: Essence versus Accident

Psychologists have long been puzzled by the human ability to discern incomplete forms immersed in complicated backgrounds. For example, no person has any difficulty in seeing as distinct the different pieces of furniture in a room. The problem is that few of the objects are completely seen; their surfaces overlap, edges of one thing may continue along edges of another, and so forth. A person can sense no effort in the process of aggregating all these edges, vertices, and regions and assigning each to the proper thing. But the "things" have to be created in the mind; the picture has only the features. A program completed by Adolfo Guzman in 1967 did this to a degree, and most of its deficiencies were finally corrected in a long series of later refinements and reformulations (see Fahlman). Once we understand the kinds of constraints that such groupings satisfy, there is no great difficulty in representing this knowledge in a program. The key point, philosophically, was to stop looking for a single, powerful, magical principle of form or gestalt or an organizing principle, and instead to ask, What does a system that can do this have to know?[q]

Context, Meaning and Language

Among the earliest ventures into computer intelligence were projects in the early 1950s whose goal was mechanical translation from one natural language to another. Since computers could not understand in any significant sense what sentences meant, it was proposed to translate by this three-step process: analyze the input sentence's syntactic structure, replace each word by a matching word of the other language, and reconstruct the sentence using matching syntactic operations in the target

q. Even today, many workers in related fields are still looking to explain such perceptual phenomena in terms of the few fragments of "global mathematics" available: Fourier analysis, holograms, minimum principles, and the like. Such holistic principles are rather treacherous, for their power comes, it is often forgotten, from the strength of the constraints upon their applicability. Holograms *are* sensitive to distortions.

language. But these word-for-word translations turned out nearly useless, because of problems with choosing the correct syntactic structure from so many possibilities and the proper word sense from so many alternatives.

Mechanical translation thus did not fare well, and the results gave the subject a bad name. It has not properly been appreciated how important this work was in developing the science of computational linguistics, which has made such enormous progress in the years since. Regrettably, a substantial schism developed between those who felt that syntactic analysis, if better understood, could solve many of those problems and those who felt that it would be better to work on translation using a different, two-step process based on meaning as well as on syntax. In this conception, the original sentence would first be "understood" in the sense that a new "conceptual data structure" would be constructed to represent things and relations between things. Then this conceptual structure (rather than the original sentence) would be used to generate a verbal description in the target language. One advantage is that successive sentences could operate with the same structure, allowing the system to work with ideas like pronoun reference that span more than one sentence.

The idea of building meanings into the programs by using implicit semantic structures—and then using them for subsequent computations—quite properly became so engaging that the older goal of mechanical translation from one language to another was largely forgotten, and the new field of making computers understand natural language was born. Bobrow's high-school algebra program was an early demonstration that even a very small system for conceptual representation could go a surprisingly long way toward resolving the syntactic ambiguity problem. But it was not really until the spectacular demonstration of Winograd in 1970 that the semantic representation approach was generally seen as scientifically plausible. Winograd's program was the first to give the appearance of being able to handle the meanings of a broad class of apparently natural English sentences; it was not so easy to see how strongly its performance depended on the very small core of semantic representation programs within it. In any case, the stage was set to show more generally that, just as Guzman and his successors showed for perceptual problems, the crystallization of meaning from text could develop from a suitable collection of processes activated by local cues; no mysterious, holistic, new antimechanical principle was required.

This does not mean that most of the problem of meaning was solved. It was not easy to combine new representations with those in Winograd's system—or with those used by the systems of Woods and others. There seems to be no clear and natural separation between the "surface" or even the "deep" syntactic structures of word-by-word language and the internal conceptual representations that they talk about. Quite possibly, some reasoning is very close to verbal reasoning, and the rules of inference for some of commonsense logic is not logic at all, but a variety of quasi-verbal transformation that the child has learned or been taught to use, usually (but not always) to produce valid conclusions.

Learning and Generalizing from Limited Examples

The problem of making computers "learn" was felt by most early workers to be the most important problem of intelligence. If a program could be made that would play chess or checkers well or do problems in calculus, well, what of it? The credit should go to the programmer, not the program. Now, if the program would learn to do that itself . . . !

This widely held opinion—that learning was the phenomenon to study—turned out to be surprisingly wrong and distracting. For it turned out that the really important issues are better expressed by the question, What sorts of programs and data structures are good to put into one's memory? If we formulate the problem this way, the remaining question of how to put those structures into the machine's memory becomes a manageable problem of engineering (although, in humans, a still quite baffling problem of physiology). The hard part of learning is not how to remember, it is deciding what to remember. The many early experiments on "pure learning" in the cybernetic era left hardly a mark because they did not address this issue squarely.

What kinds of structures can help summarize the results of an experience in order to retrieve, adapt, and apply it to a later problem not exactly like the first? We must find not just representations of experience but representations that lend themselves to the multiple views of analogy, for that is surely the key to using old solutions to solve new problems.

The first really effective demonstration of this kind of thinking appears in Winston's thesis, in which a program learns to recognize various simple structures made up of children's building blocks. The program is shown just a very few examples of each kind of structure, and it attempts to find some explicit meaning—to add or modify some particular element of a conceptual structure—for each example that it sees. If the teacher gives it poorly chosen examples in which the program cannot find a clean, simple hypothesis, then it gets nothing from the experience. If the teacher selects examples that emphasize certain features among many, then those features will usually be emphasized in the resulting structure, but only if the program has already been prepared to emphasize those kinds of elements in its perceptual description of the situation.

In Winston's system the "learned" conceptual structures are not merely stored away passively in some memory; as soon as they are constructed, they play an immediate role in describing subsequent experiences. Thus, if the program were shown a room of furniture at the start, it could do nothing with it. But once trained to recognize chairs and tables, then it might be able to characterize the scene as a group of chairs and tables. (Built into the program, from the start, are several different concepts of "group" and procedures that try to decide which one is appropriate.) This work needs to be extended toward learning procedures as well as learning data structures; for a discussion of steps in that direction, see the section entitled "Self-Knowledge and Programming Knowledge."

In any case, once the focus of attention is diverted from learning to the purpose of description, each new experience poses a question, and one that must be faced by each child, not just by the computer science researcher: What is a way to describe this? Now, what we have learned in other areas can be applied to this problem. We do not have to look for a single secret, a uniform principle of learning. Instead, we can regard each such experience as posing a problem to be solved, and we can apply any or all of our intellectual resources to the task. Learning becomes, at least for the older child, just another problem to solve, and he should accumulate appropriate special and general knowledge for this as he does for other kinds of problems. Only, he has to do it earlier—so it is not just another problem.

CONCEPTUAL REPRESENTATIONS

In all these areas, we see a progressive deepening of ways to represent knowledge and processes in programs. Today this has become central to the great network of issues studied in cognitive psychology, linguistics, and AI. We do not know how to tie this work together in a really coherent package, but the following are some of the issues that seem most important.

Knowledge about knowledge Why was it easier—or was it just earlier—to make programs expert at calculus or chess than to make infant-level block-building and scene-analysis programs? The apparent answer is almost paradoxical: the procedures we so admire in specialized human experts, however difficult they may be to discover or learn, are often quite clear and simple in the final analysis. But the knowledge and processes we acquire and use to get around our infantile physical and mental worlds is—at least so it seems—a fantastically intricate mixture of many different structures. The ingredients may not in each case be very "deep," but they are of so many different kinds that inventing procedures to exploit and control their interactions is much more difficult. The expert knowledge required to work on a particular kind of mathematical structure seems much more uniform and homogeneous.

It has been astonishingly hard to see what commonsense knowledge is composed of. How does one decide which memories are relevant to a problem? How does one distinguish between causation and coincidence?

How does one manage the interactions of time and space, of statements and motives, of probably and possibly? Philosophers and logicians have not succeeded in finding plausible rules for such matters; no one has ever been able to write down good formal logical axioms and rules of inference for any substantial body of commonsense knowledge.

The problem is complicated by a sort of paradox: the things we do earliest and best often seem the ones we understand least. For example, the processes we use to represent the visual fragments of a room (while one's head or whole body is moving about) is so familiar and reliable, and its acquisition so early in our development, that its details are invisible to us. Of course, this mechanism might very well be largely innate—genetically preassembled. That is not the issue here; as scientists we have to understand the knowledge so embedded. What are these different kinds of knowledge? To begin with, one always needs to know about the specific problem area: the rules of the game if one wants to play chess; some rules of physics if one wants to play with blocks. But whatever one does, one also has to know many commonsense things about causes and effects, time and space, parts and wholes. What is conserved and what is tentative? If one moves a block, its location and support change, but its color and shape do not. But no one ever tells that to anyone else.

Epistemological structures   Even a baby has to know a lot about the categories and hierarchies of entities. Moving chess pieces is like moving toy blocks; no one lives long enough to learn to apply the rules a second time to the same configuration. One must know that chess pieces are things, so the rules of baby physics apply to them. One must learn that such rules don't apply very well to persons (see note j)—you can't move them around by the same procedures—so the normal child's epistemological structure comes to have a dualistic separation: the baby learns about mind and matter. In any case, everyone comes to know that John is a man, x is an animal, y is a thing, and so forth. Logicians can handle the simple hierarchies of inclusion and part-of; commonsense concepts are more tangled, and there are serious technical problems about representing these relations all at once.

Knowledge interconnections   Hierarchies are crosslinked to represent relations between things. Everyone knows that alligators are like crocodiles. Everyone also "knows" that possession is like proximity in linguistic structures, as Jackendoff argued; however, we don't know enough about this kind of "knowing." It is not enough to say that two things are different or similar; one must know something about the differences. (Benches are like chairs without backs, but wider.) It is this kind of knowledge that gives one the power to make analogies, construct generalizations, and extract essentials from contexts. (See my essay, "A Framework for Representing Knowledge.")

Logical and procedural structures   We all know that things that are equal to the same thing are equal to each other. Does one use "logic" for this, applying axioms to propositions? There is another way: construct a pointer from each of the things to one of them, chosen to be the dominant one. Then reference becomes almost instantaneous, and chaining becomes unnecessary, but the commitment to the "canonical name" can cause subtle commitments. This technique of "procedural embedding"—of building knowledge into programs—is much more efficient than performing deductions, but we have hardly begun to understand the consequences of such trade-offs in this active and unsettled area of contemporary research, in which new concepts of computer science complement older psychological concepts in a dazzling excess of possibilities. (See Hewitt, "How to Use What You Know," and Rieger.)

Procedural embedding is seen clearly in Winograd's system (see chapter 4); here the distinction between "knowing what" and "knowing how" is purposely and fruitfully blurred. The "robot" in Winograd's block-building program has only one hand, which cannot pick up a block that has another one on it. There is no explicit statement about this, but in the program's "dictionary," the verb MOVE points not to a "definition" but to a program in the PLANNER language' something like

```
TO MOVE :X to :Y
1. CLEARTOP :X
2. PICKUP :X
3. MOVEHAND (LOCATION :Y)
4. OPENHAND
```

where each step is an "advertisement" for finding another program that will accomplish the stated goal. It will not try to move a block whose top is cluttered; the program will act as though it knew this. PICKUP, for example, could be:

```
TO PICKUP :X
1. MOVEHAND (LOCATION :X)
2. CLOSEHAND
3. LIFTHAND
```

and so forth.

Procedural representations can be very compact, because temporal, logical, causal, and even geometrical knowledge can be embedded implicitly in the program. If, however, one wants to reason about, instead of with, the procedure, there is a problem. Assuming that one could get access to the code—and this is itself questionable, since to take one example the muscular control programs in the human cerebellum are presumably not directly accessible—one would have to go through extra levels of deduction about what the program implies. Such a process of deduction would require knowledge of some programming semantics as well as subject-matter semantics, and this complication could be one reason that much of human knowledge is of the sort that Polanyi calls "tacit." Such subjects would be particularly hard to describe and reason about.

A current goal of AI research is to find ways to capture both the potential efficiency of procedural representation with the potential intelligibility of "declarative" representation. The path to this probably involves hierarchical "comment" structures that explicitly relate the structures of procedures to the structures of the goals for which they are designed.

Formalisms and Informalisms

Can we find uniform ways to represent knowledge? The subject changes too fast for anything but a blurred snapshot, but the following are some of the issues involved:

Atomic and molecular theories of meaning Science usually tries to deal with complication by describing things in terms of a few "atomic" or elementary entities with a limited number of interrelationships. This is also the tradition of logic, which uses more mathematical primitives. Within AI, there has also been a trend toward the development of what are called "semantic networks" (see Quillian); the best-developed systems at present are Schank's "conceptual dependency" representations for actions.

Frames and scenarios Even if concepts were constructed of primitive, atomic units, one could not operate directly with them. One cannot use too little knowledge, or too much, at one time; there must be structured chunks. Terms like "frame," "script," "schema," and "scenario" are used to suggest varying ideas of what such medium-scale structures might be like. In order to retrieve an appropriate frame, there must be some sort of combinational trigger or matching condition to evoke it, and for purposes of analogy one would want the trigger to depend on the outstandingly important features of the frame, not on unimportant accidental features or decorations. This suggests that the top levels of these structures should consist of generally useful elements of broad application, with lower levels containing more specific detail. (See my essay, "A Framework for Representing Knowledge.")

Expectations, presumptions, defaults, frames Most workers seem to agree that computational cognitive processes ought to work with expectation-oriented structures. In vision, for example, our "low-level" processes presumably convert the sensory information into something like proto-objects, automatically aggregating features into structures that can be identified (see Marr and Poggio). At some point, however, the "recognition" must involve memory as well as directly data-dependent calculations. Thus when one knows one is entering a certain kind of room, one ought to be able quickly to identify an object with some of the features of a certain kind of furniture. The frame, or schema, for that kind of room should thus preset subsidiary schemata in order quickly to make those identifications. Furthermore, the schemata can activate "default" substructures that aren't seen at all, such as the wall at the back of the room one is in. Similarly, when told that there has been a party, one is preset to interpret references to food as (probable) refreshments. Those working on these expectation-rich representations are facing a central concern: how to explain the speed of thought, the apparent smoothness of perception and comprehension. The frame-oriented theories expect to find the answer in the idea that one's currently active frame of script contains enough presumptions, orientations, and expectations for almost instant preparation of the new representations that will be needed next.

Plans Storing in memory large frames and scenarios can serve the needs of problem solving as well as those of recognition. Just as one recognizes a kind of room by a mechanism in which certain combinations of cues trigger a scheme into which the other data may be fitted, so the features of a problem one has to solve should trigger a scenario or plan depicting the major steps needed to solve the problem—or at least the steps that have solved such problems in the past. Of course, the quality of such systems will depend on the quality of the representation of the earlier experience; the steps described must be general enough to be adaptable to differences between the original experience and the current one.

Difference networks When something goes wrong with a plan, one should not be left completely at sea. A good plan will also contain "advice" about what to do if one of the steps fails to work. One simple way to do this would be to include, for each identifiable kind of failure, a pointer to another plan adapted to that difference. This idea (described in terms of recognitions rather than plans) is discussed in Winston and in my "A Framework for Representing Knowledge."

SELF-KNOWLEDGE AND PROGRAMMING KNOWLEDGE

Are "mental procedures" like the computer programs of today? Our concepts of computation are changing so fast we cannot expect current models of mind to keep up with them. Still, it would be remarkable if such basic ideas as data structure, matching procedure, local versus global assignment, priority interrupt, monitor/trace procedure execution, and so forth did not survive as permanent additions to our ways of thinking about such matters. So while we cannot set down a stationary theory of human mental organization, we can augment the community of ideas for building such theories.

Control Structures

When different mental procedures interact, how is it decided which is in charge at any moment? Ideas about such "control structure" issues have evolved far from the simple sequential instructions and subroutine calls of early programming. (The very idea that one has more control than another is a control structure concept.) For example, in the pattern-matching-based systems that are currently popular in AI research, subsidiary processes are not explicitly "called" by the currently active program. Instead, they lurk to one side and intervene when conditions seem right.[r]

But even this kind of "situation-actuated" style of programming, which is a great advance over step-by-step programs, is not the final answer. An intelligent program needs better ways to "arbitrate" when several such agents request attention, and it should be able to mediate concurrent execution of several processes. In my view, the control structures of intelligent programs are likely to come to resemble the kinds of social and

r. Winograd's project used several different programming languages, linked together within the LISP language. English sentences are "parsed" by programs in a new "PROGRAMMAR" language that allows linking between grammatical and semantic knowledge; physical problems in the world of wooden blocks are handled by programs in MICROPLANNER (see Sussman and McDermott), a derivative of the PLANNER language. Recursive definitions are allowed in all such languages; CLEARTOP is something like

```
TO CLEARTOP :X
1. FIND :Y ON :X
2. IF FAIL, RETURN
3. MOVE :Y AT (FINDSPACEFOR :Y)
4. CLEARTOP :X,
```

which will keep removing blocks from the top of X until there are no more. Of course, somewhere in the system must be the commonsense restriction that blocks that are in the way must really be removed and not just moved around. For example, "FINDSPACEFOR" must not decide to put a block right back where it came from, or where the previous block was, putting the machine into an infinite loop. Winograd's program ingeniously interlocks its subprocesses so that this will not happen. Sussman's thesis discusses kinds of knowledge that would enable a machine to learn to eliminate such bugs.

The programs written in PLANNER-like languages are really very much like collections of detached statements about what to do in different circumstances. A typical statement has the general form, CONDITION, ACTION, ADVICE. The condition describes a "pattern" of events, for example, that a statement of the form, "MOVE BLOCK A TO PLACE B," has been executed. The ACTION says what to do if the condition happened; here it might say "ERASE any existing statement that says 'A is on B,' where B is a place." The ADVICE might say something like, "In trying to perform the ACTION (presented as a goal, rather than a specified operation), give priority to using a certain specified set of statements." The point is that the specification of the procedure is highly decentralized and not at all like a FORTRAN program.

political structures that have been evolved by human communities—and perhaps for very similar reasons. There seem to be some extreme forms that are more or less inevitable: the total authority of an absolute ruler (or the total control of any active line of a FORTRAN program); the absolute democracy of a linearly additive perceptron machine; the preestablished specializations and interactions of a hive of social insects. But all such "simple" control structures have fatal limitations. As Hewitt points out in "Protection and Synchronization in ACTOR Systems," control structure problems may be seen as the conventions by which messages are passed among specialists. No one individual can have all the knowledge necessary to maintain a complex organization, so one needs specialists, and some of the specialists must be experts in "epistemological control"— they must know enough about who is competent at what to be able to decide who should be permitted to do what at different times. All societies seem to have evolved political subspecialties, operating within structures such as the following.

Election   Sometimes several weak reasons combine to be as compelling as a single strong reason.

Representation   A single individual with a strong reason for action may not be able to affect the top levels of the system, and usually quite properly so. Hierarchies of responsibility seem inevitable: the accumulation of knowledge requires partition into specialties, one needs specialists to manage interactions between the specialties, and finally one comes to need specialists in dealing with specialists.

Recourse   Most systems of justice involve appeal systems that recognize faults in local execution of the community's practices. The review by specialist higher courts is not primarily to correct unjust individual decisions—they cannot do this exhaustively—but to monitor the adequacy of the system's structure.

Codes, ideals, and censors   Societies adopt explicit and implicit codes of behavior, systems of laws, taboos, and sanctions. One cannot "legislate morality," it is often said, and I think this recognizes that there is always a disparity between the explicit bureaucratic regulations that are supposed to handle situations in general and the inevitable bugs and problems such systems cannot deal with. The multiple codes are bodies of normative knowledge and procedures in which are embedded vast expanses of commonsense knowledge about individual cases and other issues that cannot be compacted into formal, explicit structures. Our ethical predispositions, for example, are imposed upon us for the most part by social sanctions, well outside the formal codes of governments. Psychologically, at least in Freudian theory, one sees the individual ego threading its way between positive urgings from one side and prohibitions from the other: these constraints supposedly accumulate in a set of goals/standards/

imperatives derived from an introjected parent model. Some of them develop via "sensors" that detect, distract, and destroy early stages of "thinking the unthinkable." Nipping certain aspects of personal development in the bud is surely more efficient than attempting to constrain an already developed social pathology.

In the final analysis, we probably should not try to seek out the theory of a perfect, adequate, stable control structure. Both our understanding of human psychology and computational flexibility will benefit if we examine how knowledge-based systems can themselves know about their own control and learn to modify them for personal uses.[s]

Where Do We Get New Processes?

In thinking, just as in evolution, entirely new things are very rare; new concepts are really variants of old ones, and new programs arise as modifications of old ones. In programming, or any other sustained activity, old processes often fail at new puzzles. But if failure is only partial, then one tries to modify the process to maintain good features and suppress bad ones.

The art of modifying programs that don't work, whether on old or on new problems, is called "debugging"—there is no other living name for it. So this distasteful title is the one we must use for a subject of the most central importance to psychology and computer science. The subject of designing and debugging programs has only very recently acquired a scientific content, a content whose importance was never properly recognized in psychology or philosophy. It is about types of bugs; that is, about disparities between a programmer's intentions and the behavior of his program. Our thesis is that this knowledge is not proprietary to computer specialists but is a central component of all commonsense thinking. (Papert's essay in chapter 5 discusses this point of view.)

s. It has been popular in philosophy to speculate on the nature of consciousness, its phenomenology, and its material basis. I think it more profitable to approach it by speculating on its uses, which I interpret as concerned with knowing something about what is happening in one's mind. The ability to describe the course of a successful experience is, as I have noted, critical for sophisticated learning, and it would be better to be able to sense aspects of one's own control structure for such purposes. Why is it so hard for people to see how their minds work? Why is so much of our motivational structure "buried" in the subconscious? One theory that Seymour Papert and I are working out asserts that direct access to such knowledge might (as we think Freud suspected) be dangerous: careless modifications in one's own goal structure is a potentially fatal activity. On the other hand, we don't need such a negative reason to explain the difficulty. A simpler explanation is that to "know thyself" is not a simple precept of honesty or even an injunction to be observant; it is an assignment of the utmost technical difficulty. To do it one would need to develop a good theory of AI—or at least of "I"—and there is no reason to expect such a technology to be genetically available.

The Darwinian scheme of evolution evokes a decentralized process of populations, variations, and natural selection. Until recently, the most general (but least efficacious) way to generate new structures was by way of random mutation.[t] (In the 1930s Turing and others discovered nonrandom computational processes that could exhaust all structural possibilities even more effectively.) We do not believe, however, that the evolution of mind in the human infant very much resembles the course of organic evolution. Nor do we agree (with early cybernetics, for example) that the apparent trial and error of a child's exploration is a good representation of what is happening. Deeper things are going on, but one cannot see them except through the lens of a theory powerful enough to encompass the intricate self-modifying procedures that must be operating.

Are there even higher-level control structures? Does some genetic system know how to recognize certain kinds of problems and construct appropriate genetic material? We don't know of systems that literally do such things, but within the differentiation of multicellular systems there are countless instances of contingent expression of concealed genetic material. Some chromosomes may contain material accumulated over ages, presently unused, that could be a source of biologically meaningful new proteins and other mechanisms. Random DNA strings make polypeptide chains that are useless for structural purposes because they do not form consistent spatial configurations. More adaptive results would come from focusing variational activity on already functional genetic pools. Selecting such a substrate is like specifying an intermediate-level programming language. One might look for such a situation in the apparently redundant DNA material found in many species.

In the development of individual intelligence, there are more direct ways for higher-level structures to evolve once the system knows something about programs. While "diagnose and treat" would be surprising in a genetic system, it is not so hard to evaluate and reverse an intellectual experiment.

Debugging Theories

In the past few years, work in our own laboratory at MIT has focused on the conjecture that the key to intellectual growth lies in learning how to debug

---

t. The early models of evolution as completely unplanned and fortuitous no longer seem adequate. We now know several mechanisms that affect the kinds of genetic variations that occur, that stabilize and even repair certain structures concerned with basic genetic and metabolic mechanisms; these second-order regulators are themselves, of course, the product of the "day-to-day" activity of natural selection. In the short term, most evolutionary variations consist of rearrangements of and selections among existing genetic material, within and among the chromosomes.

one's own procedures. Several doctoral theses have adopted this line of attack. P. H. Winston developed a theory of concept learning in which the program compares a description of what it sees with a conceptual structure that (the machine has been told) should match. If there is a mismatch, the program tries to correct the principal disparity by making a change in the conceptual structure. Using a fixed collection of such "description" debugging methods, Winston's program was a milestone in the field of machine learning, because it could make strong and significant generalizations from very small numbers of examples. To be sure, it could do this only in its narrowly circumscribed "microworld" of simple three-dimensional constructions with children's toy blocks.

In another thesis, G. J. Sussman developed a theory in which a computer can debug its own programs. Again, the concrete subject matter is the restricted world of children's blocks, but now the focus is on the block-building programs rather than on the geometry of what they build. Sussman introduces "libraries" to be filled with knowledge about (1) types of program bugs and how to recognize them and (2) techniques for modifying programs to correct inadequacies. This kind of program might be thought to have the beginnings of a rudimentary consciousness, for it has some ability to monitor its own performance, to remember what happened (in general terms as well as in detail) and to be able to make goal-oriented modifications to itself in response to "dissatisfaction" with what it did.

Finally, I. P. Goldstein developed a theory in which a program can deal with interactions between several different conceptual representations of the same thing. In this work, the objects were childlike drawings of commonplace objects like houses, faces, trees, and figures. Goldstein's program relates a static description of a thing—"the arms are attached to the shoulders," "the feet are attached to the legs"—to a dynamic or procedural representation of the same thing: "draw a circle" (to be the head), "draw a line from a point on the circle" (to be the neck). Again the program finds disparities (bugs) in the transition from one kind of description to another. The intention is to do this in such a way that the debugging techniques can be directed not just to particular objects or particular programs but to the "schemata" or "plans" that relate them to each other.

In these systems, I think we are seeing for the first time the beginnings of useful kinds of self-knowledge in computer programs. At the same time, we are seeing a movement toward psychological theories in which self-awareness becomes functional. If we step away and view the process in terms of these scientists' intentions, I think it significant that the element of self-awareness was introduced for practical rather than phenomenological purposes. In other words, they might have constructed such theories because they wanted to explain, say, "consciousness" or how it is that machines can "know" what they are doing. In the past, theories stemming from such motives were not particularly productive. In these new theories, with their "lower-level" goals of making programs solve harder problems, the self-analysis features are emerging as the only promising practical approach.*

EDITORS' POSTSCRIPT

One of the controversial issues touched on in this essay is the role of mathematical logic in representing knowledge. McCarthy, for example, argues that a greater role can be played by mathematical logic than the one Minsky assigns it. Weizenbaum takes issue with some of the implicit projections for AI made here.

REFERENCES

Bobrow, Daniel G. "Natural Language Input for a Computer Problem-Solving System." In *Semantic Information Processing,* edited by Marvin L. Minsky, pp. 135–215, Cambridge, Mass.: MIT Press, 1968.

Borodin, Allan. "Computational Complexity: Theory and Practice." In *Currents in the Theory of Computing,* edited by Alfred V. Aho. Englewood Cliffs, N.J.: Prentice-Hall, 1973.

Clarke, Arthur C. *2001: A Space Odyssey.* New York: New American Library, 1968.

Evans, Thomas G. "A Program for the Solution of Geometric-Analogy Test Questions." In *Semantic Information Processing,* edited by Marvin L. Minsky. Cambridge, Mass.: MIT Press, 1968.

Fahlman, Scott E. "A System for Representing and Using Real-World Knowledge." MIT Artificial Intelligence Laboratory Memo no. 331. Cambridge, Mass., May 1975.

Gerrold, David, *When Harlie Was One.* New York: Ballantine Books, 1972.

Guzman-Arenas, Adolfo. "Computer Recognition of Three-Dimensional Objects in a Visual Scene." Ph.D. diss., MIT, 1968.

Heinlein, Robert. *The Moon Is a Harsh Mistress.* New York, Berkley, 1968.

Herbert, Frank. *Dune.* New York: Ace Books, 1971.

Hewitt, Carl. "How to Use What You Know." *Advance Papers of the Fourth International Joint Conference on Artificial Intelligence,* Tbilisi, USSR, September 1975. Cambridge, Mass.: MIT Artificial Intelligence Laboratory, 1975, 1:189–198.

———. "Protection and Synchronization in ACTOR Systems." MIT Artificial Intelligence Laboratory Working Paper no. 83, Cambridge, Mass.: November 1974.

Jackendoff, Ray. "A System of Semantic Primitives." Papers on Theoretical Issues in Natural Language Processing, presented to an Interdisciplinary Workshop in Computational Linguistics, Psychology, Linguistics, and Artificial Intelligence. Cambridge, Mass.: June 1975.

Jones, David F. *Colossus.* New York: Berkley, 1966.

* I am grateful to Carl Hewitt for comments on parts of the manuscript.

Knuth, Donald, and Amble, Ole. "Ordered Hash Tables." Stanford University Computer Science Department, June 1973.

Marr, David, and Poggio, Tommy. "From Understanding Computation to Understanding Neural Circuitry." In *The Visual Field: Psychophysics and Neurophysiology,* edited by E. Poeppel et al. Neurosciences Research Bulletin, in press.

Minsky, Marvin L. "Artificial Intelligence and Common Sense." In *Frontiers of Knowledge,* vol. 2 (Doubleday Lectures). Forthcoming.

————. *Computation: Finite and Infinite Machines.* Englewood Cliffs, N.J.: Prentice-Hall, 1967.

————. "Form and Content in Computer Science" (ACM Turing Lecture). *Journal of the Association for Computing Machinery* 17, no. 2 (April 1970): 197–215.

————. "A Framework for Representing Knowledge." In *The Psychology of Computer Vision,* edited by Patrick H. Winston. New York: McGraw-Hill, 1975.

————. "Matter, Mind and Models." In *Semantic Information Processing,* pp. 425–432. Cambridge, Mass.: MIT Press, 1968.

————. "Plain Talk about Neurodevelopmental Epistemology." In *IJCAI-77: Proceedings of the Fifth International Joint Conference on Artificial Intelligence.* Cambridge, Mass., August 1977, 2:1083–1092.

Minsky, Marvin L., and Papert, Seymour A. *Perceptrons.* Cambridge, Mass.: MIT Press, 1969.

Newell, Allen, and Simon, H. A. "GPS: A Program That Simulates Human Thought." In *Computers and Thought,* edited by Edward A. Feigenbaum and Julian Feldman. New York: McGraw-Hill, 1963.

Nilsson, Nils J. *Problem-Solving Methods in Artificial Intelligence.* McGraw-Hill Computer Science Series. New York: McGraw-Hill, 1971.

Polanyi, Michael. *The Study of Man* (Lindsay Memorial Lectures, 1958). Chicago: University of Chicago Press, 1959.

Quillian, M. Ross. "Semantic Memory." In *Semantic Information Processing,* edited by Marvin L. Minsky, pp. 216–270. Cambridge, Mass.: MIT Press, 1968.

Rieger, Chuck. "An Organization of Knowledge for Problem Solving and Language Comprehension." *Artificial Intelligence* 7, no. 2 (Summer 1976).

Schank, Roger C., and Colby, Kenneth Mark. *Computer Models of Thought and Language.* San Francisco: W. H. Freeman, 1973.

Sladek, John T. *The Reproductive System* (original title: *Mechasm*). New York: Avon Books, 1974.

Slagle, James R. *Artificial Intelligence: The Heuristic Programming Approach.* McGraw-Hill Series in Systems Science. New York: McGraw-Hill, 1971.

Sussman, Gerald J. *A Computer Model of Skill Acquisition.* New York: American Elsevier, 1975.

Sussman, Gerald J., and McDermott, Drew. "From PLANNER to CONNIVER—A Genetic Approach." *AFIPS Conference Proceedings* 41, pt. 2 (1972): 1071–1080.

Waltz, David. "Understanding Line Drawings of Scenes with Shadows." In *The Psychology of Computer Vision,* edited by Patrick H. Winston. New York: McGraw-Hill, 1975.

Weizenbaum, Joseph. Letter to the editor, *Science,* July 2, 1976.

Williamson, Jack. *The Humanoids.* New York: Avon Books, 1975.

————. "With Folded Hands." In *Science Fiction Hall of Fame,* vol. 2A, edited by Ben Bova, Garden City, N.Y.: Doubleday, 1973.

Winograd, Terry. *Understanding Natural Language.* New York: Academic Press, 1972.

Winston, Patrick H. "Learning Structural Descriptions from Examples." In *The Psychology of Computer Vision.* New York: McGraw-Hill, 1975.

Woods, W. A. "Progress in Natural Language Understanding—An Application to Lunar Geology." *AFIPS Conference Proceedings* 42 (1973): 441–450.

Woods, W. A., Kaplan, R. M., and Nash-Webber, B. L. "The Lunar Sciences Natural Language Information System: Final Report." BBN Report no. 2378. Cambridge, Mass.: Bolt, Beranek and Newman, 1972.

19
Current Research Frontiers in Computer Science

Alan J. Perlis

Most of the senior research scientists in the world were educated and began their research lives in a world in which there was no computer science. Some even incubated in a world in which there were no electronic computers. While modern developments have spawned new variants in sciences such as biology, chemistry, physics, and economics, their roots are still anchored firmly in the familiar pantheon. We are awed by the progress in these sciences, even somewhat unnerved by the portents they suggest, like nuclear holocausts, space colonization, and cloning. But man is unchanged—he still occupies the center of the stage, and any progress is intended for his benefit. It would seem the same would be the case in computer science, but here we are less sure. No earthshaking event, spawned from computer science, is in the offing. Yet we find that an "ecological" transformation, pulsed by computers, is underway. It is having a day-to-day effect on man and his society, here, now, and hereafter. Where the developments in physics deal with extremals (the very small, the very fast, the very large, the very short-lived, and the very distant), computer science studies the worlds we sense and create and think we understand and control. In these worlds many see computers coming to play roles as servants, junior partners, and potential masters. Although the last role must never arise, it makes sense to accept computers as servants and junior partners. The exploitation and acceptance of computers will be easier for us to digest if we understand what computer science is.

Computer science studies the phenomena that arise around, and because of, the computer. Without the one, the other would not exist. These phenomena vary in content, are dynamic, and are influenced by changes in the computer, changes in the environments surrounding computers, and, of course, results already obtained within the science itself. Com-

Alan J. Perlis is Eugene Higgins Professor of Computer Science and chairman of the Department of Computer Science at Yale University. He was for many years chairman of the Computer Science Department at Carnegie-Mellon University and is a winner of the Association for Computing Machinery's Turing Award.

puter science is developing with great rapidity. Those of us who have been privileged to witness its growth from inception to its present vital state seek to understand and exploit the pattern it has displayed. Certainly the signs are there for all to see; there is no shortage of data. What we should like to have is a model of the science's development, means for its validation, and the wisdom to evaluate and take advantage of its predictions.

The digital computer is now ubiquitous. In the future much of its presence will sink beneath our casual notice, as has the electric motor and the telephone. Note the intrusion of the computer into the home sewing machine, the radar range, and the automobile. From a world with no electronic computers to one with over half a million has taken twenty-five years, one human generation. How much of this growth has occurred because of computer science research? Most computer scientists would argue that very little of this "first growth" is a consequence of computer science research. It would seem to have been most prominently spawned from fundamental research in solid-state physics, electronics, classical numerical analysis, and mathematical logic. This is not surprising, since computer science, as an independent self-organizing system, is only about fifteen years old. It will be argued, however, that an important lubricant of this tempestuous initial growth was provided by research results in a field that was the precursor of an important part of computer science, the study of programming.

We are nowhere near the crest of the everywhere-evident flood of computer applications. Barring grotesque discontinuities in the development of our society, the computer will accelerate its intrusion into those of our personal, business, and social activities that have an appreciated and understood algorithmic component. In almost every case the intrusion of the computer into a device, a work scheme, or a recognized data-processing activity has quickly infected its host. Of course every invention has had an effect on its users, but for no other invention of our time has this effect been so quickly perceived as a first step in a sequence of translations. These changes from means, to ends, to means, leading to many unanticipated generalizations and previously unconsidered variations, make the introduction of the computer seem like stepping through Alice's looking glass into a new world, where means dominate ends, where syntax rules semantics, where everything is a special case of something more general, and where gravity is so weakened that with the expenditure of little energy or materiel, prodigious feats are ours to perform. So breathtaking are the consequences of this transformation that our need to understand it and optimize its payoff has defined the content of and much of the direction of research in computer science.

As with every other science, little but rhetorical organization is gained by isolating a fundamental group of topics and results from which all else is supposed to follow. Computer science has been variously described, and while there is no agreement on the primacy of any one view, two of them are worth mentioning here. The first sees computer science as studying the nature and consequences of the phenomena arising around and because of computers. Seen in this way it contains both theoretical and experimental components. Study is directed as much by the existing phenomena as they in turn are altered by the science. Such study involves a pragmatic mixture of at least engineering, physics, mathematics, economics, and psychology. It would seem, therefore, to be an applied activity, and not a science in the classical sense. Computer science, however, is so rich, so self-generative, and so widely applicable to the human condition, and at the same time so incompletely subsumed by any of its constituent disciplines, that we must treat it as a separate entity or risk not understanding it at all. There is little predisposition to limiting study to what can be treated formally or mathematically. It is recognized, however, that one goal of computer science research is formalization as a vital aid in identifying gradients for further research and product development.

A second view of the science springs from the subject of computer programming. By arguing that all traffic between, within, and on computers is mediated by programs, computer science is seen as being primarily concerned with studying the properties of abstract programs, called algorithms. There can be no doubt that the study of algorithms is at the core of computer science, and enormous progress has been made in this field during the last few years. A significant part of any theory of computation, computers, and analytic thought must be based on our understanding of abstract algorithms.

The two views coalesce when we recognize that what our algorithms can do on computers defines many of the phenomena that we observe around computers. Similarly, our external (to the computer, that is) needs for computers and computation suggest areas of algorithm analysis and synthesis that do not originate from within the study of algorithms themselves. As an example, what do we understand by the term *effective algorithm*? Based on the work of the logicians Post, Markov, Church, and Turing, an effective algorithm is defined as one that can be performed (done in a finite amount of time) on an abstract computer such as the Turing machine. However, the user of the computer is more attracted to a definition of *effective* that takes into account the resource requirements of algorithms. Somehow an algorithm should not be considered effective if its resource requirements grow too rapidly as its data increase in amount. The study of the resource requirements of abstract algorithms, called complexity theory, has come into existence because of the computer and the variety of tasks it performs, and not in response to problems posed purely in terms of mathematical logic.

Regardless of how we define computer science, research in its varied areas seems to follow similar patterns of development. The first efforts are directed toward appending an accomplishment to the computer—that is, to programs running on it. These first efforts are usually similar in form, technique, and purpose to those practiced in a less obviously algorithmic way by the human being. A second stage is the development of sophistication in the programs. An enormous amount of algorithmic structure is exposed. Its exploitation, matched to the computer's great speed, gives the programs capabilities that few humans can match. By the time the third phase begins, the program's accomplishments have made it a technical virtuoso, and as is the case with humans, generalizations and couplings to other human activities seem an appropriate next step. However, when we take it, the game suddenly changes. Algorithmic structure can no longer be developed in an orderly way. Either there is no evident algorithmic structure or there is too much, with no one dominant. Combinatorial chaos ensues. The programs, originally requiring little data, become dependent upon huge amounts of data that we do not have or do not know how properly to organize and supply. Progress becomes excruciatingly slow. We find ourselves depending on heuristics, rules of thumb based on weird mixtures of commonsense and knowledge deeply rooted in our technology. Each advance is not only laborious but leaves us feeling that we are farther from our initial goals than when we started. Our progress provides little comfort, since its chief and immediate consequence is to identify a need for programs we do not yet know how to organize and produce. We have embarked on a voyage through the Semantic Gulf, and research in the next decade will concentrate on methods for traversing it, just as the first decade of computer science research concentrated on the first two of the phases I have described.

Programming is a central concern of computer science. I shall treat research in the theory of algorithms separately from research in programming, for while the two topics are intimately related, their research uses different tools, has different goals, publishes in different journals, and employs different people. SIGPLAN, the Special Interest Group on Programming Languages of the ACM, now holds a yearly meeting with SIGACT, the Special Interest Group on Automata and Computability Theory, but these joint meetings may or may not have a beneficial effect on progress in coupling research in the two areas.

Programming research was first directed toward defining and producing aids to increase human programming productivity. Within the past twenty years, a vast number of programming languages has been produced. There have been languages tailored to particular audiences, like students, data-processing specialists, and engineers; languages created for particular areas of study, such as artificial intelligence, mathematical formula manipulation, and the building of programming systems themselves; and languages created to generalize sets of already existing languages, such as languages to fit tasks associated with certain types of computers. While new languages continue to be defined and processors for them implemented on computers, language invention no longer plays a major role in computer science research. We no longer believe that linguistic awkwardness is the root of our difficulties with the computer. However, mention must be made of a few recent language inventions, if only to show that such research is not moribund and its results are still of value to the field.

A group directed by A. A. van Wijngaarden of the Netherlands has created within the past few years a language of exceptional elegance—Algol 68. It generalizes in almost every way features provided by a number of earlier languages. It was designed as an "umbrella" language in the sense that all programming tasks could be "naturally" expressed in its terms. Unfortunately great resistance is being shown toward the use of this language, both in Europe and in the United States. Nevertheless, its development has focused attention on some important linguistic features: coercion, the transformations that match operators to operands; W grammar, a grammar with an unbounded number of syntactic production rules; and general parameter passing rules.

The flexibility of Algol 68 makes it possible to write programs whose correctness is hard to establish. Niklaus Wirth of Switzerland, believing that the writing of correct (i.e., probably correct) programs dominates almost every other aspect of programming, has designed a "projection" of Algol 68 called PASCAL. In a few years, PASCAL has become widely used for the expression of algorithms, and it is claimed that formal correctness proofs can be naturally organized in its terms. PASCAL is one of the few languages in wide use for which a formal semantic model exists. Whether use of PASCAL will noticeably enlarge the set of large programs whose correctness can be proved because of their linguistic and logical simplicity is yet to be determined. One observes that in many algorithms the proof of correctness depends on external theory, such as the mathematical results used in the algorithm. Hence proofs cannot be based only on the axiomatic meaning of the linguistic patterns as defined in the language.

Among the tasks requiring programming is the creation of operating systems and compilers. These are examples of systems controlling the processing of other programs. A number of languages have been defined to ease these tasks. A fundamental property of such languages is that among the programs constructible in their terms are those whose translations must match in efficiency (come close to equaling in code size and execution speed) any machine code program that might appear in a compiler or operating system. In practice, only a few such machine programs are crucial to any intended system. For the remainder of the system's programs, the language provides syntax and data structures that make their programming both simpler and less error-prone. Arbitrary machine code programs are unlikely to appear in systems. Hence one can absorb the small set of required program forms into the language by function. By affixing a suitable syntax to these functions, one may both think and program in terms of a system-building language harmoniously matched to the set of tasks for which it was created. The rub, of course, is that the set of tasks sooner or later comes to contain a "mutant" that disrupts the harmony and yet must be dealt with. Sometimes these mutants lead to extrapolative or interpolative changes of the language and its processor. An appreciation of the effect is incremental and builds nicely on our current processing model. However, there have been mutants that caused us to reorganize our vision of what our processors should be. Understanding now requires an act of generalization: we have two instances of processor structure. What is their common parent?

Users of a language abhor discontinuity. Orderly extension is what is desirable. All previously written programs should be unaffected by future change. One's current programming dilemma should be resolved to fit the distribution of one's programming requirements both now and hereafter. Perhaps the forces creating mutants are being damped out and may soon disappear. The forces leading to change include (1) radically new computer designs, (2) new user populations, (3) new applications, and (4) new understanding of the sense and purpose of computation.

Surely there must be a limit to the proliferation of new computer designs. In twenty years we have passed from large, synchronous, batch-oriented machines to the current lively mélange of computers of all sizes and specializations. Perhaps from now on, change in computers, instruction codes, and usage modes will slow down and stabilize, preparatory to ceasing. If this should occur, it will be because of economics and not because of the sterility of alternative products that applications suggest and componentry can produce. While there are some visible conservative trends in machine design, it is not the lack of radical new designs that will impede future language development. Instead, the conservative nature of user populations and the stationary nature of applications is already slowing language development. FORTRAN, glorious persistent weed that it is, not only survives, but its users become increasingly committed to it, even though theirs is often a love-hate relationship. Moreover, the style of programming and the nature of problem solving suggested by the use of FORTRAN has become so widespread that from FORTRAN has come our current view of what programming is. Languages such as Algol 60 and its derivatives serve better to structure this style. Only LISP and APL, among commonly used languages, allow for different styles of programming.

However, they are subject to pressures to conform to the FORTRAN style. Perhaps we are fortunate. In twenty years we have homed in on a stable model of programming that is natural and appropriate for our thought processes and our current and prospective needs.

As new applications arise, their constituent programs are being produced in the same FORTRAN style. New populations are educated in it. The investment in thinking, software, and hardware to support it is becoming so huge, measured by any economic index, that revolutionary change is now almost out of the question. In any case, new styles of thinking about programming do not seem to be emerging. In 1972, during a visit to China, I had hoped to find that the combination of the computer, an intelligent people, an established egocentric view of the world, and Mao's preachment of national independence and cultural isolation might have led to a view of programming substantially different from our own. Alas, Algol 60 dominated in China and is slowly being supplanted by FORTRAN.

Research in programming languages is concerned almost completely with enhancement of the FORTRAN style. What is this style? Fundamentally it produces programs that are execution-ordered sequences of weakly coupled subprograms, each of which consists of more of the same. The decomposition continues until a subprogram can be easily expressed in primitive linguistic constructs. Generally, sequencing at all levels is explicit. Few of the language operators combine in their definitions sophisticated control and arithmetic functions. Control is primitive, and there is no wish radically to extend it. When applications arise requiring new control constructs, such as concurrency within operating system descriptions, the new control structures are fitted as well as possible into our dominant model. By embedding such constructs, we are able to preserve and even reinforce our model of computation; we participate in a chain of graceful evolution. The harmony we insist upon gives the task of programming manageable proportions. Thus programming comes to be seen as an engineering activity whose progress, in all economically important directions, will be rapid and assured.

Most of the current research in programming is directed toward understanding and improving the engineering of programs, particularly large ones. A large program is seen as a system, a collection of communicating standard programs whose diverse combinations can perform a multitude of complex tasks by the setting of parameters. The initial step in the creation of such programs is specification: What is the system to do for us? Immediately we perceive a spectrum. There are systems for which our initial specification is close to our terminal expectations. Our conception of the tasks to be performed does not change much as the system comes into being; what we can do does not radically change what we will do or what we would like to do. However, there are also systems for which the act of specification cannot be divorced from the act of creation. What we do at one stage strongly determines not only what we should do next, but what we should have done already but did not. And of course there are systems whose construction history is episodic at both ends of the spectrum.

The first type of system is generally the latest in a line of a gradually evolving, and hence understood, sequences. The second type of system, just as obviously, is not. Compilers and operating systems are examples of the former. The systems erected in studying artificial intelligence problems are examples of the latter. As one would expect, the orientation of research on these two extreme types of systems is quite different. Much of the research on the first type of system is a consequence of how many and what kind of people build and use these systems, whose study is a part of what we call software engineering. Research is dominated by the desirability and necessity of standardization. We seek standard programming languages, standard decomposition techniques, standards of documentation, standards of testing, and standards for correctness proofs. We seek standard paradigms that cover the entire life history of a system, from inception to replacement by a generalization.

Our concern with structured programming, a phrase much with us these days, is but one manifestation of our need to understand and achieve standardization. It is now universally accepted that structured programming and the discipline it enforces on designer and programmer accelerates the construction of correct and stable systems. For those systems whose nature and organization we understand, an engineering discipline and industry is now coming into being. As it gathers practitioners, wealth, and prestige, software engineering will act as an increasingly conservative force on the entire subject of computer programming. This is as it should be, for standardization is a necessary precursor to increased automation of programming processes. Edsgar Dijkstra, largely responsible for exposing the importance of standardization of technique in system work, saw enforcement of structured programming (and what it implies) as the only way to stretch our limited intellects to master the ever-growing complexity of our systems.

As we have come to understand them, these systems have exposed a number of research problems of great interest. Problems arising from concurrency are being widely studied. One set of problems is concerned with minimizing the effect of "cross talk"; that is, guaranteeing the independence of multiplexed information streams that share resources. Various signaling techniques have been invented, and the plurality of these techniques has led to the study of problems of ordering their power and generalizing their capabilities. Another set of problems is concerned with maximizing the effect of cross talk, or maximizing the parallelism by which dependent tasks can be performed independently. With the advent of highly parallel computers (STAR, ILLIAC IV, STARAN), a thorough analysis of how serial algorithms can be speeded up through parallel execution is being studied.

A further set of problems arises out of the natural expansion of systems to cover computer networks. Problems arising in the management of single computer systems become aggravated when they occur in networks of computers. They are particularly difficult to solve when the networks are nonhomogeneous, as is the case with the ARPA network. Among the problems raised by computer resource sharing is guaranteeing the security of programs and the data in their systems. Not only military but internal revenue and industrial systems require secure systems. IRS is mandated by law to provide responses to some queries as long as the data requested is of a statistical nature. It is not even known if such systems can be guaranteed not to divulge specific information by analyses of sets of responses of a statistical nature.

At the other end of the spectrum are the systems we do not yet really know how to build, since they cannot be built in the same way as our familiar systems, nor are they built by the same kinds of programmers. For these systems, a basic issue is structure—discovering what it is, and inventing control structures is an important part of the design process. Redesign is likely, and highly talented programmers are needed to create such systems. The users and designers are identical. The successful systems depend very little on elaborate tool preparation intended for very general use. While successful systems certainly create their own tools whose utility is exportable, it is surprising how little these tools add to system progress. Nevertheless, the search goes on for general models that will accelerate the construction, reliability, and longevity of these systems. For example, Markov-like production systems are rediscovered every five years, and Newell has fathered a system-building language whose chief virtue is the complete control it gives the system builder over the machine on which it runs. However, no general theory of such systems exists. Each is ad hoc, and its success depends, more than anything else, on the energy and talent of the programmers. LISP is the preferred language for such systems, and its survival and general utility rivals that of FORTRAN.

Improving all aspects of system design and construction will be a continuing preoccupation of computer science. Of almost overriding importance is continuing improvement in our efficiency at writing code. Certainly we may expect both the average and maximum code size of systems to increase for the foreseeable future, as well as their logical complexity. Improving our ability to manage the larger groups of programmers required for these expanded tasks is one approach. In the long run, however, improving both individual proficiency and individual efficiency will be required. Several language efforts such as SETL and APL are directed toward providing these improvements. What is sought here is code compaction with a syntactic versatility that permits the semantic requirements of code to be expressed in a form that is universally and immediately understood. SETL, a language-design effort at the Courant Institute, seeks to obtain its leverage on controlling complexity by the use of sets as a fundamental data structure. APL and LISP use arrays and lists, respectively. The similarity of these three languages is immediately apparent: the key to complexity management is as much direct manipulation of data structures by natural operators as it is repetitive decomposition into ultimately simple standard units whose correctness is easily appreciated and demonstrated.

We observe in mathematics that successive abstractions carry their own notations. Mathematical abstractions soon attain a steady state in use of notation. The central ideas in the abstraction become expressed in a notation appropriate to the tasks undertaken and are not continually expressed in terms of lower concepts. As the abstraction takes form, so do its linguistic processors. I suspect that a similar search for syntactic equilibrium will always be before computer scientists in their pursuit of good software.

Continuing association with computers leaves one with mixed feelings of awe (so much is possible) and frustration (tasks could be accomplished so much more quickly if the proper tools were available). New tasks would demand no more than a trivial effort if the proper software were available. Furthermore, much software preparation is highly repetitious, particularly when software is shifted to new computers. Since at the present time new computers are not likely to be identical in word format and code structure to previous machines, to transfer software from an old to a new computer bootstrap techniques are commonly used. Software is programmed to be produced by a generator, and only the generator is reprogrammed for the new machine. But the generator is programmed by hand for each new machine.

Another approach is available, and it opens up a fascinating area of programming research. Suppose we have a language in whose terms we can specify computers. One such language is ISP, invented by Bell and Newell. Suppose we also have a machine-independent model of some information process. In particular, consider the process of assembling machine language programs. No model can be completely independent of some view of the computer, but suppose we can define a single program that, given an ISP description of a machine, will define an assembly language and produce an assembler for that machine. The program defines a machine assembly language and creates a translator for that language into the binary code that will execute on the given machine. We might characterize this exercise as one in automatic programming. We note that ISP was not designed for, nor was it specially adapted for, specifying machine properties in a form suited to the needs of our model. Furthermore, the set of machines to which this model applies is quite varied. We could characterize the model as being machine-independent. Assemblers map symbolic machine language into binary machine code and are very concerned with machine-dependent issues. Such an assembler generator has been created and has produced assemblers for a number of disparate computers.

This suggests a useful paradigm. We isolate a set of models (semantic descriptions) for various data-processing activities. I will name a few elementary activities: (1) control structures such as *if then else, case, while,* and *for* statements; (2) moving character strings within memory; (3) symbol table and stack management; and (4) management of certain standard data structures such as linked lists and arrays. If programs can be generated to perform functions such as these for a variety of machines, given their ISP descriptions, then the automatic creation of simple compilers for these machines will be feasible. Once we have manually constructed programs for these processes for several machines, we should be able to describe in a machine-independent way how to map their semantics into machine code. A large amount of future research in programming will deal with the creation of semantic models for information processing. These models are considerably simpler, though much like the conceptual dependency models created for natural-language processing.

Another important part of computer science is artificial intelligence (see chapters 17 and 18). While the name may offend some, the research work in this area is among the most thought-provoking in the science. Not all workers in this area are driven by the same motives, yet their results and techniques have a similarity that gives the field of artificial intelligence a strong identity. Artificial intelligence defines systems that perform functions on computers akin to those performed by human thought and considered to be creative. The research follows the same pattern of development described earlier. One can find current work struggling through each of the three phases.

As is true of no other part of computer science, the goals of some artificial intelligence research projects have caused many people to raise objections of an ethical and professional nature. Research on speech understanding can lead to programs that eavesdrop or deny us human contact in some telephone-regulated transactions. Such programs may also give the individual access to data sources that were previously only available at great expense. In any event, should the research be successful, its misuse may expose faults in our society that we are required to correct. It is not up to the programs themselves either to exploit or correct our social deficiencies.

Research progress in a highly technical activity such as creating programs to perform organic chemical syntheses does not demean the highly original art upon which program progress is based. Instead, the program provides a universally available background in which the original techniques can be organized and widely used. By contrast, research on programs that will tell simple stories in a version of the language of Shakespeare and Durrell is not literature and is not intended to be thought of as such. It is research into the attainable power of enormously replicated variation clothed in natural language. Time alone will tell whether our algorithmic creativity is sufficiently ingenious to create objects that satisfy some of our literary needs. Art interprets reality. When we confront art, sometimes we see the artist and sometimes the object, but in either case we learn not to confuse them with reality. We have learned that, for healthy people, art has at most the power to distort but not to replace reality. So it is with our evaluation of the great works of artificial intelligence and our judgments of how they relate to reality.

The study of algorithms is another aspect of computer science research. While mathematics has always dealt with algorithms—for example, Euclid's algorithm—computers have made algorithms numerous, complex, and important. Computer programs are the machine-executable representations of algorithms. Just as the study of universal computers led to the discovery of problems for which no computable function or algorithm could be found, so the study of algorithms has led to the discovery of problems for which all algorithms are inefficient. It is in the nature of our understanding of computation that these reasonable problems can possess only algorithms whose use of resources, principally time or storage, grows exponentially with the size of the algorithm's data. Naturally, a fertile area of research is to identify problems whose algorithms have exponential resource needs, to define classes of such problems, and to establish relations between classes that have similar computation efficiencies.

Every reasonable problem has a lower bound on the number of steps any of its algorithms require for solution as a function of its data, in particular as a function of how much data it has. In order to wash out the relevance of idiosyncratic red-tape operations, the resource requirements of algorithms are generally given in asymptotic terms with respect to the data. The customary mathematical notation $O(g(n))$ is used to indicate that a resource used is bounded by $cg(n)$ for a positive constant c, a data size n, and a positive increasing function of $n, g(n)$. Optimal algorithms are those that differ from the lower bound only in the magnitude of c, which may of course be of considerable practical importance for commonly occurring values of n.

While work in algorithms is mathematical in statement and technique, we should not be misled into believing that the results are of little or no importance to computer practice. On the contrary, they are fundamental. They reveal modes of problem formulation and problem solving that are and will continue to be basic tools in the thought processes of every computer scientist and specialist.

The burgeoning work in complexity has already exposed a wealth of results and problems that enrich both theoretical and practical developments in computer science. First, consider those computational processes that have arisen out of the natural discretizations of analytic processes, such as numerical solution of differential equations, zeroes of functions, and approximation theory. These processes must be reexamined to determine their complexity, and searches must be launched for optimal algorithms. Numerical analysis is becoming as concerned with computational combinatorics as with the long-standing issues of stability, order of approximation, and convergence.

One of the first surprising results of complexity theory was the result that matrix multiplications had a complexity $O(n^{2.81})$ and not $O(n^3)$, as had long been assumed and practiced. Similar bounds hold for matrix inversion and linear equations. Many of the linear system problems spring from discretization of low-order differential equations and lead to very sparse matrices. Much better results are possible for these cases than for the general situations. Furthermore, for these sparse systems the computations per step are small in number and simple, and the arrays are often large in order. The practical optimization must include the actual partitioning and transfer times between levels of computer storage.

Second, in those problems where optimal solutions are believed to be or known to be of exponential complexity $O(c^{g(n)})$, a search is being made for algorithms that yield solutions close to optimal but of polynomial complexity ($O(n^\alpha)$). Fortunately, many otherwise intractable problems yield good approximations that are computationally efficient. Obviously, we are at the threshold of important research in the "approximation of algorithms."

Third, complexity focuses attention on the importance of data organization to the performance of an algorithm. Data organization is now seen to be not primarily a matter of input convenience but a memory that is matched to the needs of the algorithm for tracking computational progress. For example, it is better for large n to have a data reorganization phase followed by a computation phase each of $O(n \log n)$ complexity than a simple computation phase of $O(n^2)$ complexity.

Fourth, complexity will have a major effect on programming languages. It is inconceivable that our current programming languages will not be altered to permit many of these grand and elegant algorithms natural and simple representation. Thus we note that Algol 60 programs for these algorithms are often quite obscure and the proofs of their correctness unnecessarily difficult. This seems to be particularly true in the case of algorithms for graph problems. A language like APL that derives its power and elegance from concurrent manipulation of array structures cannot adequately represent many of these optimal algorithms with the customary brevity of description.

Fifth, the nature of computational decomposition that these algorithms espouse is bound to affect the organization of the computer itself. In the age of integrated circuitry, the cost-effective increase in the internal complexity of our machines will be able to keep pace with the logical complexity of our good algorithms.

I remember reading a survey paper on information theory in which it was concluded that most of the theoretical developments in information theory had been ignored by practicing engineers. Two almost disjoint developments of the subject were taking place simultaneously. A similar state of affairs must not be allowed to occur between algorithms and programming.

Thus far, only a few general techniques for efficient algorithm invention have been identified. By far the most important is the principle of divide and conquer. Here a problem is divided into a small number (usually two) of smaller identical problems, and this solution process is used recursively. Often this can significantly reduce the complexity of a problem, for example, from $O(n^2)$ to $O(nlogn)$. Generally the greatest reduction is found when the reduced problems are of equal size.

Often the reduction process does not naturally lead from a problem of size n to two problems of size n/2, but instead leads to *n* problems of size n-1. In this latter case, to avoid exponential growth in complexity one often uses the method of dynamic programming to order the solution of such problems from the smallest to the largest, storing results en route so that the solution to no subproblem is ever computed more than once. Few other general techniques for reducing complexity are as yet known.

Some complexity results imply that certain problems are computationally intractable. Theorem proving by algorithms such as any of the resolution techniques has been an important activity in computer science for some time. It is an appealing approach since many computer problems can be phrased as theorem-proving tasks and the proofs used automatically to provide programs for solving the problem. Cook and Reckhow have shown that there are theorems (hence infinitely many) whose number of proof steps are exponentially long in terms of the theorem data (axioms). Some computer scientists use this and similar results as an argument against dependency on computer-driven theorem proving.

These results are an argument against theorem proving in the absence of a semantic environment organized to provide heuristics, establish subgoals, and reorganize itself as results accrue. At present only the mind of man provides such an adequate environment. Indeed only the minds of some men appear to be adequate for this task. Again a voyage on the Semantic Gulf beckons us!

Some years ago it was popular to use the phrase "man-machine symbiosis" to describe man's relationship with computer phenomena. Every advance in computer science, of both a positive and a negative character, reinforces the need to maintain some degree of partnership in problem solving between man and machine. Certainly we are continually enlarging and improving the set of programs available to us. But we must also recognize that the facile use of these environments must be continually improved by extending our individual capabilities to select, alter, and use complicated collections of programs. I would say that this is one of the fundamental activities of computer science education, at least in the university. It is not enough to educate people to understand and create algorithms. The computer scientist must be taught to manage and control the ever-shifting equilibria between our programs and our appetites. He must do so as an unashamed technologist viewing the world as much from inside the computer as he views the computer from the world without.

EDITORS' POSTSCRIPT

The reader should note that this article deals with traditional core issues in computer science. Thus relatively more specialized areas, such as artificial intelligence and scientific computation, are not extensively discussed. These topics are dealt with in the essays of Minsky and Fernbach.

V
Critiques

20
Once More: The Computer Revolution

Joseph Weizenbaum

Both the cost and the physical size of computer hardware are decreasing at an exponential rate. It follows from this that the very measures by which computers are classified as micro, mini, small, large, and very large are also constantly being readjusted. Today's so-called minis are functionally equivalent, at least roughly, to the most powerful large computers of only a decade ago, yet almost all their physical indices—for example, their bulk and power consumption—are a very small fraction of the corresponding indices of their ancestors, and so is their cost. It is almost as if the cost of computers as a function of their weight is a constant of nature—if, it must be added, the cost of much of their necessary peripheral gear is neglected. Another effect of this ongoing process is that computers of the size of the older large computers have many times as many components packed into them and are therefore functionally much more powerful while being no more expensive than their recent predecessors. This phenomenon is, of course, also reflected on the software side: the measures according to which programs are ranged from small to large are changing similarly. Programs that only a few years ago would have been classified as rather large are now shoehorned into mini and even micro computers, while on the other end of the scale, programs of hitherto unimagined size and complexity are developed for the newer giant computer systems.

One need have only ordinary, decent, American respect for the genius of the free market system in order to share the belief that these dramatic technological developments must inevitably induce a veritable flooding of the marketplace with computers. In the not too distant future computers will be as pervasive on the American scene as, for example, fractional horsepower electric motors are today. The analogy to these small engines

Joseph Weizenbaum is professor of computer science at MIT. Following technical work in the field since its early days, he is now interested in the societal consequences of computer use, a topic he discusses in detail in his book, *Computer Power and Human Reason.*

underscores, by the way, not only the magnitude of the expected flood but the fact that many of these computers will be, as are many of the motors currently in use in homes, unobtrusive parts of a wide variety of household gadgets.

The widely shared belief in technological inevitability, especially as it applies to computers, is translated by scholars and the popular media alike into the announcement of still another computer revolution. (It will be remembered that the past two decades have, according to these same sources, already witnessed one or two such revolutions.) This time, the much-heralded revolution will transform society to its very core, and a new form of society will emerge: the information society.

A question that appears to be asked only rarely is what pressing problems this inundation of technological fixes is supposed to attack. Certain problem areas *are* often identified, to be sure. There is, for example, some discussion of the drabness of modern society. This is seen by some computer scientists to be owing in large part to the deadly uniformity of most consumer goods (see chapter 3). This monotony could, it is argued, be relieved by "individualizing" products through the use of versatile manufacturing robots. Education is also raised as a problem area. Here it is occasionally argued that the visions of such thinkers as Dewey, Montessori, and Neill "fail in practice *for lack of a technological basis*. The computer now provides it" (my emphasis, chapter 5, "Computers and Learning"). But it is clear in these and other cases that the discussion is carried out in a mode of thought that has become altogether too traditional, especially among computer technologists: it begins with a great many solutions and then looks for problems. One consequence of this way of thinking is that it obscures real problems. The aimlessness of everyday life experienced by millions in modern society has deep roots in the individual's alienation from nature, from work, and from other human beings. As long as that is not understood and dealt with there can be no relief. To give everyone who can afford it a pair of shoes different from everyone else's and then advertise that achievement as a step toward the amelioration of some of society's deepest ills is not revolutionary; it is absurd. Similarly, the real problems to which people like Neill and Montessori actually addressed themselves are not functions of some "technological base," except perhaps in the contrary sense; that is, they might not be so stubborn were it not that schools exist in an already overly technological society. No fix, technological or otherwise, of the American education system that does not recognize that American schools are rapidly becoming America's principal juvenile minimum security prisons can be expected to have socially therapeutic effects. Giving children computers to play with, while not necessarily bad in itself, cannot touch this or any other real problem.

THE HOME COMPUTER

Enthusiasts for the home computer struggle with problems that could arise only as consequences of the triumph of the kind of mass-marketing techniques that gave us, for example, the multimillion-dollar deodorant industry. The product to be marketed is invented simultaneously with the dysfunction it is designed to cure. It is simply assumed that, what with the lowering of prices to below any conceivable threshold of consumer resistance, virtually every household will have a programmable computer. The "problem," then, is created by the solution itself: what are people to do with this appliance; what is it to be applied *to*? The electric carving knife, whatever its faults, at least answered that question for itself.

A typical essay on the home computer begins by assuming that there *are* computers in the home and then addresses the question of what they may be used for. The home computers foreseen are miniature versions of the kinds of computers that exist in the world at large, including, for example, freestanding computers on which anything at all may be programmed, computers equipped with prepackaged systems, and process-control computers. The issues that emerge from considerations of the computer in the home are much the same as those arising from the presence of the computer in modern society generally. Chief among these are what social—that is, political, cultural, educational, and so on—needs computers help satisfy today and what roles they are likely to play tomorrow.

Perhaps the first question to ask is just what fraction of American homes will have the kinds of computing machines typically envisioned. A standard analogy is to television. It is certainly true that essentially all American dwellings that could conceivably be called homes have at least one television set now. It appears to be true that many of the dwellings of the poor and even of the very poor have, whatever else they lack, a television set. Television, then, is an example of a technological gadget that has vindicated the marketeers who think in terms of consumer resistance thresholds below which it is possible to duck absolutely. It has to be noted, however, that the television sets of the poor are often purchased at a cost that is outrageous when measured in terms of what elementary necessities are given up.

Will the home computer be as pervasive as today's television sets? The answer must almost certainly be no. The picture of the home that emerges implicitly from the accounts of advocates for the home computer (it appears to be derived from television's own tedious so-called family dramas) is one of a middle-class, even an upper-middle-class, home (see chapter 1). The wall-to-wall carpeting needs to be cleaned by a robot; roasts are in the oven; the family is united by its preoccupation with toys, games, sports; the computer helps "the mother" pay the telephone bill; and so on. B. O. Evans, another computer scientist, imagines the same kind of home when he addresses himself to the home computer. In chapter 16 he writes,

For home use, terminals have potential for catalog ordering, activity planning, home library and education, and family health, including histories, diagnoses, doctors' specialty lists, and emergency procedures; family recreation, including music selection and games; career guidance, tax records and returns; home safety and property maintenance, including house plan retrieval, maintenance schedules, electrical and other physical facility layouts, and energy management; and budgeting and banking.

What and whose needs will be satisfied by the functions described here and by the ongoing proliferation of computers and computer controlled systems? What will be the indirect effects on a society that increasingly, possibly irreversibly, commits itself to being monitored and controlled by systems that even its own technostructure ill understands?

We may recall the euphoric dreams articulated by then Secretary of Commerce Herbert Hoover at the dawn of commercial radio broadcasting and again by others when mass television broadcasting was about to become a reality. It was foreseen that these media would exert an enormously beneficial influence on the shaping of American culture. Americans of every class, most particularly children, would, many for the first time, be exposed to the correctly spoken word, to great literature, great drama, to America's most excellent teachers, and so on. We are all witnesses to what actually happened. The technological dream was more than realized. Scratchy low-bandwidth radio was replaced by high-fidelity FM, then by stereo broadcasting of the finest sound quality. The tiny black-and-white television screen grew to impressive size and was painted in "living color." Satellite communication systems made it possible to display almost any event taking place, even in outer space, on television screens in homes anywhere on Earth. But the cultural dream was cruelly mocked in *its* realization. This magnificent technology, more than Wagnerian in its proportions, combining as it does the technology of precise guidance of rockets, of space flight, of the cleverest and most intricate electronics, of photography, and so on, this exquisitely refined combination of some of the human species' highest intellectual achievements, what does it deliver to the masses? An occasional gem buried in immense avalanches of the ordure of everything that is most banal and insipid or pathological in our civilization.

We are beginning to see this same calamitous script reenacted in terms of the home computer. Again we have the euphoric dream. But the heralds of its transmutation to disaster are already obvious: the market is inundated with computer games in which the players' main objective is to kill, crush, and destroy. We have spacewar, battleship, tank battles, and so on. I overheard an MIT graduate student who was deeply engaged in a game of spacewar with his fellow students say to them, "We ought to get more points for killing than for merely surviving." That statement seemed perfectly reasonable to all concerned. It may well be prophetic in a deeper sense than anyone present realized.

The home computer is in its current form merely a miniature version of the freestanding computers that today can be found in countless laboratories, business offices, and other enterprises. However, just as many of these computers are increasingly being interconnected to one another to form computer networks, so, according to most authorities, will home computers become, in effect, satellites of a variety of large computer networks. Only in this way would the home computers be able to access the large data bases needed for the tasks B. O. Evans visualized their function to be; for example, banking and catalog ordering. Indeed, many authorities believe that home computers that function in part as nodes of extensive computer networks will play a crucial part in the process of transforming our society into what Daniel Bell, professor of sociology at Harvard University, calls an *information society.*

THE INFORMATION SOCIETY

Bell is perhaps the foremost American social scientist to have written extensively on the information society. He sees it already: a child of the marriage between modern communication and computer technologies, of which existing computer networks are but the first issue.

Certainly, one foundation of the information society is knowledge. This Bell defines in chapter 9 as

. . . an organized set of statements of facts or ideas, presenting a reasoned judgment or an experimental result, which is transmitted to others through some communication medium in some systematic form. Thus, I distinguish knowledge from news or entertainment. Knowledge consists of new judgments (research and scholarship) or presentations of older judgments (textbook, teaching, and library and archive materials).

Elsewhere in the chapter he characterizes this definition as an attempt at an " 'objective definition' that would allow a researcher to plot the growth and use of knowledge." The inner quotes are, to his credit, Bell's.

What renders Bell's definition of knowledge nearly useless for the present purpose is that it is fatally (again, for the present purpose) circular and incomplete. What "facts," "experimental results," and "reasoned judgments" *are* is itself determined by the observer's organizing principles. This, the observer's Weltanschauung, is itself "knowledge," but a knowledge that is largely tacit and one that almost entirely escapes Bell's categories. Bell's definition is incomplete also in that it systematically excludes almost everything called knowledge in everyday life. People know a great many things that are neither products of research and scholarship nor materials in textbooks or archives, for example. They know what pleases people they see every day and what offends them. They know their way about their cities and what detours to take when the usual paths are blocked. (In fact, that kind of knowledge is closely analogous to a mathematician's knowledge of a special mathematical domain; mathematicians see shortcuts in the construction of proofs of theorems, for example, that they do not deduce logically but at which they arrive as a consequence of their deep general understanding of their domains. Taxi drivers in big cities know their domains similarly.)

Bell's perhaps unconscious willingness to exclude this kind of knowledge from consideration betrays, it seems to me, precisely the kind of parochialism that afflicts almost the entire intelligentsia, especially when it turns its attention to large-scale social problems. It betrays what for the intelligentsia is to count not only as knowledge but as fact. Bell himself gives a hint as to what these determinants are, and what they are not:

[The] upheaval in telecommunications and knowledge poses two economic-political policy problems, one structural, the other intellectual. The structural question is what kind of technical-economic organization is best designed to be efficient, meet consumer (*i.e., industrial, commercial, financial, scientific, library*) use, and remain flexible enough to *allow for continuing technological development.*

The second policy problem . . . is . . . the question of a national information policy, *particularly the dissemination of science (sic) and technical information.* [My emphases.]

For Bell, "the crucial variables of the post-industrial society are information and knowledge." And Bell with obvious approval attributes to the psychologist George A. Miller the observation that

. . . recoding is an extremely powerful weapon for increasing the amount of information that we can deal with. In one form or another we use recoding constantly in our daily behavior. . . .

Our language is tremendously useful for repackaging material into a few chunks rich in information. . . . the kind of linguistic recoding people do seems to me to be the very lifeblood of the thought process.*

I agree entirely.

What Miller had in mind when he spoke of "chunking" is the phenomenon that permits us to recall, say, the telephone area code of New York, not as the sequence of the three separate integers "2" and "1" and "2" but as the single number "212." Even more important from the standpoint of daily life, words like *mother, enemy,* and so on are not remembered merely as words, that is, letters chunked into aggregates, but as chunks that engage huge, often conflicting conceptual structures laden with emotional meanings. And of course these meanings come into play when human beings talk and otherwise communicate with one another in ordinary language. A welfare computer system may very well be able to dip

---

* This passage is from a longer version of Professor Bell's essay, to be published in 1979.

into its data bank and calculate that, say, five people occupy a particular household; it cannot understand what difference it makes in reality whether those five people are merely roomers who happen to share the rent burden, or a family. It may very well be able to deduce (from their last names, for example) that they are a family and jump, as computer specialists say, to a subroutine that treats them as a unit, in that sense chunking its data. Still, what it means in human terms to be a family cannot be part of the computed chunk.

Computer-based information systems *necessarily* induce recoding of data into information-rich chunks of precisely the sort Miller is talking about. But the recoding required for the computer, some of which computers commonly do by themselves, is such as to denude the original data of the nuances and subtleties that accompanied them and that determined their meanings while they were still cast in ordinary language. The "richness" of chunks created either by or for the computer is of a different, that is, a lower, order than that of their sources. As Bell himself says,

. . . if the purpose of a library, or of a knowledge-based computer program, is to help a historian to assemble evidence or a scholar to "reorder" ideas, then the very ambiguity of language must be confronted. Terms necessarily vary in different contexts and lend themselves to different interpretations, and historical usages shift over time (consider the problem of defining an intellectual, or the nature of ideology), making the problem of designing a "knowledge" program quite different from designing an "information" program . . . . A sophisticated reader, studying a philosophical text, may make use of the existing index at the back of the book, but if he is to absorb and use the ideas in a fruitful way, he has necessarily to create his own index by regrouping and recategorizing the terms that are employed . . . . *In this process, no mechanical ordering, no exhaustive set of permutations and combinations, can do the task.* [My emphasis.]

I believe Bell intended this passage to voice his conviction that there are limits to what computers can do, particularly that artificial intelligence cannot bring forth an artifact that exhibits the entire range of human creativity. After all, every computation is fundamentally a "mechanical ordering" based on permuting and combining its data. If that is his assessment, then I agree with it wholeheartedly. However, Bell seems to see this boundary as being relevant to only the most extreme fantasies of the leadership of the artificial intelligence community (the artificial intelligentsia), hence irrelevant to hard-nosed, practical current concerns. This is where he and I disagree.

SOME HARD QUESTIONS

The use of large-scale computer-based information systems induces an epistemology within which reigns an extremely poverty-stricken notion of what constitutes knowledge and what is to count as fact. Unfortunately, this same notion—a kind of pragmatic positivism bordering on scientism—dominates much of the thinking of modern intellectuals and political leaders. It has also, in my view, profoundly infected the thought of ordinary people. It has no *necessary* relationship to the computer; it existed, after all, long before there were computers. But the computer is its starkest symbolic manifestation. It is the instrument that, more than any other force, reifies it.

To see its influence one may turn to Bell's own examples.

Consider first the report of the Club of Rome, the *Limits of Growth* study, about which Bell writes,

What gave the Club of Rome study a degree of authority was the announcement that the authors had succeeded in modelling the world economy and carrying out a computer simulation that traced out the interconnections of four basic variables: resources, population, industrial production and pollution.*

Bell goes on to remark that the *Limits of Growth* study has been largely discredited. Nevertheless, the study had and continues to have "authority." But not every announcement of the completion of a study immediately lends that study the kind of great and far-reaching authority that the *Limits of Growth* immediately came to enjoy. It was not the announcement that lent authority to the study; it was the fact that the study was conducted by insiders of that very temple of high science and technology, MIT (which proudly characterizes itself as being "polarized around science and technology") *and* that the model being announced was done on a computer. Interestingly enough, Bell claims the *Limits of Growth* model to be discredited by the "unreliability of [its] initial data" and by "its simplified assumption of a linear, extrapolative growth." He never hints that this or any other model's difficulties might be more fundamental, located, for example, in their epistemological foundations. But then he appears to share those more basic assumptions.

Professor Jay Forrester, the main driving force behind this and similar models, has repeatedly revealed his models' epistemological foundations. For example,

. . . the human mind is not adapted to interpreting how social systems behave. . . . until recently there has been no way to estimate the behavior of social systems except by contemplation, discussion, argument, and guesswork.

The great uncertainty with mental models is the inability to anticipate consequences of interactions between parts of a system. This uncertainty is *totally* eliminated in computer models. Given a stated set of assump-

---

* This passage and the remarks in the paragraph that follows, are from the longer version of Bell's essay.

tions, the computer traces the resulting consequences without doubt or error. . . . Furthermore, any concept or relationship that can be clearly stated in ordinary language can be translated into computer model language.[1]

It is the widely shared belief in the epistemology expressed by these words that is, in my view, chiefly responsible for the acceptance of Forrester's and similar models.

Consider the impact of Forrester's words on the members of the U.S. Congress, to whom they were addressed, or on any other group of people who have no training in or intuition for formal systems. They hear that the basis of their thinking, mental models, leads to uncertainty, whereas Forrester-like computer models totally eliminate this uncertainty and all doubt or error. That is what they hear; it is not precisely what Forrester said. For he said only that given a system of well-formed equations, their solutions (if they exist) are unambiguously determined. And with that one cannot quarrel. But the word "doubt" is curiously out of place in this context. It is a word out of psychology, not out of mathematics or logic. Clearly, what Forrester really means to communicate is that because of the uncertainty inherent in them, one must doubt conclusions reached from mere thinking. Conclusions derived from computer models are valid beyond doubt.

The "stated assumptions" to which Forrester refers may be correct or they may be incorrect, but they must necessarily be incomplete. And their necessary incompleteness derives from exactly the same source as the incompleteness of the set of knowledge Bell is willing to admit into his calculus. The last sentence of the quotation reinforces this thesis; it implies that anything worth saying at all, hence worth knowing in Bell's sense, can be "clearly stated in ordinary language," hence "translated into computer model language."* It is on precisely this epistemological foundation that Bell rests his vision of the coming (or already present?) information society. For "the crucial variables of the postindustrial society," Bell argues, "are information and knowledge. By information I mean data processing in the broadest sense; the storage, retrieval and processing of data becomes the essential resource for all economic and social exchanges." Of course he envisions an extension of what is already true, namely the widespread use of computers to do the data processing in the information and knowledge society. Furthermore, almost all the processing will be done on data bases also stored in computer systems. These Bell characterizes as characteristics of populations: census data, market research, opinion surveys, election data, etc." But what about these data bases? Bell himself quotes Peter H. Schuck:

* In these circumstances one needs to recall Ionesco's remark, "Not everything is unsayable in words—only the living truth."

What is . . . disturbing, given the imminence of national economic planning, is the abject poverty of our economic statistical base, upon which a good theory must be grounded. In recent years the inadequacy and inaccuracy of a broad spectrum of economic indices—including the wholesale price index, the consumer price index, the unemployment rate, and business inventory levels—have become quite evident.*

The trouble is that the computer induces confidence (as in the Club of Rome report) and that it usually magnifies errors and their consequences enormously.

Another classic example comes from the much-touted command and control system in operation during the Vietnam War. "The mechanisms of [this system] were so complete," Bell says, "that basic tactical decisions (on military targets to bomb, or harbors to blockade) were controlled by political centers in the White House, ten thousand miles away, but transmitted in 'real time.' " However "complete" this system may have been, Admiral Moorer, then chairman of the Joint Chiefs of Staff, testified to the U.S. Senate Armed Services Committee that specially programmed computers in the field systematically lied to the Pentagon's computers with respect to the secret bombing of Cambodia. It was of course not some computer in the Pentagon that was misled by such lies—computers process information, not meanings—it was the policymaker who relied, or claimed to rely, on "what the computer says" whose decisions were gravely affected. As Admiral Moorer complained at the time, "It is unfortunate that we had to become slaves to these damned computers."[2]

It is instructive to note just how the U.S. Air Force computers in Vietnam whose function it was to maintain records of sorties flown, ordinance and fuel expended, and so on were made to lie to the Pentagon's computers in Washington. Computers in the field were programmed to automatically convert the geographical coordinates of targets struck by U.S. planes in Cambodia to coordinates of "legitimate" targets in Vietnam. Tapes of these allegedly raw though actually "cleansed" data were then forwarded to Washington to be entered into the Pentagon's computers. Highly placed Washington insiders who were permitted to see the summaries produced by Pentagon computers wrongly believed themselves to be gaining a privileged insight into what was actually happening in the field. Thus did the military create a textbook example of Orwell's Ministry of Truth; thus did it create history.

From a military point of view, this procedure raises serious questions of command and control. It raises even more general questions of responsibility and accountability in a highly technologized information society. Clearly, the technically relatively simple task of writing the coordinate

* The Schuck quote and Bell's comment on Vietnam are from the longer version of Bell's essay.

conversion programs had to be assigned by someone to someone. Perhaps the programmers who actually did the job were given their assignment in purely abstract form, without being told, that is, what the ultimate function of their product was to be; they may have been given merely a specification of a black box that was to exhibit certain input-output behavior. If so, then the programmers could deny responsibility for the consequences of their handiwork on the ground that they didn't know what they were doing. But should they not have inquired? On the other hand, perhaps they knew what they were doing but being in the military thought it their duty to follow orders—more importantly, perhaps they felt that duty removed all responsibility from their shoulders. Just what are the responsibilities of the mere technicians, or of engineers or scientists, in the information society?

Decisions crucially affecting people's lives are made with the aid of computer systems contaminated by a "broad spectrum of inadequate and inaccurate economic indices" and by systematic lies. If the programmers of these systems—and by extension their professional managers, systems analysts, and so on—are not responsible for the consequences of actions based on what these computer systems tell policymakers, and if policymakers are excused from responsibility on the ground that they merely relied on "what the computer said," then who is responsible?

This question poses what is at bottom a special case of the problem of individual responsibility and accountability that has been with us ever since human beings organized themselves into large social units. In modern times, it has manifested itself symbolically and actually most egregiously in the form of an Adolf Eichmann's claim of personal innocence based on the plea that he was "merely following orders"—as indeed were U.S. Air Force computer programmers in Vietnam—when he supervised the transportation of millions of human beings to death camps. Is there any *moral* difference between Eichmann's failure to confront what he was actually doing and the Air Force programmers' identical failure? We Americans puzzle over the circumstance that neither General Westmoreland nor Lieutenant Calley is responsible, nor is anyone else along the chain of command that unites them, for the men and women and babies Calley shot and killed with his own hand. Nor have any committees of the U.S. Congress nor anyone else been able to find any individuals in the U.S. military's chain of command who acknowledge accountability for implementing the disinformation machinery, to borrow a truly Orwellian term from the world's intelligence agencies, that systematically deceived at least some policymakers. In another sector of our affairs, we wonder how it can be that neither the workers on the assembly line nor the executives nor anyone in between is responsible when General Motors installs cheap Chevrolet engines in high-priced Oldsmobiles. Some of us can still be astonished by the spectacle of an American secretary of state publicly grieving over "the tragedy that has *befallen*" the Watergate criminals.[3] There appear to be no actors on stage, only anonymous events. We are, I believe, entitled to be at least a little skeptical of Admiral Moorer's characterization of the Joint Chiefs as victims of computers in the sense he apparently intended. Or are we to believe that the bombing of Cambodia was a secret even from them? More likely, Admiral Moorer was in this instance using the computer as an instrument to help create and preserve, in the picturesque phrase coined by the White House, plausible deniability.

The institutionalization on the most fundamental social and political levels of a systematic retreat from responsibility and accountability has no necessary relation to computers. However, the computer, and particularly the role advocated for it by many social scientists and computer intellectuals, amplifies and intensifies the problem and exacerbates its effects. Computer intellectuals are aware of this and sometimes give voice to their concern, but usually in ways that are oddly detached from present-day reality. For example, Professor Alan Perlis, head of Yale University's Computer Science Department, like most thoughtful computer scientists sees the computer as "having a day-to-day effect on man and his society," as pulsing an "ecological transformation" (chapter 19). He "sees (computer science) as studying the nature and consequences of the phenomena arising around, and because of, computers." Yet what will surely prove to be by far the most important of these phenomena, the transformations in man and society induced by the computer, are strangely absent from his and, I would say, the actual agenda of frontier research in computer science. It isn't that Perlis is totally unaware of some social and political problems that are sharpened by the application of certain computer technologies. For example he acknowledges, again as would many computer scientists, that "research on speech understanding [by computers] can lead to programs that eavesdrop or deny us human contact in some telephone-regulated transactions." (Indeed, the current press gives us abundant evidence that governments are already using computers to sort "interesting" communications from the mass of those they illegally monitor.) But then he dismisses the crucial problems raised by this development, such as the problem of responsibility and control, by saying, "It is not up to the programs themselves either to exploit or correct our social deficiencies." I suppose this is intended to absolve *programs* from any responsibility for any harm that may come from their use, just as bullets are not responsible for the people they kill. But not a word about the responsibilities of the researchers who put such tools at the disposal of a morally "deficient" society.

Professor Marvin Minsky of MIT, to give another example, confesses in chapter 18 that he is inclined to fear most the HAL scenario. [He is here referring to the computer on board the spaceship in Arthur C. Clarke's *2001*: The computer eventually wrested control from the ship's astronauts.] The first AI system of large capability will have many layers of poorly understood control structure and obscurely encoded "knowledge." There are serious problems about such a machine's goal structure: if it cannot edit its high-level intentions, it may not be smart enough to be useful, but if it can, how can the designers anticipate the machine it evolves into? In a word, I would expect the first self-improving AI machines to become "psychotic" in many ways, and it may take many generations . . . to "stabilize" them. The problem could become serious if economic incentives to use the unreliable early systems are large—unfortunately there are too many ways a dumb system with a huge data base can be useful.

Minsky believes himself to be talking about machines of the future, a future in which some of the most ambitious goals of artificial intelligence will have been very nearly realized. His "fear" is therefore abstract and has little if any influence on what he believes he or currently active workers with or designers of computer systems ought to worry about today. But if we, as we should, conceive of computer systems as including the people who manage and maintain them, then it becomes clear that the "unreliable early systems" Minsky rightly fears are already very much with us and that the economic incentives to use them are, for many organizations, already insuperably large. And millions of people would probably agree that our self-improving "machines"—where that word is taken in the large sense—have already become psychotic. But do we have the many generations' time to "stabilize" them? Are these, indeed, the systems we want stabilized?

It is simply a matter of fact that almost all very large computer systems in use today *have* "many layers of poorly understood control structure and obscurely encoded knowledge." It is simply no longer possible for these systems' designers—or for anyone else—to understand what these systems *have* "evolved into," let alone to anticipate into what they *will* evolve.

Large computer systems typically are not designed in the ordinary sense of the word *design*. To be sure, they begin with an idea—a design, if you will—which is then implemented. But they soon begin to undergo a steady process of modification, of accretion to both their control structures and their data bases, which changes and continues to change them fundamentally. Typically too, this sort of surgery is carried out not by the original programmers but by people who come and go from and to other assignments. As a result, there are, again typically, no individuals or teams of people who understand the large systems to which they have contributed their labors. Modern large-scale systems have no authors; they have, in Minsky's words, simply *evolved into* whatever they have become. Robert Jastrow, director of NASA's Goddard Institute for Space Studies, boasts of systems of precisely this sort, in complete disregard of the dangers inherent in their use. when he asserts, "Computers match people in some roles, and when fast decisions are needed in a crisis, they often outclass them."[4]

Professor Minsky long ago absolved *programmers* of credit and responsibility for whatever effects may issue from the incomprehensible systems they may create on precisely the ground that their systems *are* incomprehensible:

[The] argument, based on the fact that reliable computers do only that which they are instructed to do, has a basic flaw; it does not follow that the programmer therefore has full knowledge (and therefore full responsibility and credit) for what will ensue. For certainly the programmer may set up an evolutionary system whose limitations are to him unclear and possibly incomprehensible.[5]

What does it mean to understand a computer system at all? In chapter 18 Minsky correctly points out that "[to] 'understand' . . . implies . . . some sort of schematization—a getting at the basic principles rather than attending equally to all details, however small. In that sense, 'understanding' means understanding an idealized model of something rather than the thing itself." Minsky comes very near to saying here that to understand something complex is to have an economical theory of the thing—and in this I would agree with him. To know every line of the code that constitutes a large computer program is not necessarily and not even probably to understand the program. A theory of what the program is supposed to do is required in order to be able to tell, for example, when the program is malfunctioning; in other words, to understand it. But it is precisely this form of understanding that is rendered impossible by the very way large computer systems are constructed—unless, that is, the computer systems in question are based on robust theories from their inception to their current state of evolution. There are very few such computer systems outside the domain of scientific computing. We are thus in precisely the situation Minsky fears: designers cannot anticipate what their machines will evolve into. And that is, as Minsky observes, a "serious problem." Once one understands the seriousness of the problem, one must surely be led to wonder what Bell had in mind when he wrote, "Obviously, the information explosion can only be handled through the expansion of computerized and subsequently automated information systems." Perhaps a better course would be to attempt to contain the information explosion. Programmers can make a contribution and in the process gain a sense of responsibility and dignity by refusing to add to systems whose purposes and theories of operation cannot be explained to them. How else, by the way, could programmers possibly be sure that they are not working on systems to whose ultimate purposes they could not reconcile their consciences?

Are there technical solutions to the problem presented by essentially incomprehensible computer systems? It seems to me there are not. Clearly, to accept one's responsibilities is a moral matter. It requires, above all, recognition and acceptance of one's own limitations and the limitations of one's tools. Unfortunately, the temptations to do exactly the opposite are very large. It is true, as Minsky observes, that even dumb systems can be of considerable use. Their uses are encouraged when, in the short run, they benefit their users, while the harm they cause to others is remote and largely invisible. Moreover, architects of systems that initially appear to function well are usually richly rewarded until and often even long after their systems' faults have become obvious and the harm they have done has become irreversible. This last observation holds true even for systems that have nothing directly to do with computers: witness, for example, the fate of the coterie of American "statesmen" who led America into the Vietnam war.

On the other hand, the impressive number of comprehensible though large computer systems that exist in the scientific domain, in chemistry, physics, mathematics, and astronomy, teach us that incomprehensibility is not a necessary property of even huge computer systems. The secret of their comprehensibility is that these systems are models of very robust theories. One can tell when they go wrong, for example, because the errors they then produce result in behavior that contradicts their theories. What this should teach us is that the construction of reliable computer systems in the social and political sphere awaits not so much the results of research in computer science as a deeper theoretical understanding of the human condition. The limit, then, of the extent to which computers can help us deal with the world of human affairs is determined by the same thing that has always determined such limits: our ability to assess our situation honestly, and our ability to know ourselves.

ARTIFICIAL INTELLIGENCE

No discussion of the role computers are to play in the emergent information society would be complete without an appraisal of the state of and the hopes for artificial intelligence (AI). This must be because the ethos of so much of the rest of the computer practicum is now pervaded by the spirit—and by what little substance there is—of AI. There is talk not simply of robots but of intelligent robots, not simply of home computers but of intelligent home computers; kids in school will have AI at their disposal and even help create more of it. Dr. Sidney Fernbach, previous head of the Lawrence Livermore Laboratory's Computation Center, one of the world's largest computation facilities, in chapter 8 invokes an absurd vision of AI's potential use in science and in education that gives an idea of what leading computer managers expect from their instruments:

The scientist experiences and learns to understand physical phenomena throughout his entire life, but his most active years for thought are relatively few. The experiences of large numbers of scientists can be put into the data banks of computer systems, and *the computers can then be programmed to sort through all this information and come up with "original" ideas. . . .* Thus far I have provided for bookkeeping functions, data retrieval, problem solving in both numeric and analytic bases, and *a reasoning system stocked with all the scientific knowledge in the world.* This latter system should not be restricted to science alone. Our educational facilities in general need to have the information in the Library of Congress at the fingertips of teachers and students. This could be the greatest educational tool in the world. [Emphases mine.]

Artificial intelligence, much like real intelligence, has been extraordinarily resistant to attempts to define it with precision. But there seems to be general agreement that however else intelligence manifests itself and whatever else it may be, a necessary property of it is that it must be able, to use Fernbach's words, to "come up with "original" ideas." There is also a widespread consensus that the production of original ideas has much to do with the application of analogies and metaphors. As Minsky says, ". . . in analogy lies the secret of really useful learning, a way to apply something learned in one situation to a problem in a quite different area." Minsky then goes on to discuss a program written by Thomas Evans, then one of his students, "that proposed solutions to geometric analogy IQ test problems and achieved performances resembling those of teen-agers— although, of course, only in this restricted microworld." Obviously, Minsky thinks this program to be of very great importance to AI. I know of few papers or books Minsky has written or talks he has given since this program was written (1964) in which he has not emphasized its importance.

This is not the place to discuss the Evans program in detail. Suffice it to say here that the program is given descriptions of two geometric figures A and B, the source figures, and a small set of target figures, say C, D, E, and F. The problem is to select one of the figures D, E, or F such that C is to the selected figure as A is to B. A and B may be related in that, for example, some subfigure of A, A1, is *above* another subfigure of A, A2, while in B the corresponding subfigure B1 is to the *right* of B2. The possible relations between the subfigures of A are above, left, and inside. A2 may also be smaller or larger than A1, or it may be rotated or reflected or be some combination of these relationships. Given that the set of possible relationships of subfigures to one another is very small, it is possible to specify rules that govern how source figures are transformed. The program's problem then becomes to find a rule that transforms C into one of the target figures, such that that rule most closely resembles the rule that transformed A1 into A2 in the original problem statement.

A metaphor is fundamentally a borrowing between and intercourse of thoughts, a transaction between contexts.[6] The extent of the creative analogical reach of a metaphor is always surprising. Its power to yield new insights depends largely on the richness of the contextual frameworks it fuses, on the potential mutual resonance of disparate frameworks. Newton fused the contextual framework consisting of the behavior of everyday objects in the material world, like apples falling to the ground, with that of the solar system, and produced the remarkable idea that the moon is falling to Earth.

Do the processes embodied in Evans's program have much to do with whatever processes may exist for coming up with original ideas by the use of analogy and metaphor? This is an extraordinarily important question in view of the stress Minsky places on Evans's program, for in effect Minsky claims that Evans's program and those that have followed the general methods it pioneered are achievements in a progression that terminates in the realization of true computer creativity. We recognize that the firecracker of the ancient Chinese was such an achievement in the progression of technologies that led to the moon landings, but that mountain climbing, no matter how much nearer it brings the climber to the moon, can never be such a step. The question then is whether the kind of analogy programs on which Minsky appears to be betting so heavily are more like firecrackers than like mountain climbing.

The answer seems to me to be obvious. Truly creative thought, to the extent that it is based on analogical and metaphorical reasoning—and it is a very large extent—gains its power from the combination of hitherto disparate contexts. The act of creation is that of selecting from among the infinitude of similarities shared by every pair of concepts precisely those two frameworks that shed the maximum illumination on one or both of them. The AI community will readily agree that the analogical reasoning programs AI has produced so far are *given* the relevant criteria of similarity they need—that is, the two frameworks that are to be fused. This is not to criticize the quite clever programs produced to date; it is rather to illustrate on what profoundly and fundamentally misguided bases some of the most crucial concepts of AI are built.

CONCLUSION

The computer in its modern form was born from the womb of the military. As with so much other modern technology of the same parentage, almost every technological advance in the computer field, including those motivated by the demands of the military, has had its residual payoff—fallout— in the civilian sector. Still, computers were first constructed in order to enable efficient calculations of how most precisely and effectively to drop artillery shells in order to kill people. It is probably a fair guess, although no one could possibly know, that a very considerable fraction of computers devoted to a single purpose today are still those dedicated to cheaper, more nearly certain ways to kill ever larger numbers of human beings.

What then *can* we expect from this strange fruit of the human genius? We can expect the kind of euphoric forecasting and assessment with which the popular and some of the scientific literature is so abundantly filled. This has nothing to do with computers per se. It seems rather to be characteristic of a peculiarly American tradition of thought. We have seen many other examples of it, and these may be instructive. Americans thought that universal schooling—not to use the term education—would lift the masses by their bootstraps and ensure a happy, prosperous, democratically governed society. This dream was realized in substance; that is, almost all American youngsters are today forced to attend school during the whole of their adolescence. But the American primary and secondary school has become not a center of learning, not even a center where elementary reading and writing can be taught. It has become, as I noted earlier, a minimum security prison in which millions of children and adolescents are contained for a considerable fraction of each of their days. Government reports document that America's young people are largely functionally illiterate. As a university professor, I can testify that not many youngsters recruited from among the best and the brightest can compose a single paragraph of standard English prose. As for democratic governance, a recent HEW study revealed that nearly half the sampled high school graduates did not know that their representatives in the Congress were elected, let alone who they are or what terms of office they serve. Other examples of dreams that have been realized in a technical sense but have spawned disasters in place of the social bounties they foretold can be cited from medicine, urban planning and architecture, mass transportation, and so on.

We can also expect that the very intellectuals to whom we might reasonably look for lucid analysis and understanding of the impact of the computer on our world, the computer scientists and other scholars who claim to have made themselves authorities in this area, will, on the whole, see the emperor's new clothes more vividly than anyone else. They will shout their description in the most euphoric terms. Some of us will find their accounts unrealistic, not because of mere differences of opinion but because their accounts are plainly silly. For example, in chapter 11 the distinguished Princeton professor of public and international affairs Robert Gilpin writes,

. . . in order to exercise power, a nation must be able to process vast amounts of data. The classic case in point is the Arab petroleum boycott against the West following the October 1973 Arab-Israeli war. Without sophisticated data-processing capabilities, the Arab oil producers *could not have* kept track of Western oil tankers, refinery output, and all the other information needed to enforce the embargo. Moreover, given the complexity of the oil industry and the potential for cheating by cartel members, it is doubtful if the Organization of Petroleum Exporting Countries (OPEC) would remain intact without the benefit of electronic data processing. [Emphasis mine.]

Oil tankers spend weeks at sea. An old-fashioned clerk with a quill pen could keep track of them on the back of a few large envelopes. And there have been effective cartels since at least the rise of modern capitalism, long before there were any electronic computers.

It is not necessary to credit computers for accomplishments with which they have nothing to do. They can be realistically credited with having made possible some easing of the lives of some people. Modern airline reservation systems, for example, have made it easier for me to travel. Herbert Simon believes that computers are raising the level of expertness in decision making on complex matters (see chapter 10). I would suggest, however, that Admiral Moorer might be asked his opinion on that point. There is no question that computers have helped enormously to extend our vision of our corner and even the farther corners of the universe; I have in mind both that computers have radically transformed many aspects of astronomy and that without computers space flight, hence the dramatically symbolic picture of the earth floating in space, would have been impossible. Many other examples could be given of how and in what ways the computer has done some good. But some questions are almost never asked, such as, Who is the beneficiary of our much-advertised technological progress and who are its victims? What limits ought we, the people generally and scientists and engineers particularly, to impose on the application of computation to human affairs? What is the impact of the computer, not only on the economies of the world or on the war potential of nations and so on, but on the self-image of human beings and on human dignity? What irreversible forces is our worship of high technology, symbolized most starkly by the computer, bringing into play? Will our children be able to live with the world we are here and now constructing? Much depends on answers to these questions.

NOTES

1
United States, Congress, House, Committee on Banking and Currency, Hearings before the Subcommittee on Urban Growth, October 7, 1970, 91st Congress, 2nd session, pp. 205–265.

2
New York Times, August 10, 1973.

3
"The Wide World of Watergate," *Newsweek,* August 20, 1973, p. 13.

4
"Toward an Intelligence beyond Man's," *Time,* February 20, 1978, p. 59.

5
"Steps toward Artificial Intelligence," in *Computers and Thought,* ed. Edward A. Feigenbaum and Julian Feldman (New York: McGraw-Hill, 1963), p. 447.

6
I. A. Richards, *The Philosophy of Rhetoric* (Oxford: Oxford University Press, 1936), p. 93.

A Reply to Weizenbaum   Daniel Bell

To invoke an old Russian proverb, Mr. Weizenbaum is knocking down an open door. He sets up a confrontation between the "technologist" and the "humanist" and, having recently made the crossover, he is angry and harsh with those who seemingly do not share his new enthusiasm. More regrettably, he adopts the tactic and even the tone of the heresy hunter to sniff out—usually by pouncing on statements taken out of context—technological hubris and to berate this attitude as being morally blind. That is a pity. Since I share many of Mr. Weizenbaum's concerns, I wish he had written with a pen, not a large paintbrush.

In his thick strokes, Mr. Weizenbaum fails to make some necessary distinctions. The first centers on the understanding of the word *knowledge*. Mr. Weizenbaum, like any tyro in epistemology, begins with the statement that "acts," "experimental results," and "reasoned judgments" are themselves determined by the observer's organizing principles. He seems to think that such a statement necessarily disproves the idea of objective knowledge. But this is to confuse the source of knowledge with its validity. Would he have us believe that all knowledge is completely relative? That there is *no* basis for deciding which knowledge is better than other knowledge? He points out, quite understandably, that much knowledge is tacit knowledge. But the scientist-philosopher who did most to establish the idea, Michael Polanyi, then went on to assert most emphatically that tacit knowledge becomes translated into public knowledge by the process of open discourse—debate, testing, and evaluating—which is the very process of science, what Polanyi has called "the republic of science."

Since Mr. Weizenbaum does not follow through with the logic of his own argument, it is not clear what he is driving at. He would seem to be saying that what everyone knows may be knowledge, and it is only the parochialism of the "intelligentsia" that would rule out the knowledge that the "masses" (i.e., the taxi drivers) possess. This is the kind of populism that would lead us to abolish all schools in favor of the street knowledge that the tough minds pick up so readily as "street smarts."

If I can make sense of his remarks, let me distinguish between two issues. First, Mr. Weizenbaum is coming close to the argument that there is probably no objective knowledge, is seemingly (I have to make these qualifications, for none of his arguments is fully stated) equating objective knowledge with fixed or absolute knowledge. But clearly this would be an absurdity. The stoutest defender of the idea of objective knowledge in the contemporary philosophy of science, Sir Karl Popper, is also the strongest proponent of the argument that all knowledge is tentative, conjectural, hypothetical, exploratory, incomplete. In fact, in dealing with Hume's challenge to inductivism, Popper admits that no theory can ever be accepted as true. Then what is objective knowledge? It is knowledge that is *testable* by its ability to set up some criterion by which it could be falsified. As Popper has said, "*Ad hoc* explanations are explanations which are not independently testable; independently, that is, of the effect to be explained. . . . the testability of a theory increases and decreases with its *informative content* and therefore with its *improbability* (in the sense of the calculus of probability). . . . a man of practical action has always to *choose* between some more or less definite alternatives, since even *inaction is a kind of action*. Which theory shall a man of action choose? Is there such a thing as *rational choice*? . . . . there is no 'absolute reliance'; [yet] since we *have* to choose, it will be 'rational' to choose the best-tested theory."[1] The controlling term for both Polanyi and Popper (though the two differ in many significant respects) is critical rationalism. That is the basis for "objective knowledge."

The second issue Weizenbaum raises is why, in my definition of knowledge, I excluded such street knowledge as the taxi driver's or the intuitive knowledge of a mathematician regarding proofs of a theorem. The simple point is that a definition is related to a purpose. I was not giving an absolute definition of knowledge. The purpose was instrumental, namely, what kinds of knowledge could be measured, stored readily, retrieved, and used within an instrument that could be designed for that purpose. I do believe that judgmental knowledge and evaluative knowledge cannot be ordered in the form that some computer scientists believe. Mr. Weizenbaum, who is apparently so fearful of any concessions to the computer, italicizes a phrase of mine to indicate that I am making only "limited" concessions to the "most extreme fantasies." Mr. Weizenbaum is simply pushing harder on the open door.

If Mr. Weizenbaum is a cognitive relativist in one realm, he is a moral absolutist in the other, and as simplistic in the latter as he is in the former. Leaving aside the heavy-handed analogy between Eichmann and the Air Force programmers—another use of a paintbrush rather than a pen—there are two distinctions that arise in the relation of technology to society and technology to moral problems. The first is the point that technology is not a "reified thing" or some abstract "logical imperative" but is embedded in a social support system, and it is the support system, not the technology, that determines its use. One can, with the same technology, design totally different outcomes by designing different social support systems. To take the example of the automobile, one can have a system of complete private ownership and the large degree of personal mobility it affords yet suffer a large social cost in the amount of garage space needed or pollution of the air. But another system deploys automobiles as a public utility; one takes an automobile from widely dispersed pools or stations throughout a city, uses it as needed, and leaves it at another station near one's destination. The technology is the same, yet the pattern of use is highly dissimilar. The crucial decisions are sociological, not technological.

The second problem, however, arises from that very fact. It is often said, "We have been able to go to the moon, why can't we build better houses, or design a better curriculum, or assure a better health system?" The point is that getting to the moon is largely a technical problem, but the other, social questions frequently involve a difference if not a clash of values. We may say that individuals have a right to determine the decisions that affect their lives, yet if a community insists that busing its children to schools outside the neighborhood disrupts its own community patterns, the problem is compounded because we have a conflict here between community decisions and racial integration. Or if we say that places in a medical school should be allocated on the basis of cultural disadvantage to a stipulated number of minority persons, even at the expense of the merit principle, it is not a matter of right versus wrong but of right versus right. This is what makes moral decisions so difficult. And these are the hard questions.

I fear that Mr. Weizenbaum has misread my essay. In my work on postindustrial society, I have reiterated the point that a change in the technoeconomic order (and that is the realm of information) does not *determine* changes in the political and cultural realms of society but poses questions to which society must respond. In the Commission on the Year 2000, which I chaired for a decade, the insistent point of the enterprise was that the effort to plot alternative futures or the likely outcome of the present is not to stipulate the future but to widen the sphere of moral choices. In my essay in chapter 9—and it is a single essay, not the world—I have sought to deal with the way in which a change in the infrastructure of a society—in this instance, the expansion of a communications system—begins to have societal effects whose consequences must be understood in order for a society to make intelligent policy choices.

I can understand Mr. Weizenbaum's moral concerns, but he puts these forward with the hyperbolic fervor of a convert, and in this case I fear that his sermon is misdirected. Many years ago, Norbert Wiener wrote a book with the fetching title *God and Golem.* Mr. Weizenbaum fears that the computer may be a Golem, a clay monster into whom life has been breathed. That may well be, though I doubt it. In any event, fearing the Golem, one should not try to play God, or his prophet. The secular tasks of the world are difficult enough.

NOTE

1
Karl R. Popper, *Objective Knowledge* (Oxford: Clarendon Press, 1972), pp. 15–16, 17, 21–22.

Another Reply to Weizenbaum

Michael L. Dertouzos

Weizenbaum's main premise is his concern with ". . . a mode of thought that has become altogether too traditional, especially among computer technologists: it begins with a great many solutions and then looks for problems." This chastizing of technological opportunism is particularly appealing to the public in today's climate of dwindling energy resources, questionable nuclear reactor safety, and other technology-related problems of our increasingly complex and technology-dependent society. It further suggests the existence of a far more appealing methodology: worthy societal goals are first identified and then relentlessly pursued with the massive resources of scientific research.

Unfortunately it is not the technologist but rather science itself that cannot always satisfy preset goals, as evidenced by our as-yet-unsuccessful attempts to overcome cancer. As many scientists know, scientific discovery is very often the result of a well-timed accident or the by-product of the pursuit of an altogether different goal. Even the intended use of a scientific discovery does not necessarily forecast the consequences of subsequent uses. Take for example radar, which was developed during World War II. Application of the implicit Weizenbaum doctrine would have characterized that development as societally questionable, since its intended function was to help wage war. Yet, the safety of today's worldwide air transportation system rests on that earlier development.

What is it then that we as technologists should do? To begin with, we should not engage in technological research that clearly violates our moral and legal codes, as in the use of human guinea pigs in potentially dangerous experiments. However, the bulk of scientific and technological research is not blessed with such clear and early indicators. Take the internal combustion engine, for example, or nuclear power, or behavior-changing drugs. If we ask ourselves today whether these developments have, on balance, helped or hindered the pursuit of worthy societal goals, we are at best in a quandary even though we have lived with these technologies for many years. How, then, in view of such retrospective ignorance can we ever hope to assess the prospective benefits of a contemplated invention let alone look purposefully for a beneficial one that will solve some of our problems?

To my mind, we should follow a dual policy: encourage scientific discovery and control its applications as they evolve. Only through such an approach can we ensure that we will neither miss potentially useful, nor abuse potentially harmful, applications. Accordingly, the motivation of the technologist, whether in trying to solve pressing problems or looking for problems that fit solutions, is more a question of personal preference than a determinant of ultimate results. More specifically, we have no compelling reasons at this time to suppress the development of technologies that will make possible information networks, computers in the home, or, my favorite theme, computer individualization of products and services. To do so is to assert that the consequences of these developments will be more hazardous than beneficial—and we do not know that at the present time. Instead, both the scientists and the lay public should be encouraging research as well as increased awareness and continuous scrutiny of foreseeable consequences of our technological breakthroughs. The controlling mechanisms of society—be they preferential, legal, or economic —will then determine what applications we should or should not pursue.

Contributors

Kenneth J. Arrow
Harvard University, Cambridge, Mass.

Daniel Bell
Harvard University, Cambridge, Mass.

Marvin Denicoff
Office of Naval Research, Arlington, Va.

Michael L. Dertouzos
Massachusetts Institute of Technology, Cambridge, Mass.

B. O. Evans
IBM Corporation, Valhalla, N.Y.

Sidney Fernbach
Lawrence Livermore Laboratory, Livermore, Calif.

Robert G. Gilpin
Princeton University, Princeton, N.J.

J. C. R. Licklider
Massachusetts Institute of Technology, Cambridge, Mass.

John McCarthy
Stanford University, Stanford, Calif.

Marvin L. Minsky
Massachusetts Institute of Technology, Cambridge, Mass.

Joel Moses
Massachusetts Institute of Technology, Cambridge, Mass.

Nicholas P. Negroponte
Massachusetts Institute of Technology, Cambridge, Mass.

Roger G. Noll
California Institute of Technology, Pasadena, Calif.

Robert N. Noyce
Intel Corporation, Santa Clara, Calif.

Seymour A. Papert
Massachusetts Institute of Technology, Cambridge, Mass.

Alan J. Perlis
Yale University, New Haven, Conn.

Martin Shubik
Yale University, New Haven, Conn.

Herbert A. Simon
Carnegie-Mellon University, Pittsburgh, Pa.

Victor A. Vyssotsky
Bell Laboratories, Piscataway, N.J.

Joseph Weizenbaum
Massachusetts Institute of Technology, Cambridge, Mass.

Terry Winograd
Stanford University, Stanford, Calif.

Index

Programming research, 425–426
current emphasis on improving program engineering in, 428–429
differences in research in theory of algorithms and, 425
new area of, 431–432
Programming system types, 429
Programs, 46
control structures and, 414–416
distinction between programming and
use of, 62–63
proving, 383
reproducibility of, 393
ways to represent knowledge and pro-
cesses in, 408–409
Project Charles, 243
Project Hartwell, 243
Project Vista, 243
Propaedia, 192
Propagation delays, 329
Proprietary commercial functions, 92
Proxima Centuri, The (artwork), 31
Public opinion, 223–226
Public policy, 218, 266–270
Public transportation, computer-
monitored, 113
Public utilities, 88
Public utility regulation, classic, 254–
255
Pythagoreans, 192

Qualitative areas, 405–406
Quantum chemistry, 147
Quasi-information industries, 183
Queuing models, 381
Q-32 computer, 373
Quillian, 412
QWERTY phenomenon, 79–80

Radar warfare, 98
Radio communication, 158
Radner, Roy, 311
Railroads, 232, 272
Rake's Progress, The, 303
Ramsey, Frank, 307
Rand Corporation, 244, 371
Random-access memory, 130, 144
Random-access storage hardware, 91
Random-walk theory, 173–174
Range, computer-controlled, 8
RCA, 367
Reactor physics, 147
Reading machines for the blind, 108
Real-valued utility function, 307–308
Reasoning
and computers, 377
by analogy, 405–406

Regulated competition, 271, 273
Regulated industry, 259
Regulation
alternatives to, 266
definition of, 254
increase in prices and, 272
increased total profits and, 274
making a case for, 271–272
need to know effects of, 196–197
problem of defining boundaries of,
278–279
short-term market conditions and demand for, 273
technological innovation and, 196
Regulation planning, 202
Regulatory agencies
concentration on a few indexes of performance by, 260
conservative bias of, 259
limited control over government agencies by, 268–269
threat to financial viability of regulated
firms and, 260
Regulatory functions, 87, 103–106
Regulatory proposals, 254–255
Relevant structure concept, 171
Remote access, 220
Remote batch controllers, 347
Remote communication lines, 152
Remote data bases, 363
Remote networks, 156
Research
algorithms and, 433
in artificial intelligence, 400–409
in automatic programming, 96
in computer aids, 32
computer use in government sponsorship of, 148
current interest in interactive systems
in, 66
Department of Defense and, 119
and development, of software, 121–
122
explanation systems and, 68–69
hardware/software devices and, 382
in knowledge-based programs, 44–45
in machine recognition of elemental
visual objects, 44
in natural language and communication, 63–66
in performance measurement, 381–
382
in programming language, 96
interactive network communications
and, 176
large file systems and, 385
MULTICS project impact on, 372